PRIDE IN MODESTY

Modernist Architecture and the Vernacular Tradition in Italy

MICHELANGELO SABATINO

PRIDE IN MODESTY

Modernist Architecture and the Vernacular Tradition in Italy

UNIVERSITY OF TORONTO PRESS
Toronto Buffalo London

© University of Toronto Press Incorporated 2010
Toronto Buffalo London
www.utppublishing.com
Printed in Canada

ISBN 978-0-8020-9705-7

Printed on acid-free paper with vegetable-based inks.

Toronto Italian Studies

Library and Archives Canada Cataloguing in Publication

Sabatino, Michelangelo, 1969–
    Pride in modesty : modernist architecture and the vernacular tradition in
    Italy / Michelangelo Sabatino.

    Includes bibliographical references and index.
    ISBN 978-0-8020-9705-7

    1. Vernacular architecture – Italy – Influence.   2. Architecture – Italy –
    History – 20th century.   I. Title.

    NA1118.S22 2010   720.945'0904   C2009-907107-X

This book has been published with assistance from the Graham Foundation
for Advanced Studies in the Fine Arts and the New Faculty Research
Program of the University of Houston.

University of Toronto Press acknowledges the financial assistance to its
publishing program of the Canada Council for the Arts and the Ontario
Arts Council.

University of Toronto Press acknowledges the financial support for its
publishing activities of the Government of Canada through the Book
Publishing Industry Development Program (BPIDP).

Contents

Figures

Foreword
The Extraordinary Role of Ordinary Things

One of the world's truly astounding modern buildings opened as the Crystal Palace on the occasion of the *Great Exhibition* of 1851 in London. Colossal in every way, but delicate and almost evanescent in its effects, its canopy melted into the cloudy sky, the way Camille Pissarro later painted it, while shrouding mature trees, fountains and enormous orchestras under its gossamer web of glass. While blending into the weather, it also created its own climate and atmosphere. Where modern nations proffered their products to a new kind of public that shared metropolitan anonymity and ancient curiosity, who would have expected anything old, not to say primitive, within the sparkling shell of the palace? Whether he expected it or not, the German architect Gottfried Semper (1803–79), living impecuniously in his London exile, discovered a Caribbean hut that left him dumbfounded (Fig. F.1). Its simple platform and thatched roof required only a few bamboo poles and woven mats to partition its space.[1]

Architectural theorists from Vitruvius to Abbé Laugier had long speculated about the very earliest manifestations of architectural ideas. They sought to locate them on the threshold between nature and the first social groups banding together in a dark and distant past. Cutting and tying branches to cover a patch of ground for comfort and safety was thought to have inaugurated an evolution leading ultimately to the Parthenon and on to Gothic cathedrals. Gottfried Semper, on the other hand, was less enthralled by such fables than by a true phenomenology of architecture. That is to say, he sought in the very nature of building the conditions for useful speculation about it. Eking out a living in London, he added to his meagre earnings by designing displays for nations

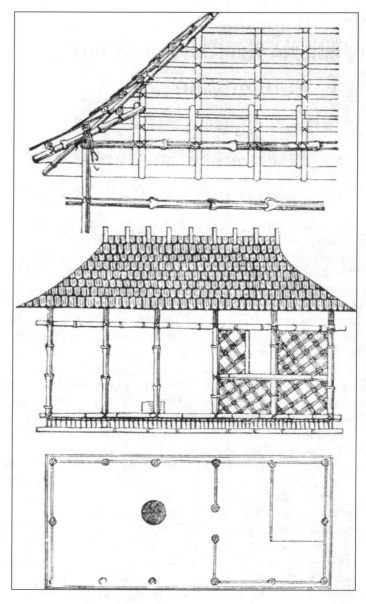

Fig. F.1 Illustration by Gottfried Semper, of the Caribbean hut in the Great Exhibition of 1851, London, from *Der Stil in den technischen und tektonischen Künsten* (1863), 263.

such as Canada and Turkey, thoroughly familiarizing himself with their unusual exhibits.

In the case of Canada, the displays consisted mostly of First Nation artifacts, kayaks, oars, tools, and ornamented hides. Semper's eyes were primed for a fresh look at ethnographic objects, such as the Aboriginal construction that caught his attention. The Caribbean hut he found so arresting when he came upon it under the bell jar of the Crystal Palace possessed, in his view, the character of a real building while handing down the legacy of all human construction. As a highly educated architect who was versed in mathematics and knowledgeable in history, he might also have been jaded, blind to such a *discovery*. For what one discovers always needs to have been there all along but gone unrecognized for what it is. A discovery tends to be something we've been after without knowing what it may hold. Semper was looking for architecture *tout court*, and when he beheld the Caribbean hut it appeared to him to be both a fossil and a representation in a nutshell. One would be justified to think of the hut as a *seed* of architecture, something capable of springing into life and propagating in all its nascent variety. For beginnings, like genetic origins, bifurcate into bewildering manifestations before gradually narrowing down to a limited range.

When Semper pondered the origins of architecture, time took on far greater force in his reflections, as it did in the thoughts of some of his contemporaries. Just as his composer friend Richard Wagner extended the Tale of the Nibelungen into hours and finally days, so Charles Darwin's *On the Origin of Species* (1859) slipped deep into unfathomed time. The fairly tight mesh of calendric periods that conventional history cast over the past was now being stretched beyond comprehension. How deep in the past lie those beginnings that have survived in remote areas of the world, themselves only recently 'discovered'? How vast are the periods separating an increasing number of archaeological finds from the present? In what way are primitive organisms or buildings related to their modern counterparts? Why do they exhibit such continuity beneath a plethora of manifestations?

In Semper's mind, the Caribbean hut embodied a scheme that cannot be reduced any further without losing coherence. It stands not only for a single building but its very species. Its elements are both independent of one another and yet united by a single purpose. In Semper's own words, "each [of these] elements of construction speaks for itself" while contributing its part to an ensemble.[2] In this regard his thinking still echoed Marc Antoine Laugier's summary description of a *petite cabane*

Fig. F.2 Johannes Rabe, view from the east of the Gardener's House (Das Gärt-nerhaus von Osten) Potsdam (gardens of Sanssouci), 1847, from Claudia Sommer, ed., *Die Römischen Bäder in Bleistift, Feder und klasserfarbe* (Berlin: Stiftung Preussische Schlösser und Gärten Berlin-Brandenburg), 38.

rustique when he wrote, "I see only columns, a plinth, and a roof," but it removed the idea from a casual reading of history.[3]

Semper did intuitively what the French anatomist Georges Baron Cuvier had done systematically before him and what palaeontologist do to this day: they derive the actual find before them from its antecedents by means of its evolutionary transformation. They reach back in time as far as the fossil record will carry them, or as far as their speculations help them dot in the lines that nature may have hidden or effaced. By dint of such reasoning, Semper not only found in the hut what we might call the anatomy of geometrically regular structures, but also he felt he was touching on the very origins of building. If you move forward in time, it is easy to see that the diagram Semper recognized in the hut also continues to underpin many recent buildings, even some of the most advanced in the twentieth century, such as Mies van der Rohe's Farnsworth House.

Examined in the light of open-ended time, rather than confined to

periods, as historians were increasingly wont to do, primitive buildings invite anti-hierarchical speculation and synchronic comparison.
With this study of vernacular tradition in modern times, Michelangelo
Sabatino is careful to respect the calendar of his agenda when he chroni-
cles the return of long-forgotten or simply overlooked buildings in
twentieth-century Italy, but he does expand his horizon beyond their
chronology. Customary differences such as those between polite and
vernacular architecture spell out a distinction in terms of social classes
no less than in the categories of buildings. When these distinctions took
hold, they began to get in the way of contact and exchange. Applied to
architecture, high and low often rehearse the comedy of upstairs-down-
stairs, separating building types and finishes, filleting the fine from the
crude, distinguishing the hand of the author from the pattern of the
craftsman. To be sure, an occasional mixing of parts or playful switch-
ing of roles can add flavour, but will only confirm the gulf that allegedly
separates the knowledgeable design of buildings from their fate in the
hands of the untutored. By contrast, a serious investigation of history in
the long term suggests filiations and inter-relationships of another kind,
recognizing latent possibilities in the elementary and the primitive.
More than just a repository of past building practices, vernacular structures intrigue the knowing eye as a seemingly spontaneous coincidence
of thinking and making.

It is no surprise that Semper, once recommended by Karl Friedrich
Schinkel for employment in Dresden, turned to Schinkel's captivating
architectural paraphrases of rural Italian houses (as seen in Potsdam in
the gardens of Sanssouci) when he designed a small villa right on the
border between Switzerland and Italy in 1863 (Figs. F.2, F.3).[4] In its subtle inflection of regularity and exception, the Villa Garbald springs from
the tension between type and individuality, recalling simultaneously
and symbiotically open lofts from Tuscany and pergolas and external
stairs from Capri. Northern Europeans responded to Italian vernacular
buildings with a loving appreciation of their stark volumes and their
abundant variety of pergolas, trellises, terraces and stairs, balconies,
shutters, and chimneys. What distinguishes a modern comprehension
of the primitive from mere lore is precisely the recognition that everything *does* have primitive antecedents and even highly evolved things
still preserve patterns and codes from long lost moments of the past.
Instead of adding ballast or hampering the flight of ideas the primitive
reclaims its share of the present. It may well be that modern ideas in
architecture are often little more than old ones in disguise. That is why

architects periodically rediscover what may, on the face of it, have been around for as long as anyone can remember, but gone unrecognized for that very reason.

When the Crystal Palace was dismantled and reassembled at the periphery of London, in Sydenham, a few years after the close of the *Great Exhibition*, startling discoveries had been made in the English soil. The anatomist Richard Owen attributed fossilized bones to a prehistoric creature, the Iguanadon, a lizard-like dinosaur. For the Park at Sydenham, science and entrepreneurship were joined momentarily in the person of Benjamin W. Hawkins who had Iguanadons and similar extinct creatures sculpted in concrete over metal scaffolds for display below the sloping terrain at the foot of the Crystal Palace. Splendid fountains lent a grandiose atmosphere to the setting before cascading into a recreated primeval marsh where visitors could wander among the biggest landlubbers and glimpse into the "abyss of time."[5] To look up from the Iguanadon's waterlogged haunt to the crowning splendor of the Crystal Palace meant peering into time at the scale of millions, even hundreds of millions, of years. The bubble of familiar historical time burst into droplets and fed the expanding pool of eons that ultimately melt into the unfathomable age of the universe itself. This awe-inspiring view, perhaps the first that offered a truly sublime comprehension of time on the scale of the sky's nocturnal infinity, betrays a curious liability. When we learn that Hawkins advertised the park's recreation of a Mesozoic setting as a glimpse of "those vast forms and gigantic beasts which the Almighty Creator designed with fitness to inhabit and precede us in possession of this part of the earth called Great Britain," we encounter a claim that continued to be made for many pre-historic artifacts. If the Iguanadon is "British" by location of its modern fossil find, then no proprietary claims can be barred, even if nothing remotely like the British Isles existed in that distant period of the earth's history. But precisely claims of such nationalist kind continue to be made throughout the twentieth century for objects free of any such affiliations. Primitive house forms, typologies of barns, artisan's tools, fabrics and even spoken dialects were marshaled in pursuit of chauvinist and racist ends. If Swiss historians, mostly of the amateur variety, fantasized about a Gotthard house as the mother of all Swiss peasant houses, or Austrians invested wood construction with moral integrity, Germans romanticized steeply inclined roofs as the guardians of their *voelkisch* character, and Italians endowed marble with heroic qualities they claimed to possess themselves, then

Fig. F.3 Photograph by Michelangelo Sabatino, Gottfried Semper's Villa Garbald, Castasegna, Switzerland, 1864.

these appeals to atavism are not much different from the British claiming "their" dinosaurs.

The study of things primitive has long been haunted by the specter of aggressive, even belligerent and racist ideologies, but such distortions may only give a measure of importance, not of truth, in the matter. While most pre-modern artisans are innocent of such political and racist convictions, twentieth-century ideologues were quick to appropriate them for their own ends. Since the Larousse dictionary defined "primitive" as that which "possesses the simplicity of the earliest times,"[6] owning the primitive was to claim the legacy and value of its "simplicity" as a superior quality, superior to what must then be thought of as modern "complexity." Such arguments not only distort the past, they also disfigure the present, for the modern becomes especially "complex" precisely where it contends with what is not of its ilk.

The discovery of primitive forms of construction – such as Semper's Caribbean hut – can be compared with the virtually contemporaneous unearthing of fossils that opened a door into the depth of time. The study of simple rural structures that dot the background of Italian paintings from the fourteenth and fifteenth centuries also casts architect-designed buildings of the time into a different light. Instead of underscoring the distinction between polite and vernacular modes of building, fundamental continuities begin to emerge. The architect and publicist Sebastiano Serlio (1475–1554) paid the most convincing tribute to this view when he connected the primitive with the evolved, the rural with the urban. Compiling his unpublished treatise on "human habitation," Serlio intuited that vernacular and polite architecture share more of their DNA than a superficial inspection might suggest.[7] Beginning with the simplest thatched huts and ending with a grandiose proposal for a royal palace, he not only retraced his own life from humble origins to service at the court of France, he also ascended from the shepherd's temporary shelter to the dwellings of artisan and patrician classes before reaching the highest echelon to which an architect might aspire. Simple buildings of the Renaissance began to fetch attention in modern scholarship when the actual circumstances of construction in the past and present invited comparison beyond the evidence held in archives.[8]

Anonymous structures of diverse kind, the tightly knit organization of small towns, and the clever layout of rural dwellings fascinated proponents of the modern no less than custodians of the past. Many architects took along their cameras, historians sketched half-abandoned

Fig. F.4 Photograph by Ugo Pellis, built-in-stove, from "Il focolare a terra e alto," *Usellus,* 2 June 1934; republished in Alessia Borellini and Francesco Paolo Campione, eds., *Uomini e cose: Ugo Pellis Fotografie, Sardegna, 1932–1935* (Florence: Giunti, 2009), 83. Copyright MCL/ALI/SFF.

localities, and glottologists sought out the "last inhabitants" of remote and depopulated linguistic regions. To avoid a second death, after the loss of self-sustaining communities in many remote regions, words, objects, and buildings were entered into vastly expanding inventories. From linguists turned ethnographers, such as Ugo Pellis who explored the remotest corners of Sardinia in the 1930s, to architects such as Giuseppe Pagano, the Castiglione brothers and later Aldo Rossi, a vivid interest in vernacular buildings, simple objects of daily use, and practices of habitation rekindled scholarly curiosity and stimulated architectural imagination (Fig. F.4).[9]

If our ears still ring with the claims of modern art and architecture – claims to rationality, realism, and the public good – it is their peremptory demand to discard time-honoured things and ideas that gave them the lie. Brand new will make it better, the precision of the machine replace the rule of thumb and the judgment of the eye, but the new all too often makes a poor substitute for the old whose simplicity may recommend it before and after the present moment. The story Sabatino tells with persuasive evidence brings home what has threatened for a century to slip into the quaint residue of holidays in the countryside or linger in nostalgic recollection. More than an antidote to schematic modernization, the legacy of the primitive proved essential for the very emergence of the modern, which, in its early stages, often sought to "restore building to what it has always been. Building."[10] It may come as a surprise that these are the words of Mies van der Rohe, the man who coldly dispatched anything superfluous until, with the Farnsworth House, he had pared building down to a version of the "hut." The essentially modern reassumed the guise of its primitive origins. Imbued with "the simplicity of the earliest times," but made of the stuff of its own industrial age, such a building exposes into nature what Semper discovered at a great remove from it under the glass canopy of the Crystal Palace.

Ringraziamenti/Acknowledgments

Like a coming-of-age novel, one's first sole-authored book is accompanied by the growing pains associated with inexperience and at times, paralyzing self-doubt. During the time it has taken to complete this project – from dissertation to this book – I have lived on two continents and in three countries. The research and writing required for this study have been the two constants in an otherwise variable journey that has taken me from Toronto to Venice, through Boston, and finally to Houston. As the literary critic Northrop Frye once noted – likely in response to Marshall McLuhan's insistence that "the medium is the message" – "print has a unique power of staying around to be read again, presenting, with unparalleled patience, the same words again however often it is consulted." I have learned first-hand that patience and perseverance are the foremost ingredients of lasting scholarship.

I could not have sustained this multi-year effort were it not for the counsel and assistance of a number of academics and the financial support of American and Canadian universities and research institutions. The origins of this book can be traced to the discoveries I made as a student of architecture and history at the Istituto Universitario di Architettura di Venezia (IUAV). It was during this time that I developed my interest in twentieth-century art and architecture. Had I not chosen to study in a place so defined by its plurisecular traditions, perhaps I would not have been compelled to understand how the built environment of Italy profoundly shaped its modernist architecture and urbanism. During my time as a student, the individual whose life and work had the greatest influence on my own was Manfredo Tafuri. Though I do not subscribe entirely to his approach, I am forever indebted to this severe, yet kindhearted master of doubt, for his mentorship. Even now, his work and example continue to resonate with me in my daily life, thousands of miles removed from where I first met him. In Italy, I encountered a host of scholars who contributed in various ways to my training and have continued to offer assistance over the years. My thanks go to Professors Marco Biraghi, Donatella Calabi, Maristella Casciato, Giorgio Ciucci, Francesco Dal Co, Cesare De Seta, Terry Kirk, Vittorio Magnago Lampugnani, Marco De Michelis, Manuela Morresi, Paolo Nicoloso, Massimiliano Savorra, Hermann Schlimme, and Guido Zucconi.

If my architectural education in Italy fostered my interest in twentieth-century art and architecture, it was in the Department of Fine Art of the University of Toronto that I found a supportive and stimulating environment in which to pursue my doctoral research. I received assistance and encouragement from my former supervisor, Professor Alina A. Payne. While I was in Toronto, Professors Marc Gotlieb, Michael Koortbojian, Alexander Nagel, Douglas Richardson, and Philip Sohm were inspiring interlocutors. Professors Larry Wayne Richards and George Baird of the University of Toronto's John H. Daniels Faculty of Architecture, Landscape, and Design were generous with their guidance as dissertation committee members. As was Professor Barry Bergdoll of Columbia University (and the Department of Architecture and Design at the Museum of Modern Art) who served in the role as external reader.

During my term as instructor at the Yale School of Architecture, I gave a graduate seminar on Italian modernism. This teaching appointment provided a welcome opportunity to share my research with the students and to profit from the lively discussions that ensued. Thanks are due to those students, as well as to former colleagues such as Professors Thomas Beeby, Kent Bloomer, Edward Cooke, Peggy Deamer, Peter Eisenman, Stephen Harby, Dolores Hayden, Sandy Isenstadt, Eeva-Liisa Pelkonen, Emmanuel Petit, Alan Plattus, and Vincent Scully. I offer special thanks to Dean Robert A. M. Stern for his support and to Professor Kurt W. Forster for his ongoing mentorship.

As a post-doctoral research associate in the Department of History of Art and Architecture of Harvard University, I learned much from my continued dialogue with Alina A. Payne and the opportunity to engage in discussion with Professors James S. Ackerman, Yve-Alain Bois, Neil Levine, David J. Roxburgh, and Henri Zerner. During my time at Harvard, my friendship with Todd Pittinsky made exploring Cambridge and the Cape enjoyable. The librarians at Harvard (as well as those of

Yale, the University of Toronto, and the University of Houston) also deserve special thanks for their assistance. In the United States, several scholars offered me guidance at different junctures of the project. I am grateful to Professors Anthony Alofsin, Jean-Louis Cohen, Ruth Ben-Ghiat, Sibel Bozdogan, Emily Braun, Richard Etlin, Mia Fuller, Diane Ghirardo, Mark Jarzombek, Brian McLaren, Jean-François Lejeune, Francesco Passanti, Jeffrey Schnapp, Paolo Scrivano, Paul V. Turner, and Gwendolyn Wright.

Financial support for my doctoral and post-doctoral work was generously provided by SSHRC (Social Sciences and Humanities Research Council of Canada), the Department of Fine Art (University of Toronto), and the Graduate School of Arts and Science (Harvard University). A travel grant from the Vernacular Architecture Forum and a Caroll Meeks Travel Fellowship from the Society of Architectural Historians provided welcome opportunities to present my research to a scholarly audience. A fellowship at the Wolfsonian-FIU in Miami Beach allowed me to continue my research and writing in a relaxing and engaging environment. Director Cathy Leff, Marianne Lamonaca (Associate Director, Curatorial Affairs and Education), and fellowship coordinator and curatorial research associate Jon Mogul merit special mention for making my stay productive. The Graham Foundation for Advanced Studies in the Fine Arts provided funding for costs related to the translation and the editing of primary texts from Italian into English. I also received a publication grant from the University of Houston's New Faculty Research Program. At the Gerald D. Hines College of Architecture of the University of Houston, thanks go to Dean Joe Mashburn for his unfailing support and to all of my colleagues who have helped me to grow as a teacher and researcher. Alessandro Carrera of the UH Department of Modern and Classical Languages has been a reliable interlocutor. Thanks go to the undergraduate and graduate students who attended my courses and seminars for allowing me to share my research interests with them. Stephen Fox of the Anchorage Foundation of Texas has been by far the most selfless and generous individual I have had the good fortune to encounter while in Houston. Professor Carlos Jimenez of the Rice University School of Architecture has helped me appreciate this sprawling yet fascinating city. At the University of Toronto Press, Ron Schoeffel was patient and helpful throughout the entire process, as were Anne Laughlin and Beth McAuley.

Although my father is not here to see this book to press, I wish to thank him and my mother for the financial support that made living and studying in Italy possible. Both my parents and my maternal and paternal grandparents unknowingly played a crucial if indirect role in instigating this research project. From when I was a child, it was they who brought me to Italy and first introduced me to the hill towns of the South, where they were born and once lived. As a young boy, I was both fascinated and frightened by the "primitively" built environments and rugged rural landscapes inhabited by my ancestors and living relatives. These intense images and memories of my youth, enriched later by years of study in Italy, offered me new and enduring perspectives with which to understand the complexities of the vernacular tradition and its impact on so-called pedigreed design. Through my family, I learned about the Italian customs of ordinary people. Not unlike Italo-Canadian novelist Nino Ricci whose *Lives of the Saints* (1990) explores a world removed yet ever present for his immigrant parents, I too was challenged and strengthened from a similar experience. Finally, although Serge Ambrose joined at the tail end of this journey, his insights, humour, and assistance have made the difficulties both easier and more joyful. To him, I owe much more than words can express.

I dedicate this book to James S. Ackerman and Manfredo Tafuri.

PRIDE IN MODESTY

Modernist Architecture and the Vernacular Tradition in Italy

Listen to me, the poets laureate
walk only among plants
with rare names: boxwood, privet and acanthus.
But I like roads that lead to grassy
ditches where boys
scoop up a few starved
eels out of half-dry puddles:
paths that run along the banks,
come down among the tufted canes
and end in orchards, among the lemon trees.

Eugenio Montale, *I limoni / The Lemons* (1922)

It is possible to recognize a common ground in the way these authors feel about the new architecture. They all detest ornament, embellishments, and the superfluous. The best of them detest elegance, deceit, secrets. That they equate this feeling with a fight against aesthetics is of little importance. Such a feeling may also end up as the true moral core of any work of aesthetics. With these authors, what matters is the desire for simplicity, the repudiation for all types of exterior wealth: in sum, it is *pride in modesty*.

Lionello Venturi, "Per la nuova architettura"
(Toward a New Architecture), *Casabella* 6:1 (January, 1933): 2–3.

Introduction

History has its rules, though they are not always followed even by professional historians; poetry, too, has its laws. The two are not necessarily irreconcilable.

Marguerite Yourcenar, *Mémoires d'Hadrien* (1951)[1]

Italian modernist architecture and urbanism of the twentieth century emerged in a cultural context characterized by distinct and competing regional traditions, unified primarily by a deep-seated agricultural heritage that had since antiquity coexisted with the urbane aspirations of city dwellers.[2] American architects and theorists Robert Venturi, Denise Scott Brown, and Steven Izenour noted in their study entitled *Learning from Las Vegas* (1972) how the vernacular and classical traditions coexist in Italy: "The Italian landscape has always harmonized the vulgar and the Vitruvian: the *contorni* around the *duomo*, the *portiere's* laundry across the *padrone's portone*, *Supercortemaggiore* against the Romanesque apse. Naked children have never played in our fountains, and I.M. Pei will never be happy on Route 66."[3] Although the key events and issues that shaped Italy's modernity are by now well known, little scholarly attention has been given to looking at how the rediscovery and appropriation of ordinary things – often anonymous, preindustrial, vernacular buildings and objects – informed and transformed the practice and discourse of architecture and urbanism from the 1910s well into the 1970s. This book looks at why and how the robust volumes, basic plans, unadorned facades, and modest local materials of extant vernacular buildings (whether individual or aggregates) that constituted the lion's share of hamlets, villages, and hill towns throughout the Italian peninsula provided formal, practical, and poetic inspiration for modernist architects during a period of sixty years and spanning two major world wars and two different regimes such as fascism and democracy. It seeks to examine how, in parallel with the rise of the urban working proletariat, modernist art of architecture entered into a new dialogue with informal building traditions that challenged the influence of classical architecture, and how class divisions that distinguished city dwellers and peasants fuelled a new ethos for architecture that led from political resistance to synthesis of thought and action.[4] Lionello Venturi's expression "pride in modesty" ("*orgoglio della modestia*"), borrowed and used extensively by architect Giuseppe Pagano during the 1930s, captured the subversive essence of this synthesis.

With some exceptions, most histories of twentieth-century Italian architecture have focused upon either the interwar or the postwar years.[5] Despite shifting social, political, and economic contexts and differing points of view, the influence that vernacular buildings exerted on modernist architects cannot be submitted to such neat time frames. Over the *longue durée* (to use a concept dear to Lucien Febvre of the French Annales School of history), from the 1910s through the two world wars and the postwar period of reconstruction, and even into the 1970s, it seems only logical to look at this phenomenon as one that gained momentum in Italy but also as an international phenomenon.[6] In Italy, the vernacular tradition informed modernist (as well as nostalgic, antimodernist) design practices, inspired critical debates and the production of exhibitions and publications, and also spurred legislation pertaining to the preservation of traditional buildings and sites.

As a study of a single pervasive architectural phenomenon, seen in the wide cultural context of the Italian peninsula and the Mediterranean region at large, this book attempts to reread Italy's engagement with the vernacular tradition and its rural heritage during the period when rustic, pastoral environments were being effectively wiped out by industrialization and the lure of modern urban life. Insofar as the vernacular tradition is associated with relatively stable and even static rural societies, it might be viewed as antithetical to a modernity based on the very notion of rapid change. If, in the American context, commercial vernacular (i.e., popular) roadside architecture responded to competitive market forces that dictated constant change, and barns and grain silos remained remarkably constant over time, in Italy during the same period, creative tension between agrarian and urban cultural realms was played out in debates concerning single-family dwellings and apartment blocks concentrated in the periphery of Italian cities, densifying ex-urban zones bordering the rural countryside. Films of the postwar period engaged this tension between the *remote* or rural and the urban: from the solitary paradise of Capri to which the characters in Jean-Luc Godard's *Le mépris (Contempt)* (1963) retreat, gathering at the Casa Malaparte to escape the studios at Cinecittà in Rome, or the desolate volcanic island off the coast of Sicily in Michelangelo Antonioni's *L'avventura (The Adventure)* (1960) where a group of Italians take refuge during a yachting trip, to the Roman settings of Federico Fellini's *La strada (The Road)* (1954) and *La dolce vita (The Sweet Life)* (1960) or Antonioni's *La notte (The Night)* (1961) and *L'eclisse (The Eclipse)* (1962) in which scenes alternate between the old city centre and newer developments at the periphery. In fact, both the Casa Malaparte on Capri's Punta Massullo, completed in 1942, and the housing estates of the Tiburtino and Tuscolano neighbourhoods, built in the periphery of Rome after the Second World War, conflated pastoral and urban forms, building types, and materials.

The *marginality* of modernist architecture and urbanism born during the interwar and postwar years of this new dialogue with the vernacular building traditions of Italy is determined by quantitative issues as well as spatial ones, insofar as even those buildings and housing estates realized were often located in peripheral sites: even more egregious is the marginalization in the historiography of twentieth-century architecture, of the builders (i.e., *authors)* of vernacular forms who are typically considered to be anonymous while architects who appropriated their principles are given most of the credit. Marginality is thus an undercurrent of this book. While a number of architects who identified with the rationalist movement and were critical against the fascist regime's interference with the arts still managed a form of resistance in their celebration of the inherent modesty of vernacular tradition, few built projects were realized, and most of them were single-family residences like the emblematic Casa Malaparte. Although the neovernacular *case coloniche* (tenant farmers cottages) realized as part of the fascist-era New Towns of the Agro Pontino such as Aprilia, Latina (formerly Littoria), and Sabaudia are part of this undercurrent since they relied on mimesis of extent models rather than the transformation of vernacular sources, they often achieved distinction in urban planning and not architectural terms. However, if the vernacular tradition was marginal compared with the ubiquitous classical tradition in public architecture of the interwar period, it gained a new momentum during the postwar years.

For the architectural historian writing in English about a phenomenon of appropriation that unfolded in specific political and cultural
contexts of Italy, and whose manifestations were expressed equally specifically in Italian, uses of a blanket expression like *vernacular tradition*
in another language threatens to blur or even obliterate vital nuances
that distinguish highly diverse practices and intentions over time. In
translation, it is important to capture what Benedetto Croce referred
to as "vibration."[7] Lucien Febvre's dictum "it is never a waste of time
to study the history of a word. Such journeys, whether short or long,
monotonous or varied are always instructive" has relevance for historians exploring the impact of vernacular buildings on modernist architecture and theory in Italy and beyond.[8] So, too, do terms like peasant
and "the people."[9] Perhaps nowhere so much as in the Italian language
is the definition of what in English is called *vernacular architecture* so
elusive. Some of the expressions employed over a sixty-year span are
fabbricati etnografici (ethnographic buildings), *architettura minore* (minor
architecture), *architettura naturale* (natural architecture), *architettura rurale* (rural architecture), *architettura rustica* (rustic architecture), *architettura popolare* (popular architecture), *architettura spontanea* (spontaneous
architecture), *arte paesana* (peasant art), *arte popolare* (popular or folk
art), and *arte rustica* (rustic art).

Depending on the perspective of the writer or speaker, the same category could be assigned different value. For example, negative antimod-
ern attributes were ascribed by rationalist architects during the 1930s to
the Italianized term *folklore*, but not to *architettura rurale*. These differences are especially interesting within the context of the Anglophone
world, where folklore, folk art, and folk architecture are generally considered to be synonymous with the vernacular tradition.[10] In the Italian
context, expressions like *architettura rurale* referred to architecture, *arte
paesana* to arts and crafts, and *tradizioni popolari* referred to folklore in the
English sense. Furthermore, unlike a number of other groups, rationalist architects in Italy often attributed positive values to the primitive, a
quality they typically attributed to extant vernacular building.[11]

One is hard-pressed to summarize debates of this period in Italy,
which generated a variety of charged terms reflecting political and cultural stances. The English term vernacular is borrowed from linguistics,
where it refers to dialect, a common native language. The etymology of
the word *vernacular* is rooted in class distinctions: the Latin *verna* refers
to the status of *slave*. More importantly, in almost all cases, the appropriation of the vernacular tradition by professionally trained architects

helped negotiate class division that surfaced in architectural history up until then between style-driven historicist or classical and vernacular buildings. In the romance languages, various words for *peasant* allude to the pastoral context, stemming from the Latin root *pagus*, meaning *village*. Thus, not only is the vernacular tradition lower on the totem pole when it comes to class divide, because villages and their inhabitants were typically considered peripheral to the city, the subject and spatial conditions in which this tradition most thrived are two times removed from centres of power. The American folklorist John Michael Vlach's important study *Back of the Big House: The Architecture of Plantation Slavery* (1993) astutely points out how the vernacular environment of the slaves is strategically marginalized and given less visibility behind the classically inspired estates (i.e., Big Houses) of the antebellum South.[12] While the perception that the vernacular simply *serves* the art of architecture handicaps the study of vernacular on its own terms, it also creates new opportunities for reflection on hybrid practices within modernist and contemporary architecture by individuals who straddle professional practice and history or criticism.[13] The plurality of expressions coined by practising architects, critics, and historians to describe the phenomenon of modernism indebted to appropriations of the vernacular tradition implies the multifarious readings it received as well as the disparate approaches of designers. For example, the vernacular tradition has inspired such diverse movements as Expressionism and National Romanticism in the first half of the twentieth century and various forms of Regionalism in the second half. Whereas practising architects who study the vernacular tradition almost inevitably produce distorted interpretations based on personal design agendas – what literary critic and theorist Harold Bloom has coined as *poetic misprision* and Manfredo Tafuri described as *critica operativa* (operative criticism) – the expectations for historians and folklorists tend to be more inclusive and less self-serving.[14]

To a certain extent, this book's methodological framework is indebted to the efforts of art historians like George Kubler, whose pioneering study on the history of things bridged the divide between art and material culture:

> Let us suppose that the idea of art can be expanded to embrace the whole range of man-made things, including all tools and writing in addition to the useless, beautiful, and poetic things of the world. By this view the universe of man-made things simply coincides with the history of art.[15]

Kubler's teacher and author of the seminal *The Life of Forms in Art* (1934), Henri Focillon welcomed the advent of serious scholarship on the vernacular tradition in his introduction to the proceedings of the first Congrès International des Arts Populaires (International Congress of Popular Arts) held in Prague in 1928: "For the first time, one can begin to sketch a vast system of comparisons and relationships that tend to demonstrate, despite the variety of races and backgrounds, a kind of common source, an emotion and a collective wisdom."[16] Focillon and Kubler believed that the vernacular tradition was not static, but rather self-transforming. While my project is necessarily embedded in the tradition of architectural history, it is also indebted to the fields of ethnography, anthropology, and geography in which the pioneering investigations of vernacular building and objects were first located.

The subordinate and often times problematic relationship between vernacular buildings and those works by professionally trained architects can be traced back to Sir George Gilbert Scott (1811–78) and his appropriation of the term *vernacular* from linguistics to describe domestic architecture.[17] In all of those instances in which modern architects, in Italy for example, valorized the vernacular tradition, what needs to be stated clearly, however, is the fact that the process of appropriation led them to refer to their work as architecture rather than neovernacular. If Giuseppe Pagano referred to extant vernacular buildings as *architettura rurale* (1936), he spoke of his own contemporary architecture as rationalist. If Giancarlo De Carlo employed the term *architettura spontanea* (1951) to refer to vernacular buildings of cityscapes and actively encouraged participation by the end-user, he ultimately spoke of his work in terms of architecture.

In light of its dialogue with the vernacular and classical traditions, the trajectory of twentieth-century architecture and urbanism in Italy is broadly characterized by its ambivalent "relationship with history," one that has inspired modern and contemporary architects to look to the past for creative inspiration, with results ranging from nostalgic and kitsch to compelling.[18] The scope and results of this relationship have changed according to political regimes from fascist to democratic. In mapping the history of Italian architects and intellectuals during the twentieth century, it is useful to reflect on Julien Benda's concept of "treason," which targeted intellectuals who betrayed the *super partes* neutrality of the scholar as clergyman with their involvement in politics.[19] Not only did intellectuals subscribe to fascism; so, too, did socialists and communists during the interwar and postwar years pursue agendas that shaped Italian modernism.[20] The most principled and least opportunistic instances of Italian architects who soiled themselves with politics in both inter- and postwar years were those who engaged in one way or the other with the tradition of realism in the arts, whose roots can be traced to nineteenth-century French painter Gustave Courbet's celebration of "the people."[21] For example, the gritty materiality of Rome's Tiburtino neorealist housing estates designed for the working class (1950–4) by Mario Ridolfi, Ludovico Quaroni et al., is preempted by politically charged figurative works such as the *Crocifissione (The Crucifixion*, 1941) produced by the anti-fascist painter Renato Guttuso to denounce the violence perpetrated on the "common man" in times of war.[22]

Due to its relationship with the fascist regime and its ongoing dialogue with the classical and vernacular traditions, Italian modernism has occupied an uneasy position in histories of architecture both inside and outside of Italy, at least until the 1960s and 1970s, when a major shift occurred in assessments of the Modern Movement and International Style.[23] Furthermore, the years following the fall of fascism gave architects and scholars some emotional detachment so they could begin to evaluate more objectively the architectural debates (i.e., culture) and production of the interwar years.[24] The rise of a new generation of historians and critics during the 1960s has been just as important to the legacy of modernism as its original protagonists.[25] In 1960, a decade after the publication of Bruno Levi's influential history, Leonardo Benevolo gave Italy under fascism an important overview under the rubric of "political compromise and the struggle with the authoritarian regime."[26] From the mid-1930s until the end of the Second World War, Italian modernism experienced a lukewarm reception among militant critics who defined modernity exclusively in terms of its repudiation of the past (*tabula rasa*), exemplified in the embrace of abstraction and the abandonment of figuration as well as an alignment with leftwing utopian ideals based upon ideas of progress and technology.[27] The tension between tradition and modernity in Italian culture (whether art, architecture, or literature) in the arts worked to create the perception of ambivalence and a lack of coherence.[28] By reinventing tradition, Italian architects, during and after fascism, constructed a hybrid modernity that was at odds with avant-garde radicalism and its insistence on the "eclipse of history."[29]

Militant critics identified futurism as Italy's foremost contribution to modernity. Antonio Sant'Elia's *Città Nuova* (New City, 1914) and

Giacomo Mattè-Trucco's Fiat Lingotto factory in Turin with its rooftop automobile track (1915–39) featured prominently in international avant-garde journals and books throughout the 1920s and 1930s.[30] More recent accounts of Italian modernism have been less focused on futurism. As English architect and historian Alan Colquhoun recently noted in his overview of architecture in Italy from 1920 to 1965,

> The strong connection between the architectural avant-garde and Fascism in Italy during the "heroic" period of modern architecture has always been an embarrassment to architectural historians … The Modernist architects, for their part, sympathized wholeheartedly with a movement that shared their dislike of nineteenth-century liberalism and their desire simultaneously to modernize and return to ancient roots.[31]

Just as the interplay of totalitarianism and democratic forces led Palmiro Togliatti, the leader of Italy's Communist Party from 1927 to 1964, to describe fascism as an "eclectic ideology," many different ideological positions were occupied in the name of modernizing and returning to ancient roots.[32] Under fascism, the vernacular tradition was appropriated by second-generation futurists and rationalists who were reacting against historicism and sterile classicism imposed by party officials known as *gerarchi* and epitomized by state-sponsored sites in Rome like the Esposizione Universale Roma (E42, 1938–42).[33] These rationalist architects were critical with the fascist regime's interference with the arts and architecture and deployed the vernacular tradition to help undermine anti-urban and anti-modernist attitudes. Whereas second generation futurists infused mechanization with the primitive expressivity of vernacular buildings and landscapes, rationalists appropriated extant vernacular buildings as a source of *Mediterraneità* or *Mediterranean-ness* to broaden the parameters of what constituted *Italianità* or *Italian-ness* according to the fascist regime. During the 1950s, neorealist architects adopted spatial and material qualities of extant vernacular buildings to counteract the alienation and displacement they imagined to be experienced by peasant farmers turned working-class proletariat moving *en mass* from rural and village dwellings into new urban housing projects, and likewise patterned the design of public spaces on the experience of hamlets and hill towns. In both cases, memory was engaged, but nostalgia was avoided. Rationalist architects who aspired to *Mediterraneità* in the 1930s admired the whitewashed surfaces and serially repeated forms of vernacular buildings typical of the seaside towns along the Mediterranean coast of Italy, Spain, and

Greece. Their counterparts of the 1950s were inspired by the hill towns of central Italy, where exposed brick and pitched roofs clad with terracotta tiles evoked the rugged vitality of rural environments from whence the new working-class proletariat came. In the 1960s and 1970s, Italy's vernacular heritage provided neorationalists with a tool to sidestep what Aldo Rossi dismissed as "naive functionalism."[34]

Writing in the late 1960s, architect and theorist Vittorio Gregotti (1927–) was one of the first to acknowledge continuity in the interest for the vernacular tradition between the 1930s and the postwar era:

> Interest in spontaneous architecture had long existed in Italy. Since Giuseppe Pagano's and Guarniero Daniel's book *Architettura Rurale Italiana* (1936), this architecture had been considered as naturally connected with rationalist architecture, inasmuch as it related the natural and functional styles of building. The ninth Triennale (1951) devoted substantial research to spontaneous architecture and dedicated a remarkable exhibition to it. Its extraordinary formal repertory had for many years a direct influence on the attempts of Italian architecture to make contact with the working class.[35]

Whereas in Germany under Adolf Hitler, modern artists and architects fled to America or other European countries, in Italy, most of those who identified with the Left as well as the ultra-nationalist right wing of Benito Mussolini's fascism remained and continued practising after the war.[36] In some aberrant instances, projects started but not completed under fascism were actually realized under the new postwar democratic government. A case in point is Marcello Piacentini's (and Attillio Spaccarelli's) Via della Conciliazione (Road of the Conciliation) that connects Saint Peter's Square to the Castel Sant'Angelo, which replaced extant historic buildings of the Borgo with sterile classicism. Another example is the classically inspired Museo Nazionale delle Arti e Tradizioni Populari (National Museum of Arts and Popular Traditions) at the E42 in Rome by Massimo Castellazzi, Pietro Morresi, and Annibale Vitellozzi.[37] Many buildings erected under Hitler's reign of terror, especially in Munich, were attacked after the fall of the Nazi regime; in Italy, fascist monuments were subject to hostility and acts of vandalism, but not targeted with the same degree of physical violence and the practice of *damnatio memoriae*.[38] Furthermore, there was no legal process in Italy that can be equated with the Nuremberg Trials in Germany.

Italian architects who worked under fascist patronage but took issue with bombastic classicism sought to appropriate vernacular sources as a form of resistance; these were regarded with respect by the Left-leaning architects who identified with the social reform agenda of the regime and served as examples for those who felt they could persuade the regime to adopt a progressive Italian modernism. A case in point is Giuseppe Pagano (1846–1945), who pleaded with fascist officials to embrace the "pride in modesty" exemplified by extant vernacular buildings he and Werner "Guarniero" Daniel showcased in the 1936 exhibition Architettura rurale italiana (Rural Italian Architecture) installed at the Milan Triennale. In reaction to the visual and spatial hysteria of the Mostra della rivoluzione fascista (Exhibition of the Fascist Revolution) mounted in 1932 in the nineteenth-century Palazzo delle Esposizioni at Rome, Pagano and Daniel abandoned the "museum in motion" approach of Giuseppe Terragni's Sala O, and the monumentality of Mario Sironi's Sala Q, in favour of a more somber exhibition design aimed at drawing attention to the social and architectural problems of their time.[39] Their straightforward and modest exhibition eschewed visual drama in favour of simplicity, and convincingly demonstrated the extent to which vernacular buildings and urban forms suggested vital, functionalist design solutions in contrast to the stale, historicizing tendency of official fascist architecture. Although Pagano died as a political prisoner of the fascist regime he once supported, his endorsement of Italy's rural vernacular architecture as a means of tempering the oftentimes facile rhetoric of classicism was inspirational for architects like Franco Albini (1907–77) and Giancarlo De Carlo (1919–2005), who perpetuated his passion with their Mostra dell'architettura spontanea (Spontaneous Architecture Exhibition) in 1951 at the Milan Triennale.

During the years that Albini and De Carlo were championing Pagano's legacy, the relationship between writers and the public led Italian architects to address the needs of everyday working-class people, especially in the realm of housing.[40] In fundamental ways, the arts and architecture of the twentieth century – in Italy and beyond, and in democratic as well as totalitarian regimes – was characterized by the new prominence and participation of the masses.[41] Although the populace was ostensibly on Mussolini's mind and figured prominently in his political reforms regarding healthcare and education, there was no shared governance. Whereas politics and ritual associated with classicism was elevated to the level of a new religion under fascism, after the war, Italians were anxious to return to more local, grass-roots forms of governance and sought to rid themselves of the mystical fervour and authoritarian presence of its former leader.[42] It is not surprising, then, that Italo Calvino (1923–85) and Pier Paolo Pasolini (1922–75) focused on the folk (i.e., popular) poetry, fables, and songs of an agrarian culture threatened with extinction by incipient industrialization and the progress brought forward by the Italian economic miracle.[43]

While the primary aim is to identify and analyse key examples of texts and buildings, the secondary aim is to situate the Italian architect's engagement with the vernacular tradition within the broader context of modernist practices outside of Italy. For example, during the late 1930s, as the novelist Curzio Malaparte built his Casa Malaparte on Capri in collaboration with rationalist architect Adalberto Libera and stonemason Adolfo Amitrano, Finnish modernist Alvar Aalto designed and realized the Villa Mairea in Noormarkku.[44] Whereas Malaparte embraced the ultra-nationalist ideology of the right-wing milieu of the journal *Il Selvaggio*, his architectural proclivities for bold volumes and sweeping views of the surroundings were essentially modernist in opposition to the prescriptive attitudes towards "tradition" and *Italianità* that prevailed under fascism. National Romanticism in Finland, on the other hand, was an invented tradition, experienced as a democratic phenomenon.[45] While the villas of Aalto and Libera were produced in vastly different political contexts, there was in both cases a creative engagement with materiality and forms based on extant vernacular buildings.

During the twentieth century, Scandinavian historians, architects, and critics ranging from Christian Norberg-Schultz to Juhani Pallasmaa have discussed the practical and poetic qualities of the vernacular in relationship to Nordic buildings and landscape.[46] Aalto's eclectic embrace of organic forms and artisanal (handcraft) techniques and materiality parallels the dynamics underlying the Casa Malaparte.[47] Aalto drew inspiration from wood buildings typical of Finland (and Scandinavia), whereas Libera and collaborators relied upon the know-how of indigenous stone construction to create a flat roof structure that echoed reinforced concrete constructions of the time.[48] What is key to both of these experiments – northern modernism versus that of Mediterranean modernism – is the common interest in drawing upon and rethinking the context (site, culture, climate) in order to temper the universal qualities of modernity with regional characteristics embodied in the extant vernacular.

Such appropriations of the vernacular tradition enabled architects such as Libera to effectively challenge the hegemony of classicism and historicism in Italy. Since Italian unification in 1861, classicism was routinely invoked to represent Italian identity within national boundaries and beyond, at international exhibitions and fairs.[49] During the last decades of the nineteenth century, the pursuit of collective representation in Italy's largest cities coincided with the perception that classicism best embodied the virtues of a modern urban civilization in the throes of industrialization. Ernesto Basile's Parliament Building (1903–18) and Giuseppe Sacconi's *Altare della Patria*, the national monument to Vittorio Emanuele II (1911), are two prime examples in Rome. While National Romanticism in the Scandinavian countries, England, Germany, and central Europe was in part inspired by a rediscovery of vernacular traditions, Italy based much of its cultural legitimacy on classicism and its various iterations, ranging from neo-Renaissance and *Cinquecento* to Beaux-Arts.[50] It was not until the 1910s with the rediscovery of the vernacular-built domain by ethnographers, anthropologists, and geographers that its influence began to be felt in the discourse and practice of architecture.

That the allure of classicism was very strong in Italy during fascism is not surprising, given the legacy of Antiquity and the Renaissance. In his *Crowds and Power* first published in 1960, Elias Canetti observed that "Italy may serve as an example of the difficulty a nation has in visualizing itself when all its cities are haunted by greater memories and when these memories are deliberately made use of to confuse its present."[51] Benito Mussolini's instrumentalization of the Roman legacy is best revealed in a speech delivered only three years after he illegally seized power during the 1922 March on Rome: "Today, on this well-prepared ground, a new and great art can be reborn that is both traditionalist and modern. We must create, otherwise we will merely exploit our heritage. We must create a new art for our time, a Fascist art."[52] Despite his encouragement to look beyond Italy's heritage, Mussolini exploited the language of classicism, its rhetorical power having been appropriated over centuries by emperors, kings, oligarchs, and popes, as the dominant vehicle of propaganda and self-aggrandizement.[53] Despite the populist claims of the fascist regime, its official architecture tended to embrace the elitism of classicism. Oscillating between nostalgia for the past and *tabula rasa* renewal, Mussolini's regime went from instituting a new calendar based on "fascist time" to the systematic appropriation of ancient Roman buildings and sites in service of his "Third Rome."[54] Whereas numerous studies have been devoted to the relationship between right-wing totalitarian regimes, the aesthetics of power, and classicism during the interwar years, from Nazi Germany to Stalin's Soviet

Union, no comprehensive cultural and design history has considered why or how the vernacular tradition shaped the arts and architecture of the fascist years.[55]

Against the backdrop of Italy's changing political context during the twentieth century, architects engaged both classical and vernacular traditions. Studies of Italian modernism have taken great pains to distinguish between a banal classicism in the service of nationalist politics, and the more sophisticated classicizing tendencies that motivated the *Novecento* and rationalist movements during the 1920s and through 1940s.[56] This distinction has been made by scholars, architects, and critics who reconstructed the relationship of modernism to classicism beyond the Italian context. For example, many have pointed out that the abstract classicism of Mies van der Rohe shares nothing with the megalomaniacal monumentality of Albert Speer's new Berlin.[57]

Furthermore, the work of rationalist architects built during the interwar period was saved from the wrecking ball of history because they worked against banal and historicist classicism. The Venice Biennale Architecture in 1976 under Vittorio Gregotti's leadership was an important benchmark in this shift. Framing the issue of *progressive* architecture realized in fascist Italy, historians, architects, and critics were able to skirt the matter of collaboration with the regime.[58] In spite of their direct involvement with fascism, the classically inspired *Mediterraneità* of Giuseppe Terragni was salvaged, while the classicism of Mussolini's architect Marcello Piacentini was deemed unworthy of anything but cursory study.[59] In recent years, Piacentini, like his German counterpart Speer, has received considerable scholarly attention.[60] Foregoing outright condemnation in favour of more rigorous analysis shed new light on the matter. The understanding that emerged during this time was that there were a number of different approaches. On the one hand, there was architecture realized *for* fascism which symbolized the regime, while on the other hand, there was architecture realized *during* fascism which was critical of the regime and tried, unsuccessfully, to redirect its course.[61]

Although the impact of classicism on Italian modernism has been examined in depth, the vernacular tradition has not received the same intense scrutiny as a force in the Modernist Movement.[62] Just as classically inspired modernist buildings had "many souls," to use a felicitous expression of architectural historian Giorgio Ciucci, ranging from the metaphysical *Novecento* to Rationalism and the stripped monumentality of *Stile Littorio*, the appropriation of vernacular forms generated a number of different expressions.[63] For example, in the act of reassessing Rationalism and *Mediterraneità*, with all of its attendant regional, national, and transnational implications, architects and scholars drew attention to the role played by both classical and vernacular traditions in shaping Italian modernism during fascism.[64] In their influential overview of twentieth-century architecture and urbanism published in 1976 in Italian, Manfredo Tafuri and Francesco Dal Co claimed:

> The single factor linking the varied points of view was the definition of a "national art." This constituted a common ground where proposals for renewal and reactionary tendencies could meet. In the rationalist position, the concern with preserving a bond with tradition while still achieving a renewal of forms became the occasion for reproposing Mediterranean myths or the antirhetoric of purportedly spontaneous or peasant-style architecture.[65]

To be sure, the use of "spontaneous or peasant-style architecture" was not limited to the interwar years, or to Italy, for that matter.

An indication of shifting attitudes towards modern architecture in Europe and North America, coupled with a growing awareness of the role played by the "anonymous" vernacular tradition, surfaced after the war in 1957 with British architect James Stirling's seminal essay "Regionalism and Modern Architecture."[66] Stirling wrote, "The most visually stimulating chapters of Kidder Smith's recent book *Italy Builds* were not those on Italian Modern and Italian Renaissance but that on the anonymous architecture of Italy."[67] Stirling appreciated American architect and critic George Everard Kidder-Smith's association of traditional buildings and urban spaces with examples of Italian modernist architecture realized between the 1920s and the 1950s. Stirling had previously written an article on Le Corbusier's recently completed chapel of Nôtre Dame du Haut in Ronchamp in which he discussed the Franco-Swiss architect's interest in the "farm buildings" of the Mediterranean:

> ... If folk architecture is to re-vitalise the movement, it will first be necessary to determine what it is that is modern in modern architecture. The scattered openings on the chapel walls may recall de Stijl, but a similar expression is also commonplace in the farm buildings of Provence. The influence of popular art is also apparent in the priest's house and the hostel buildings.[68]

The discovery of Le Corbusier's Mediterranean-inspired work in both interwar and postwar years – from Villa de Mandrot (1931) to Maisons Jaoul (1956) and Ronchamp (1954) – led to a gradual loosening of tensions that had arisen between the modernism of the industrialized North and that of the agrarian South.[69] Le Corbusier and Italian rationalists were part of a strain of Mediterranean modernists who tempered functionalism with culture and context. Within this framework of hybridity, geography (and geopolitics) has been used to define arts as well as culture.[70] Colonialism was equally instrumental in strategically perpetuating these stereotypes. Postcolonial studies have subsequently worked to deconstruct these to show the underlying power structures that prompted them. As Edward Said has argued in his orientalist critique and as Antonio Gramsci has espoused in his concept of the "Southern Question," geography can perpetuate stereotype and power struggles.[71] Furthermore, as Jared Diamond has deomonstrated, geography can be used to explain deep-seated patterns of disequality.[72]

Tensions and competitive exchanges between the North and the South, defined as a geographic and cultural region that unfolds across the Mediterranean basin, have been present in the historiography and criticism of art and architecture since the sixteenth-century artist and critic Giorgio Vasari referred to the Goths as "barbarians" in his *The Lives of the Artists*. In the nineteenth century, English artist and critic John Ruskin distinguished between what he believed to be the active and contemplative dispositions of northern and southern artists of the past and, in so doing, perpetuated a number of stereotypes:

> So that, in the twelfth century, while the Northern art was only in need of direction, the Southern was in need of life. The North was indeed spending its valor and virtue on ignoble objects; but the South disgracing the noblest objects by its want of valor and virtue.[73]

More recently, critics and historians of Scandinavian architecture and approaches to building have conceptualized a Nordic identity around conditions such as shared climate.[74] In the introduction to his *Nightlands: Nordic Building*, Christian Norberg-Schulz wrote:

> The book's subtitle, Nordic Building, has been chosen to emphasize that architecture is primarily something built, and that built form becomes an art when it gathers and represents the world to which it belongs. The Nordic art of building thus manifests what it means to "live poetically" under

Nordic conditions, whereby the word *poetic* acknowledges the qualitative identity of the environment.[75]

Although some parallels to define identity through geography do exist with regard to the American Southwest and the West, few critics and historians have actually discussed the South as it relates to architecture. Lewis Mumford's *The South in Architecture* (1941) is an exception. Mumford identifies adaptation to climate as key:

> Take for example a capital matter: adaptation to our trying American climate, with the extremes of temperature that prevail in the North and the sub-tropical conditions that exist in large portions of the South ... The forms of building that prevail in any region reflect the degree of social discovery and self-awareness that prevails there. [76]

American architect and writer Charles W. Moore, who spent his professional life working in California, Texas, and Connecticut, defined southernness in his article "Southernness: A Regional Dimension" as "a kind of scaled-down urbanity that seems to me, a Northerner, the most powerful southern image."[77] Shortly after the publication of his book, Mumford found himself defending regionalism in the midst of heated debate and controversy at the Museum of Modern Art (MoMA).[78] Moore led the turn from modernism to postmodern by vindicating the importance of ordinary places: the "scaled-down urbanity" of the design of Kresge College at the University of California, Santa Cruz (1964–74) evoked a continuation of the building types and spatial configurations typical of Mediterranean vernacular environments.[79]

Although the vernacular tradition was associated with a pre-modern "primitive" era by virtue of its pre-industrial building techniques and materials, it also comprised a *regional* heritage shared by other countries bordering the Mediterranean, a geographical area that touches three continents – Europe, Asia, and Africa. While the pioneering narratives of the modern movement that surfaced in the 1920s and 1930s authored by figures such as Nikolaus Pevsner acknowledged the role of the pre-industrial vernacular tradition of the North in the emergence of modernity, most ignored the impact of vernacular architecture of the Mediterranean region on modernists such as Le Corbusier in France and José Luis Sert in Spain.[80] In the work of these architects the vernacular tradition was subsumed into modernist, rationalist buildings, in contrast to the Mediterranean revival practices of protagonists such as

Addison Mizner in Florida, just to name one. Ironically, Paul Schultze-Naumburg's comparison of a Mediterranean village with the Weissenhof and Schönblick housing estates in *Das Gesicht des deutschen Hauses* (The Appearance of the German House) (1929), and the racist collage in the Bund für Heimatschutz's *Schwäbisches Heimatbuch* (Swabian Yearbook) (1934), in which the Weissenhof housing estate was likened to an *Araberdorf* (Arab village), reveal the resistance to Mediterranean modernism among a group of northern architects.[81] On the whole, from William Morris and Charles Voysey in England to Hermann Muthesius in Germany and Alvar Aalto in Germany and Finland, the role that vernacular architecture played in reforming northern (and central European) modernist practice has been acknowledged, whereas that of the South has not.[82]

The conflation of modernity and the vernacular tradition raises issues of anonymity and authorship for theorists and practising architects. The notions of timelessness and anonymity that have adhered to the vernacular tradition contrasted with picturesque rusticity in the nineteenth century, when artistry and authorship established the value of a work of art or architecture. For avant-garde practitioners of the twentieth century, timelessness and anonymity came to be revered as an antidote to historicism and individualism. As James Maude Richards wrote in 1937,

> The more immediate cause of decay was a cultural – a socio-psychological one; a phenomenon that may be summarized as a diffusion of purpose, manifested in a divorce of art as an individual achievement from art as a vernacular expression. The bane of the nineteenth century was the celebrity-architect: the Renaissance idea of the individual glorified over the Renaissance sense of artistic unity. And architecture cannot afford to be an affair of the individual. It is only when the individual innovation becomes assimilated into a regional tradition that it can be regarded as culturally valid ... Such a unity of purpose allows the establishment of a unity of cultural language – the widespread vernacular, in the case of architecture, already referred to.[83]

Well before Richard's embrace "unity of cultural language," Arts and Crafts Movement theorist and designer William Morris celebrated the lack of self-consciousness of "ordinary things" of pre-industrial vernacular traditions. In his *The Revival of Handicraft* of 1888, Morris wrote,

The art of making beautifully all kinds of ordinary things, carts, gates, fences, boats, bowls, and so forth, let alone houses and public buildings, unconsciously and without effort, has gone; when anything has to be renewed among these simple things the only question asked is how little it can be done for, so as to tide us over our responsibility and shift its mending on to the next generation.[84]

Frank Lloyd Wright, who shared Morris's interest in the vernacular, while still sympathizing with the individualism which Richards was to dismiss, famously wrote in his "The Sovereignty of the Individual" (1910):

Here as elsewhere, nevertheless, the true basis for any serious study of the art of Architecture still lies in those indigenous structures; more humble buildings everywhere being to architecture what folk-lore is to literature or folksong to music and with which Academic architects were seldom concerned. In the aggregate of these simple buildings lie traits which make them characteristically Italian, French, Dutch, German, Spanish, or English as the case may be.[85]

Le Corbusier, who also trained within an Arts and Crafts milieu in La Chaux-de-Fonds, Switzerland, but took a more conciliatory stance in relation to industrial production, also advocated *l'art paysan* or *folk art* as a source of contemporary design.[86] One need only recall his Maison Blanche (1912) as an early indicator of what would be a lifelong interest.[87] Le Corbusier's own struggles to come to terms with modernity without forgoing tradition altogether are at the heart of complex debate over "Art, Craft, Technology" spearheaded by the likes of Adolf Behne.[88]

A number of architects who disavowed nineteenth-century historicism on the basis of its academic character looked to the vernacular as a tradition that had developed outside of the academy and was authentically Rational and thus modern. Hungarian-born Marcel Breuer (1902–81) identified "old peasant houses" as a source of modern architecture in 1935:

At this point, I should like to consider traditionalism for a moment. And by tradition I do not mean the unconscious continuance and growth of a nation's culture generation by generation, but a conscious dependence on the immediate past. That the type of men who are described as modern architects have the sincerest admiration and love for genuine national art, for old peasant houses and for the masterpieces of the great epochs in art, is a point which needs to be stressed.[89]

During the 1960s Bernard Rudofsky's book and exhibition *Architecture without Architects: A Short Introduction to Non-Pedigreed Architecture* (1964) and Myron Goldfinger's *Villages in the Sun, Mediterranean Community Architecture* (1969) drew attention to the Mediterranean vernacular tradition outside French, Italian, Greek, and Spanish circles. John Maas hailed Rudofsky's study as a book "of transcendent importance to architectural history" because "the architectural historians do not yet pay attention to the anonymous architecture of early and rural societies."[90] Both practising architects, Rudofsky and Goldfinger were among a growing number of architects who challenged modernist architecture in thrall of a contextual formalism. In the introduction to his book, Rudofsky, who lived and worked in Italy until the mid-1930s, lamented the general lack of familiarity with what he termed "non-pedigreed architecture" of the Mediterranean region and beyond, and adumbrated a number of possible adjectives, including "vernacular," "anonymous," "spontaneous," "indigenous," and "rural."[91]

Ironically, Rudofsky's exhibition was held at the Museum of Modern Art in New York, the same institution that only three decades earlier offered its audience the International Exhibition of Modern Architecture (1932).[92] In the book that came out after the exhibition, Philip Johnson and Henry-Russell Hitchcock featured, among others, André Lurçat's North-South hotel on the island of Corsica (1931), a work clearly indebted to the serial whitewashed vernacular housing of the Mediterranean region with its flat roofs and unadorned walls.[93] Despite this affinity with the extant vernacular tradition, the curators chose to emphasize its formal affinities with the New Architecture of Germany and Holland. The curators also selected Luigi Figini and Gino Pollini's *Casa elettrica* or "Electric House" in Monza (1930). While the nautical elements of the house were seen to express universal machine-age qualities, Johnson and Hitchcock made no reference to the fact that the house was painted Pompeian red to evoke the vernacular and classical Mediterranean that had so engrossed Figini and Pollini as well as other members of the Gruppo 7.

The chapters that follow map the emergence and unfolding of a diverse set of approaches to vernacular architecture within the modernist tradition as it developed in Italy and was viewed from outside the nation's borders. Their dynamic interaction and the debates that ensued within a volatile and shifting political, economic, and social context is traced from its prehistory, so to speak, in the ethnographic projects that first brought to public attention the heritage of anonymous vernacular traditions in the 1910s, through the 1970s.

The first chapter, "In Search of *Italianità*: Ethnography and National Identity," looks at how and why the vernacular tradition initially became the focus of ethnographic and anthropological study of Italy's disparate regions in response to the need to forge a national image that included all Italians, both city and country dwellers. This chapter focuses on educational as well as heritage-driven initiatives, such as state-sponsored exhibitions and legislation aimed at preservation of the built domain and the folk objects that had rarely found a place in the museums of Italy. While ethnographic exhibitions took a documentary approach, drawing upon the materials and forms of extant vernacular buildings and objects, there was also a tendency to search for poetic expression in the work of artists and craftsmen like Duilio Cambellotti. In sum, the first chapter maps the discourse on the vernacular tradition as it surfaced primarily outside of architecture in exhibitions, publications, and public discussions with nationalistic and social agendas.

Chapter 2, "The Picturesque Revival: Rusticity and Contextualism," examines how and why interest in the vernacular tradition gained momentum in architectural discourse and practice after the First World War. Expanding upon early initiatives of ethnographers, architects including Gustavo Giovannoni and Piacentini began to appropriate elements from the vernacular tradition in the design of single-family dwellings and housing estates during the 1920s such as Garbatella and Aniene in Rome, at a time when Italy was on the threshold of transformation from a liberal to a fascist state. This chapter takes into account how the appropriation of vernacular forms paralleled the prevailing influence of classicism while architecture schools, independent of engineering schools, finally began to be professionalized with the implementation of the so-called Riforma Gentile, approved in 1922.[94] Since most of the individuals discussed in this chapter were either historicists or embraced *Stile Liberty*, their appropriations of the vernacular tradition revealed an interest in rusticity but eventually developed into the more comprehensive concept of contextualism. The issues raised in their approach paralleled experiments in the realm of object design that were also inspired by vernacular traditions, and debates over the merits of artisanal and industrial production.

The third chapter, "*Tabula rasa* and Tradition: Futurism and Rationalism between Primitivism and *Mediterraneità*," explores architectural developments of the 1920s and 1930s against the background of Benito Mussolini's *ruralesimo* (ruralism), focusing on the fascination that vernacular architecture, natural landscapes, and artisanal objects held for a second-generation of futurist artists and rationalist architects in parallel with the rise and consolidation of fascism.[95] It explores the ways artists and architects negotiated values like regionalism, nationalism and its other side, internationalism, at a time when fascist rhetoric on the new Italy dominated official and non-official discourse.[96] Competing attitudes emerge here, too, among architects who embraced fascism with varying degrees of commitment to the ideology. A case in point is the Island of Capri. As it became the subject of debates over the preservation of its natural landscape and built environment in the face of rampant tourism, futurist artists made it the object of their paintings and rationalist architects designed modern-day villas.

The fourth chapter, "Engineering versus Architecture: The Vernacular between New Objectivity and Lyricism," analyses tensions that developed under fascism between engineers and architects with different attitudes towards the role of individualism within the design process. While rationalist architects of the Gruppo 7 appropriated the Mediterranean's extant vernacular traditions along with its classical heritage in their pursuit of the subjective and lyrical in design, others like Pagano fought to uphold modesty and anonymity as a counterpoint to virtuosity in design. Despite their differences, they all opposed propagandistic rhetoric aimed at selling *Italianità*; in sum, these engineers and architects also projected a new ideal of simplicity and frugality that undermined the overblown classicizing aesthetic of the fascist regime. Against the grain of fascist policies promoting rural values as an antidote to urban vices, architects like Pagano who cocurated with Daniel the watershed exhibition Architettura rurale italiana (Rural Italian Architecture) at the Milan Triennale of 1936 sought to temper modernity with tradition while opposing all forms of historicism.

The final chapter, "Continuity and Reality: The Vernacular Resumed in Postwar Architecture and Urbanism," looks at Italy's transformation from fascist dictatorship to democracy with the end of the Second World War. For many architects, the austere reality of the postwar years under the American-sponsored Marshall Plan and the need for a great deal of new public housing to accommodate the influx of agrarian dwellers from the countryside to urban areas led them to look at the extant forms of Italian hill towns to rethink housing in its social dimension.

If neorealist film captured the everyday struggles of ordinary people, with directors often choosing amateur actors, so, too, the new housing estates that made up the lion's share of architectural production during those years became a canvas on which the hopes of working-class Italians were depicted. These years also witnessed the gradual move away from entrenched Catholic values in favour of a new secular outlook of Italian society, despite the constant resistance by the ever-powerful church. The chapter also looks at the role Italian architects played in shaping debates about how modern architecture could embrace an aesthetic of poverty.

In closing, the epilogue maps Italy's contribution to debates in Europe and America in an era of growing disenchantment with the modern movement. Giancarlo De Carlo, Ernesto N. Rogers, Enrico Peressutti and Aldo Rossi are among the prominent Italian architects who entered into dialogue with architectural milieus outside of Italy and shaped the outcome of practice by rethinking the role of tradition in modernist architecture.

Writing in the same year that he abandoned the fascist party, Giuseppe Pagano explained that the design of what was to be his last completed work, a weekend home in Viggiù, near Milan (1942), was motivated by his desire to make something that did "not offend the landscape" and that was truly "una cosa qualunque" (just an ordinary thing).[97] Indeed, ordinary things offered a number of progressive Italian architects the possibility to combine modernism with tradition while avoiding banal nostalgia. Lionella Venturi's "pride in modesty" was both a call to arms and a design strategy to help counteract pompous showmanship in architectural practice. Nearly 70 years after Pagano's Viggiò house was completed, the legacy of the vernacular tradition continues to offer architects and designers in Italy and beyond lessons with which to transform the commonplace by conflating local and global matters.

1 In Search of *Italianità*: Ethnography and National Identity

A language cannot be rebuilt in one stroke, and the arts are also a language. As Italian architecture manifestly must have a national appearance and temperament, it should be connected in some way to one or more Italian architectures of the past; and because presently this connection does not exist, they are in effect all there ... Must one cling to one past style in order to mimic it? Let's not dream of it, for imitation makes everything colder, poorer, more shriveled, and renders everything unbearable.

Camillo Boito, "On the Future Style of Italian Architecture" (1880)[1]

Italy's national unification, with Rome becoming the capital of the kingdom in July 1871, took place in the context of a political sea change that swept Europe, transforming empires into nations and altering relationships among countries throughout the Continent and around the world.[2] Neither was Italy immune to the quarrel over "Style-Architecture and Building-Art" that defined European architectural debates in thrall of historicism during the last decades of the nineteenth century.[3] To be sure, the ideological search for a language of national identity and the "challenge of tradition" powerfully propelled the arts.[4] During the fractious years following unification, classicism, in its ancient as well as its neo-Renaissance, neo-Baroque, and Beaux-Arts iterations, became the architectural language of choice to express a new civic consciousness for Italians within national boundaries.[5] If some exceptions occurred at home in Italy, when it came time for international exhibitions and fairs, the common language of the *Stile Nazionale* (national style) was unequivocally classicism and its derivations.[6]

For intellectuals as well as political leaders, classicism was consid-

Fig. 1.1 Poster by Galileo Chini, *Roma – 1911* – Esposizione Etnografica. Courtesy Archivio Chini – Lido di Camaiore.

ered a national and universal language, a veritable *lingua communis*. This is not surprising, as the invention of a national, even international, identity in a culturally diverse context depends on the suppression of regional diversity and its subordination to a common language.[7] Despite regional variations, Antiquity and the Renaissance were synonymous with Italian identity in the arts and architecture. While the vernacular buildings and artisinal crafts of the rural masses as well as the cultural legacy of the Middle Ages heavily influenced National Romanticism in the Scandinavian countries, England, Germany, and central Europe, Italy's self-identification with classicism during the founding years of the Kingdom of Italy resulted in the marginalization of both regional vernacular traditions and medieval sources.[8] However, despite the long shadow cast by classicism, Italian architects active in the last decades of the nineteenth and the first decades of the twentieth century began to revalorize and appropriate the medieval as well as the vernacular architecture of the various regions of Italy. Already in 1875, architect, theorist, and preservationist Camillo Boito (1836–1914) exhorted architects to abandon classicism *stricto senso* in favour of neomedievalism: "If we want to avoid academic classicism (which only has an icy modernized Roman quality anyhow) we need to leave it alone in Rome, and latch onto a different type of architecture."[9] In an article on the 1873 Universal Exhibition in Vienna, Boito described the Russian farmhouse as the most interesting architectural feat after the Palace of the Viceroy of Egypt. In his commentary on the exhibition, Boito also marvelled at the Swedish fisherman's hut, the Norwegian pavilion, and the Hungarian church. For him, their ingenuity demonstrated that even among peoples who had not produced "a very advanced art," one could find "concepts that were grand, or in their rusticity, elegant."[10]

In Italy, the interest expressed by Boito in vernacular buildings began to resurface in the 1910s, long before the rise of fascism, in animated debates leading up to a groundbreaking exhibition of ethnographic material – the Mostra di etnografia (Exhibition of Ethnography) – gathered from Italy's diverse regions and showcased in Rome in 1911 (Fig. 1.1). The Future Style of a new country was forged across a large territory laden to the point of being burdened with regional diversities: Italy had witnessed the rise of the Roman Empire, its fall and occupation by invaders from the North, and the gradual definition of independent kingdoms and city-states that competed with one another for dominance. The architectural culture of Italy sharply reflected specific regional traditions rooted in the diverse climates and terrains that go from the Mediterranean basin to the Alps. Whereas the kingdoms and city-states of Italy that banded together to form the new nation shared broadly defined cultural traditions, the coastal and southern regions shared more with other countries bordering the Mediterranean Sea, and likewise, Italian regions bordering France, Switzerland, Austria, and what is today Slovenjia shared traditions generally associated with northern Europe. The shared architectural heritage of regions once dominated by the Roman emperors provided an inviolate basis for such a common language. While the neomedievalism that Boito championed as a source of a national language was no match for the power of classicism, regional variations of this tradition challenged the perception of homogeneity.[11]

Given the deep-seated cultural and economic differences that so sharply distinguished the agrarian South from the increasingly industrialized North from the early twentieth century onwards, resentment, suspicion, and outright animosity threatened to erode the edifice of the newly unified nation. During fascism, Italian intellectuals, artists, architects, and cultural promoters viewed *vernacular* or *folk* traditions as vehicles for bridging "ancient regional divisions" in favour of a more cohesive nationalism.[12] On the eve of the First World War, Giovanni Crocioni (1870–1954) argued in *Le regioni e la cultura nazionale* (Regions and National Culture, 1914) that the construction of Italian national culture could be facilitated by increased awareness of its diverse regional cultures.[13] For Crocioni, the folk traditions of the Italian masses were an ideal unifier because they embodied a moral code with which all the inhabitants of different regions could identify.[14] Paolo D'Ancona's 1921 essay "Artigianato regionale e arte decorativa in Italia" (Regional Craftsmanship and Decorative Arts in Italy) echoed Crocioni's approach as did a number of magazines and journals that combined culture and tourism with more subtle regional political agendas.[15] Not only did Crocioni's book promote regionalism and advocate the appreciation of vernacular expressions, but also it anticipated federal legislation of 1921 granting a certain degree of political autonomy to the various regions of Italy just one year before Benito Mussolini's blackshirts illegally seized power during the March on Rome.[16]

While national ideals unified Italy politically, vernacular culture and language (i.e., regional dialects continued to be used throughout the country) became the focus of three interrelated fields of activity: ethnography, preservation, and design (architectural and object-based).

Geographers, ethnographers, historians, and linguists studied and analysed the living conditions and art forms of the agrarian peasant class and its relationship to the agrarian landscape.[17] Along with Italy's classical heritage, preservationists and cultural administrators shifted from an exclusive focus on the historic architectural remains of Roman antiquity to include vernaculars, dwellings, and objects. In parallel with preservation efforts, architects studied these previously ignored buildings and published their findings to raise public awareness of vernacular traditions.

As Italy consolidated its political identity within an unstable Europe on the brink of the First World War, there was a move to transform the agrarian peasant into an Italian citizen who would take an active part in the country's collective identity. Partly in response to this initiative, the Italian government mounted the Esposizione del cinquantenario (Fiftieth Anniversary Exhibition) in Rome in 1911 to celebrate the first fifty years of Italian unification. In Rome, the Esposizione was composed of the Esposizione regionale ed etnografica (Regional and Ethnographic Exhibition) and the Esposizione internazionale di Belle Arti (International Exposition of Beaux-Arts). They asked Rome-based architect Marcello Piacentini (1881–1960) to oversee the master plan and design some of the key exhibition buildings (Fig. 1.2).[18] With its satellite installations in the former provisional capital cities of Turin and Florence, the Italian Esposizione was staged as a large-scale, multi-site international cultural event. Whereas the Prima esposizione internazionale d'arte decorativa moderna (First International Exhibition of Modern Decorative Art) held in Turin in 1902 had resulted in international exposure for Art Nouveau and in particular for Italy's Stile Liberty artists, architects, and designers, the 1911 Esposizione was decidedly more political and was regarded, not by coincidence, as a "testimony of love for the fatherland and for the living faith in the future destinies of Italy."[19] Eventually demolished, Raimondo D'Aronco's imaginative pavilions realized for the 1902 Turin exhibition symbolized the swan song of an era.[20] By the time the 1911 Esposizione was over, Stile Liberty, with its embrace of cosmopolitan formal aspirations and regional craftsmanship, had lost the leadership in architecture, interior design, and objects.[21]

The Mostra di etnografia (Exhibition of Ethnography) organized by pioneering ethnographer Lamberto Loria (1855–1913) was one of the installations mounted in Rome in 1911.[22] According to the original plans spearheaded by Loria, the outdoor Mostra di etnografia was to replace the Museo di etnografia italiana (Museum of Italian Ethnography) he

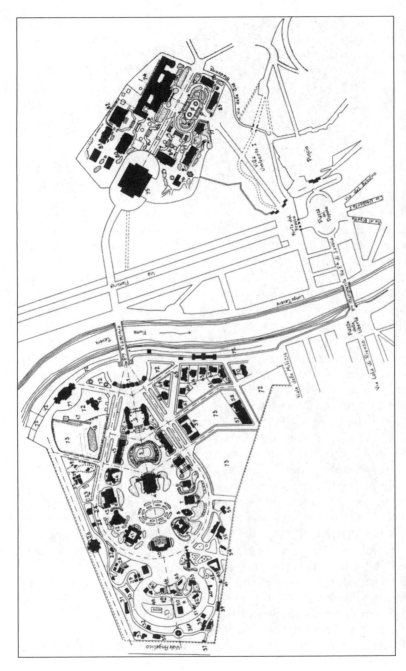

Fig. 1.2 Plan of Fiftieth Anniversary Exhibition, Rome, 1911, from Daniele Donghi, *Manuale dell'Architetto*, vol. 2 (Turin: UTET, 1925), 497.

Fig. 1.3 Postcard, view of Casa colonica (demolished) (Lucca, Tuscany), Exhibition of Ethnography, Augusto Giustini and Angelo Guazzaroni, Rome, 1911. © Wolfsonian – Florida International University.

helped to establish together with Count Bastogi and Pasquale Villari in Florence in 1906.[23] During the first decade of the twentieth century, Florence, one of Italy's Renaissance centres, spearheaded ethnographic studies. A lack of funding thwarted Loria's plans at the time, and in due course the Piazza d'Armi site was demolished to make room for new residential buildings.[24] Funding problems, Loria's premature death, and difficulties that continued through the fascist period conspired to cause a delay of decades before the Museo Nazionale delle Arti e Tradizioni Popolari was inaugurated in Rome under the directorship of folklorist Paolo Toschi (1893–1974).[25] By that time, the open-air museum concept deployed by Loria had been abandoned, and, ironically, his collection was housed in a classically inspired building erected for the Universal Exhibition originally planned to open in 1942.[26]

Typical rural dwellings described as *fabbricati etnografici* or ethnographic buildings by historian Francesco Baldasseroni (1879–1923) who edited the exhibition catalogue and which represented the thirteen regions of Italy that had been established up to that point (today, Italy has twenty regions). Abruzzo, Calabria, Campania, Emilia-Romagna, Lucania Liguria, Lombardy, Marche, Piedmont, Puglia, Sardinia, Sicily, Tuscany, Umbria, and Veneto were constructed as part of a *living museum* in Piazza d'Armi across the Tiber from the Villa Borghese.[27] Postcards produced for the exhibition show vernacular building types such as the *casa colonica* or cottage, typical of Lucca in Tuscany, flanked by haystacks and adorned with corn braids alongside stone *trulli* (stone dwellings with conical roofs) of Alberobello in Puglia (Figs. 1.3, 1.5).[28] Buildings such as these were redolent with regional identity, using local materials and building methods that had been developed in response to specific climatic and topographic conditions. The installation should thus be seen as an inclusive strategic gesture at a moment when the politics of national unity were, in reality, in their infancy.

The individual regions were grouped together into geographic areas of the Italian peninsula and the two islands of Sardinia and Sicily (Fig. 1.4). Italia Meridionale (southern) was the first in the visitors' itinerary once they passed the ceremonial foro followed by Italia Settentrionale (northern), Italia centrale (central) ending with Sardinia and Sicily. It was clear that the diversity of building types reflected the efforts of organizers to catalogue and convey differences as well as similarities in the vernacular traditions of the Italian peninsula. The organizers laid out different routes to be followed by the visitors according to whether or not they were interested in folk and vernacular culture of the Mostra di Etnografia (Ethnography Exhibition) or if they preferred the style-driven pavilions of the so-called Mostra regionale (Regional Exhibition). The ethnographic buildings were aligned around the margins of the site whereas the so-called regional pavilions occupied the centre core.

Not unlike Skansen, Arthur Hazelius's pioneering open-air museum in Stockholm, founded in 1891, featured meandering roads along with fauna and flora typical of the different geographical regions of Italy.[29] Despite its aspiration to promote the nationalist notion of *Italianità*, the installation design combined the naturalness of English picturesque garden-city tradition with a loosely organized axial plan.[30] While most of the public may have been familiar with the classical fora of antiquity, the experience of following a meandering path dotted with vernacular buildings and so-called regional (style-driven) pavilions was new, a phenomenon ushered in by the world fairs from the late nineteenth century onwards.[31] Summing up the Mostra di etnografia, Arduino

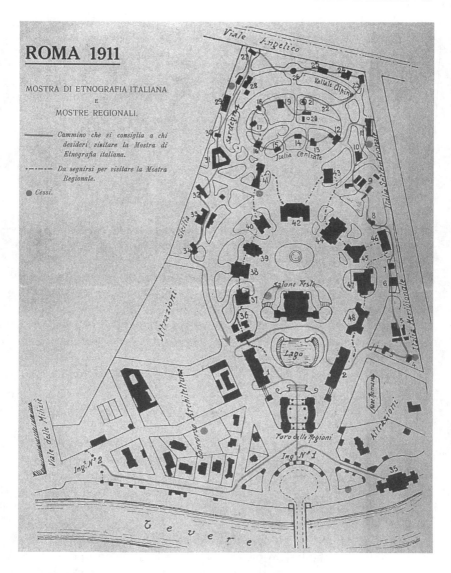

Fig. 1.4 Plan of "Mostra di etnografia italiana e mostre regionali," from *Esposizione Etnografica Italiana a Piazza d'Armi – Guida sommaria e pianta* (Rome: Tipografia Nazionale G. Berteri, 1911).

Fig. 1.5 View of Trulli of Alberobello, Exhibition of Ethnography, Augusto Giustini and Angelo Guazzaroni, Rome, 1911, from Francesco Baldasseroni, *Catalogo della Mostra di etnografia in Piazza d'Armi* (Bergamo: Istituto Italiano d'Arti Grafiche, 1911), 157.

Colasanti (1877–1935) called it "Una esposizione in azione, dunque un grande museo di vita" or an action-packed exhibition, great museum of life, specifically drawing attention to the fact that it featured building types still in use, and everyday lifestyles still being practised in Italy at the time.[32] Installed outdoors, the exhibition showcased architecture and quotidian objects not typically on display in traditional museums, with peasants on site re-enacting their daily lives, in a didactic presentation that also embraced arts and crafts.[33] While ethnographic and sociological interests drove the documentation and display of the "material life" of the Italian peasantry, it also laid the groundwork for enlarging traditional art historical boundaries to what George Kubler poetically described as "the shape of time."[34]

Engineers Augusto Giustini and Angelo Guazzaroni, in collaboration with Associazione artistica fra i cultori di architettura (in Rome) along with others, headed by Piacentini and Gustavo Giovannoni (1873–1947), worked alongside Loria in carefully selecting the vernacular building

types. A lack of architectural drawings in the otherwise quite rich exhibition archive suggests that the buildings were realized on site in collaboration with local masons.[35] Little other than schematic plan drawings
outlining total area (in square metres) but not elevation drawings sur-
vive to illuminate the process; this curious documentary lacuna is not
especially surprising given the empirical process of realizing vernacular
buildings. Geographer Renato Biasutti (1878–1965), who went on to edit
a multi-volume series of books devoted entirely to the rural dwellings of
different regions of Italy, observed, "One of the most interesting aspects
of the exhibition was the reproduction of traditional rustic buildings of
the Italian regions, selected almost always with a satisfactory criterion
and faithfully reproduced in their exterior forms, and in rarer instances,
also in the interior layout as well as interior furnishings."[36]

It is important to draw attention to the fact that, unlike the wooden
vernacular buildings that were disassembled and transported from
their original sites to be displayed in the pioneering open-air museums
of northern countries where wood was abundant, masonry buildings
typical of the southern and central regions of Italy had to be recreated or
simulated, and as such, no real historical value would ever be assigned
to them. Biasutti's observation that the buildings had been "faithfully
reproduced" is an important one because it speaks to the somewhat
static nature of vernacular buildings. The fact that most building types
had not changed significantly over time was a double-edged sword:
for some, it reflected continuity and cultural coherence and was thus
worthy of praise; for others, it suggested inferiority, a patent absence
of the transformational impetus that characterizes the *art* of architecture. While reproduction was desirable in the documentary context of
an ethnography exhibition, it was not considered an asset in academic
architecture debates where historical styles had since the Renaissance
been appropriated and transformed through artistic invention. On the
other hand, it was argued, the vernacular belonged to a living tradition
and continued to be replicated because it continued to serve certain
unchanging functions. Promoters of peasant (or folk) traditions defended it from detractors who claimed it was merely mimetic and not
inventive. Baldessaroni wrote in defence of the "fresh fantasy" of folk
art while still revealing his role as observer and "outsider": "Imitation
in folk art is never ostentatious or servile; if it is true that the people
invent little or nothing, all of us know how many stimuli manage to
pass through their uncultivated but ready spirit, and that they transform them with limited yet fresh fantasy so that their products appear

spontaneous and original."[37] Despite his earnest defence, his choice of words and the very fact that he felt compelled to defend folk art betray deep-seated divisions regarding culture and artistic creation typical of the first decades of the twentieth century in Italy.

As an indication of these divisions, alongside the Mostra di etnografia of 1911, and in contrast to its ethnographic focus, another exhibition was installed, the Mostra regionale (Regional Exhibition) comprised of historicist, style-driven pavilions that reflected periods of greatest political and artistic clout for the regions. Whereas Giustini and Guazzaroni simply replicated extant vernacular buildings, the Mostra regionale attracted prestigious architects who were commissioned to design regional pavilions in historicizing styles. The vernacular buildings of the Mostra di etnografia were likely considered by organizers and politicians to be of a lesser "artistic" order, the subject of ethnographic research, than the architectural examples designed for the Mostra regionale. Baldasseroni inverted the hierarchy in his review of the two exhibitions, drawing attention to the aesthetic import of the ordinary buildings showcased in the Mostra di etnografia, and significantly, remarking on their operative relevance for contemporary Italy in comparison with the retrospective quality of the Mostra regionale, which had been financed by each of the regions whereas the ethnography exhibition had been financed with the funds of the organizing committee:

> The regional pavilions have been conceived as part of a retrospective exhibition; they showcase the historic contribution of architecture and the arts from the different parts of our country. The *Italian Exhibition of Ethnography*, on the other hand, reveals the beauty that Italy has to offer in the traditions and customs of its people. Its aim is to give new impulse to research on these traditions and costumes, as well as reviving the activities and forms of vernacular art and architecture that have long since been forgotten and have nearly disappeared.[38]

The contrast between the promotional (and self-aggrardizing) quality of the pavilions and monuments inspired by historic styles planned for the 1911 celebrations and modesty of the Mostra di etnografia buildings could not be more obvious. Giuseppe Sacconi's Altare della Patria (National Monument to Vittorio Emanuele II), inaugurated in 1911 and completed in 1935, symbolized Italy's public face to the world, which stood in sharp contrast to the vernacular buildings in

Piazza d'Armi.[39] Pavilions dressed in the styles of the past to evoke, for example, a highly ornate neomedieval town hall building from Puglia designed by Vittorio Pantaleo, stood in stark contrast to the domestic vernacular buildings of the same regions, as was the case with the *trulli* of Puglia (Fig. 1.5). Other dramatic comparisons include the neo-Baroque pavilion of Campania by Antonio Curri and the multi-level urban housing typical of Naples, and the neomedieval bell tower designed by Max Ongaro representing Piazza San Marco in Venice and the "Gruppo caratteristico Veneziano – Palazzetto Von Axel," a typical vernacular residential neighbourhood of Venice.[40] In all these instances, different architects designed the regional pavilions and the team of Giustini and Guazzaroni executed the vernacular version.

An anti-academic and romanticized association of the vernacular with "spontaneous" know-how transmitted through hands-on learning over the centuries was expressed in contemporaneous comments generated in response to the Mostra di etnografia. While discussing carved objects made of wood by a shepherd of Abruzzo, Baldasseroni referred to the "primitive ingenuity" of a statue of Saint Eustache.[41] The civil engineer Luigi Angelini (1884–1969) praised the "alpine simplicity and primitive grace, rustic strength and effortless lightness" of vernacular buildings and objects.[42] The fact that Angelini praised the buildings and wares of artisans and farmers at the Mostra di etnografia and over the course of his life spent quite a bit of effort publishing articles and drawing vernacular environments of his hometown Bergamo and surrounding area, suggests that peasant environments began to acquire status among practising architects and intellectuals after the 1911 exhibition.[43] Unlike the English-language usage of primitive as a derogatory quality, in Italian, the term was associated with the Romantic notion of primordial, so that when Italian intelligentsia used the term, they were thinking along these lines. The parallel between peasants, or the working rural class, and primitivism was an iteration of a recurring controversial theme in the history of art of the nineteenth and the first half of the twentieth centuries.[44] Primitivism also became emblematic of marginalization and rebellion amongst the peasants turned social bandits in Italy.[45]

Not only the buildings and their contents but also genuine peasants were on display at the Mostra di etnografia as the *other*, as *specimens*, following a practice that was common in the nineteenth and early twentieth centuries. Whether it was peasants from European countries or so-called savages from exotic lands under colonial rule, expositions of other peoples occupied a central yet problematic place in the histories of modern art, architecture, and design.[46] From the beginning, the organizers of exhibitions and fairs century struggled to obfuscate an agenda falling somewhere between self-promotion and dutiful pedagogical service to the peoples of the world, that is, the desire to display scientific, technological, and cultural commodities. The sight of of actual peasants in ethnographic exhibitions was often a novelty for bourgeois city-dwellers who didn't typically wander into the countryside, allowing them to observe *primitive* (often illiterate) peoples contextualilzed in simulations of their indigenous settings. Yet the display of European peasants was fundamentally different from, for instance, Paul Gauguin's experience of viewing *exotic* dancers in the Javanese village at the Universal Exhibition held in Paris in 1889. Shortly after, Gauguin left for his first trip to Tahiti, and when he came back to Paris, he proudly described himself as a "savage."[47] Tahiti and its inhabitants remained a place far removed from the places the European peasantry inhabited, often removed from the city-dwellers. The increased interest in "the people" (i.e., farmers) might be traced to the thrust of Jean-Jacques Rousseau's *First Discourse* of 1750, where the "savage" was "noble" and who found his ideal environment in the wilderness or the rural countryside, not in the social and physical constraints of the city: "It is in the rustic clothes of a farmer and not beneath the gilt of a courtier that strength and vigour of the body will be found."[48] Gustave Courbet echoed Rousseau's admiration for rustic people in his seminal self-portrait entitled *Bonjour Monsieur Courbet* (1854). In a letter dated 31 July 1850, he asserted: "Yes, dear friend, even in our so civilised society, I must lead the life of a savage. I must break free from its very governments. The people have my sympathy. I must turn to them directly. I must get my knowledge from them, and they must provide me with a living. Therefore I have just embarked on the great wandering and independent life of the bohemian."[49]

At this same fair in Paris where Gauguin experienced the Javanese village, in the shadow of the Eiffel Tower, the Histoire de l'Habitation exhibition of over forty different types of dwellings organized by architect Charles Garnier (1825–98) proved that domestic architecture, and not just monuments, was of increasing interest to a broad audience and not only specialists. Garnier redesigned examples of typical domestic structures from around the world in a number of very distinct styles, with their interiors and landscaping recreating real-life context. This landmark exhibition was a veritable encyclopedia of the domestic

Fig. 1.6 Capanne romane bislunghe (oblong Roman huts) from Charles Garnier and Auguste Ammann, *L'abitazione umana,* trans. Alfredo Melani (Milan: Pubblicazione del *Corriere della Sera*, 1893), 287.

architecture of the world. Alongside signature designs for housing by known architects, some of which appropriated vernacular sources, were the indigenous dwellings of primitive peoples that coexisted alongside idealized interpretations of Roman and Greek villas.[50] Garnier's evolutionary (Darwinian) approach was largely based on Eugène-Emmanuel Viollet-le-Duc's blueprint for the *Histoire de l'Habitation Humaine depuis les temps préhistoriques jusqu'à nos jours* (Paris: J. Hetzel, 1875), a book intended for young adults.[51] Both Viollet-le-Duc's *The Habitations of Man in All Ages* (English translation by Benjamin Bucknal, Boston, 1876) and Garnier and Amman's co-authored study were translated into Italian in 1877 and 1893, respectively.[52] Alfredo Melani (1859–1928), an architect and critic often associated with Boito's circle, oversaw the abridged Italian translation, *L'abitazione umana*, published only a year later in

1893 and distributed as a gift to subscribers by the leading Milan-based daily newspaper *Corriere della Sera*.[53] This Italian edition contains a number of illustrations that range from a Roman-style house rebuilt for the Paris exhibition to the oblong Roman huts common to peasant communities in the Roman countryside (Fig. 1.6).[54]

Along with exhibitions held outside of Italy, the events that paved the way for Mostra di etnografia of 1911 in Rome came from Sicily, an island that was rich in rural culture and a host of vernacular art and architectural traditions. Sicilian folklorist Giuseppe Pitrè (1841–1916), whose legacy was the impetus of a museum in his native city of Palermo, organized the Mostra etnografica siciliana (Sicilian Ethnographic Exhibition) on the occasion of the Esposizione nazionale (National Exhibition) of 1891–2 held in Palermo only two decades after unification.[55] As the first ethnographic exhibition after Italian unification, it presented a wide range of folk arts and crafts produced by the Sicilian peasantry. Although Pitrè's exhibition and accompanying catalogue focused on the dwelling in terms of customs and traditions as well as the production of arts and crafts, he only marginally addressed vernacular buildings (Fig. 1.7). At the Palermo exhibition, his collection was displayed in a modest Stile Liberty pavilion by Sicilian architect Ernesto Basile (1857–1932), who also designed the large pavilion next to it, which combined Arab-Sicilian stylistic elements with Beaux-Arts rationality.[56] No attempt was made to replicate traditional peasant housing to host Pitrè's collection. However, next to the building that housed the Sicilian Ethnographic Exhibition stood a duplicate that hosted the Mostra geografica (Geography Exhibition), which showcased the ethnographic collection of Count Antonelli of objects made by the Shoan people of Ethiopia.[57] Political ambitions and propaganda fuelling Italy's colonial expansion into Ethiopian Africa were the reason reed huts made their debut at the Palermo exhibition in the open-air Mostra eritrea (Eritrean Exhibition). An "Abyssinian village" with cone-shaped reed huts was reconstructed and situated at the edge of the main pavilion next to an "Arab café" to heighten the exoticism of the presentation (Fig. 1.8).[58] Also in Palermo at the exhibition, the Capanna della mostra del Club Alpino (Alpine Club Exhibition Cabin) recalled the vernacular chalets typical of the Alps. Nothing could have appeared more exotic in the balmy Mediterranean climate of Palermo than the pitched roof, timber framing, and straw roof of a building typical of alpine regions in Austria, Germany, Northern Italy, and Switzerland.

Fig. 1.7 Catalogue cover page, Giuseppe Pitrè, *Catalogo illustrato della Mostra di Etnografica Siciliana* (Palermo: Stabilimento Tipografico Virzi, 1892).

Fig. 1.8 Drawing by Gennaro Amato, *View of the Eritrean Exhibition*, from *Palermo e L'Esposizione Nazionale del 1891–92*, Issue No. 15 (Milan: Fratelli Treves, Editori, 1892), 117.

Pitrè's study of the Sicilian folk traditions found support among literary figures. Writing in 1891, Girolamo Ragusa-Moleti (1851–1917), who would later write the book *La poesia dei selvaggi* (1897) on the poetry of "savages and barely civil" (that is, non-Western) individuals, recalled the sceptical reactions to ethnography and the pioneering work of Pitrè:

> I remember the burst of laughter with which ten years or so ago greeted Pitrè's work. Even though he received little recognition from the fatherland, he worked on his own tirelessly so that eventually the majority of those naysayers regretted having criticized him because they were ignorant of the work he was doing gathering materials for a science that was not included in the encyclopedias they were already familiar with.[59]

Many years after Pitrè's death, the writer Italo Calvino (1923–85) credited the Sicilian folklorist for not merely transcribing but also preserving the "inner poetry of the stories" collected in his monumental twenty-five volumes of Sicilian folk and fairy tales, which were published between 1870 and 1913.[60] At the same time that Pitrè was exploring the complex world of the peasantry of Sicily, the *verista* writer Giovanni Verga (1840–1922), published two collections of short stories, *Vita dei campi* (1880) and *Novelle rusticane* (1883), which focused on the ordinary yet fascinating qualities of Sicilian rural life while echoing one of Honoré De Balzac's seminal works, *Sons of the Soil* (1840).[61] Calvino also wrote that "Pitrè did in folklore what Verga had done in literature." In his *Vita dei campi*, Verga was interested in depicting the unaffected primitive qualities of his fictitious yet realistic characters such as Turiddu Macca ("Cavalleria rusticana"), Jeli the Shepherd, Rosso Malpelo, and the She-Wolf. The drama and vitality of Verga's most well-known short story went itself to opera in the interpretation of Pietro Mascagni, which premiered in 1890 in Rome. Verga's account in "Cavalleria rusticana" ends with the following description of Turridu which evokes animal-like qualities: "Turridu pawed the air for a while amid the cactuses, then dropped to the ground like a stone. The blood foamed up with a gurgling sound into his throat, and he couldn't even get out the words, 'Ah, mamma mia!'"[62]

Interpreters of the literary and social culture, whose writings served as the textual equivalent of the spatial and visual texture of vernacular art and architecture, anticipated the architect's participation. So, too, did the work of geographers, linguists, and ethnographers lay down the foundations of what was to come. Coinciding with the 1911 Mostra di etnografia was the First Congress of Italian Ethnography. It was held to coincide with the opening of the exhibition. A year later, the journal *Lares* (named in honour of the Roman deities who protect the house and the family) was founded, and joined *Folklore*, under the editorial direction of Raffaele Corso (1883–1965), in becoming one of Italy's premier ethnography journals. These journals featured articles on folk arts and vernacular architecture that had been previously discussed in geography journals such as the *Rivista Geografica Italiana*, founded in 1894. *Lars* and *Folklore* (subsequently changed to *Il Folklore italiano*) inspired, in the first decades of the twentieth century, a number of symposia and congresses on folk art and increased the circulation of information through their publications. As this specialized academic knowledge gradually spread, it awoke a new interest in the subject on the part of artists and architects anxious to glean cues to apply to their contemporary work. Up to this point, experts of vernacular architecture had not existed within the discipline of architecture. Not by coincidence, Aristide Bara-

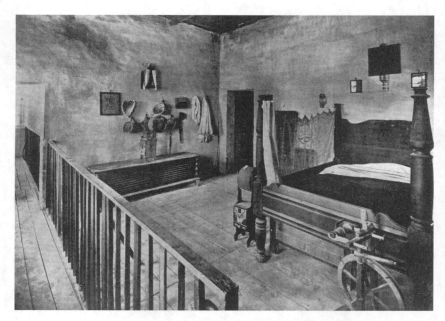

Fig. 1.9 Photograph by Ins. Ital. Grafiche, Bergamo, of a peasant's bedroom in Sarre, Piedmont, from Charles Holme, ed., *Peasant Art in Italy* (London: The Studio, 1913), 16.

giola (1847–1928), who was trained in philosophy and linguistics, was the only individual asked to address participants on the *casa villereccia* (rural house) at the First Congress of Italian Ethnography.[63] As can be expected from the type of expertise presented by ethnographers, geographers, and linguists, the emphasis was on the built environment and traditions of the peasantry as a whole, not architecture. To be sure, during the early 1910s in Italy, there was little dialogue between the world of geographers and ethnographers and that of practising architects and artists.

Aside from gaining attention within academic circles, vernacular art and architecture studies gained further momentum thanks to the initiatives related to the growing leisure industry and changing patterns of mobility. In the preface to *Peasant Art in Italy* (1913), Sidney J.A. Churchill, an art scholar who had settled in Naples, explained: "The changes in the local customs are due to the development of railway communication and emigration" (Fig. 1.9).[64] Although the introduction of a transportation infrastructure lent a great service to Italy in terms of mobility, it also disrupted the rural landscape which had remained undisturbed for centuries.[65] Already in 1894, the Touring Club Italiano (TCI), Italy's primary tourism agency, had been founded and, a year later, it launched its official journal *Le Vie d'Italia*.[66] In fact, the new culture of leisure that expressed interest in the picturesque qualities of the landscape and vernacular buildings brought advantages, not only disruption, to the idyllic landscape and its indigenous population. TCI also pursued an ambitious guidebook-publishing campaign that revealed to architects and their future clients the rich diversity of previously ignored regions of Italy.[67] These TCI publications offered a uniquely Italian perspective on the peninsula, which was distinct from the model Karl Baedeker and others had established in northern Europe. Improved access by train and car, thanks to the realization of rail lines and roads, encouraged anyone who was interested to explore the territory outside cities and towns, especially destinations such as the Alps, the rugged Mediterranean coast, lake regions, and even remote islands where vernacular architecture abounded.

Another important travel and leisure association that abetted, albeit indirectly, the growing awareness of folk art and architecture, primarily of the northern Alpine regions of Italy, was the Club Alpino Italiano (CAI), founded in 1863 in Turin on the model of the Austrian, German, and Swiss Alpine clubs.[68] In 1865, the CAI established, like the TCI, its own journal. Many architects, including Luigi Angelini, were members of these organizations, which sustained their professional as well as personal interest in the Alpine environment and culture. The CAI was perhaps the most visible promoter of Alpine vernacular architecture at various national exhibitions, commissioning a prominent pavilion at the 1884 Turin exhibition, for example (Fig. 1.10). Their wood and stone kiosk was sited next to the neomedieval castle and village designed by Alfredo D'Andrade. The club sponsored an Alpine village for the 1911 exhibition, also in Turin, in which an Alpine church was featured alongside a *rascard*, a wood-and-stone building typically used to store grain and house animals. Other exhibitions, not directly related to the CAI, such as the Villaggio tirolese (Tyrolean village) designed by Trieste-based Wagnerschule architect Max Fabiani in 1906, drew attention to the regions of northern Italy in the foothills of the Alps which did not normally figure in the romantic vision of a resplendent Italy bathed in Mediterranean light.[69]

In contrast to the exploration of the countryside and its primary in-

Fig. 1.10 Drawing by Ettore Ximenes, view of the Italian Alpine Club pavilion, 1884, from *Torino – L'esposizione italiana* (Milan-Turin: Fratelli Treves, 1884), n.p.

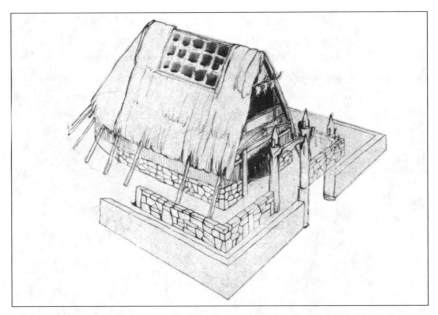

Fig. 1.11 Duilio Cambellotti, ink drawing, axonometric, *The Main Hut of the Roman Agro*, Exhibition of the Roman Agro, Rome, 1911. © Cambellotti Collection.

habitants by the leisure class, the 1911 celebrations in Rome offered Duilio Cambellotti (1876–1960) an opportunity to explore his long-standing interest in the marginalized peasantry of the Roman *campagna* (countryside).[70] Writing in 1948, towards the end of his life, Cambellotti romanticized the marshlands surrounding Rome before they were "sanitized" and appropriated by the fascist regime for large-scale agriculture:

> For most, up until a half-century ago, recalling the Roman countryside evoked squalor, pain, and malaria fever. For those who had an evocative spirit however, for those who had a sense of art, of culture, and for the poet or the artist, it was a place of dreams, of tragedy, of heroic atmosphere.[71]

Cambellotti's fascination with the *primitivism* of its inhabitants and built environments made him the most qualified to rebuild replicas in proximity to the ethnographic pavilions of the monumental reed huts

Fig. 1.12 Chest manufactered by Agro peasants (photographer unknown), on display inside the main reed hut of the Exhibition of the Roman Agro, Rome, from *La casa* (1 October 1911), n.p.

traditionally inhabited by the rural working class of the Latium region. Although the reed huts of the Mostra dell'Agro Romano (Exhibition of the Roman Agro) were also part of the vernacular tradition from where ethnographic pavilions by Giustini and Guazzaroni were sourced, Cambellotti's interest in dwellings made of reed and mud made in the place of masonry made his work much more subversive (Fig. 1.11).[72] The cavernous, two-storey central hut, with a facade adorned by three ox skulls as a symbol of the toil of the fields, was flanked by several smaller huts enclosing exhibitions on peasant literacy initiatives and displays of building techniques of the reed huts, all of which were intermingled with objects gathered by Cambellotti from the Roman countryside (Fig. 1.12).

This exhibition promoted the efforts of reformist intellectuals such as Giovanni Cena (1870–1917) and Alessandro Marcucci (1876–1968) who, like many socially minded artists they befriended, were seeking to improve the squalid living conditions (and high illiteracy rate) of the Italian peasantry by supporting education and building schools in the countryside. Rather than expect the children of the working rural class to travel to cities, Cena, Marcucci, and Cambellotti wanted to bring the schools to the countryside and often promoted modest yet interesting schoolhouse designs (Fig. 1.13).[73] Along with advancing this socio-political agenda, the organizers of the exhibition drew attention to the "heroic atmosphere" of the primitive dwellings and folk art.

The ethnographic buildings and Cambellotti's Roman Agro exhibition of small peasant communities of the Roman countryside were located opposite the Villa Borghese urban park, where various buildings of the International Fine Arts Exhibition were showcased in newly designed buildings inspired by classicism. Just as vernacular architecture was typically found beyond the protective walls of the cities where open fields and winding country roads led to hamlets, villages, and towns (or in the case of the malaria-infested swamplands) surrounding Rome, these two exhibitions occupied the outskirts of the presentation. In this context, their physical marginalization reflected the prejudice against folk art and architecture typical of art and architect circles in Italy during the last decades of the nineteenth century. The sidelining in Italy of the vernacular tradition despite the efforts of those few who courageously sought to modify the status quo was mainly class-driven. Even though enlightened leaders of liberal persuasion sought to balance the profound cultural, social, and economic differences between regions (especially between the increasingly industrialized North and agrarian South), there remained deep-seated resistance to the disenfranchised working peasant class that was considered illiterate and even savage by some.

The 1911 Mostra di etnografia gave new visibility to vernacular architecture and arts, which slowly began to emerge as an alternative to more traditional expressions of Italian identity based on classicism. The divisionist artist later turned futurist, Giacomo Balla (1871–1958), displayed his relief painting *Contadina davanti a due capanne* (Peasant woman in front of two [reed] huts, 1910) as one of a series of twelve in Cambellotti's central reed hut (Fig. 1.14).[74] Balla's emphasis on the grace and humility of a female peasant viewed against the backdrop of gritty reed

Fig. 1.13 Agro school designed by Duilio Cambellotti with Giovanni Cena and Alessandro Marcucci (photographer unknown), from Vittorio Morpurgo, "Gli edifici e la minerva," *Architettura e arti decorative* 1:2 (November–December, 1921), 373.

Fig. 1.14 Painting by Giacomo Balla, *Contadina davanti a due capanne* (Peasant woman in front of two [reed] huts), 1910, Private collection.

huts (he had added coarse sand to the oil paint to enhance through granularity their tactile quality) suggests his solidarity with the peasantry who lived outside the cities and towns. Among the twelve works in the series was Balla's portrait of Leo Tolstoy, whose seminal work *What Is Art?* (1897) had been translated into Italian in 1900. Cambellotti's socialist-minded circle in Rome, frequented by Balla and many others, sought to broaden the traditional boundaries of art to include material culture.[75] They were particularly taken by Tolstoy's expansive definition:

> We are accustomed to regard as art only what we read, hear, see in theatres, concerts and exhibitions, buildings, statues, poems, novels … But all this is only a small portion of the art by which we communicate with one another in life. The whole of human life is filled with works of art of various kinds, from lullabies, jokes, mimicry, home decoration, clothing, utensils, to church services and solemn processions. All this is the activity of art.[76]

Elsewhere in Italy, artists such as Giuseppe Pellizza da Volpedo (1868–1907), Giovanni Segantini (1858–99), Gaetano Previati (1852–1920), and Angelo Morbelli (1853–1919) produced divisionist paintings that showcased the agrarian landscape of Italy: arcadia and anarchy, alienation and solitude are reoccurring themes in these paintings.[77] These artists, identifying with the peasants' status as outcast, depicted their daily hardships in a sympathetic way. In so doing, they hoped to combat the bourgeois contempt or indifference directed at this underprivileged group, whose illiteracy and political disempowerment closed off its members from the civil life of the country. Pellizza da Volpedo II's *Quarto Stato* (Fourth Estate) (1901) (Fig. 1.15) depicts workers on strike marching forward proudly and with determination towards a new dawn of progressive politics for the marginalized working rural classes. In literature, Gabriele D'Annunzio (1863–1938) celebrated the power of natural forces in his *Laudi del cielo, del mare, della terra e degli eroi* (1899) as well as the heroic qualities of the peasantry in his *The Daughter of Jorio: A Pastoral Tragedy* (1902).[78] Loaded with symbolism, D'Annunzio casts the peasants as clichés of uncontrollable passions typical of irrational peoples; in her introduction to the English translation, Charlotte Porter wrote, "An elemental savor of the savage blood of the ancient race clings to the country of the Abruzzi [sic]. This elemental quality, intensely impressional and tragic, underlies the light sensitive beauty and bright artistic grace characteristic of Italy in general."[79]

Cambellotti's work, too, evoked a dark, sublime beauty of the countryside lands inhabited by the peasants in D'Annunzio's tales, in contrast to the grandiosity of the urban heritage of the caesars of Imperial Rome or the legacy of magniloquent popes. The difficulty of escaping from this Janus-type duality of the classical-vernacular and the urban-rural is best exemplified in the posters designed by artists to advertise the 1911 celebrations. Despite his active interest in the peasantry, one of Cambellotti's posters for the exhibition featured two bold imperial eagles perched on freestanding columns. In contrast, Gallileo Chini's poster (and postcards) advertising the Exhibition of Ethnography is a playful, colourful rendition of peasant women in their traditional regional dress (Fig. 1.1).[80] The difficulties encountered by Cambellotti in defending the peasantry by embracing cues from the natural and built environments they inhabited are just one part of the bigger problem of acceptance. In his overview, Manfredi Nicoletti described the "brutal realism" of Duilio Cambellotti's monumental reed hut. He saw Cambellotti's efforts as emblematic of the difficulty encountered by *Stile*

Fig. 1.15 Painting by Giuseppe Pellizza da Volpedo II, *Quarto Stato* (Fourth Estate), Milan, 1901. Permanent Collection, Galleria d'Arte Moderna, Milan.

Liberty artists and architects who vindicated creativity without wanting to surrender their ideological affiliations.[81] In fact, Cambellotti's reed huts seem worlds apart from Raimondo D'Aronco's extravagant pavilions at the 1902 Turin Exhibition.

Taking his cue from the failed attempt to transform the Mostra di etnografia of 1911 into a permanent open-air museum and with an awareness of the destruction that the Great War brought to Italian cities and landscapes, Arduino Colasanti (1877–1935) disseminated his *Circolare n. 13. Raccolta di elementi decorative italiani di arte paesana* (Circular No. 13: Collection of Decorative Elements of Italian Peasant Art) on 12 January 1920. In this document, Colasanti, an Italian Renaissance scholar who had been recently appointed general director of the Department of Antiquity and Fine Arts in Rome, urged superintendents, directors, gallery inspectors, artists, and students of art to begin collecting peasant art before it was forever lost or destroyed.[82] Colasanti's *Circolare* was widely distributed among Italian architects, artists, critics, historians, and literati, generating interest as well as controversy.[83] A copy of Coloasanti's *Circular* no.13 document was immediately reprinted in the right-wing journal *La Fionda*, founded in 1920 and directed by Salvatore Lauro.[84] A small yet committed group of enthusiasts at *La Fionda* trained a keen focus on vernacular art and architecture: this group included artist and architect Adolfo De Carolis (1874–1928), folklorist Corso, and writer D'Annunzio.Throughout De Carolis's involvement with the journal, he demonstrated that he was equally committed to safeguarding the material and spiritual values embodied in peasant arts and crafts, which he referred to as *arte popolare*, as well as using vernacular architecture sources in contemporary design. De Carolis wrote:

> The new homes of the common people must all have some sign of love and faith. In order that one can remember that one does not live off bread alone, in order to remember that one does not live under the sun forgetful of eternal images that are the gifts and flowers of the soul. If for centuries the common people have loved their images, is it possible that today they no longer have any value? Is it really true that the crown, the dove, the star, the fountain, the lamp, the ear of grain, the heart, the lamb, the name of the woman who Dante invoked *e mane e sera*, no longer have anything to say.[85]

De Carolis's interest in the vernacular tradition was in part influenced by his religious fervour, implicit in his reference to the passage

Fig. 1.16 Frontispiece by Adolfo De Carolis, *La figlia di Iorio: Tragedia Pastorale* (The Daughter of Jorio: A Pastoral Tragedy), 1904 (Milan: Fratelli, 1927).

of the Gospel of St. Luke 4:4: "That man shall not live by bread alone, but by every word of God." He brought to the vernacular a moral compass that was based on Christian and not secular values. His fascination with the symbols in peasant art is especially significant. As xylographer of the 1904 edition of D'Annunzio's pastoral tragedy in three acts, *The Daughter of Jorio*, he created images associated with the agrarian life of the peasant, lambs, grain, grapes, and flowers (Fig. 1.16).[86] De Carolis's choice of using the rudimentary but expressive technique of woodcut to illustrate D'Annunzio's text is not surprising in light of his interest in pre-industrial qualities of much of peasant art.[87] The same approach was taken by other artists with a much more radical agenda, such as Wassily Kandinsky and Kasimir Malevich, whose interest in the peasantry was both political and visual.[88] The association between the artistic endeavours of the peasants and Italy's spiritual and artistic rebirth after the debacle of the First World War was of fundamental importance during the 1920s. This tension between politics and aesthetics, culture and primitivism that unfolded in the work of D'Annunzio, for example, was at the heart of the debate that propelled discussions around the vernacular tradition in design into the 1920s when the rise of fascism was about to put new pressures on architects to to create designs that would service politics.

2 The Picturesque Revival: Rusticity and Contextualism

> It seems to me that next to the new aristocratic tendencies emerging today there could be an important place for other more modest forms of folk art that has thrived among the people for a long time; when one compares them to new expressions of internationalism they appear really spontaneous and indigenous. They are like wild flowers with the scent of the fields next to garden flowers that have been carefully cultivated.
>
> Gustavo Giovannoni, "The New Art and Folk Art" (1904)[1]

With the impetus of the end of the First World War the 1920s witnessed an ongoing debate surrounding the role that the vernacular tradition could play in shaping Italian architecture and urbanism. Taking Gustavo Giovannoni's lead, Marcello Piacentini distinguished between "aristocratic" and "peasant" art.[2] In 1921 Piacentini collaborated with Giovannoni and Vittorio Morpurgo (1890–1966) on mounting a modest yet topical Mostra di arte rustica (Exhibition of Rustic Art) as a way of fostering debate around the new possibilities that "rustic art" could offer to contemporary designers.[3] All three architects and curators gravitated around the Associazione artistica fra i cultori di architettura (Artistic Association for the Cultivation of Architecture), an offshoot of the Società amatori e cultori di belle arti (Society of Friends of the Fine Arts). The three-room exhibition (Rooms 46 through 48) was presented to the public in conjunction with Rome's 50th anniversary as the capital of the newly unified Italy at the Beaux-Arts Palazzo delle Esposizioni designed by Pio Piacentini on the new thoroughfare of Via Nazionale (Fig. 2.1). The curators of the exhibition, working under the aegis of the recently founded Scuola superiore di architettura di Roma, would come to be identified with the promotion of studies on extant *architet-tura minore* or minor architecture, a group of picturesque, modest-sized vernacular buildings as well as *toned-down* classical ones dating from the fifteenth and sixteenth to the eighteenth centuries.[4]

Writing a year after the modest-sized exhibition closed, Piacentini announced the Associazione's intent to publish a series of books under the title *Architettura minore*. The first two volumes, both titled *Architet-tura minore in Italia* (Minor Architecture in Italy, 1926) focused on Rome with examples ranging from the Casa Guidi in Via Botteghe oscure (vol. 1, p. 67) to a Convent in Via del Lavatore (vol. 2, p. 80).[5] The im-portance of such an initiative should not be underestimated, especially if one thinks that the lion's share of publications (whether books or arti-cles) regarding Rome and its surroundings up to this point were almost always dedicated to classical monuments and sites. This fact is under-scored in the introduction of the first volume, which reads:

Fig. 2.1 Photograph of mostra di arte rustica (Exhibition of Rustic Art), Palazzo delle esposizioni, Rome, 1921 (photographer unknown), from Antonio Maraini, "L'architettura rustica alla cinquantenale romana," *Architettura e arti decorative* 1:4 (1921), 384.

If one could identify and share with the reader what this publication contributes, it would be that it fills a lacuna: although publications abound regarding solemn expressions of art, there is very little on more modest expressions of architecture ... Nothing is to be found among publications on the minor architecture of our past; by minor architecture we mean those architectural manifestations found in our cities that don't necessarily fall under the rubric of monuments ... but are modest works like houses, groups of buildings, edicules, etc., that is – architectural prose alongside poetry.[6]

The committee charged with selecting the examples of "architectural prose" included Contessa Maria Pasolini, the architects Luigi Ciarrocchi, Mario De Renzi, Mario Marchi, and Plinio Marconi (1893–1974), as well as Giuseppe Astorri, president of the Associazione.[7] The third volume of the minor architecture series, *Lazio e suburbio di Roma*, appeared much later, in 1940, no longer under the aegis of the Associazione but rather under that of the Centro nazionale di studi di storia dell'architettura.[8] The cursory introductions to these rather large-format publications and the reliance upon photography rather than detailed plans and sections indicate that they were intended to function as visual sourcebooks for practising architects and perhaps even as coffee-table books for the general public. Compared to the reliance on drawings of most of the publications during those years, the choice of photography is timely and daring.[9]

Based on the broad selection of architects' drawings from a number of regions in Italy as well as a number of photographs gathered together by preservationist Contessa Maria Pasolini, it is clear that the curators of the Mostra di arte rustica attempted to be as inclusive as possible of artists and regions. Not unlike Loria's 1911 Mostra di Etnnografia, Giovannoni, Morpurgo, and Piacentini acknowledged the similarities and differences among peasant arts, crafts, and architecture of northern, central, and southern Italy. The list of contributors who submitted drawings to the exhibition (as published in the catalogue) included Giulio Ferrari, Camillo Jona, Angelo Guazzaroni, Arturo Viligiardi, Luigi Angelini, Paolo Mezzanotte, and Cornelio Budinich. Although the architects who participated were based all over Italy, in terms of the curators, there was a clear bias towards exponents of the nascent Scuola Romana (Roman School), comprising a distinct group interested in promoting the *architetto integrale* (integrated architect) by collapsing the figures of historian, restorer, and designer into one.[10] Especially in-

Fig. 2.2 Drawing by Duilio Cambellotti of a reed hut, from Ercole Metalli, *Usi e costumi della campagna romana – Seconda edizione riveduta e notevolmente ampliata con disegni orginali di Duilio Cambellotti* (Rome: Tipografia della Reale Accademic Nazionale dei Lincei, 1924), 13.

teresting is the presence of Angelo Guazzaroni, who together with Augusto Giustini had been the designers of record for the reconstruction of typical vernacular (i.e., ethnographic) buildings at the 1911 Exhibition of Ethnography. The politically motivated balance the triad of curators sought is also evident in the samples of arts and crafts selected by Giovanni Ferri from the collection of Lamberto Loria, at that point still awaiting a permanent exhibition space and temporarily housed in the Villa d'Este at Tivoli, which functioned as a provisional museum of Italian ethnography after the failed attempt to keep the 1911 Piazza d'Armi "living museum" open on a permanent basis. Objects like amphorae, blankets, baskets, and chests originating from the Island of Sardinia and from Piedmont to Abruzzo and Calabria were displayed with the drawings of various artists and architects. The overall effect of the exhibition suggested picturesque variety and not any rigorous visual order.

Significantly, there were no architectural drawings or ceramics by the Roman-based artist Duilio Cambellotti on view, despite his well-known efforts to celebrate the *atmosfera eroica* (heroic atmosphere) of the vernacular environment.[11] Cambellotti's work on the 1911 Mostra dell'Agro Romano testified to his commitment to elevate the lot of the Italian peasantry living in primitive reed dwellings in the Roman countryside; unlike the Scuola Romana exponents, he was uninterested in the brick-and-mortar permanency of the *architettura minore*. Just shortly after the Mostra d'arte rustica closed its doors, the second edition of Ercole Metalli's seminal study *Usi e costumi della campagna romana* was published with Cambellotti's airy and vivid architetural drawings (Fig. 2.2).[12] Although drawings of the dramatic, cavernous reed dwellings that populated the Roman territory were not displayed in the Mostra di arte rustica, drawings by Giulio Ferrari (1858–1934) of houses in Reggio Emilia and a number of other sites were selected by the curators for inclusion. Ferrari was an artist, historian, and teacher who would go on to write the comprehensive study *L'architettura rusticana nell'arte italiana* (Rustic Architecture in Italian Art, 1925) (Fig. 2.3).[13] Although it included a chapter on huts, he clearly held in higher esteem the more *evolved* permanent dwellings made of brick and mortar from the thirteenth century onwards.[14] The book was subdivided into seven chapters, including one chapter on huts and six on different groups or regions of Italy: Latium, Emilia–Toscana–Umbria–Marche, Abruzzo–Sicily–Sardinia, Piedmont–Lombardy, Veneto, and Canton Ticino. Ultimately, Ferrari's interest in craft and more permanent vernacular expressions informed his work as curator of Rome's Museo Artistico Industriale (Museum of Art and Industry), an important institution that not only collected objects but also held programs for teaching traditional *métiers*, which paralleled the experiences of similar institutions throughout Europe.[15]

Writing in 1926, Renato Biasutti observed that the contribution of his fellow geographers to the study of the vernacular tradition, which he referred to as the *abitazione rurale in Italia* (rural dwellings in Italy), had waned in recent years.[16] He acknowledged in the place of geographers,

Fig. 2.3 Drawing by Giulio Ferrari, view of Casa rustica in Via di Porta Latina in Rome, from Giulio Ferrari, *L'architettura rusticana nell'arte italiana* (Milan: Ulrico Hoepli, 1925), 83.

artists, and architects had now taken the lead. Many of the individuals cited by Biasutti, such as Edwin Cerio, Giulio Ferrari, Camillo Jona, Guy Lowell, and Plinio Marconi, had been involved in the Mostra di arte rustica in Rome and had sustained research with their new publications.[17] Biasutti identified an important shift in the focus of research driven by architects and artists. A similar opinion was expressed by Antonio Maraini, artist and leading promoter of *l'arte paesana* or peasant art, in his review of the Mostra di arte rustica, in which he argued that *architettura rustica* (rustic architecture) was relevant to contemporary Italian design. Maraini pointed out that the rustic house was not only economically viable, but also, as a *tipo regionale* (regional type), it was well suited to the climatic conditions and lifestyles of each region.[18] In this same review he described vernacular architecture as an "anonymous building fashioned according to secular traditions handed down from generation to generation."[19] He saw this regional quality as distinct from nationalism insofar as it was "spontaneous" rather than grounded in ideology. Maraini emphasized the importance of reconciling individual authorship, a prominent feature in contemporary architecture, with the anonymity of the traditional, anonymous builder, and argued for creative synthesis of extant sources so that the contemporary expressions of architecture would avoid banal mimesis.

If Maraini's review was favourable, others were not. The Mostra di arte rustica was sharply criticized in an unsigned review in *La Fionda*, presumably by Corso and De Carolis, on the grounds that no experts had been called in to select the peasant arts and crafts to be displayed with the drawings of extant buildings.[20] The growing number of individuals who dedicated themselves to "scientific" study and display of peasant art considered it worthy of the same rigour demanded of other specializations in the history of art and architecture. While art critic Arturo Lancellotti praised the *"bella semplicità"* ("beautiful simplicity") of the rustic architecture on view, he also alluded to the fact that the selection and display could have been better.[21]

Before Marcello Piacentini fell into disrepute because he opportunistically served as Mussolini's architect during the 1930s, he produced several interesting designs inspired by the forms and materiality of *architettura minore*.[22] Piacentini's Villa Nobili (1916–18) in the Parioli residential neighbourhood of Rome drew inspiration from the type of large Roman farmhouse often referred to as a *casale* (Fig. 2.4).[23] With its elementary massing, stucco surface, terracotta tiles, and limited use of ornament, his Villa Nobili was one of the few examples of contempo-

Fig. 2.4 Photograph of Marcello Piacentini's Villa Nobili, Rome, 1916–18 (photographer unknown), from Antonio Maraini, "L'architettura rustica alla cinquantenale romana," *Architettura e arti decorative* 1:4 (1921), 383.

rary architecture featured in the Roman Mostra di arte rustica of 1921. Other examples of domestic architecture in which Piacentini appropriated cues from extant buildings of Rome and its surrounding countryside are his Villetta del Critico d'arte Arturo Jahn-Rusconi (1914–17) (now demolished) and Casa Giobbe della Bitta (1922–5). In an obituary on Piacentini following his death in 1960, the critic and historian Bruno Zevi (1918–2000) viewed some of these early designs as expressive of Piacentini's creative verve before his earlier symbolic "death" (i.e., his collusion with fascism and his embrace of monumental classicism).[24]

Piacentini was not as interested in the scholarly study of peasant art and architecture as he was in the influence of the tradition on contemporary design. During the early 1910s, there was little dialogue between the specialized and often guarded academic world of geographers and ethnographers and that of practising architects and artists. There is evidence to suggest that artists and architects found little guidance in existing studies for taking an operative approach to folk art and architecture as a source for contemporary design, and sought to define it themselves. Piacentini's advocacy for vernacular art and architecture predated the rise of fascism. He eventually abandoned the vernacular in favour of classicism. It is important to note that the important developments in the emergence of interest in the subject – such as the publication of Colasanti's *Circolare* no. 13 (1920) and the *Mostra di arte rustica* (1921) – occurred *before* the March on Rome in 1922. During the first years of fascism, Mussolini had very little direct influence on the direction of Italian contemporary art and architecture. Arguably, it was his "Arte e civiltà" (Art and Civilization) speech of 1926 that offered a first, albeit approximate, outline of his platform.[25] Though Mussolini did not make any explicit reference to peasant art in this speech, what clearly emerged was his desire to use the past as a benchmark for contemporary achievements.

Scholars have largely ignored Piacentini's extensive interest, during the early years of his career, in peasant art and the domestic architecture it inspired. They have preferred to focus on his high-profile classically inspired designs under fascism that wreaked havoc on Italy, especially several pompous and heavy-handed architectural interventions in Rome (E42, 1938–42) and other Italian cities such as Brescia (Piazza della Vittoria, 1928–32), and Turin (Via Roma nuova, 1934–8). A lengthy article Piacentini published in 1922 is essential to understanding his interest in the vernacular tradition. In "Influssi d'Arte Italiana nel Nord America" (Influences of Italian Art in North America), he discussed recent examples of contemporary American architecture that he felt absorbed cues from *architettura minore*.[26]

During the 1920s, Piacentini often used the expression *architettura minore* (minor architecture). It is a term that would exercise an enormous influence on Italian modern architecture from the 1920s to the 1950s among both progressive and conservative architects who were interested in appropriating cues from hill-towns and rural farmhouses. In his 1922 article, he used the term to describe Italian architecture, mostly domestic, which over the ages was "non-monumental, but practical, that responds to the modest needs of life, that are common to all men, and as such, closest to us."[27] During those same years, many Anglo-American authors had already used the adjective *minor* (often interchangeably with *small*) to describe houses and farms of the Mediterranean basin, mainly in rural France and Spain, that were not monumental and were lesser known because they were located in the smaller towns rather than urban centres, hence the use of the term *provincial*.[28]

Piacentini also introduced the concept of *prosa architettonica* (architectural prose) to describe designs that appropriated vernacular architecture "with modest intentions, with local material, with minimal means, with an approach of peasant art that is simple, easy, and spontaneous, and free of all presumption" and should be "of little personal content, but collective, anonymous."[29] He felt it would thus combat what he viewed as the *foggie architettoniche* (sterile historicist architecture) of the past decades. If Piacentini's statement of 1922 is analysed in light of his Beaux-Arts designs for the 1911 Roman jubilee celebrations and his role as Mussolini's architect during the 1930s, we can assume that for him, "architectural prose" was more appropriate for domestic architecture than for the architecture of the state, which called for monumentality.

Piacentini's distinction between building and architecture (i.e., prose and poetry) was already addressed by Giovannoni in two essays published prior to the outbreak of the First World War: fairly briefly in "Arte nuova ed arte popolare" (New Art and Folk Art) of 1904, and in greater depth in "Vecchie città ed edilizia nuova" (Old Cities and New Buildings) of 1913.[30] This in-depth article was expanded and published in book form in 1931.[31] To some degree, Piacentini's concept recalls Giovannoni's concept of *ambientismo* or contextualism, an approach based on the *architettura minore* of the urban fabric as well as on *arte rustica* as its main ingredient.As newly appointed professor of *edilizia cittadina ed arte dei giardini* (civic buildings and garden art), Piacentini – taking his cue from Giovannoni – acknowledged the importance of minor architecture. His inaugural address on 9 November 1921 at the Regia Scuola Superiore di Architettura di Roma went under the rubric of "Nuovi orizzonti dell'edilizia cittadina" (New Horizons in Civic Building).[32] Clearly his interest in peasant architecture, which he expressed first in his 1920 article "Arte aristocratica ed arte paesana," in his 1922 article "Influssi d'arte italiana nel nord america," and in his 1921 address, informed his conception of architecture and urbanism that he based on *ambientismo* and minor architecture: "I think that we should study the city in its comprehensive shape starting with the numerous buildings aligned in the streets that up until recently seemed bland, and that in a word are minor architecture. That which, I recently called architectural prose should become the daily focus of our work."[33]

Piacentini's early domestic work was influenced by a scaled-down

Fig. 2.5 Photograph by David Gebhard of Smith House #1 by George Washington Smith, Montecito, California, 1916, from David Gebhard, *George Washington Smith, 1876–1930: The Spanish Colonial Revival in California* (Santa Barbara: Santa Barbara Art Gallery, 1964), n.p.

vernacular "prose" that shared affinities with California architects George Washington Smith (1876–1930) and, to a lesser extent, Irving Gill (1870–1936). It is obvious that by minor architecture Piacentini was referring not only to vernacular sources but also to a scaled-back classicism. In his designs, he offered a synthesis different from that of Smith, who often simply replicated the vernacular models of Spain and rarely referenced a classical vocabulary. Smith's first house – the Heberton house in Montecito, California (1916) – which was selected by Piacentini as one of the examples of North American designs illustrated in his "Influssi" article is a case in point (Fig. 2.5). Smith aspired to have a "consciousness of simplicity":

> Cézanne and Gauguin gave me the most inspiration, although the Spanish and Italian primitives thrilled me also. So much so that, after I got my blood filled with the modern idea of painting, I began to regard all

the other forms of art with the same consciousness – the consciousness of simplicity.[34]

Some years later, and within a significantly more charged political context, Carlo Enrico Rava, one of the founders of the modernist Gruppo 7, expressed his appreciation for the "Latin spirit" of American architects like Gill and Smith.[35]

In his "Influssi" article Piacentini cited the examples of contemporary architecture that he thought not only best exemplified the *Stile Italiano* (Italian style) in America. He also acknowledged and praised the efforts of American architects who studied from real life (*dal vero*) the villas and peasant houses (*ville e case paesane*) of the Italian peninsula. Piacentini was impressed that these architects made visits to Italy in order to sketch and photograph the examples that were included in their publications. At the time Piacentini was writing, there was still little documentation of extant rustic architecture. Apart from the catalogue for the 1911 Exhibition of Ethnography in Rome, the book *Peasant Art of Italy* (1913), which used photography to document typical examples of vernacular buildings in different regions of Italy, and the two collections of drawings published by architect Camillo Jona in 1920 on Mediterranean and Alpine "rustic architecture," no other comprehensive pan-regional publications had yet been prepared.[36] Ferrari's comprehensive study of 1925 had still not materialized.

Although Piacentini does not state it explicitly, he is without a doubt referring to two widely circulated sourcebooks published in the United States by the Boston architect Guy Lowell (1870–1927):[37] *Smaller Italian Villas and Farmhouses* (1916) and *More Small Italian Villas and Farmhouses* (1920) (Fig. 2.6).[38] These were published before Piacentini wrote his article in 1922 and were the only American sourcebooks frequently cited during the 1920s by Italian writers.[39] They were the first attempt at documenting an architectural type (the *villa* and house or *casa*) in order to circulate it among practising architects and inspire contemporary design in various areas of the United States, especially California.[40] While Lowell does not address arts and crafts he does include farmhouses and toned-down classically inspired "minor" villas that were fairly modest in scale and detailing. The accompanying text in his book is rather short and implies that the substance lies in the visual information the photographs provide.

The emphasis on smaller villas and farmhouses as models for upper-middle-class patrons who could not afford to emulate imperial or

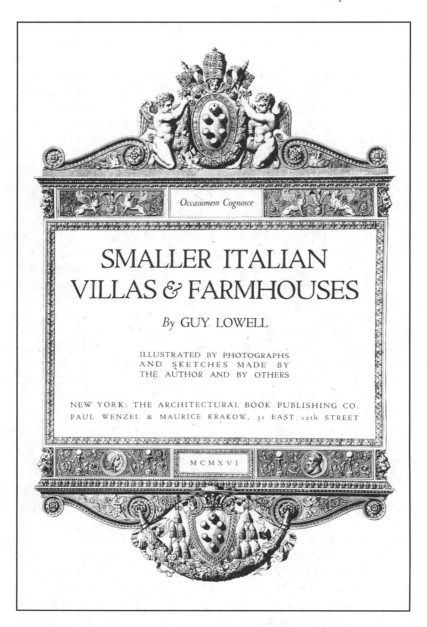

Fig. 2.6 Guy Lowell, *Smaller Italian Villas and Farmhouses* (New York: The Architectural Book Publishing Co., 1916).

princely palaces is fundamental to the debate over late nineteenth- and early twentieth-century domestic architecture in America as well as Europe.[41] The fairly modest scale of Lowell's examples offered an alternative to the Beaux-Arts estates designed by firms such as McKim, Mead, and White for wealthy industrialists and bankers. Lowell's publications were followed by others prepared by architects interested in the Mediterranean revival in the American South and Southwest, particularly California and Florida. A notable example is *Farmhouses and Small Provincial Buildings in Southern Italy*, published in 1925 with a text by Katharine Hooker (1849–1935) and the regionalist architect Myron Hunt (1868–1952).[42] Rexford Newcomb's *Mediterranean Domestic Architecture in the United States* (1928) demonstrated the recent enthusiasm for Spanish and Italian prototypes that were adapted to the American context and customs.[43] While the Mediterranean revival architect Bertram Grosvenor Goodhue (1869–1924) did not write books on the subject, he did contribute prefatory texts to studies on Mediterranean architecture.[44] In Florida, the Mediterranean revival of Addison Mizner and urban-scale initiatives such as the city of Coral Gables did much to generate interest in the documentation of European sources, mainly using photographs, though sometimes drawings.[45] Thus, Lowell's publications are part of a larger body of work aimed at bringing the vernacular and scaled-down classical buildings of the Mediterranean to North America.

If the focus of American architects was primarily on domestic single-family dwellings for the upper middle classes, in Italy, a number of architects who expressed interest in minor architecture began thinking about the urban and collective housing scale. Commenting on the 1911 ethnographic exhibition, Giovannoni, known for his promotion of *ambientismo*, referred to the buildings as emblematic of *"forme artistiche liberamente germogliate nelle città e nei borghi d'Italia"* ("artistic expressions freely sprouted in the cities and villages of Italy").[46] Just prior to the opening of the *Mostra di arte rustica*, Giovannoni and collaborators looked to these "freely sprouted" extant models as a source for the design of the working-class neighbourhoods familiarly known as La Garbatella (1920–22) and while designing the Città-Giardino Aniene at Montesacro (1920).[47] Giovannoni with the help of other architects started planning the picturesque neighbourhood of Garbatella on the outskirts of Rome to serve the working-class families of local industry, with meandering streets and stylized multi-family dwellings comprising ornamental rusticated bases and pitched roofs clad with terracotta tiles (Fig. 2.7). The rustic detailing of the facades reflected Giovannoni's

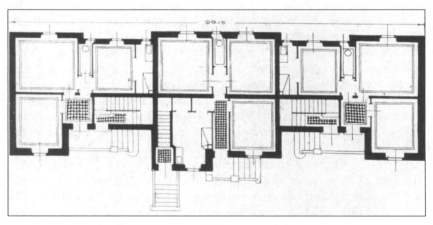

Fig. 2.7 Photograph of external view and floorplan of housing type "I," Lotto 3, Fabbricato 9 (photographer unknown) by Camillo Palmerini, 1920–3, planner Gustavo Giovannoni, Garbatella housing estate, Rome, 1920–3, from Innocenzo Costantini, "Le nuove costruzioni dell'Istituto per le case popolari di Roma: La borgata giardino 'Garbatella,'" *Architettura e arti decorative* 2 (November 1922): 119–37.

and his collaborators' commitment to minor fifteenth-century domestic architecture of Rome, on which he had written abundantly.[48] Giovannoni was not so much interested in the basic dwellings found in the countryside, such as the reed huts that Cambellotti had so valiantly studied and recreated. Nor did his architecture share the spirit of a forced economy of means that characterized the vernacular buildings realized by and for peasants. His quaint and stylized interpretation of hill towns and rural hamlets (referred to as *borghi*) typical of the Roman countryside (Garbatella, from the Italian *garbatezza*, suggests well-mannered or pleasing) can be understood as a Roman-centric response to picturesque English garden-city traditions.

The Garbatella and Aniene neighbourhoods, which were inspired by extant regional sources, were part of a growing interest in a national "Italian" architecture that could be tempered with regionalist cues. To be sure, institutional regionalism, in part based on the rediscovery of the vernacular tradition, emerged in the arts and crafts *before* architecture. In a letter to Milan's Mayor Emilio Caldara written on 20 December 1917, socialist parliamentarian Guido Marangoni (1872–1941) called for the founding of a "great exhibition of decorative art" to ensure that the "decorative arts which once were the pride and distinguishing mark of each Italian region" would be revived.[49] The Monza Biennial exhibitions of 1923, 1925, and 1927 were centred on promoting regional crafts and identity, and featured, among other things, the glass-blowing and lacemaking of Venice, the ceramic industry of Tuscany, the rugs and baskets of Sardinia, and so on. Each region displayed its products in a separate space within the Palazzo Reale in Monza. Evidence of the diffuse interest in *arte rustica* at the Monza exhibitions appears in the publication *L'arte decorativa contemporanea* (Contemporary Decorative Art, 1923), written by prominent Italian artist and critic Carlo Carrà.[50] The Monza Biennial exhibitions of the 1920s were mounted in the context of other cultural initiatives valorizing peasant arts and crafts as the residue of an idealized, if remote, Italian past that was seen as important to contemporary design reform. The Monza Biennial exhibitions eventually were modified into Triennials when the organization moved to Milan in 1933. This renewal of interest in Monza, and subsequently in Milan, provided the impetus for Italian decorative and industrial arts at a time when industrialization had already begun to disrupt the secular traditions and social assets of the Italian peninsula.

The Esposizione italiana d'arte decorativa e popolare (Italian Exhibition of Decorative and Peasant Art) held in Stockholm in 1920 was an important occasion on which the two impulses of contemporary design and collecting were brought together. The Mostra di arte rustica (Exhibition of Rustic Art) held in Rome in 1921 presented drawings of extant vernacular buildings and objects alongside a selection of the contemporary architectural designs. The Mostra Internazionale delle arti decorative (International Exhibition of Decorative Arts) held in Monza in 1923 combined peasant arts and crafts with the work of contemporary artists and artisans, suggesting the possibility of continuity between the past and the present. This thesis was clearly the impetus behind another exhibition, L'arte popolare italiana Ars (Italian Folk Art), held in Rome that same year.[51] The 1925 Mostra Internazionale delle Arti Decorative (International Exhibition of Decorative Arts) in Monza also showcased the "*arte dei pastori*" (art of the shepherds) along with contemporary Italian design.[52]

While the exhibition of 1911 in Rome jump-started the rediscovery of folk art and architecture from the point of view of ethnography, it was the Italian Exhibition of Decorative and Peasant Art held in Stockholm under the auspices of the Swedish Society of Arts and Crafts, directed by Gregor Paulsson, which acknowledged the tradition's artistic value outside of Italy.[53] By displaying contemporary design alongside arts and crafts of the Italian peasantry, this event offered a new interpretation of the heritage of Italy (Fig. 2.8).[54] The exhibition opened on 13 November 1920 and closed at the end of December the same year. It was installed in Carl Bergsten's (1879–1935) Nordic classical Liljevalchs Konsthall (Art Gallery) built in 1916, located on the island of Djurgården, opposite one of the main entrances to Skansen. The exhibition on Italian peasant arts and crafts could not have been more appropriately sited, considering the proximity to the pioneering open-air ethnographic museum in which Sweden's peasant architecture, arts, and crafts were displayed.[55] Oddly, vernacular architecture (even in the form of models or photographs) was excluded from the thirteen galleries dedicated to the exhibition; documentary images attest to the attempt to loosely recreate an informal domestic environment in which extant Italian peasant arts and crafts were commingled with contemporary decorative arts to create the illusion of a continuum from past to present. Women dressed in traditional costume greeted visitors to the opening events.

Many of the circumstances surrounding the genesis of the exhibition remain unknown. It may have been that the Italians were prompted by the ongoing difficulty of establishing a national ethnographic museum in Rome to search for alternative venues of display.[56] Perhaps, too, the

Fig. 2.8 Photograph of the Italian Exhibition of Decorative and Peasant Art (photographer unknown), from Remigio Strinati, "L'esposizione italiana di arte decorative a Stoccolma," *Rassegna d'Arte antica e moderna* 4 (April 1921): 137.

publication of *Peasant Art in Italy* (1913) in the London-based Studio Series played a small but significant role in bringing Italy to the Swedes' attention.[57] Whatever the reasons, the composition of the committee formed to organize the exhibition in Stockholm demonstrates the seriousness with which the Italian government took this task: the group included prestigious artists and designers Guido Balsamo-Stella (1882–1941); the prominent folklorist Raffaele Corso (1883–1965); and art critics and historians such as Pompeo Molmenti (1852–1928), Lionello Venturi (1885–1961), Eugenio Barbantini (1884–1952), and Arduino Colasanti (1875–1935). The absence of an architectural historian on the committee is indicative of the absence of a section dedicated to vernacular buildings. Stella and his wife Akerdhal (both of whom had lived in Sweden) participated in the selection of objects, as did Barbantini and Colasanti and two Swedish members of the selection committee, Amelie Brazdova and Maja Sjöström.[58] According to an Italian observer, the Swedish members of the committee selected objects not necessarily on account of their intrinsic quality or historic importance but rather on the basis of their appeal to a Swedish audience.[59]

In his pioneering study *Tappetti rustici italiani* (Italian Peasant Rugs, 1922), Albert Sautier recognized the importance of the Stockholm exhibition as a catalyst for subsequent events in Italy:

> In 1920, the exhibition of decorative art in Stockholm, in which rustic art received the importance it deserved, was for foreign countries an exceptional surprise. Sweden, which also possesses a branch of rustic art, both rich and original, to which, for many decades, she has dedicated love and fervid study worthy of being imitated, was able to appreciate all the beauty especially of the woven woolen blankets of Abruzzo, and the success of this exhibition had a loud echo in Italy – so loud as to encourage the architect, Marcello Piacentini, in the spring of 1921, to dedicate to rustic art three rooms in the Roman Biennial Exhibition.[60]

Others, like Antonio Maraini, would cite the Stockholm exhibition as being one of the most influential exhibitions of the 1920s through the 1940s.[61]

The Stockholm exhibition, like that in Rome, presented the most representative crafts of various regions in order to show off their accomplishments and celebrate Italy's diversity.[62] While all displays valorized traditional craftsmanship, works by artisans and peasants were

Fig. 2.9 Cover, Eleonora Gallo, *Peasant Art in Italy* (Florence: G. Giannini and Figlio, 1929).

displayed side by side with works produced in contemporary artisanal workshops that had thrived for hundreds of years in Italian cities: handmade glass by the Venetian artisan Vittorio Zecchin (1878–1947),[63] and from firms such as Vetreria Artistica Barovier and Fratelli Toso; children's toys by Guido Cadorin; textiles by Lorenzo Rubelli and Bevilacqua; lace by Jesurum;[64] and the cooperative Aemilia Ars society in Bologna headed by architect Alfonso Rubbiani.

The desire to suggest continuity between decorative arts of the past and those of the present that surfaced in Stockholm and a number of exhibitions in Monza was fuelled by a renewed interest in promoting regionalism by way of traditional *métiers*. Whereas the practise of architecture, even the construction of vernacular buildings, was the exclusive domain of males, crafts were associated with women. In many respects, this division of labour between men and women – physical and intellectual – reflected the rigid gender-based hierarchies that structured the production of peasant buildings and arts and crafts. Men traditionally worked hard materials (brick, iron, stone, wood, and sometimes reed) while women were responsible for soft materials like lace and textiles. While the Arts and Crafts Movement did bring women to the forefront, it also reinforced stereotypes of "crafty" women.[65] The contribution to the study and revival of arts and crafts made by the women who manufactured lace was particularly significant in Italy, where men dominated the arts. Women's active participation in the making of crafts and the writing of histories on the subject tended to reinforce their association with the minor arts. One notable Italian example of a female taking an active role in documenting and analysing craft is Elisa Ricci, wife of influential art and architectural historian Corrado Ricci (1858–1934). She was asked by Charles Holme to write a piece for his *Peasant Art in Italy* (1913) because she was considered an expert on women's crafts. Ricci was extremely prolific throughout the first three decades of the twentieth century and wrote several important books on lace, one of which was translated into English.[66] Eleonora Gallo wrote the comprehensive *Arte rustica italiana* (Peasant Art in Italy), simultaneously co-published in Italian and English in 1929 (Fig. 2.9).[67] She wrote and illustrated the text of this important study of peasant art in different regions of Italy, which focused mainly on arts and crafts to the exclusion of architecture. The special care Gallo took in designing the binding and pages of the book recall the very influence of the folk art she had meticulously documented. In 1934, Emma Calderini wrote and illustrated *Il costume popolare in Italia* (Folk Dress in Italy), contributing to the emergence of yet another female voice in a largely male-dominated critical debate.[68]

Part of this increased interest in documenting and analysing both the objects and buildings of the vernacular environment can be traced to Colasanti's *Circolare* no. 13, which encouraged Italians to safeguard their folk heritage. His initiatives were met with positive reception on the part of Marcello Piacentini in his "Arte aristocratica ed arte paesana" (Aristocratic and Peasant Art), published in April 1920 in the Rome-based daily newspaper *La Tribuna*.[69] Piacentini's review was published just two months after Colasanti's *Circolare* no. 13 appeared, and only a month after publication of Antonio Maraini and Ojetti's public disagreement also voiced in the pages of *La Tribuna*.[70] Ugo Ojetti (1871–1946) was an influential critic who voiced his opinions on nationalism in art and architecture with passion and persuasion. Piacentini openly supported Maraini's efforts to promote the study of *arte paesana* as a source for contemporary design practice in Italy. Piacentini embraced the different qualities of aristocratic and peasant art, ultimately suggesting a negotiation between the two. He betrayed a class awareness that was especially significant in Italy at a time when the struggle between liberal and conservative factions was intense.

Maraini's first article, "L'arte popolare" (Popular Art), appeared in *La Tribuna* on 3 April 1918 followed by another one, "Arte popolare e stile decorativo nazionale" (Popular Art and National Decorative Art) on 28 February 1920. As art editor for the newspaper, Maraini was slowly emerging as an apologist for the study of peasant arts and crafts in Italy, especially in relation to the debate over the reform of art education. Maraini published a definition of peasant art in his entry to the 1929 *Enciclopedia italiana di scienze, lettere ed arti*,[71] and he wrote numerous articles in which he articulated his position on reform of artistic education. Keeping in mind the Arts and Crafts movement in England, Germany, Scandinavia, and central Europe, his recommendations for educational reform were largely based on the rediscovery of the methods and techniques of peasant art.[72] Some years after Maraini, Marconi published an entry aimed at completing the picture set forth by his colleague in the *Enciclopedia italiana* that focused exclusively on *architettura rustica*.[73] He clearly distinguished rustic architecture from so-called *costruzioni rurali* (rural buildings), which he claimed belonged to a functionalist, engineer-based tradition quite different from the autonomous rustic architecture of peasants in various regions of Italy.

In "Aristocratic and Peasant Art," Piacentini referred to the *cortese duello* (polite quarrel) that had surfaced between Maraini and Ojetti in the *Tribuna* text: "I'm absolutely convinced that there could not be more necessary and efficient promotional work to be done in Italy so that our domestic architecture can be born (and not reborn)."[74] In the same essay, Piacentini mentioned the drawings of *motivi architettonici rustici* (rustic architectural motifs or accents) of the Neapolitan Gulf region of southern Italy by the German émigré and architect Ernesto Wille (1860–1913).[75] Wille was the only non-Italian member of the Associazione artistica fra i cultori di architettura in Roma and was widely respected by his Italian peers. He was one of the first architects practising in Italy to appropriate Italian vernacular architecture in his work. The drawings Piacentini referred to were in personal notebooks from his travels to the Island of Ischia and elsewhere, which Wille had assembled but never published, despite plans to do so.[76] Based on his observation of Wille's work, Piacentini claimed it was largely indebted to Italian peasant art and architecture, which he described as both "mystical art" and, with an air of ownership, as "our humble material."

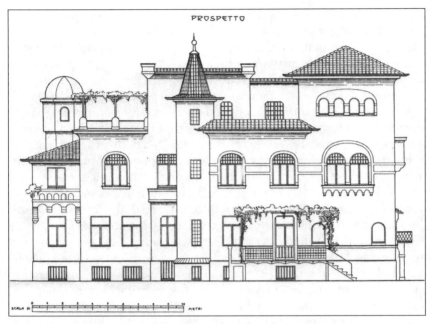

Fig. 2.10 Elevation drawing by Ernest(o) Wille, Villino Wille, Via Andrea Cesalpino, Rome, 1906–8, from Luigi-Federico Babini, *Ville moderne in Italia – Ville di Roma – Facciate – Particolari – Piante – Raccolte* (Turin: C. Crudo and C. Società Italiana di Edizioni Artistiche, 1915), 15.

Wille designed several fair-sized multi-storeyed villas (or *villini*, smaller-sized villas), mainly for well-to-do German families residing in the neighbourhood known as Villa Patrizi in Rome.[77] The most notable are Villino Celestino Meurer (1899), Villa Amelung (1904), Villino Federico Spiro (1904), Villino Thérèse Nast-Kolb (1905), and his own residence, known as Villino Wille (1906–8) (Fig. 2.10).[78] These quaint and elegantly detailed villas and *villini* were mostly two-storey buildings in which he used traditional materials like brick and made abundant use of stucco in place of stone ornament. Wille introduced architectural elements like loggias and terraces that allowed the inhabitants to enjoy the Mediterranean climate and surrounding views. Despite neomedieval attitudes to asymmetrical massing and roofs, the smooth abstract facades echo the simplicity of vernacular buildings. The 1915 portfolio of *Ville moderne in Italia – Ville di Roma* includes two of Wille's designs, likely referred to as *villini* (his Villino Wille in Via di Andrea Cesalpino and Villino Federico Spirino in Via di Villa Patrizi) because of their toned-down "minor" quality and above all their lack of ostentatious classical ornamentation.[79] A comparison of the *villini* by Wille and Spiro with other contemporary examples also reproduced in this publication reveals the novelty of Wille's interest in replicating the sophisticated yet informal quality of extant Mediterranean vernacular buildings.[80]

Throughout these discussions tensions surfaced over national, regional, and international identity in the arts and architecture discourse. As Piacentini was actively involved in the debate over appropriating the vernacular tradition in contemporary architectural practise, Ojetti was quick to respond in the realm of the arts to the criticism provoked by his debate with Maraini, published as "L'arte in campagna" (Art in the Countryside) in the widely read Milan-based daily *Corriere della Sera* in March 1920, immediately following the publication of Colasanti's *Circolare* no. 13. Ojetti expressed lukewarm support of peasant art and its possible contribution to contemporary design. Sometime later, he also published an appraisal of recent trends identifying Lamberto Loria as Italy's premier ethnographer.[81] At the time, Ojetti was considered one of Italy's most influential critics, a self-appointed defender of the academic and timeless values of Italian classicism. Although he supported measures for safeguarding the patrimony of peasant art, he did not overenthusiastically endorse reviving the influence of peasant art in contemporary art.[82]

Like Colasanti, Ojetti was a scholar of the Italian Renaissance as well as a historian of nineteenth-century art. His outlook had deep roots in the culture of historicism. As editor of *Dedalo*, he published an essay on Alpine art by the writer and poet Piero Jahier (1884–1966).[83] Following the example of noted folklorist Jules (Giulio) Brocherel (1871–1954), Jahier was one of the very few to draw attention during those years to the Alpine regions of Italy and to the peasant arts, crafts, and architecture found there.[84] Much of the focus until then had been on central and southern Italian peasant art and architecture. In many ways, Jahier's work undermined the stereotype of an Italy defined exclusively by its Mediterranean shores. His article did not address architecture, a lacuna he was later to acknowledge.[85] Jahier was already known by critics for his seminal novel *Ragazzo: Il paese morale* (1920), which concerned the spiritual regeneration of Italy through the timeless morality and enduring legacy of the rural values of the "common man."[86] Jahier's celebration of the moral virtues of the Italian peasantry shared much with Francesca Alexander's account of *Christ's Folk in the Apennine:*

Fig. 2.11 Photograph by Piero Jahier of an Alpine milking stool, Valle Varaita, from *Arte Alpina* (Florence: Vallecchi, 1961), n.p.

Reminiscences of Her Friends among the Tuscan Peasantry (1887) edited by John Ruskin. Jahier's interest in common people and objects such as milking stools manufactured by peasants recalls, like Cambellotti's a decade earlier, Tolstoy's expansive definition of art that included material culture (Fig. 2.11). Jahier described the milking stool in this way: "The rustic milking stool, carved and shaped by an ignorant hand, but one that was thirsting for beauty, called to mind Italy."[87] The idealistic tone and moral fervour of Jahier's description of Alpine art finds parallels in Bruno Taut's *Crystal Chain Letters* and his *Alpine Architektur* (1919), as well as in the paintings of Ernst Ludwig Kirchner during his self-imposed exile in the Swiss mountains of Davos during the 1910s and 1920s.[88]

Shortly after Ojetti published Jahier's essay, he printed other articles on peasant art. His *Commenti* article of 1920, already mentioned, offered an overview of recent developments in the study of what he refers to as peasant art, and its implications within the realm of contemporary design. Ojetti discussed the aims of the recently founded organization Lares (and its eponymous journal) headed by Maraini and Baldasseroni. Lares was conceived to promote the contemporary production of a peasant art that was deemed the most interesting and at the greatest risk of disappearing. In his *Commenti*, Ojetti credited the First World War with drawing attention to the need for the study and preservation of peasant art, as it allowed Italians of various regions, especially the Alpine regions, to discover one another and share their *"riti più segreti della loro cucina casalinga"* ("the most secretive rites of their domestic cuisine").[89] Ojetti understood the importance of the kitchen in the family life of Italian peasants. The First World War had led to much destruction, especially in the Friuli region, where a great defeat was suffered by Italian troops at Caporetto and where a rich peasant life existed.

In his *Commenti*, Ojetti also mentioned that the publisher of *La Fionda* intended to produce a series of books under the direction of Adolfo De Carolis and Raffaele Corso devoted to various types of peasant art. The Bottega d'arte popolare italiana (Workshop of Italian Popular Art) – for which Gabriele D'Annunzio designed a heart-shaped logo bisected by a plant somewhere in between flower and palm tree, probably together with De Carolis – set forth an ambitious program to publish ten volumes that would range from studies on textiles and wood carvings to lace and architecture (Fig. 2.12).[90] The editorial agenda was published in October 1920:

Fig. 2.12 Logo by Gabriele D'Annunzio for Bottega d'arte popolare italiana, from "La prima bottega d'arte popolare italiana," *La Fionda* 3 (October 1920): 43.

> The workshop was and will be the small museum that we want, in order to give value to the documents that we gather for the volumes on popular art. The production of the humble peoples will thus be saved from dispersion, will be gathered for study, will be displayed as an example of beauty which is profound within the Italian spirit and that can give, provided it is renewed and diffused, newfound freshness to national art. Gabriele D'Annunzio has given thought to this font of spiritual energy while tracing the outline of the new setup of the free state of Fiume.[91]

Art historian Bernard Berenson (1865–1959), whose interest lay mainly in the Renaissance, praised the efforts of De Carolis as well as the Workshop initiative:

> I would like to say that the article by Adolfo De Carolis awakes my keen interest, as do your plans for the Workshop, and the volumes which are to be published on Italian popular art. Please keep me informed regarding everything you plan to do, because I am willing to give all my assistance

... My studies regard art. That is the art of Italy. But the art of the people is of profound interest to me, as is ethnography.[92]

As an American in Florence, Berenson was initially exposed to peasant art through Loria's efforts to establish the first ethnographic museum in Florence in 1906, though the Franco-Swiss architect and designer Le Corbusier did not list Florence on his map of places of interest for *l'art paysan*.[93] To be sure, despite Berenson's interest, his comments reveal a hierarchical vision of high art versus art of the "people."

Raffaele Corso's *L'arte dei pastori* (The Art of the Shepherds) (1920) was the first of the series to be announced, but was published only in an excerpt.[94] Volumes on textiles by Adolfo De Carolis, ceramics by Duilio Cambellotti, as well as books on rustic architecture and others were scheduled, but never published. Though this series did not materialize, another was produced by editors Piantanida and Valcarenghi in Milan, starting in 1922, which included volumes (translated from Italian into French and English) on decorative arts such as Giuseppe Capitò's novel study on the "architecture" and ornamentation of Sicilian carts, *Il carretto siciliano* (The Sicilian Cart) (1923) and Albert Sautier's *Tappetti rustici italiani* (Rustic Italian Rugs) (1922).

The link between the artistic endeavours of the peasantry, the so-called *umile gente* (humble peoples) and Italy's spiritual and artistic rebirth after the debacle of the First World War is of fundamental importance during the 1920s for the making of Italian political history. The debate ignited by D'Annunzio over Fiume (modern Rijeka), the city almost lost following the war, was at the heart of the "myth of regeneration" that contributed to the momentum that ultimately consolidated the fascist coup.[95] Fundamental, too, in promotion of integrating politics, art, and culture typical of Italian modernism, especially from the 1920s onward, were the supporters of the Workshop program.

While Ojetti was cautiously supportive of the publications and other initiatives, he clearly did not feel that they were enough to lead to a *resurrezione dell'intirizzita arte decorative italiana* (resurrection of the stagnating Italian decorative arts). He believed that structural innovations were necessary to establish state-operated schools similar to those founded in Britain, Germany, and Austria. Ojetti held these schools responsible for the rebirth of the decorative arts in their respective countries and was adamant about helping along reform in arts education in Italy. In 1920, together with Colasanti, De Carolis, and others, he wrote a memorandum directed to public officials.[96] Following his complaint and the initiative of Guido Marangoni, the Università delle Arti Deco-

Fig. 2.13 Elevation drawing by Giulio Ulisse Arata, of Rione Ovolaccio, Caso-lari Binati (double farm buildings), Désulo (Barbagia), *Arte sarda* (1936), plate 247.

rative, which later transformed into the Istituto Superiore per le Indus-trie Artistiche (ISIA), was founded on 12 November 1922 in Monza, to be housed in the same building where the Mostra internazionale delle arti decorative (International Exhibitions of Decorative Arts) took place every two years until 1930.[97] Ironically, it was at Monza, not far from Milan, Italy's industrial centre, that the peasant arts half-heartedly en-dorsed by Ojetti were valorized on the basis of the insight they could provide for contemporary Italian industrial and decorative arts that were both modern and rooted in the past.

Piacentini's complaint during the early 1920s that Italian architects were not using the lessons of *architettura minore* in their contemporary designs was repeated shortly thereafter by architect Giulio Ulisse Arata (1881–1962). In the first of a series of three essays on Sardinian rustic arts published in 1921 in the journal *Dedalo*, directed by Ojetti, Arata assert-ed that Italians had been slow to take up the subject of *l'arte rustica delle masse rurali* (the rustic art of the rural masses).[98] These three essays were eventually expanded and published as *Arte sarda* (1935) in a large-format edition bound in jute to echo the humble spirit and hand of peasant art, and amply illustrated with architectural drawings, photographs, and paintings by Giuseppe Biasi (1885–1945).[99] Biasi, the co-author of *Arte sarda*, devoted his life work to the painting of the Sardinian peasantry.[100] Having no personal ties with Sardinia, Arata may have chosen it as his subject because it was an island removed from industrial northern Italy; it thus offered him a virgin, primitive fountainhead – as the island of Sicily did for Pitrè – of inspiring materials. While Arata was an outsider, he was nonetheless Italian. In 1927, some years before the publication of Arata and Biasi's *Arte sarda*, the German photographer August Sander (1876–1964) visited Sardinia.[101] Sander did not stop with the *nuragh*, the primitive stone dwelling type which came to symbolize the mysterious island in the eyes of outsiders, but turned his lens on other forms of domestic and religious architecture, as well as peasant dress and ornaments. Since the beginning of the century, Sardinia had fascinated visitors. D.H. Lawrence visited the island in February 1921 for some days and afterward published his vivid travel account of the port city of Cagliari, *Sea and Sardinia*:

> The spirit of the place is a strange thing. Our mechanical age tries to override it. But it does not succeed. In the end the strange, sinister spirit of the place, so diverse and adverse in differing places, will smash our mechanical oneness into smithereens, and all that we think the real thing will go off with a pop, and we shall be left staring.[102]

Arata too shared Lawrence's distaste for banal mechanization. His first essay is focused on jewellery and carved utensils, the second on rugs and lace, and the third on furniture and furnishings. Arata, a practising architect, viewed Sardinian folk art as a holistic, organic phenomenon that embraced different realms of architectural and artistic culture. In the introductory paragraphs of the first essay, he encouraged the appropriation of rustic architecture as a source of new vitality within contemporary architecture. Arata praised the agrarian *casolari rustici* (rustic houses) because he believed that they could provide a cue for "new structures and architectural masses." He admired the inherent flexibility of the structures, noting that they were not the result of "fixed rules" or "awkward historicism," but rather of "the natural faculties of intuition."[103] Arata claimed that the vernacular source could lead to the optimal results of "commodity and well-being while still maintaining as vital those ethnographic characteristics with which the origins of architecture are marked."[104]

Arata incorporated aspects of rustic architecture in his own work, especially from the 1910s and 1930s, first in dialogue with the *Stile Liberty* typical of the Wagnerschule and later through forms of abstracted classicism.[105] Since the beginning of his professional career, when he focused on domestic architecture, Arata was attentive to the local vernacular and interested in the interaction with the topographic conditions of the site. He even planned to publish a book – *L'architettura rurale laziale* (Rural Architecture of Latium) – on measured drawings of Roman and Latium farmhouses.[106] His *Arte Sarda* featured a considerable number of drawings of extant vernacular buildings (Fig. 2.13). Given Arata's support early on for a creative dialogue between ethnography and architecture, it is not surprising that art and architecture critic Alfredo Melani (1859–1928), who also expressed an early interest in these two disciplines, would write the preface to the first volume of Arata's villa designs (1913), many of which were never realized.[107] Arata's interest in vernacular traditions was already evident in his Villa Ricciardi (1909–10) and, to a lesser extent, in his designs combining peasant art with local medieval references for the Banca Popolare Piacentina (1923–4) and the Agricultural Pavilion in Milan (1927–8).

Arata's interest in rustic Sardinian art was not merely scholarly. He was asked to put his knowledge and skill to use by designing a retrospective exhibition at the Mostra internazionale delle arti decorative at Monza in 1923.[108] The second Biennial exhibition was held from 17 March through 30 June 1923, and included a substantial exhibition of folk arts and crafts. Like the Stockholm exhibition of 1920, the show featured both contemporary Italian decorative arts and historic exempla from select regions. The juxtaposition of peasant arts and crafts with contemporary design at the Monza exhibition sent a clear message: this was not a detached report but an explicit invitation to contemporary artists and architects to make the connection between past and present. Artists who represented their native regions – Arezzo, Calabria, and Sardinia – were asked to select historic examples to accompany their work. The Sardinian arts and crafts room at the 1923 Monza exhibition was decorated by Sardinian artist Melkiorre Melis (1889–1982), under the supervision of Arata, and included Melis's own signature work of both ceramics and paintings alongside anonymous exemplars (Fig. 2.14).[109] It is interesting to note how, despite seemingly different agen-

Fig. 2.14 Photograph of a Sardinian exhibition curated by Giulio Ulisse Arata (with Melkiorre Melis) (photographer unknown), Bienniale Exhibition, Monza, 1923, from Anty Pansera, *Storia e cronica della Triennale* (Milan: Longanesi & Co., 1978), 140.

das, Fortunato Depero's Sala Futurista (Futurist Hall) shared many similarities with the "primitivism" of folk arts and crafts.

In the first of a three-part review of the Monza exhibition published in *Architettura e arti decorative*, architect and historian Paolo Mezzan-otte (1878–1969) discussed Arata's work and the role of rustic art and design in light of contemporary *rinnovamento artistic* (artistic renewal) and renewed interest in the "ingenuity of Italy's primitives."[110] In the first of the three articles, Mezzanotte praised the retrospective exhibition curated by Arata "with the love of a scholar and the intellect of an artist." Mezzanotte also gave an overview of developments outside Italy. He considered the political consequences of empowering the *muz-*

hik (Russian peasant), and noted instances in which peasant art was used as a vehicle for encouraging a national art that could resist foreign importations. Like Ojetti before him, Mezzanotte made reference to Colasanti's *Circolare* no. 13, which had passionately encouraged the study of peasant art in Italy; Mezzanotte lamented that these initiatives had led to little change. He had to admit that his own plan to present examples of *arte rustica* from the eastern part of Italy had failed, with the exception of one article he wrote and personally illustrated on the hearth of the Friuli region (Fig. 2.15).[111] Mezzanotte concluded by explaining that the *primitivi* of the *arte rustica* tradition could make just as much of a contribution to the art of *forme meglio evolute* (more advanced forms). He positioned classicism alongside rustic art as part of a mutually inclusive phenomenon. Mezzanotte had manifested his interest in the vernacular by participating with Enrico Agostino Griffini in the Ercole Marelli competition of 1919 for the *piccole case rurali* (small rural houses) that would replace the Alpine homes that had been destroyed during the First World War. Yet, Mezzanotte, like many others of his ilk who proclaimed love for the peasantry, looked to classicism when it came to designing public buildings under the fascist regime: recall his Milan Stock Exchange completed in 1924.[112]

The rediscovery of peasant art was aimed at reforming design as well as architecture. Yet while reform was trumpeted as the driving force, the recasting of rustic life in the twentieth century often remained fundamentally elitist, nostalgic, and sentimental. Although Piacentini's and Wille's early villas echoed the forms and materiality of peasant art, they catered to wealthy patrons. As his power in the fascist regime's apparatus increased, Piacentini moved away from his previously held concern about *ambientismo* towards an interest in appropriating classicism for both public and domestic architecture. One disagreement with Giovannoni (his former ally in the advocacy of "minor" architecture and contextualism) was over the demolition of the historic Spina del Borgo neighbourhood, which he championed in order to realize his plans (with Attilio Spaccarelli) for the monumental via della Conciliazione on axis with St Peter's Basilica [113] Another was the progressive disappearance of articles dedicated to rustic architecture once he took over the editorship of *Architettura* in 1932 and eliminated the decorative arts component of the former "Architettura e arti decorative" title. As new editor of the journal *Palladio*, Giovannoni, on the other hand, continued to devote ample space to the subject under a special rubric for minor architecture.

Fig. 2.15 Drawing by Paolo Mezzanotte of a peasant house and hearth at Villa Vicentina, from "Il focolare friulano," *Edilizia Moderna* 26:12 (December 1917), 67.

As the picturesque revival in Rome moved between rusticity and contextualism, it began to confront itself with changing political realities. In one way or the other, the quaint shapes and modest scale of the best of the period served as an antidote to the eclecticism of the nineteenth century. The peasantry and its arts and crafts were to lead Italian contemporary art and architecture out of the impasse by providing new stimuli. But, whether or not vernacular architecture as idealized by a group of architects was enough to really reform architecture in

Italy was another matter. The Italian participation in the Exposition Internationale des Arts Décoratifs et Industriels Modernes (International Exhibition of Decorative and Industrial Arts) in Paris in 1925 brings home the point: Armando Brasini's classicizing pavilion, despite Arduino Colasanti's involvement and coordination of the presentation, demonstrates the lack of commitment to rusticity and contextualism when it came to showcasing Italy abroad.[114] The behaviour of Italian officials at this and other exhibitions reflected their reluctance to portray Italy as a nation of peasants and their preference to present it as a nation of Caesars, popes, and princes. Despite this bias there followed an acceleration in studies regarding peasant art and architecture, which fostered appropriation. The entire process raised many more questions than it answered. Many of these unresolved issues would later emerge in the heated debate surrounding Rationalism and its appropriation of classical and vernacular traditions during the 1930s in Italy.

3 *Tabula rasa* and Tradition: Futurism and Rationalism between Primitivism and *Mediterraneità*

Rome is the modern world, the West; Capri, the ancient world, nature before civilization and its neuroses.
    Godard on Godard: Critical Writings by Jean-Luc Godard (1972)[1]

Our art will probably be accused of tormented and decadent cerebralism.
    But we shall merely answer that we are, on the contrary, the primitives of a new sensitiveness, multiplied hundredfold, and that our art is intoxicated with spontaneity and power.
    Umberto Boccioni, Carlo Carrà, Luigi Russolo, Giacomo Balla, and Gino Severini, *Futurist Painting: Technical Manifesto* (1910)[2]

Discourses on primitivism, the vernacular, and *Mediterraneità* played a vital role in shaping futurism and rationalism in Italy between the 1920s and early 1940s; these concepts helped artists and architects combine the abstract qualities of the machine with organic, natural qualities of the vernacular tradition, while engaging competing notions of *Italianità* that surfaced during the fascist regime.[3] Although the futurist and rationalist movements were fundamentally at odds, from the mid-1920s onward, their trajectories coincided in a shared appreciation of vernacular traditions that invoked authenticity and the notion of origins. The ideal of *Mediterraneità* was grounded in a dialogue with Italy's ancient classical past as well as its pervasive vernacular architecture, the anonymous building traditions that have persisted over centuries across the diverse regions of the Italian peninsula and the Mediterranean basin, a geographical area that embraces the three continents of Europe, Asia, and Africa. A number of the architects who dedicated themselves to the perpetuation of *Mediterraneità* during the fascist period subscribed to a design approach that rejected *a priori* styles typical of nineteenth-century historicism in favour of a rationalist approach that took program, context, and site as the catalysts for design. Although the importance of vernacular architecture for rationalism and *Mediterraneità* has been studied, classicism has dominated critical analysis up to the present.[4] The rhetorical and representational power associated with classical architecture has preoccupied historians anxious to deconstruct the volatile relationship between architecture and politics during the interwar years in Italy.[5] Unlike the vernacular tradition, which has only been recognized as a category by architects and historians over the course of the last 100 years, classicism consolidated its meanings in history, theory, and practice from the Renaissance to the Grand Tour in parallel to the rise of the profession of the architect.

If the pursuit of geometry as a metaphysical expression as well as a practical tool for architects resurfaced seductively in Italian *Novecento* and rationalism in Italy during the 1920s and 1930s, the anti-classical bias of futurists led them to a common appreciation of the non-academic *primitive* vernacular environments of Italy.[6] Despite their differences over the role of the machine and the relevance of classicism to modernity, inspiration from the forms and materiality of the pre-industrial environments of central and southern Italy and the Mediterranean basin, allowed futurists and rationalists to briefly share some common ground. During the 1920s and 1930s, both groups began to look to tradition while aligning themselves with the avant-garde in its rejection of nineteenth-century academicism. Extant vernacular was viewed as outside of the flux of history because it had not deeply entered the official discourse of architectural history in thrall to monuments of the past. During this period, competing notions of *Italianità* surfaced under the fascist regime and gradually tempered the rhetoric of *tabula rasa* that had gained momentum among futurists before the catastrophe of the First World War with the publication of the *The Foundation and Manifesto of Futurism* in 1909 by Filippo Tommaso Marinetti (1876–1944).[7]

More than a decade after the polemics of 1909 exploded and under considerably different political working conditions dictated by fascism, futurist and rationalist artists and architects with cosmopolitan leanings gravitated to the *remote* Island of Capri for – "the ancient world, nature before civilization and its neuroses" – in reinventing origins that stood somewhere in between *tabula rasa* and tradition. The fascination for Capri lay in its compelling natural and constructed environment and its location, which was not too far from the mainland but removed enough to give a sense of isolation from the political and social realities of Italy. Sites like the Grotta Azzurra (Blue Grotto) gave Capri its reputation as a land of compelling and magical beauty that was also perpetuated by the continuing fascination for islands in classical literature, starting with Ulysses.

For futurists and rationalists under the spell of nationalism, the quest to rediscover their own *Italianità* through the natural and built environments of Capri as well as other sites along the Gulf of Naples like Amalfi meant a return to origins that was not driven by nostalgia or historicist approaches. Although futurists and rationalists adopted fundamentally different positions towards the role of tradition, they shared a common interest in the stark yet expressive qualities of simple, even crude vernacular forms that signalled *Italianità*, in opposition to the universalizing objectivity of the machine. If futurism aspired to heightened expressivity by undermining convention and bourgeois timidity, rationalism sought a more ethereal lyricism by drawing upon culture and context. Although Capri was the site of classical retreats such as the Villas Damecuta, Jovis, and Lycis, the prevalent type of architecture found in the two major towns of Capri and Anacapri and their environs is the modest one- or two-storey stone and masonry whitewashed domestic buildings.

In Reyner Banham's seminal study of the origins of modern architecture and urbanism, futurism is credited with spurring the rise of modernism and anticipating the "anti-functionalist mood of Le Corbusier and Gropius in the Twenties."[8] Characterized by utopian ideals that reconsidered the city in terms of new types in order to accommodate new modes of transportation (rail, automobile, or air), the driving principles of futurism were in sharp contrast to the reality of Italy's multilayered and fragile historic environments. Although Antonio Sant'Elia's *Città Nuova* (New City, 1914) is considered by some critics to build upon the formal precedent of *Stile Liberty* and Wagnerschule, most narratives of futurism have continued to stress the movement's anti-traditional stance and dedication to verticality and the culture of the machine. During the 1920s and 1930s, Sant'Elia's drawings for his *Città Nuova* were featured in avant-garde publications as were images of Giacomo Mattè-Trucco's Fiat Lingotto factory in Turin (1915–39).[9] During those years, futurism and rationalism were often viewed as complementary expressions of Italian modernity, especially from critics and architects outside Italy. The Lingotto was not conceived as a

Fig. 3.1 First page of Sigfried Giedion, "Situation de l'architecture contemporaine en Italie," *Cahiers d'art* 9:10 (1931): 442–9.

futurist building, but its rooftop track and massive urban presence lent itself to be described as such.[10] Le Corbusier reproduced three views of the Lingotto to illustrate the second-last page of his *Vers une architecture* (Toward an Architecture, 1923).[11] In an essay assessing contemporary Italian architecture published in 1931, Sigfried Giedion (1888–1968) identified futurism with the origins of Italian modernism, and drew a visual analogy between Guarino Guarini's seventeenth-century San Lorenzo in Turin and an Alfa Romeo radial aircraft engine of 1930 to prove it (Fig. 3.1).[12] Giedion used a collage technique to suggest that the ingenuity of the past was being replaced by a more "evolved" modern-day engineering.

In recent years, scholars in Italy and elsewhere have continued to dedicate attention to futurist architecture, especially in terms of its problematic affiliation with fascist ideology.[13] Most scholarly accounts on aspects of futurism have rarely focused on the role of the vernacular and the primitive. Mechanization and its role in the break with the past have become a standard topos for many scholars. Yet the rise of fascism precipitated within the futurist movement a concern over *Italianità* and opened up possibilities that point to a less static futurism that changed over time. As the obsession with mechanization of the early 1910s began to wane, the rediscovery of Italy's *Meridione* or South, and in particular the Island of Capri, caused futurists to rethink their attitudes about the past.[14] For second-generation futurists and rationalists focusing their attention on *Italianità*, the primitive character of vernacular forms infused the rationalist dimension of mechanistic aesthetics with an organic, expressive, sculptural quality that went beyond ethereal transparency.

From the late 1920s onwards, architects in Italy used the term rationalism to describe a movement within modern architecture that prioritized function but not at the expense of individual expression and tradition. Although the rationalists identified with the utopian impulse sustaining Sant'Elia's *Città Nuova*, they all agreed on the need to move beyond the contestation or the *tabula rasa* phase of futurism.[15] Sant'Elia's *Manifesto dell'architettura futurista* (*Manifesto of Futurist Architecture*, 1914), defined futurist architecture as "the architecture of calculation, of audacious temerity and of simplicity; the architecture of reinforced concrete, of steel, glass, cardboard, textile fibre, and of all those substitutes for wood, stone and brick that enable us to obtain maximum elasticity and lightness."[16]

The debate between Giulio Ulisse Arata, one of the founding members of the Nuove Tendenze group established in Milan in 1914, shortly before the outbreak of the First World War, and Antonio Sant'Elia is worth recalling. Arata was initially supportive of Sant'Elia, whom he described as a "young artist of great genius," and encouraged him to participate in the group's first exhibition and to write a preface to the catalogue. But Arata later condemned Sant'Elia's Manifesto, of *Futurist Architecture* of 1914, published in the 1 and 15 August 1914 issues of *Lacerba*, arguing that architecture was intimately related to ethnography and geology, and therefore could not break completely with tradition as Sant'Elia advocated. From the mid 1950s, architecture scholars have demonstrated that Sant'Elia's "Messagio" amplified from his Nuove Tendenze catalogue essay was radicalized by Marinetti before being published in *Lacerba*.[17]

According to Adalberto Libera (1903–63), the architect who worked with Curzio Malaparte and Adolfo Amitrario to realize the iconic Casa Malaparte in Capri, rationalism critically engaged with innovation and tradition and he defended it against Italian politicians and critics who viewed the movement as betraying fascism's nationalist agenda. Libera maintained that rationalism could fulfil, unlike Marinetti's early futurism, both nationalist and international aspirations:

> It might seem that Rationalism in architecture is synonymous with internationalism. However, even though qualities associated with commonly accepted international standards regarding technology, comfort and culture are intrinsically part of Rationalism, those associated with nationalism like climate and ethics will also continue to exist alongside these.[18]

Between 1928, when the first exhibition of rationalist architecture was organized by the Movimento Italiano per l'Architettura Razionale (MIAR), and 1931, when the MIAR'S second and final exhibition at which Pier Maria Bardi showcased his *Tavolo degli orrori* (a highly controversial collage targeting eclectic and historicist architecture in Italy) prompted Rationalism's demise as the state-endorsed movement, debates raged over the agenda and validity of the movement with respect to the Fascist political agenda. After repeated attempts of entering into a dialogue with the *gerarchi*, the Fascist leadership, "progressive fascist rationalists" like Libera, who embraced *Mediterraneità* (which synthesized both vernacular and classical traditions) found themselves at odds with the regime's growing insistence on prescriptive attitudes that banalized classicism in state-sponsored buildings. Libera and others architects like Giuseppe Terragni (1904–43), whose Casa del Fascio in Como completed in 1936 had absorbed the lessons of classicism without succumbing to banal mimesis, felt betrayed by a regime that gradually abandoned both futurism and rationalism.

Although the critic Edoardo Persico (1900–36) endorsed rationalism as a broader European phenomenon, he criticized Italian rationalists for their political and professional opportunism and what he perceived as ethical compromise with the nationalistic and self-aggrandizing agenda of the fascist regime. In a vitriolic essay published in *Domus* in 1934, Persico treated *Romanità* (Roman-ness) with the same disdain as he regarded *Mediterraneità*:

> Italian Rationalism is unable to share the vigour of other European architecture because of its intrinsic lack of faith. And so, the Europeanism of early experiments of Rationalism is diminished, by the cold reality of practical situations into the "Roman" and the "Mediterranean," right down to the last proclamation of corporate architecture … The history of Italian Rationalsim is the story of an emotional crisis.[19]

The Island of Capri was in the heart of the Mediterranean and it occupied a special place in discussions of futurism and rationalism. Before them, the Austrian Secession architect Josef Hoffmann (1870–1956) – following the lead of Karl Friedrich Schinkel (1781–1841), John Ruskin (1819–1900), and Charles Rennie Mackintosh (1868–1928) – began to appreciate vernacular buildings in southern Italy as much as classical monuments and sites.[20] In 1911, the same year that the Le Corbusier travelled to the eastern Mediterranean and discovered its *art paysan* (folk art) and vernacular architecture, Hoffmann presented a talk in which he described the experience of travelling in 1896 to places that included Capri and Anacapri as a turning point in his architectural education and career:

> Finally I fled into the Campagn [*sic*] and refreshed myself at the simple peasant buildings, that without pomp and without stylistic architecture nevertheless give the land its special character. There, for the first time, it became clear to me what matters in architecture; henceforth I studied all the little places on my way with fiery zeal.[21]

On returning to Vienna from his travels, Hoffmann published in *Der Architekt* – a journal that circulated widely in Italy – his travel sketches of modest-sized vernacular dwellings in Capri and Anacapri, which he had observed first hand. These were accompanied by a brief explanatory text in which he helped spread interest in the Mediterranean among colleagues; Hoffmann's discovery of the Mediterranean vernacular informed the shapes and textures of a number of his designs as well as various other Viennese architects during those years, grappling with reform of modern domesticity.[22]

By the early 1920s, Capri had become an important pilgrimage site of leisure and intellectual stimuli for artists and architects who looked with interest at its vernacular buildings, rocky limestone topography, scarcely inhabited and verdant landscape for a number of different reasons. After the First World War, due to the efforts of the island's charismatic mayor Edwin Cerio (1875–1960), an engineer turned politician, Capri became, like the French Riviera and other Mediterranean destinations, a haven, and not only for Italian and foreign nobility but also for artists, architects, and writers. Futurists including Marinetti, and a number of others such as Fortunato Depero (1892–1960), Virgilio Marchi (1895–1960), and Enrico Prampolini (1894–1956) visited Capri on a regular basis during those years. Rationalist architects including Libera, Giuseppe Capponi (1893–1936), and Luigi Cosenza (1905–84) dedicated considerable time to exploring its rocky terrain and developing designs for buildings there.[23]

Capri even became a destination site for preservationists and naturalists. In an address delivered there on the occasion of the 1922 *Convegno del Paesaggio* or Symposium on Landscape, an initiative motivated by preservation of built environments and natural landscapes, Marinetti praised the *Stile Pratico* (practical style) of the indigenous architecture found there.[24] Ironically, the futurists who had sought to break with history and who even evoked the destruction of "past-loving" cities like Venice, which Marinetti dismissively labelled the great sewer, found themselves embroiled in discussions about the architectural patrimony and environment of Italy simply by being there in the midst of the symposium. Although the futurists were not interested in preservation per se, the debate that ensued certainly made them aware of the country's vernacular traditions. Marinetti celebrated the island's local vernacular architecture for its bold sculptural rather than picturesque qualities and asserted,

> I believe that this is a Futuristic island; I feel that it is full of infinite originality as if it had been sculpted by Futurist architects like Sant'Elia, Virgilio Marchi, painted by Balla, Depero, Russolo, Prampolini, and sung and made musical by Francesco Cangiullo and Casella![25]

More than a decade after Marinetti's war cry to "free this land from its smelly gangrene of professors, archaeologists, *ciceroni* and antiquarians," he now exonerated vernacular buildings, sparing them his anti-historicist wrath and proclaiming the vernacular to lie outside the flux of historical styles.[26]

Marinetti saw movement and dynamism in the dramatic and unpredictable landscape of Capri because it rejected, as he put it, "any kind of order reminiscent of Classicism," and embodied a dazzling "variety."[27] Marinetti made his love for Capri known so much that Francesco Cangiullo even wrote a short book entitled *Marinetti a Capri*.[28] Capri, and the whole terraced quality of the Amalfi coast for that matter, has a multilayered quality to its topography. Furthermore, the bright light and colours as well as the extremes of mass and nothingness (land and air/water) confer a dramatic visual and spatial quality that make it as visually exciting today as it was for the futurists. Its craggy landscape evoked the sublime, combining beauty with the forbidding. Thus, the futurists gradually discovered the primitive character of vernacular architecture and peasant art in their sojourns to Capri and other parts of southern Italy, which was notoriously agrarian and far away from the spatial characteristics of the industrial cities of Milan, Turin, and Genoa.

Although the interest in primitivism that surfaced in the 1920s among futurists overlapped with the interest for the archaic dimension of classicism typical of the *Valori Plastici* milieu of painters and intellectuals – Alberto Savinio (1891–1952), Giorgio De Chirico (1888–1978), and Carlo Carrà (1881–1966) – this trend remained fundamentally anti-classical. Praise for the vernacular did not imply an end to the avant-garde, but rather a reframing of its objectives somewhere in between tradition and modernity. Alessandro Del Puppo has stressed how archaism, primitivism, and classicism coexisted in Italy during the 1910s–1920s.[29] During the years immediately following the First World War, artists like Carlo Carrà who identified with futurism during the 1910s turned to metaphysics by way of the archaic or primitive.[30] While Carrà did not look to Capri, his depictions of solitary cottages – often windowless – have metaphysical overtones. Archaism, primitivism, and classicism overlap in Carrà's work. The atmosphere of *La Crevola* (1924) and *Il mulino delle castagne* (1925) evokes the mysterious world of Italian Trecento primitives like Giotto (1267–1337) and of naive painter Henri Rousseau (1844–1910), both of whom Carrà wrote about (Fig. 3.2).[31] These examples show that during the early 1920s interest in peasant art was not

Fig. 3.2 Painting by Carlo Carrà, *La Crevola* (1924), Private Collection.

restricted to apologists for *architettura minore* and *arte rustica* such as Giovannoni and Piacentini but infiltrated Italy's avant-garde. In contrast to these picturesque revivalists, the artists Balla, Depero, Marchi, and Prampolini, who either identified with or were previously influenced by futurism, looked to the pre-industrial peasant arts, crafts, and architecture of Capri and elsewhere in Italy as a source of inspiration for their work.[32]

The appropriation of primitive folk art and architecture by Italian avant-garde artists has parallels in the practices of the German expressionists of Der Blaue Reiter (the Blue Rider) group.[33] Like Picasso in France, Franz Marc not only looked to Oceanic and African art, but also delved deeply into the imagery of the European peasantry. With the exception of painter and sculptor Amedeo Modigliani (1884–1920), whose first major retrospective in 1922 at the Venice Biennale appeared alongside Carlo Anti's exhibition on Arte Negra (Negro Art), the classicizing Eurocentrism of Italian art resisted the influence of the *other*. Anti's exhibition showcased objects and sculptures ranging from Sierra Leone to Benin.[34] Even as futurists subsumed the primitive within their mindset, the memory of Italy's Trecento *primitivi* was not far removed, especially since decades earlier the Pre-Raphelite Brotherhood had done much to revive the work's currency. Right-wing art critics Ardengo Soffici and Ugo Ojetti attacked the phenomenon of neoprimitivism as foreign to the Italian national character.[35] Even when Italy embarked on its colonial imperialism in Africa, the arts of *Africa Nera* (Black Africa) were not explored by Italian artists or architects with any depth, and more often than not were actually used for racial slurs, and to show Italian superiority.[36]

Alongside the musings of the futurists, a number of concerned citizens worked to preserve Capri's heritage from the destructive force of ignorance and eccess. Cerio's *Convegno del paesaggio* in Capri, coincided with an important year for the preservation of vernacular architecture. The organizers announced the recent passing of a law on 11 June 1922 to defend Italy's heritage.[37] This legislation, which focused on *le bellezze naturali e immobile di particolare interesse storico* (natural environments and buildings of historic interest), was the first to safeguard both the natural and built environment. It is not difficult to see why the fragility of Capri made it a priority for the legislators. In 1939, the fascist regime modified the 1922 law and, at the same time, approved legislation to further safeguard Italy's artistic and architectural patrimony.[38]

The 1922 legislation drafted by writer and environmentalist Luigi Parpagliolo (1862–1953), vice-director of the Department of Antiquity and Fine Arts in Rome under the leadership of Colasanti, stressed the intimate relationship between vernacular architecture and the landscape that testified to an anthropological history of place.[39] Praise for Cerio's *Convegno* and various other initiatives aimed at "the development of a true consciousness regarding the landscape" came from many different sources. A commentary published in *Architettura e arti decorative*, probably written by either Marcello Piacentini or Gustavo Giovannoni, openly praised the conference, although it is unclear if they were actually in attendance.

> That which is delightful and useful, and should be looked upon as a hopeful promise, is the development of a true consciousness regarding the landscape. That is to say, the formation of a nucleus of people, who consider these issues, that up until now practical men ignored and disregarded, as essential to the life of the nation. Men that consider these elements worthy of interest through which they might extract useful input for new buildings which can thus be saved from the vulgarity of schematic

geometry and from a design which does not take the environment into consideration.[40]

In the same year that the Symposium on Landscape was held in Capri, Edwin Cerio published his important study entitled *La casa nel paesaggio di Capri*, a book on vernacular domestic architecture of the island (Fig. 3.3). Cerio employed the term "minimal" to describe the vernacular literature of Capri in a number of articles that appeared along with his book.[41] Plinio Marconi's "Architettura minime mediterranee e architettura moderna" (Minimal Mediterranean Architecture and Modern Architecture) (1929) was one of the last articles published on the topic of the Mediterranean vernacular shortly before Piacentini assumed the editorship of *Architettura* and steered the magazine towards classicism. Marconi's and Cerio's use of the adjective "minimal" is especially significant in relation to its use by the radical architects associated with the Congrès International d'Architecture Moderne (CIAM) who called for a break with tradition in favour of an objective response to the program. In his article, Marconi effectively compared ancient minimalism with contemporary design practices.[42]

The use of the term *casa* in Cerio's title is significant in a discussion of the hierarchies of domestic buildings, as the *casa* was less grand and less formal than the villa and was customarily identified with the peasantry and the vernacular tradition. Instead of illustrating the text himself using photography, Cerio enlisted the help of a Venetian artist living in Capri, Gennaro Favai, who would go on to produce his own book on the subject in 1930, entitled *Capri*. Favai's red chalk drawings emphasize the dramatic earthy tones of Capri's natural landscape and the whitewash of its extant vernacular. That same year, Cerio, Parpagliolo, and the artist and architect Giovanni Battista Ceas collaborated on an impressive book entitled *Capri: Visioni architettoniche di Gio. Batt. Ceas* (1930). A number of other books focused on the vernacular buildings of Capri and other places in the south of Italy were published during those years, including Camillo Jona's *L'architettura rusticana nella costiera d'Amalfi* (1920), and later, Roberto Pane's *Architettura rurale campana* (1936). Together, these studies on the vernacular buildings of southern Italy constituted a critical mass of publications that gave the anonymous tradition a legitimacy that was formerly the exclusive purview of classicism. Significantly, these books were written and illustrated by architects rather than ethnographers or geographers, positioning the vernacular squarely in the field of operative critical discourse driven by design.

EDWIN CERIO

LA CASA
NEL PAESAGGIO DI CAPRI

CARLO SIVIERIO - Capri - (La Certosa).

LE PAGINE DELL'ISOLA
COLLEZIONE BIBLIOGRAFICA CAPRENSE

EDITORI ALFIERI & LACROIX - ROMA
MILANO - FIRENZE - NAPOLI

Fig. 3.3 Cover page, Edwin Cerio, *La casa nel paesaggio di Capri* (Rome: Editori Alfieri & LaCroix, 1922).

In his article "L'architettura minima nella contrada della Sirena" (1922), Cerio featured a photograph of a local stonemason, thereby drawing attention to typically neglected players in architectural narratives. Cerio's preference for local builders in the place of architects was echoed by Swedish physician Axel Munthe (1857–1949), whose widely circulated autobiographical novel *The Story of San Michele* (1929) also inspired interest in the earthly paradise of Capri. Munthe's novel recounts his experience of living on the north side of the island near Anacapri, and most importantly, his personal involvement with the construction of his own home – San Michele. Munthe prided himself on the fact that he did not hire an architect and that he laboured along with the *maestro* (master stonemason-bricklayer) and his workers, who could not read or write. He sensitively described the relationship of the house to the surrounding natural elements:

> As I saw it again I thought San Michele looked more beautiful than ever. The house was small, the rooms were few but there were loggias, terraces and pergolas all around it to watch the sun, the sea and the clouds – the soul needs more space than the body. Not much furniture in the rooms but what there was could not be bought with money alone. Nothing superfluous, nothing unbeautiful, no bric-à-brac, no trinkets. A few primitive pictures, an etching of Dürer and a Greek bas-relief on the whitewashed walls.[43]

Interest in Capri and the Mediterranean basin during the 1920s among English-speaking architects and historians who shared little of the futurists' and rationalists' enthusiasm for minimalism or primitivism is attested to by the growth of the permanent settlement of cosmopolitan residents of the leisure class and the proliferation of articles in English magazines that ranged from the scholarly to the touristic. Three brief articles on Amalfi, Ravello, and Capri by the architect and critic Renato Paoli appeared in the British journal *The Architect* in 1920 and 1921. Paoli's picturesque design agenda is revealed in his own villa, L'Amalfitana, built in the suburbs of Rome several years later. Paoli – not unlike Ernesto Wille before him – employed such elements as loggias and decorative motifs typical of the rustic architecture of Amalfi.[44]

In addition to being as politically active as the mayor and leader of the local preservationist movement, Cerio also designed several houses employing vernacular vaulting traditions. Giuseppe Capponi (1893–1936)

Fig. 3.4 Drawing by Edwin Cerio, Il "Rosaio," Capri, 1920–1, from Giuseppe Capponi, "Architettura ed academia a Capri – Il 'Rosaio' di Edwin Cerio," *Architettura e arti decorativ* 9:1 (September 1929): 177–88.

considered il "Rosaio" as one of Cerio's most important works (Fig. 3.4). Cerio was open-minded and encouraged rationalist architects like Capponi, who didn't necessarily share his taste, to design homes for the island. Capponi's villa was completed in 1928.[45] Like many other architects sympathizing with rationalism, Capponi was captivated by what he called the *semplicità primitiva* (primitive simplicity) of the rural architecture of Capri and Ischia. His interest in incorporating this element in his drawings, paintings, and photography informed his unique brand of expressionist rationalism. He incorporated his distinctive line drawings in the brief article "Motivi di architettura ischiana" (Motifs in Ischian Architecture, 1927), which investigated the architecture of the Island of Ischia and was intended to be expanded into a book, but never was.[46]

The Casa Malaparte (1938–42) on Capri's Punta Massullo (Fig. 3.5) evolved into a collaboration between writer Curzio Malaparte, rationalist architect Adalberto Libera, and master builder Adolfo Amitrano.[47]

Fig. 3.5 Photograph by Petra Liebl Osborne of Casa Malaparte, Punta Massullo, Capri, 1938–42, from *Casa Malaparte* (Florence: Le Lettere, 1999).

Bruce Chatwin decribed it as "one of the strangest habitations in the western world."[48] It is emblematic of the overlaps between futurism and rationalism. With its combination of machine-age nautical references (a rooftop veil, a blunt bow looking out to the Mediterranean sea, and a graduated stern) and indigenous stone masonry techniques, the Casa Malaparte exemplifies how futurists and rationalists drew from Capri's environment to construct a new hybrid of Italian modernity that combined the future with the past. While the first round of futurism celebrated the machine-age automobile and a total break with the past, this new interest in Capri seems to speak to a more conciliatory attitude towards the past. Although Capri's natural and built landscape shared little with the verticality of Sant'Elia's *Città Nuova*, its remoteness from civilization fuelled the creative impulses of "the primitives of a new sensitiveness."[49] After filming *Contempt* (Le Mépris, 1963) on location at the Casa Malaparte, Jean-Luc Godard wrote, "Rome is the modern world, the West; Capri, the ancient world, nature before civilization and its neuroses."[50]

Between 1938 and 1942, Curzio Malaparte worked with Libera and Amitrano to design and build his stone house there on a dramatic promontory:

> I was the first to build such a house. And it was with reverential trepidation that I set myself to the task, helped not by architects or engineers (save for legal issues, legal formalities), but by a simple master builder, the best, the most honest, the most intelligent, the most upright that I have ever known ... For months and months, teams of masons worked on that farthest balcony of Capri, until the house began slowly to emerge from the rock to which it was married, and as it took shape, it revealed itself as the most daring and intelligent and modern house in Capri.[51]

Malaparte's praise of his "simple master builder" is not surprising. He abandoned Massimo Bontempelli's cosmopolitan journal *Stracittà "900": Cahiers d'Italie et d'Europe* to adhere to Mino Maccari's journal *Il selvaggio strapaese*, a platform that promoted the values of the Italian peasantry (*strapaese*) in opposition to cosmopolitan urban values (*stracittà*).[52] Malaparte published his *Italia barbara* (Barbarous Italy) in 1925 for the Turin-based publisher Piero Gobetti, writing that "the time has finally come to praise Italy's barbarians – the creative and free spirits of the peasantry who have remained loyal to their traditions and customs."[53] His barbarian peasants are the protagonists of vernacular culture, and Malaparte is clearly deferential to them despite his use of the pejorative adjective. Although the two movements *Strapaese* and *Stracittà* are usually discussed as diametrically opposed factions, Carlo Carrà, for one, combined classicism with the primitivism of rural buildings to express a simplified and cosmopolitan solemnity. With its massive rustic walls and modern flat roof, the Casa Malaparte evoked the hermetic quality of some of Italy's most expressive extant vernacular buildings. Yet it also conjured up powerful metaphysical associations: the building appears like a floating ship. Despite the allusion to movement by way of the nautical reference, here architecture surrenders to its rootedness.

In 1922, the futurist architect and set designer Virgilio Marchi (1895–1960) lauded the vernacular architecture of Capri and the Amalfi coast as a source for contemporary designers in "Primitivismi capresi" (Capri Primitivisms), a short, illustrated essay he published in *Cronache d'attualità*, Anton Giulio Bragaglia's avant-garde journal. Two years later, in his book *Architettura futurista*, Marchi praised the "innate virtue of primitive builders" as he discussed the relationship between the vernacular tradition and contemporary design. On the cover he showcased a design he conceived for a hydro-electric station, one of the most modern of twentieth-century architectural buildings that echoes the sculptural, stereotomic qualities of the vernacular types of the Capri and Amalfi coast (Fig. 3.6), with their external staircases and multifaceted volumes, which he had recorded in a drawing onsite a few years earlier. In this book, as well as in his sequel *Italia nuova architettura nuova* of 1931, Marchi expressed admiration for the "ingenious spontaneity" of the architecture of Capri. With *Architettura futurista* (Futurist Architecture) and *Italia nuova architettura nuova* (New Italy, New Architecture),[54] Marchi tried to position himself as the heir to Sant'Elia, and as the promoter of futurist architecture after the latter's death in 1916, although he realized none of the buildings he had envisioned in a series of drawings produced in the 1910s and 1920s.

The artist, artisan, and set designer Fortunato Depero also took inspiration from Capri and from Italy's "retrograde" *Mezzogiorno* in paintings of the peasantry and their built environs in his *Portatrice caprese* (1917), *Tarantella* (1918–20), and *Paese di tarantelle* (1918), all of which had a lasting influence on Italian modern art (Fig. 3.7). Depero's interest in the vernacular has been the object of several scholarly publications.[55] His enthusiasm for "peasant ingenuity" extended to such folk customs as the *tarantella*, a lively dance typical of southern Italian towns. De-

Fig. 3.6 Cover page, Virgilio Marchi, *Architettura futurista* (Foligno: Franco Campitelli Editore, 1924).

scribing his travels to the "paradise of Capri" and the Amalfi coast in 1917, Depero wrote:

> After four hours of sailing from Capri we landed in Positano on the Amalfi Coast … On one side of this small port we noticed a simple windmill that was inactive for many years and that was transformed into a home … It looked like a primordial machine made of wood built with peasant ingenuity.[56]

Fig. 3.7 Painting by Fortunato Depero, *Paese di Tarantelle* (1918), Private Collection.

When he set up his professional workshop in Rovereto in the Alto Adige region, he brought to his spirited cubo-futurist reading of the layered qualities of the northern Italian vernacular landscape the colour and excitement he had experienced in Capri. Depero's depictions of hill towns to the east of Rovereto, including *Serrada* (1920) and *Lizzana* (1923), show his interest in the organic relationship between vernacular environments and the natural landscape. This dialectic relationship is manifested in his Bestetti Treves Tuminelli book pavilion, realized for the third Monza Biennale (1927). In certain ways, it recalls the sculptural qualities of the layered, interlocking stone and masonry of the southern Italian vernacular built environments, such as the *trulli* of Alberobello in Apulia, interconnected and anchored to each other and the earth from which they rise.

Depero was one of a handful of modernist artists who felt that one could respond to the future without ignoring the rich heritage of the past, a move most militant critics at the time deemed impossible. Additionally, Depero's own craft extended beyond painting to the applied arts. His so-called Casa del Mago (House of the Magician) in Rovereto was a workshop in which local artisans produced tapestries, ceramics, and furniture inspired by traditional models and using local materials and artisanal methods. In Depero's workshop, women had a prominent albeit cliché role in the making of items that required sewing tapestries, cushions, clothing, costumes, and textiles.[57] Although he oftentimes depicted urbane worlds of glass and steel (especially after visiting New York), Depero employed traditional organic materials such as wood and ceramics and techniques such as weaving to forge a novel synthesis of modernity and primitivism.

Depero's portrayals of Italy's rural landscapes and peasant life are indebted to the figurative tradition that he abstracted by way of simple volumes and bold colours. He was interested in such farm machines as the boldly painted horse-drawn carts typical of rural communities of southern Italy, which also interested the architect Giuseppe Capitò, who published a study on the topic in 1922 (Fig. 3.8). Depero's framing and use of colour also could have been inspired by the vibrant geometric ornament typical of Sicilian and Neapolitan carts. Fishermen's vessels were likewise ornamented with bright colours by local artists (as well as the vessels' owners themselves). Depero's painting *Carretto napoletano* (1918), whose contemporary was *Paese delle Tarantelle*, depicts the peasant cart documented by Capitò and others as an ancient machine of considerable dynamism and vitality. During the late 1930s, Depero

Fig. 3.8 Photograph by Giuseppe Capitò, Sicilian horse-drawn cart, from Giuseppe Capitò, *Il Carretto Siciliano* (Milan: Editori Piantanida Valcarenghi, 1923), 25.

supported the fascist *autarchia* laws enforcing the use of indigenous materials to compensate for the economic sanctions of the European community following Italy's invasion of Ethiopia in 1936. In his furniture design, Depero seized on Buxus, an organic corklike material newly invented in Trentino, to manufacture folk objects like hope chests.

Wassily Kandinsky (1866–1944) discovered, before Depero had, the material and spiritual qualities of the "great wooden houses" and folk objects of the Russian peasantry during a visit to Vologda in 1889.[58] Kandinsky claimed that his pursuit of the "hidden" had saved him "from the harmful side of folk art," presumably its sentimental or picturesque aspects.[59] Kazimir Malevich (1879–1935) responded to the lifestyle and arts of the Russian peasantry as well: "The whole peasant life attracted me strongly."[60] This interest is evident in his bold shapes and colours of *Peasant Woman with Buckets and Child* (1912) and *Head of a Peasant* (1928–32).[61] Romanian sculptor Constantin Brancusi (1876–1957) is another unequivocally modern artist who looked to folk traditions (such as funerary pillars) in his interpretation of primitivism, as in his Endless Column monument in Târgu Jiu, Romania, completed in 1938 from sketches and models of two decades earlier.[62]

Another prominent futurist painter and aspiring architect, Enrico Prampolini, offered a synthetic "atmosphere-structure" interpretation in his painting *Architettura cromatica di Capri* (1921), in which he depicted the intrinsic relationship between vernacular architecture and landscape of Capri.[63] Throughout his artistic life, Prampolini looked to the landscape, light, and water of Capri as a source of poetic inspiration. His multistorey and multifaceted futurist pavilion in Turin (1927) was drawn from the sculptural and colourful vernacular landscape of Capri and southern Italy (Fig. 3.9).[64] His pavilion echoes the tensions between reality and dream that surfaced in the imagined landscape and art configurations produced during those years by the Danish artist Maurits Cornelis Escher (1898–1972), who also drew attention to the sites of the Gulf of Naples and the Amalfi Coast. Between 1922 and 1935, Escher combed central and southern Italy, and during this time made drawings of Tyrrhenian communities such as Atrani and Amalfi. The extraordinary cohesion of vernacular architecture and Mediterranean landscape at these sites would continue to inspire the work of Escher throughout his life.[65]

Although some of the interests and concerns of futurists were also shared by the rationalists, especially when it came to the vernacular tradition, what set them apart was their disagreement over the creative potential of classicism. The influential artist and writer Carlo Belli (1903–91) reflected on *Mediterraneità* and classicism, or "*Grecità*":

The theme of *Mediterraneità* and *Grecità* … this was our orienting star. We soon discovered that a bath in the Mediterranean would have exposed us once again to values that had been submerged by Gothic superimpositions and academic fantasies. There is a substantial exchange of letters between myself, Pollini, Figini, and Terragni on this theme. There are also my articles in various journals, which were especially polemical with Piacentini, Calza Bini, Maraini, and others who were possessed by a cult for the Roman littoral … We studied the construction techniques of the

Fig. 3.9 Enrico Prampolini, Futurist Pavilion, Turin, 1927 (photographer un-known), from Ezio Godoli, *Il futurismo* (Rome: Laterza, 1983), 55.

vernacular of Capri, in order to understand why they were built that way. We discovered their traditional authenticity and we understood that their perfect rationality also coincided with optimum aesthetic values.[66]

In many ways, the enthusiasm for *Mediterraneità* was spurred by the increased financial freedom of the Italian leisure class, which permitted its members to commission weekend and vacation homes along the Adriatic, Ionian, Ligurian, Mediterranean, and Tyrrhenian Seas. All the

Fig. 3.10 André Lurçat, Hotel Nord-Sud, Calvi, 1931, from Henry-Russell Hitchcock and Philip Johnson, *The International Style: Architecture since 1922* (New York: W.W. Norton, 1995), 177.

most important examples of Italian domestic architecture that looked to classical and vernacular traditions were designed for these sites, as were numerous recreational and therapy colonies created under the auspices of the fascist regime.[67]

Precisely because of its affiliations with right-wing politics of fascism, Italian, and other expressions of Mediterranean modernism were either eclipsed or misunderstood in influential narratives of the 1930s. Philip Johnson and Henry-Russell Hitchcock's 1932 exhibition The International Style: Architecture since 1922 and the book that accompanied it are a case in point. Although Johnson and Hitchcock included André Lurçat's Hotel Nord-Sud (Hotel North-South) of 1931 in Calvi, along with Le Corbusier's De Mandrot villa in Le Pradet (1931), they failed to acknowledge Lurçat's explicit engagement with a Mediterranean vernacular tradition characterized by smooth whitewashed surfaces and flat roofs (Fig. 3.10).[68] Contemporary commentators in Italy like Gio Ponti (1891–1979) were quick to notice the "perfect Mediterranean character" of André Lurçat's building.[69] In Ponti's estimation, this was not at odds with the *schietto stile moderno* (straightforward modern style) of the work. To be sure, Johnson and Hitchcock's omission is not surprising in light of the fact that they were not really interested in recognizing the pan-regional or national iterations of modernity because it would have weakened their curatorial argument that modern architecture should reflect an international style.

Progressive architects working in fascist Italy and beyond appropriated extant vernacular models to undermine the bombastic monumentality of classicism. For example, although national issues no doubt factored heavily in Josep Lluís Sert's and Libera's works and writings, their primary concern was that the New Architecture should achieve a transnational character as Mediterranean. Sert expressed his interest in standard Mediterranean vernacular architecture while comparing extant row houses to J.J.P. Oud's Stuttgart housing estate for the Weissenhof Siedlung (1927) (Fig. 3.11). Commenting on indigenous, pre-industrial standardized dwelling units in Spain's San Pol de Mar, on the Catalonian coast, Sert noted, "The standard becomes evident. The absence of all aesthetic concerns: fantasy, originality, historical styles, scholastic culture, individualism. The same needs, the same characteristics, taking advantage of modern building techniques."[70] Oud's architecture could be interpreted as Mediterranean. Though the quest for *Mediterraneità* was not exclusive to the progressive front of the rationalist movement, these architects found themselves under constant attack from both the left and right; right-wing academic architects complained on the grounds that their designs were inspired by non-Italian sources and were thus a betrayal of Italian and fascist culture. Left-wing architects outside Italy complained rationalists were collaborating with the fascist government. Enrico Peresutti, a member of the Studio Architetti BBPR founded in 1932, responded to such claims and reminded these critics that while the rediscovery and appropriation of the vernacular may have been spearheaded by foreigners, this architecture was the inheritance of the indigenous population. In his article "Mediterranean Architecture," published in *Quadrante* in 1935, Peressutti wrote:

> Here they all are, recreated in the houses of Biskra, in the houses of Libya, in the houses of Capri. Here is a heritage that we Italians all too often ignore, or want to ignore; a patrimony which we have confined to the archives, a patrimony which we have neglected, as if it were merely a document which has only historical value.
>
> A patrimony which, rediscovered by Gropius, Le Corbusier, Mies van der Rohe, has been disguised as an innovation of northern origin, as a twentieth-century invention. And many have been deceived. Many have mistaken this disguise for a real novelty, for a universal law. Without real-

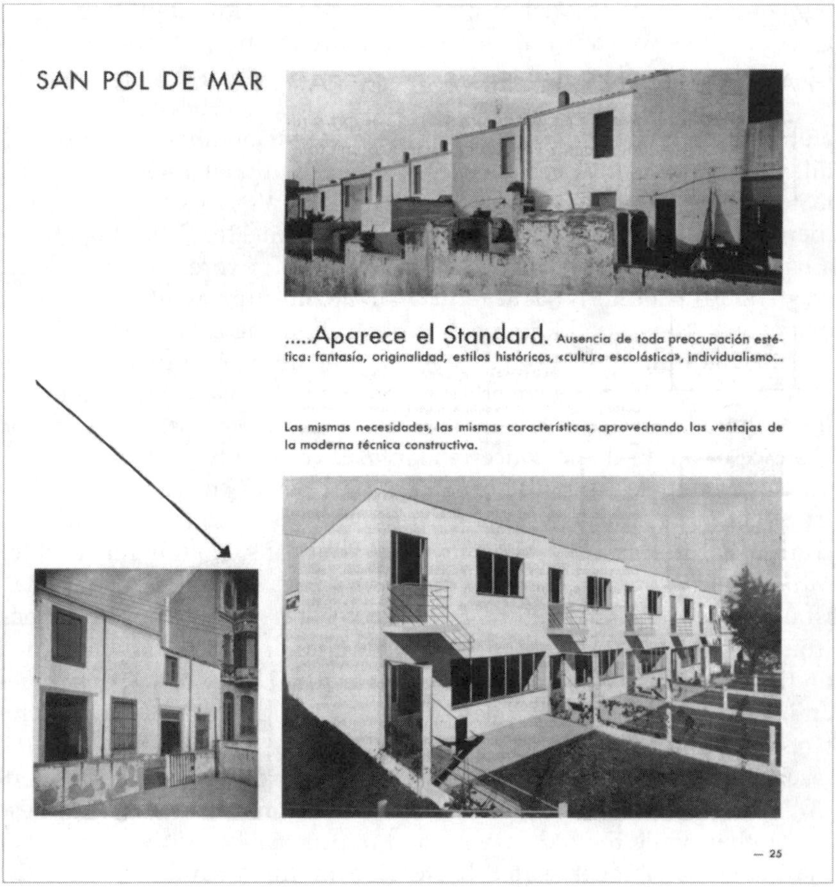
SAN POL DE MAR

.....Aparece el Standard. Ausencia de toda preocupación estética: fantasía, originalidad, estilos históricos, «cultura escolástica», individualismo...

Las mismas necesidades, las mismas características, aprovechando las ventajas de la moderna técnica constructiva.

— 25

Fig. 3.11 Article by Josep Lluís Sert, "San Pol de Mar," *AC – Revista Trimestral,* Publication del "G.A.T.E.P.A.C." 1 (1931), 25.

> izing that this novelty lacks the life, lacks the language, lacks the song of the Mediterranean.[71]

Peressutti was writing in reaction to the nationalist tensions that surfaced during the fascist years. Comments from critics outside Italy confirmed Peressutti's observations that modern German architects had appropriated Italian and Mediterranean traditions. Paul Schultze-Naumburg's comparison of a Mediterranean village with the Weissenhof and Schörblick in his *Das Gesicht des deutschen Hauses* (The Appearance of the German House) (1929) and the racist collage in the Bund für Heimatschutz's *Schwäbisches Heimatbuch* (Schwabian Yearbook) (1934) in which the Weissenhof housing estate was compared with an *Araberdorf* (Arab village) is a case in point.[72] Schultze-Naumburg acknowledges this appropriation and chastises his German colleagues for betraying the values of their Heimat. Unlike these racist attacks, Peressutti's observation showed a deep understanding of the shared heritage of Mediterranean architecture and its relationship to a site and culture. Peresutti (and Gio Ponti only a few years later) cited examples of not only Italian vernacular but also those of neighbouring cultures that prospered along the Mediterranean.[73]

Despite the profound differences between futurism and rationalism over issues of classicism and the machine, the vernacular architecture and landscape of the Mediterranean (Capri, the Gulf of Naples, and beyond) provided both groups with a source of common inspiration. Although rationalist architects negotiated classical and vernacular sources, futurists rejected the former on the basis of its elitism and associations with academic historicism. Although most of the rationalists active during the 1920s and 1930s were involved with projects for public buildings and housing, the pursuit of a Mediterranean modernism allowed a small minority of them to oppose the fascist regime's manipulative rhetoric and "aestheticization of politics," to use Walter Benjamin's fulminating expression, with anthropologically layered dwellings tailored for a specific climate and geographic area.

In the 1930s, a number of Italian rationalist architects enthralled by the poetics of *Mediterraneità* expressed interest in the Pompeian (and thus Mediterranean) courtyard or patio house. Belonging as much to the classical tradition as the vernacular, the courtyard house proved to be adaptable to the functional requirements of modern dwelling, but it also facilitated a traditional Mediterranean lifestyle that involved spending parts of the day outdoors.[74] For wealthy and working-class clients, the courtyard house, with its common elements (atrium and blank external walls that protect the house rather than represent its owners through an elaborate facade), lent itself to repetition and anonymity. For rationalists, this architecture was an expression of economical planning with limited space; for the nationalists and historicists (Pier Maria Bardi's *culturalisti*), it was an expression of *Italianità* that could be flaunted to the rest of the world. By comparing the different appropriations of the courtyard house (creative interpretation versus stylistic copying), one can easily understand the different strands (rationalist versus historicist revivalism) of Italian modernism from the 1920s until the end of the Second World War.

Writing in the early 1930s for the short-lived periodical *Arte Mediterranea*, then architect Giovanni Michelucci (1891–1990) stressed how the design of the Pompeian house was based on a humanist scale. He went on to criticize Pompeian revivalism, which he called "Pompeianismo," as being more about style than the experience of space. Michelucci emphasized the rational, logical dimension over the ideological: "As man felt the need for shelter, he created an environment that responded to his needs. Humanist principles of design are the key to Pompeian architecture."[75] Although Michelucci did not design a patio house himself, his appreciation for the basic principles of its design reveals that he was not interested in Pompeian style but rather in how architecture could facilitate modern ways of dwelling.[76]

Although it remained only a prototype, the villa-studio for an artist designed by Luigi Figini (1903–84) and Gino Pollini (1903–91) for the Fifth Milan Triennale in 1933 was one of the first examples of rationalist architecture that revealed the architect's commitment to Mediterranean modernism (Fig. 3.12). Figini and Pollini's one-storey, flat-roofed patio house was organized around several open-air courtyards that could give the inhabitant the opportunity to enjoy external spaces as extensions of the interiors. Significantly, their plan did not replicate the axial symmetrical qualities of a typical *domus*, with its atrium as the dominant spatial element. The architects recreated spaces that gave the inhabitant exposure to open-air and shaded outdoor spaces, one of which contained an *impluvium*.[77] Whitewashed surfaces on the exterior elevations were juxtaposed with exposed brick. Walls painted light blue, brown, and peach echoed the sky and the earth. Here, Figini and Pollini achieved a synthesis of modern building technologies with traditional models that created dwellings like the courtyard house.[78]

A subtle yet important difference regarding the use of technology between futurist and rationalist architects working in Italy (and other Mediterranean countries) and their counterparts working in northern Europe is seen in the different attitudes towards light. Although such slogans as "light, air, and openness" gave northern functionalists many opportunities for architectural expression (i.e., large plate-glass surfaces), in the South, the pursuit of light and shadow was less technocratic and more spiritual.[79] The glow of natural light that bathed the Mediterranean shores starkly contrasted with the gleaming electric light of the

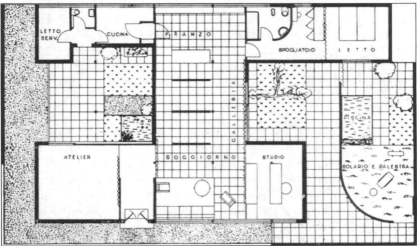

Fig. 3.12 Period photograph by Luigi Figini and Gino Pollini of the patio and plan for "Villa-studio per un artista" (Villa-studio for an artist), Milan, V Triennale, 1933, from Alberto Sartoris, *Encyclopédie de l'architecture nouvelle – Ordre et Climat Méditerranées*, vol. 1 (Milan: Ulrico Hoepli, 1948), 247.

machine age, and carried a number of symbolic associations for southern artists and architects who looked at the Mediterranean basin as the birthplace of primitive or archaic vernacular and classical traditions. It is no coincidence that art historians have written extensively on the topic of southern light and the brilliant colours of the Mediterranean landscape in paintings from Paul Cézanne to Pablo Picasso, Giorgio De Chirico, and beyond. When Adalberto Libera employed deep red stucco in the Casa Malaparte in Capri, he intended to forge a direct link between the local vernacular tradition with the not-too-distant ruins of classical Pompei.

More than fifteen years after the villa-studio was designed (and eventually dismantled), Figini's writings on Italian and Mediterranean vernacular demonstrate both a lingering anti-futurist attitude and a continuity between interwar and postwar interests. In two articles on architecture in Ischia and Ibiza, Figini seized the opportunity to reflect on recent trends in the historiography of modern architecture.[80] Citing Sigfried Giedion's *Raum, Zeit, Architektur: Die Entstehung einer neuen Tradition* (Space, Time and Architecture: The Growth of a New Tradition, 1941), Figini pointed out that many commentators on modern architecture had the tendency to overemphasize the contribution made by technology and abstraction. Figini reproached critics for their reluctance to acknowledge what he felt was the equally significant contribution of the South. Examining the intellectual premises of *Mediterraneità* in the development of rationalism, Figini saw it as instrumental in the *smeccanizzazione* (demechanization) and *sgelo* (defrosting) of modernism. He concluded his essay with a reminder about the fundamental value of vernacular architecture:

> A lesson of morality and of logic (simplicity, sincerity, modesty, humility, adherence to necessity, renunciation of the superfluous, adaptation to human scale, adaptation to local and environmental conditions). A lesson of life (vast employment of "intermediary" elements between open-air and indoor living: loggias, terraces, porticoes, pergolas, patios, walled gardens, etc.). A lesson of style (anti-decorativism, love of smooth surfaces, and for elementary sculptural solutions, the site and "framing" of buildings in the landscape).[81]

If Figini and Pollini's design for the villa-studio appropriates the Mediterranean courtyard or patio house, with its mixture of classical and informal vernacular elements, feeling no compulsion to overtly clas-

STANZA DELLE COLOMBE
NELL'ALBERGO DI SAN MICHELE
ALL'ISOLA DI CAPRI

FACCIATA SUL MARE

Fig. 3.13 Drawing by Gio Ponti and Bernard Rudofsky, "Room of the Doves," Hotel San Michele (unbuilt), Capri, 1938. Archivio Ponti, CSAC, Parma.

sicize it, Gio Ponti's design for a one-storey *Villa alla pompeiana* (1934) was altogether different.[82] With its perfectly square plan, central courtyard, open on one side and to the sky above, Pompeian-red stucco facade, and low-pitched roof, Ponti's villa is closer to the classical spirit typical of *Novecento* than the classical vernacular of Figini and Pollini's villa-studio. It is possible that his collaboration with Bernard Rudofsky on the design of Hotel San Michele on Capri in 1938 with numerous whitewashed and flat-roofed vernacular and open-air *case-stanze*, or room-size houses, led Ponti to rethink his dependency on the classical language of *Novecento* in favour of a less affected and stylized approach to modernism (Fig. 3.13).

Although Ponti's approach to the Italian domestic interior comes across as more pragmatic than ideological, his approach to national identity was overtly political.[83] In the opening editorial of *Domus*, he wrote:

> The Italian-style house is not a crammed and closed refuge against the harshness of the climate, as it is for those who live on the other side of the Alps, where for many long months people seek to conceal themselves from inclement weather. The Italian house is made for us to enjoy the beauty that our land and our sky bestow upon us during the long seasons.[84]

The Pompeian courtyard house was of interest to traditionalists and modernists in northern and southern countries alike. For example, in his *Une cité industrielle* (An Industrial City, 1918), Tony Garnier (1869–1948) had adopted the courtyard house.[85] Drawing on his journey to the Mediterranean in *Vers une architecture* (*Toward an Architecture*, 1923), Le Corbusier projected modern *existenz minimum* values onto the Casa del Noce in Pompei, which he visited and sketched:

> Out of the clatter of the swarming street, which is for every man and full of picturesque incident, you have entered the house of *a Roman*. Majestic grandeur, order, a splendid amplitude: you are in the house of *a Roman*. What was the function of these rooms? That is outside the question. After twenty centuries, without any historical reference, you are conscious of Architecture, and we are speaking of what is in reality a very small house.[86]

Le Corbusier's expressed interest in the Pompeian house was especially significant in the context of Figini and Pollini's villa-studio. Both architects were founding members of the Gruppo 7 and had collectively drafted the first manifestoes published in 1926 and 1927. Their writings were largely indebted, both in style and content, to Le Corbusier's *Vers une architecture* and heralded the advent of a *nuova epoca arcaica* (new archaic era).[87] These writings powerfully endorsed Le Corbusier's rejection of academic historicism and acceptance of a living relationship with the architectures of the past.[88] Le Corbusier's curiosity towards classical and vernacular traditions is key to understanding why he was so important a mentor to Italian architects who sought to rethink the "spirit" of the past and not merely mimic it. A passage from the Gruppo 7's 1926 manifesto *Architettura* reads:

Here, in particular, there exists a classical foundation. The spirit (not the forms, which is something different) of tradition is so profound in Italy that evidently, and almost mechanically, the new architecture will preserve a stamp which is typically *ours*. And this is already a great force, since tradition, as we said, does not disappear, but changes appearance.[89]

Tradition and lyricism (i.e., artistic flight) were what allowed these rationalists to go beyond functionalism and futurism. Lyricism was also closely associated with the concept of *Mediterraneità* espoused by members of the Gruppo 7 during the late 1920s, who later went on to endorse the Mediterranean proclivities of the journal *Quadrante*. Though Gruppo 7 had dissolved by 1930, its founding members were joined by several other architects in clarifying and defending their approach to rationalism in the *Programma*, published in the first issue of *Quadrante*.[90] The program of *Quadrante* was endorsed by Piero Bottoni, Mario Cereghini, Luigi Figini, Gino Frette, Enrico A. Griffini, Pietro Lingeri, Gino Pollini, Gian Luigi Banfi, Lodovico B. Belgiojoso, Enrico Peressutti, and Ernesto N. Rogers. This journal advanced their own design agendas, including an anti-academic approach to classicism and *Mediterraneità*:

> A clarification is required about the characteristics of Italian Rationalism. We appreciate Classicism and *Mediterraneità* on the grounds of their spiritual dimension and not merely as tools for stylistic exercises or picturesque revival. We view Classicism and *Mediterraneità* as antagonistic to certain approaches of Northern architects, Baroque revivals and arbitrary Romanticism, which also characterize some of the new European architecture.[91]

The architects working in the circle of *Quadrante* wanted to engage the powerful, dream-like visual and spatial qualities of the sun-drenched Mediterranean environment (both vernacular and classical) and the cultural heritage that had already fascinated artists for centuries beforehand. In 1933, several Italian delegates of the CIAM, Giuseppe Terragni, Figini and Pollini, met Le Corbusier onboard the ship *Patris II* as it sailed from the port of Marseilles to Athens. From its founding in 1928 to 1959 when it was disbanded, CIAM offered important opportunities for Italian architects who identified with rationalism and *Mediterraneità* to build alliances with like-minded colleagues outside Italy.[92] After reading Le Corbusier's *Vers une architecture* (1923), Carlo Enrico

Rava, a founding member of the Gruppo 7, wrote to him: "The origin of our ideas is to be found within yours; consequently, our intellectual debt is to you."[93] It is not surprising that these Italians, who were enthralled by rationalism, would revere the Parisian architect who fused antiquity and *art paysan*, and whose villa for CIAM's patron, Madame de Mandrot (1931), synthesized *Mediterraneità*.[94]

While architects in Italy during the 1930s found it increasingly difficult to reach a consensus on how to appropriate the classical and vernacular traditions in the realm of large-scale public works, they found leeway in domestic architecture as well as in the seaside, the mountains, and sun-therapy colonies.[95] Architects who undertook such vacation colonies included Giuseppe Vaccaro for Cesenatico (Fig. 3.14); Daniele Calabi for the Lido of Venice; the Studio Architetti BBPR for Legnano; and Carlo Luigi Daneri for Genoa, and they all in some form or other incorporated elements of the local vernacular.[96] Particularly for the buildings of the sun-therapy and vacation colonies, these architects dissolved the boundaries between exterior and interior spaces. As in the vernacular tradition, despite their formal diversity, the designs responded to the site, its topography, climate, and local materials. These colonies emerged from nineteenth-century notions of paternalistic goodwill, and had a moralizing intent that also linked the historical workers' villages with New Towns.

Articles on seaside, mountain, and sun-therapy clinics, written in the 1940s by the architect and critic Mario Labò (1884–1961), offer insight into contemporary critical discussion on the topic.[97] He referred to the "moral code" underlying the "communal life" of such facilities, which he described as a "calm and comfortable atmosphere." In describing a seaside village that Mansutti and Miozzo designed at Marina di Carrara, he mentioned the "rural gaiety" and "regional orientation" provided by the extensive use of brick, pitched tile roofs, and eaves with the gutters ornamented with trellises. He then hastened to clarify that despite these regional characteristics, the design escaped being folkloristic. Making the distinction between the successfully emulated vernacular tradition and its sentimental imitation was a constant preoccupation of rationalist architects. In his discussion of Daneri's mountain colony Rinaldo Piaggio at San Stefano d'Aveto, he observed that

the rustic intentions are not concealed, but are free from any softness or folkloristic reference. They proceed through allusions alone, and one should not let oneself be deceived by the copious use of materials, such

Fig. 3.14 View of Giuseppe Vaccaro's Agip Recreation Colony, Cesenatico, 1938 (photographer unknown). Archivio Giuseppe Vaccaro.

as stone and wood, which is usual among peasants. These materials are applied with a wholly modern sense of malice.[98]

Thus, for Labò and other rationalists favourably disposed towards the appropriation of the vernacular tradition, Giuseppe Pagano foremost among them, creative integration of allusion was more effective than banal mimesis of nostalgia.

In translating anonymous vernacular sources into signature styles during the 1920s to the 1940s, futurists and rationalists transformed the traditions they appropriated, which had been constructed by and for common people, often socially and economically marginalized from the urban bourgeoisie. In Capri and other idyllic southern Italian locales, futurist and rationalist artists and architects were able to transform the dramatic expressiveness of vernacular forms in order to align themselves with the avant-garde rejection of historical eclecticism while engaging contentious and competing notions of *Italianità* that surfaced under Italy's fascist regime. These futurists and rationalists embraced *tabula rasa* and tradition, and in so doing achieved a unique synthesis that was suspended precariously between primitivism and *Mediterraneità*.

4 Engineering versus Architecture: The Vernacular between New Objectivity and Lyricism

Do not build in a picturesque manner. Leave that kind of effects to the walls, the mountains and the sun. A person who dresses picturesquely is not picturesque, but a clown. Country folk do not dress picturesquely, but they are picturesque ... Do not think about the roof, but about rain and snow. That is how the country folk think and why in the mountains they give their roofs the shallowest pitch their technical experience tells them is possible.

Adolf Loos, "Rules for Building in the Mountains" (1913)[1]

From the mid-1930s, a small but vocal group of Italian rationalist architects and engineers, including the likes of Giuseppe Pagano and Ignazio Gardella who identified with neither futurism nor *Mediterraneità*, turned to *architettura rurale* or rural architecture in their search for new design methods. Heeding the admonitions of Austrian architect and theorist Adolf Loos (1870–1933), who revered vernacular buildings but abhorred the picturesque, these architects and engineers embraced modernity and nationalism while eschewing the overtly chauvinistic overtones of fascist ideology. Identifying with the rationalist elements in both the classical and vernacular traditions of the Italian peninsula, they rejected monumentality on the grounds of its deceptive rhetoric – even those architects who collaborated with the regime. In opposition to the pompous character of most classically inspired, state-sponsored architecture realized from the mid-1930s onward, they favoured understated designs. While they shared some affinities with the advocates of *Mediterraneità*, on the whole these architects aligned themselves with the pragmatism of engineering and preferred the spirit of new

Fig. 4.1 Cover page, *Agro Pontino*, Anno IX–XV, Ente Nazionale Industrie Turistiche, showing a montage of Benito Mussolini harvesting grain against the backdrop of a "New Town." (1938).

objectivity to the expressive agitations of the futurists or the lyricism of Mediterranean modernists of the Gruppo 7 milieu, such as Giuseppe Terragni, just to name one of the most talented.

One of the most influential figures was Giuseppe (Pogatschnig) Pagano (1896–1945),[2] in whose thought and design practice tradition and modernity merged seamlessly. Pagano's approach was aligned with the ideals of the rationalist movement, yet rationalism was never a unilateral movement in Italy. Most of the architects of the Gruppo 7 who subscribed to *Mediterraneità* also identified with rationalism. Most of its proponents did not conceive it as a language or *style*, but rather a *method*. As a result, the formal characteristics associated with rationalist architecture were heterogeneous: the rustic realism of Adalberto Libera's Casa Malaparte (1938–42) shared little with the straightforward rationalism of Giuseppe Pagano's Bocconi University Campus in Milan (1938–42). Different attitudes and interpretations rendered it difficult for critics both within and outside Italy to precisely define *rationalism*.[3] Pagano's rationalism from the mid-1930s onward was deeply indebted to the tradition of *architettura rurale*, at a time when Benito Mussolini routinely celebrated the *Homo rusticus* as "the most reliable type of *Homo sapiens*."[4] It is no coincidence that Mussolini was routinely photographed working the fields (Fig. 4.1). With his appointment as co-editor (with Edoardo Persico) of *Casabella* in 1931, Pagano had substantial freedom to address and promote the vernacular tradition of *architettura rurale*. The single most important event he organized during this time was the exhibition Architettura rurale italiana (Italian Rural Architecture), which he curated with Werner Daniel for the Milan Triennale in 1936.

Pagano's endorsement of *architettura rurale* as an antidote to classicizing monumentality was not encumbered by the appeal of *rusticity*, but instead fuelled his interest in the rational processes underlining affordable housing and the role that industrialization could play. His combination of pragmatism and idealism, the tension between utility and art, objectivity and subjectivity can be traced back to the years he spent training as an architect at the Regia Scuola di Ingegneria (Royal School of Engineering, later the Turin Polytechnic) before the Riforma Gentile of 1922 unified and standardized the training of architects in Italy. Pagano's architectural education was thus a hybrid of training in architecture and engineering; this laid the groundwork for his basic approach to design, in which the pragmatic was just as important as the aesthetic.[5] The most significant differences that emerged between the modernist architecture of Pagano, a committed and active member of the Italian Fascist Party, and the Gruppo 7's emphasis on *Mediterraneità*, which owed much to literature and mythology, was their different attitudes towards the role of design in architecture – in other words, the role of subjectivity in the discipline of architecture. For Pagano, as for Loos, the vernacular tradition was a repository of rational methods of building, not romantic notions of place or space derived from literature and myth. As such, he viewed Italy's vernacular tradition and regional particularities as concrete expressions of the abstract notion of *nationalism*, which was typically expressed in the language of classical architecture. Without altogether condemning classicism, Pagano valorized the economy of means underlying the unselfconscious activity of anonymous builders, whom he viewed as a repository of uncorrupted moral values.[6] He also admired the vernacular tradition for its "marvelous spirit of *primitivism*."[7] Pagano's primitivism had little to do with formalism and much more with the pursuit of "pride in modesty" (*orgoglio della modestia*), to use Lionello Venturi's poignant expression.[8]

In his 1946 tribute to Pagano entitled "Catarsi" (Catharis), Ernesto N. Rogers (1909–69) referred to him as a *domenicano battagliero* (combative Dominican).[9] In light of what Rogers referred to as Pagano's "moralizing impulse," the reference to the order of mendicant friars committed to poverty and preaching was apt.[10] To be sure, moralizing approaches to architecture and historiography are deep-seated, from Jesuit intellectual and polemicist Marc-Antoine (Abbé) Laugier (1713–69) to the critic and historian Nikolaus Pevsner, just to name a few.[11] Although it is unclear whether or not Pagano was versed in Laugier's writings (or Carlo Lodoli's, for that matter), what is interesting is that Laugier's rationalism was promoted from a moral point of view and that his "primitive hut" (*"cabane rustique"* in the original French-language edition) collapsed vernacular and classical models.[12]

Pagano's reputation as a moralizing architect committed to austerity, a tendency he shared with many utopian modernists of the Left throughout Europe and the United States during those years, was in no small part due to his promotion of *architettura rurale*. The modest-sized but incisive 1936 exhibition he co-organized with Werner (Guarniero) Daniel at the VI Milan Triennale was a watershed event in shaping the ongoing debates about the rationalist movement among Italian modernists and their interest in the vernacular tradition (Fig. 4.2).[13] It was one of the many exhibitions during those years that set out to influence public opinion.[14] Architettura rurale italiana was mounted at the Milan Triennale in the year Italy invaded Ethiopia, the event that ultimately

Fig. 4.2 View of Giuseppe Pagano and Werner Daniel's Exhibition of Rural Italian Architecture, VI Milan Triennale, 1936 (photographer unknown), from Anty Pansera, *Storia e cronaca della Triennale* (Milan: Longanesi & C., 1978), 290–1.

led to Italy's isolation from Europe and the infernal alliance between Mussolini and Hitler under the Iron Pact, which brought with it major implications for the arts and architecture, and a strategic alliance between Piacentini and Albert Speer.[15] Pagano's Architettura rurale italiana came fifteen years after the Mostra d'arte rustica (1921) organized by Piacentini, Giovannoni, and Morpurgo in Rome, and demonstrated a radically different approach to the appropriation of vernacular culture.

The exhibition and its catalogue, entitled *Architettura rurale italiana*,[16] presented buildings and sites spanning the entire Italian peninsula (Fig. 4.3). While it was the most comprehensive exhibition of its kind mounted during the 1930s, the concept was by no means unprecedented. Already, Giulio Ferrari's comprehensive *L'architettura rusticana nell'arte italiana* (1925) included buildings from all of the regions of Italy, was organized chronologically, and emphasized the great diversity of traditional buildings from the northern, central, and southern regions of the peninsula.[17] Ferrari's was distinguished by its ambitious breadth; for the most part, studies documenting the vernacular tradition were mo-

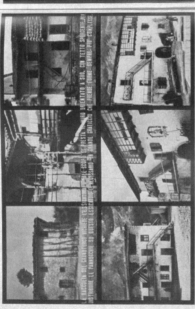

57 · INIZIALI FASI DI EVOLUZIONE DEL GRATICCIO IN LEGNO USATO PER L'AS-CIU-GATURA DEL GRANOTURCO NELLE CASE DELLA VERSIGLIA, DEL TRENTINO E DEL BIELLESE

58 · LOGGIA PRIMITIVA AD IMPALCATURA DI LEGNO PER L'ESSICATURA DEL GRANO-TURCO DI PRIMOLANO, DI PERGINE (TRENTO) E DI GANDINO NELLA VAL SERIANA

lustrazione della fig. 28). Analoga osservazione può essere fatta per le grandi masserie del golfo di Taranto (fig. 29 e 30), costruite in teneri blocchi rettangolari di tufo che si prestano ad eleganti soluzioni di volte. L'evoluzione della casa mediterranea dalla copertura di paglia al trullo, dal trullo alla cupola, dalla cupola al padiglione, alla botte e finalmente al terrazzo è ormai completa nelle sue tappe evolutive. Ma un esame formale alquanto particolareggiato può trovare ancora nell'architettura rurale dei motivi funzionali che spronano alla concezione di determinate soluzioni, che danno origine, alla loro volta, a ritmi estetici particolari. Esempi ci sono forniti dalla evoluzione della colombaia in loggia a torre, e dalla il-

64

fluenza esercitata dalla coltura del granoturco per la creazione dei ballatoi e dei loggiati. La forma primitiva della colombaia è a pianta circolare (fig. 43): una torre che sporge dal tetto, forata all'intorno, ad uno o più piani e con delle cornici sporgenti che collegano i fori e che servono da appoggio ai colombi. Questo motivo si evolve in forme turrite specialmente nel Lazio, nella Campania e in certe zone del latifondo meridionale (fig. 44), quasi abbinandosi a necessità di difesa. Dalla pianta rotonda si passa alla quadrata e si sviluppano, a poco a poco, delle vere necessità estetiche suggerite da questo appariscente elemento architettonico. Importantissimo è quello suggerito dalla cornice che creò l'abitudine di una

65

Fig. 4.3 Two-page spread of the catalogue for the Exhibition of Italian Rural Architecture, by Giuseppe Pagano and Werner Daniel (Milan: Hoepli Editore, 1936): 64–5.

tivated by regional or local interests and written by historians or architects who either worked or lived in the same region.[18] What emerged from Ferrari's overview was the great diversity of the vernacular traditions of the different regions. Italy's diverse climatic, geographic, and topographic conditions, along with the availability of materials ranging from stone to wood, and different rural traditions made it virtually impossible to extract one dominant *national* type. Like dialectics in language, the vernacular was a regional phenomenon.

Departing from the chronological approach adopted by Ferrari, the Pagano and Daniel overview of Italian vernacular architecture is typologically driven, and chronology is of much less importance. This absence of temporal framework and the decision to group the buildings into types was more typical of an architecture-engineering mindset than a historian of art like Ferrari. Thus, in Pagano and Daniel's curatorial vision, the vernacular tradition is portrayed as timeless, as the authors resisted any notion that vernacular buildings could be dated. This approach also resisted the notion of period style, which typically distinguished architecture for historians at the time. It is not surprising, then, that the historian and preservationist Guglielmo De Angelis D'Ossat would later criticize Pagano's book precisely on the grounds of its weak "historical-critical" point of view.[19] Referring to the state of studies on the same topic years later, Giovannoni did not even mention Pagano, and declared that Ferrari's study was "the most extensive and well-known."[20]

While Architettura rurale italiana followed in the path of other exhibitions, mainly by way of its clearly operative scope, it did so in a profoundly different spirit. Pagano attempted to draw attention to vernacular traditions as a source of regional types and materials for a new Italian architectural syntax, free from *picturesque* or folkloristic references, and from the excesses of rhetoric of a certain *pompier* classicism:

> The analysis of this large repository of building energy, which has always existed as an a-stylistic undercurrent, can hold for us the joy of discovery of qualities of honesty, of clarity, of logic, of building health, in the place of perceptions of the past in which it was viewed as a source of arcadia and folklore.[21]

Although the 1936 Triennale came to be known as "Persico and Pagano's Milan Triennale," one need only compare Pagano's Architettura rurale italiana with Edoardo Persico's Sala d'onore (Hall of Honour) to understand how the two were tackling contemporary debate using different perspectives.[22] While Persico "the inscrutable" referred to Grecian-inspired models for his exhibition designs, Pagano "the populist" sought to present vernacular models as a source for conceptually modern building systems that could be appropriated in the design of villas, mass housing, and other building types such as hotels and schools. It is no coincidence that the introductory exhibition panel stresses the functionalism of the rural house, and does not draw further attention to the overtly nationalistic Italian qualities of these examples.

Architettura rurale italiana relied exclusively on photography, and did not include any sketches or drawings; while it is likely that Pagano avoided the sketch in order to discourage any picturesque, sentimental readings of the vernacular, he could have opted for the documentary "measured and drawn" technique adopted by the Austrian, German, and Swiss architect and engineer association publications during the 1910 through 1930s. Although Pagano was certainly not the first to employ photography to document vernacular architecture in Italy, as Cesare De Seta has pointed out, in terms of his interest in vernacular objects he was something of a trailblazer (Fig. 4.4).[23] His black and white documentary photography, absent of human figures, echoes the silent, barren cityscapes depicted by the Alinari brothers decades earlier.[24] He rarely even photographed the interiors of the houses. An air of suspended reality pervades these images, which fall somewhere between Neue-Sachlichkeit of Albert Renger-Patzsch and August Sander in Germany.[25] Yet, by displaying them as a sequence of horizontal bands that was reminiscent of filmstrips, he introduces movement into the otherwise static and detached Alinari views. Despite his social activism and the fieldwork involved in selecting the examples and photographing them, Pagano never included inhabitants in his frames as did the Farm Security Administration photographers during the 1930s and 1940s in America.

In 1936, the same year that Pagano published the catalogue for the Architettura rurale italiana featuring photographs of vernacular buildings, Neapolitan architect and historian Roberto Pane published his *Architettura rurale campana*.[26] In the introduction, Pane addressed the relevance of studying extant rural buildings and argued that the "*architetto contadino*" (peasant architect) still had much to teach the contemporary architect. Clearly, the operative trajectory of his study (i.e., Pane's readership was mainly practising architects) replaces the pure documentary or historical approaches and continues to dominate discussions on

Fig. 4.4 Photograph by Giuseppe Pagano, Vessels, *Litoceramica* 26:1 (undated), from Cesare De Seta, ed., *Giuseppe Pagano Fotografo* (Milan: Electa, 1979): 31.

vernacular architecture during the 1930s. The Milan Triennale venue is especially important for this, because even when it staged historic exhibitions, its appeal to practising artists, architects, and designers was quite different from that of museums.

Pagano's interest in using the knowledge of the extant vernacular tradition to influence contemporary expressions of architecture in cities as well as New Towns was shared by a small minority of high-ranking officials in the fascist regime. Guglielmo De Angelis D'Ossat offered an interesting summary of the IV Congresso nazionale di arti e tradizioni popolari (Fourth National Congress for Popular Arts and Traditions) held in Venice 8–12 September 1940.[27] The committee charged with the task of discussing rural buildings in contemporary Fascist architecture and urbanism included Michele Gortani, Marino Lazzari (who served as president), Giulio Ulisse Arata, Giuseppe Pagano, and Giovanni Sacchi. They all participated in discussions in the session on *architettura rustica mediterranea*, or rustic Mediterranean architecture, a hybrid term which suggested that *architettura rustica* was a generic term and Mediterranean and Alpine were adjectives that qualified specific regional conditions.[28] At the time of the 1940 congress, D'Ossat and others like folklorist Paolo Toschi had already taken on the task of organizing an ethnographic exhibition, the Mostra delle tradizioni popolari, or Exhibition of Popular Traditions, for the 1942 universal exhibition to be held in Rome.[29]

The coexistence of different positions even among the participants of the 1940 Congresso session is especially telling of the richness of interpretations which the vernacular tradition fostered and the different political positions it engendered. Pagano viewed rural architecture as a source of an anti-academic, anti-pompous approach to Italian identity in the arts under fascism, which came to be identified with conservative critics like Ugo Ojetti and Ardengo Soffici. He was openly supportive of Giuseppe Bottai's (1895–1959) leftist vision of Fascism.[30] Giuseppe Bottai was a widely respected fascist minister of National Education from 1936 to 1943. He was considered by most a progressive supporter of the arts among the *gerachi*. In his keynote address at the 1940 Congresso, he stigmatized romantic sentimentalism about contemporary popular traditions.[31] He urged contemporary artists, artisans, and architects to respond to the real needs of human tradition in the domain of the practical and cultural needs of the times. In sum, he argued that contemporary popular art and architecture produced under the fascist regime should respond to the *Zeitgeist* of the time, and not simply retreat into nostalgia. It is unlikely that Bottai really endorsed the propaganda of the Opera Nazionale Dopolavoro (OND), whose mandate was to organize cultural events for the "people." Studies of folklore in Italy alternated over the years between the openly propagandistic and the purely historical,[32] but the OND's mandate was not only to promote popular (i.e., folk) traditions through special festivals but also to provide community recreation programs and exhibitions.[33] Within the umbrella organization of the OND, the Comitato Nazionale per le Arti Popolari organized symposia on folklore in Florence (1929), Trento (1934), and Venice (1940); they were restarted in the 1950s under the auspices of the Congresso Nazionale delle Tradizioni Popolari. In effect, they led to the publication of important studies on Italian vernacular art and architecture, as well as popular (folk) traditions.[34]

All of these spectacles around the folk were dismissed as sentimental and kitsch by rationalist architects like Pagano, who embraced the functional, typological, and material qualities of the vernacular tradition without endorsing the picturesque.[35] Pagano's trajectory was a direct continuation of Loos' statement, encouraging architects not to "build in a picturesque manner." For Pagano, vernacular traditions could not be boiled down to rusticity. He dedicated an entire issue of *Casabella* to villas in 1933, and in a brief introduction, he lamented the deficiency of recent Italian examples that incorporated cues from extant vernacular buildings in comparison with those being built in the United States. In order to prove his point, he assembled illustrations that compare villas by Frank Lloyd Wright, Charles Voysey, and Walter Gropius with a *"costruzione rustica su di una spiaggia del mediterraneo"* ("rustic building on a Mediterranean beach").[36] Implying that, unlike Wright, Voysey, and Gropius, recognized architects in Italy had still not produced anything that was of better quality than extant vernacular architecture. These comments also reveal how vernacular traditions of northern Europe had already played a strategic role in the reform of modern domestic culture.[37]

Loos' admonition to emulate the spirit and not the exterior forms of vernacular architecture is reflected in the writings of Pagano and several others. Art and architectural historian Mario Tinti (1895–1957) published an important study entitled *L'architettura delle case coloniche in Toscana* (1934), with thirty-two commissioned drawings by the artist Ottone Rosai (1895–1957), who was mesmerized by archetypal haystacks and the stoic qualities of the solitary Italian cottage (Fig. 4.5).[38] Tinti's position is aligned with Pagano's:

> In its primitive and simplified structuralism, the *casa colonica* follows organic laws similar to those that rationalist architects have consciously adapted when they have wanted to subtract themselves from the rhetoric of style and the aestheticism of facades.[39]

Fig. 4.5 Drawing by Ottone Rosai, Casa colonica in Laterina (Arezzo) in Mario Tinti, *L'architettura delle case coloniche in Toscana* (Florence: Rinascimento del Libro, 1935): 24.

This publication on the *casa colonica*, a two-storey house inhabited mainly by tenant farmers and common to central Italy which incorporated agrarian functions along with dwelling functions, was anticipated with a polemical essay in which Tinti referred to the trend of *rusticismo di maniera* (rustic style).[40]

An insight into precisely how Pagano viewed *architettura rurale* in contrast to the rusticity or contextualism of the Garbatella and Aniene neighbourhoods completed in Rome during the 1920s can be gleaned from an article he published in *Casabella* in 1935 entitled "Rural Houses."[41] Here, Pagano attempted to provide an overview of the debate surrounding the rediscovery of the vernacular tradition, dividing the proponents of it into two camps. The first was represented by what Pagano described as "lovers of local color, of folklore, and the history of minor buildings."[42] Though Pagano did not name anyone specifically, it is clear that he was referring to Piacentini and Giovannoni, both of whom had been extremely active in Rome promoting *architettura minore* in the 1920s through publications, exhibitions, and above all, design projects. The second camp was represented by "agrarian associations who approach the building of the modern rural house by simply up-dating extant models in technical and economical terms, as well as introducing hygienic improvements that any civilized man deems nec-essary."[43] Pagano characterized this interest as predominantly techni-cal, that is to say, strictly guided by functional (or rational) motivations, and not aesthetics or ideology. In so doing, he was implicitly express-ing a value judgment in favour of the later group, typically identified with *ruralistica* or ruralism, whose work ethic reflected a commitment to straightforward professionalism in responding with efficient but not self-consciously artistic buildings.[44] Thus, Pagano's subtle distinction between sentimental rusticity or contextualism and *architettura rurale* might easily be lost.

Pagano's appreciation of *ruralistica* as a repository of vernacular know-how that could enrich contemporary architectural professional practice by providing practical insights into design and urban planning was not unprecedented. During the late nineteenth and early twentieth centuries, there was ample discussion on the *casa colonica* of Latium, Padania, and Tuscany in numerous do-it-yourself technical manuals.[45] In Italy, Archimede Sacchi's *Le abitazioni* of 1886 comprises numerous chapters dedicated to *fabbriche rurali* or rural buildings. Sacchi was trained as an engineer and architect, which is significant because of the technical nature of his book. Aesthetics were of little concern to Sacchi. Isidoro Andreani's *Case coloniche* of 1919 was another important contri-bution to the literature on the subject. Especially significant in the ex-amples offered by Andreani is the simplified, unornamented character of the rural buildings displayed. Both of these texts were published by Ulrico Hoepli in Milan, a publisher largely known for technical, how-to manuals that straddled the theoretical and practical domains.[46] The functional associations of the Italian *casa colonica*, which was not re-served for leisure of the upper middle classes for which the villa was the preferred dwelling, was still associated with peasants and agrarian economies.

Pagano's interest in contemporary designs modelled upon the ver-nacular *casa colonica* is best summed up in his comments on Mario Asnago and Claudio Vender's Tenuta Castello, constructed near Pavia in 1937 (Fig. 4.6):

Casabella–Costruzioni gladly features this modest rural architecture de-

Fig. 4.6 Photograph of Mario Asnago and Claudio Vender, Tenuta Castello Housing Estate, Pavia, 1937, in Giuseppe Pagano, "Le case coloniche nella pianura padana," *Casabella* 146 (February 1940): 25–6. (Courtesy Robert Hill).

signed by two young, lively and committed rationalists. This project is being featured not so much as a new invention as to teach all the *mosche cocchiere* [pompous flies] of Cremona and Florence that one can produce good and modest work without relying on falsity and folklore.[47]

During the 1930s, the fascist regime exploited the *casa colonica* typology because it offered a cost-efficient, easily repeated model for domestic architecture and could be offered to farmers (i.e., peasants) once regional variants were introduced in the proximity of New Towns on the Roman littoral – Sabaudia and Littoria (today's Latina) – and elsewhere like Carbonia in Sardinia. Yet, unlike the examples of numerous rationalist architects who appropriated vernacular elements in their designs, most of the New Town initiatives presented neovernacular expressions that did not creatively transform extant vernacular buildings but simply repeated them after a number of minor modifications were made with some regional variants in mind. The detailed attention to the design of company towns for agriculture demonstrated to what degree Benito Mussolini meant business in exploiting agriculture.[48] The advantages to be had were always framed within the fascist ideology of "a return to rural values" so closely associated with its idealized moral code. Thus, the domestic architecture of the *casa colonica*, which many of them employed, came to be identified with peasants of regions of central Italy like Latium and Tuscany. It is no coincidence that these economical housing schemes were usually placed in proximity to the denser urban centres of the New Towns for which various recognized architects were employed to provide more complex designs.

The origin of the *casa colonica* was contested between Tuscany and Latium.[49] In light of the strong sense of regional pride in Tuscany, numerous intellectuals who saw in the *casa colonica* a modern primitivism not devoid of tradition had staked claims to its paternity. Advocates and defenders of this paternity were found primarily in Florence, where the existing strata of culture gave life to an interesting competition between rural and metropolitan values (*Strapaese* and *Stracittà*) that surfaced in the journal *Il Selvaggio* edited by Mino Maccari between 1924 and 1943.[50] The discussion on the *casa colonica* polarized the attention of Tuscan architects, artists, and critics like Giovanni Michelucci, Corrado Pavolini (1898–1980), Ardengo Soffici (1879–1964), and Tinti. Different positions surfaced. Soffici argued that classical influence was at the heart of the *casa colonica*, an argument which belittled the contribution of the anonymous builder, whether artisan or peasant, whom progressive architects like Pagano, Pane, and Cerio did much to celebrate. Soffici's complaints that the anonymous builders of the *casa colonica* were being idolized and that many of the examples being cited were actually designed, or at the very least inspired, by architects fell upon deaf ears.[51] Even so, Soffici would look almost exclusively to the Tuscan hill towns and agrarian landscapes in which these peasant buildings were to be found as the subject of his own paintings throughout his entire life.[52] Both Pavolini and Tinti hailed the Tuscan *casa colonica* as an inspired choice for rethinking contemporary design.

Most of these critics, architects, and artists, like Pagano in Milan, discussed the appropriation of the *casa colonica* with regards to contemporary concerns over rationalism and its relationship to Italian identity.[53] Thus, Corrado Pavolini argued in 1933:

> When a rationalist architect seeks to be inspired by these concepts, that is, to understand the good dose of realism and of warmth that comes from the Tuscan house, I will say then that he will have produced a rational

design (conceived according to reason and function). In sum, he will have designed a work that is alive, natural, and beautiful. [54]

But Pavolini did not limit his analysis to Tuscany; he also praised the then recent efforts of Giovanni Ceas, who had published a book on the vernacular architecture of Capri, and that Pavolini defined as a triumph of *"razionalismo spontaneo"* (spontaneous rationalism).[55] This debate on the *casa colonica* allowed for the possibility that an Italian cottage could be both national and regional.

This is also the position adopted by the Tuscan architect Giovanni Michelucci, who added to the choir of voices of those who saw in the *casa colonica* a model of contemporary rationalism that could fulfil the needs of functionalism without alienating Italian identity, history, or the pursuit of modest beauty. This was especially important at a time when critics of rationalism claimed that Italian architects were betraying Italian creativity by looking to examples of international and avant-garde "Bolshevik" architecture, whose very anti-traditionalist stance posed a threat to the fascist regime. As editor of *Domus* in 1932, Gio Ponti published a series of articles by Michelucci in which he drew attention to points of contact between ancient and modern architecture and emphasized an operative interest in the past. The most significant of these articles was "Fonti della moderna architettura italiana" (1932) (Sources of Modern Italian Architecture), which argued in favour of the Tuscan *casa colonica* as an *Italian* model for modern architecture (Fig. 4.7).[56] His aim was to establish a genealogy linking traditional Tuscan vernacular with contemporary practice. To underline his point, he redrew the *casa colonica*, eliminating the typical pitched roof and replacing it with a flat one, to show that the core elements of vernacular building could undergo a transformation using modern materials such as reinforced concrete while still maintaining strong affinities with Italian traditions.

The interest in the modest size and understated qualities of the *casa colonica* during those years was part of an ongoing discussion about the reform of domestic architecture. In his 1931 article published in *Casabella*, Edoardo Persico referred to the recent design by two *"costruttori torinesi"* (builders from Turin), Pagano and Gino Levi-Montalcini (1902–74), as a *cottage*.[57] The cottage was the weekend residence of the Colli family in Rivara (1929–31), a small town in the Canavese region of the Alps, close to Turin (Fig. 4.8). The English term "cottage" was used by Persico in an attempt to downplay what was normally referred to as a villa. With its classical hints in the symmetry of plan and facades, its

ARCHITETTURA ITALIANA

qualunque commento, in quale errore si cada con-
dannando delle costruzioni che differiscono dalle antiche o comunque da quelle generalmente accettate ed
ammirate soltanto per la sostituzione della terrazza,

elemento antichissimo, elemento mediterraneo, (in
molti casi più pratico) al tetto e per un maggior
nitore o senso di pulizia che dir si voglia, che tanto
offende gli amatori del vecchio ad ogni costo.

GIOVANNI MICHELUCCI

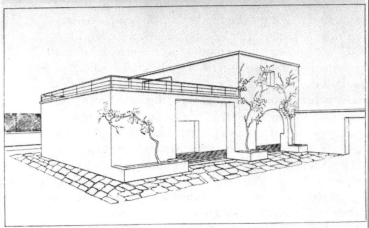

Casa colonica
nella villa
Salviati (ora
Hagermann)
nei dintorni
di Firenze

Fig. 4.7 Giovanni Michelucci, "Fonti della moderna architettura italiana"
(Sources of Modern Italian Architecture), *Domus* 56 (August 1932): 460–1.

Fig. 4.8 Giuseppe Pagano and Gino Levi-Montalcini's Colli "Cottage," Rivara, Turin, 1929–31 (photograper unknown), in Edoardo Persico, "Un 'cottage' nel Canavese," *Casabella* 45 (September 1931): 17. Courtesy Robert Hill.

podium-like base, and the incorporation of vernacular elements typical of Alpine regions, including the one-storey wood loggia on the second floor, the Colli cottage effectively combines urban and rural cues.[58]

Like Perisco, Pagano had employed the term builder when he referred to Wright as a *"poeta costruttore"* (poet-builder) thereby emphasizing the contribution of this role in the place of the architect. For both Pagano and Persico, the role of the anonymous builder was important because it resonated with the vernacular tradition upheld by peasants and artisans who produced their products for and by themselves. Both critics tended to confer even more importance to the builder than to the architect, suggesting that there was a significant poetic value to be found in construction techniques. Pagano and Persico were not alone in their admiration for the so-called peasant architect. Years earlier, in an unprecedented move that foreshadowed the builder's rise in importance, Edwin Cerio included a photo of a bricklayer in an article on Capri's vernacular architecture.[59]

In one of the first post–Second World War studies published on Pagano after his death, Carlo Melograni claimed that the Colli cottage

Fig. 4.9 Drawing by Camillo Jona ("Fienile") of grain storage with "mush-room" piers at Castelli, in Camillo Jona, *L'architettura rusticana in valle d'Aosta* (Turin: C. Crudo & C., 1920): 7.

initiated Pagano's interest in the possibilities of integrating rural archi-tecture with classical references.[60] This sort of loggia is typical of the wood-and-stone buildings of Valle d'Aosta, whose *architettura rusticana* (rustic architecture) had been amply documented by the Trieste-based architect Camillo Jona (1886–1979) and would later be photographed by Pagano in order to include them in his *Architettura rurale italiana* publication of 1936. Jona's *L'architettura rusticana in Valle d'Aosta* was published in Turin in 1920, while Pagano was still a student, and it was the first text to bring attention to Alpine vernacular (Fig. 4.9). After that, the vernacular art and architecture of Valle d'Aosta was investigated in the sustained efforts and extensive writings of Jules (Giulio) Brocherel (1871–1954), which culminated in his large-scale 1937 exhibition Arte popolare valdostana (Peasant Art of the Valle D'Aosta).[61]

If one considers that the site was within easy commuting distance from Turin, the definition of villa or weekend-vacation cottage seems appropriate. The combination of the proximity of Turin and Milan to the Alps as well as the presence of a wealthy bourgeoisie – Thorstein Veblen's leisure class – who could afford weekend and summer homes was a catalyst for rural architecture studies in relationship to contemporary design in domestic architecture.[52] The rediscovery of the vernacular tradition of the Alpine regions also served as a stimulus for other kinds of buildings, including hotels, hiking retreats, ski lodges, and health colonies. This rediscovery of the vernacular tradition, in conjunction with a growing middle class, generated a new demand for weekend or vacation homes. The access to previously remote regions of Italy, thanks to the automobile and the railroad, allowed future patrons to see vernacular architecture in its natural environment, and then refer to it as a source of their own vacation homes and villas. Therefore, it is no coincidence that it was in the Alpine regions of northern Italy, and in proximity to the most industrial, and thus the wealthiest cities such as Milan and Turin, that architects like Pagano but also Gio Ponti, Piero Portaluppi (1888–1967), and others first began to operate. If architects appropriated the vernacular for the design of villas and *case*, it was due to this incentive. Afterwards, it also found plenty of room to develop in the realm of housing.

Persico's brief commentary on the cottage, especially on the modesty and appropriateness to its location invokes John Ruskin's description of "*L'air noble*," the trait he assigned to the Italian lowland cottage in *The Poetry of Architecture* of 1873, translated into Italian in 1909:

> Now, this simplicity is, perhaps, the principal attribute by which the Italian cottage attains the elevation of character we desired and expected. All that is fantastic in form, or frivolous in detail, annihilates the aristocratic air of a building: it at once destroys its sublimity and size, besides awakening, as is almost always the case, associations of a mean and low character. The moment we see a gable roof, we think of cock-lofts; the instant we observe a projecting window, of attics and tent-bedsteads. Now, the Italian cottage assumes, with the simplicity, *l'air noble* of buildings of a higher order; and, though it avoids all ridiculous miniature mimicry of the palace, it discards the humbler attributes of the cottage. The ornament it assumes is dignified; no grinning faces, or unmeaning notched planks, but well-proportioned arches, or tastefully sculptured columns. While there is nothing about it unsuited to the humility of its inhabitant, there is a gen-

eral dignity in its air, which harmonizes beautifully with the nobility of the neighbouring edifices, or the glory of the surrounding scenery.[63]

Both Persico and Pagano were well versed in Ruskin's appreciation of the Italian cottage at least by 1935, if not earlier. In his essay entitled "Archittetura rurale in Italia" published in December 1935, just months before the opening of Architettura rurale italiana, Pagano amply cites Ruskin's *Poetry*, using his "l'air noble" expression and notion of "higher order."[64] Yet the classical-vernacular synthesis of the cottage for the Colli family shares little with Ruskin's rejection of classicism in favour of neomedievalism. What is interesting about Pagano and Persico's appreciation of Ruskin's moralism is that both of them demonstrate a willingness to engage with theories and practices that are not exclusively Italian, thus demonstrating that not all the architectural debate in Italy during fascism was provincial or inward-looking.[65]

The geometry of the plan of the Colli cottage is based on the rectangle: the plan is symmetrical, and a distinctive open central of hall that is of double height functions as an interior courtyard. A living room and dining room are located on either side of the central hall. A kitchen, with an informal dinning and resting room in the two corners, is part of the first-floor amenities. The main volume of the cottage is placed upon an elevated plinth, or podium (referred to in the drawings as a terrace); access is gained by centrally located steps, along with two sets of symmetrical lateral steps. The second floor of the cottage spills out into a partially covered loggia that wraps around three sides of the four-sided structure; instead of the marble balustrades traditionally associated with loggias, one finds wooden bands typical of the rural architecture of the region, as well as built-in flower boxes. A hipped roof covered in local slate recalls extant vernacular buildings. The synthesis of both classical and vernacular elements which the Colli cottage embodies recalls the work of Adolf Loos. The most obvious Loosian building that shares these affinities is the Landhaus Paul Khuner of 1929–30 in Austria.[66] While it is not certain that Pagano and Levi-Montalcini actually saw this project, there is an undeniable similarity with the two-storey entrance hall of both designs.[67]

Despite his vehement attack of folklore and the picturesque, Pagano had already experimented with appropriations of Alpine vernacular "accents" just a year earlier. In his 1928 pavilion in Turin which hosted the Mostra della caccia e pesca (Exhibition of Hunting and Fishing), he used logs to clad the entire surface of the building. Armando Melis described it as having *un simpatico sapore rusticano* (a pleasant rustic taste).[68] It was Pagano's designs for the 1928 Turin exhibition, largely indebted to Beaux-Arts planning methods despite the rustic cladding, which would alienate him from a protagonist and promoter of Italian *architettura funzionale* (functional architecture) in Italy, Alberto Sartoris (1901–98).[69] On the basis of what he deemed to be Pagano's retrograde Beaux-Arts approach, Sartoris attacked Pagano in the introduction of his influential publication *Gli elementi dell'architettura funzionale* (1932), claiming that he was betraying the tenets of modernism.

The pursuit of a synthesis between classical and vernacular is especially evident in the work of another architect from the Giuseppe Pagano milieu and similar age bracket, Ettore Sottsass Sr. (1892–1953), who was based in Rovereto. The Colli cottage was completed in 1931, during the same year Pagano and the *Gruppo torinese* of the Movimento Italiano Architetti Razionalisti (MIAR) which also included Ottorino Aloisio, Umberto Cuzzi, Ettore Sottsass and his collaborator Gino Levi-Montalcini, designed the classicizing monumental scheme for the Via Roma in Turin. (It would be realized eventually by Marcello Piacentini between 1934 and 1938.) This scheme is important to note because it demonstrates to what degree this group of architects who worked together began exchanging ideas and approaches to combine classical and vernacular traditions. For example, Sottsass' project of 1936–7 for a *villino* in Turin includes his four solutions that explore vernacular and classical options by alternating between a flat and pitched roof (Fig. 4.10). Sottsass demonstrates that it is possible to swing back and forth between the two traditions.[70]

Trained as an architect at the Academy of Fine Arts of Vienna, Sottsass was one of the most important architects working in northern Italy who constantly experimented with the incorporation of cues from extant Alpine vernacular into his work.[71] He eventually moved away from those literal uses of the rustic model, evidenced in his early Progetto di villa in Bolzano (1923) and his rustic designs for a kitchen at the Monza Biennale. His entry for a competition in war-torn areas of Trentino was a significant, if austere, attempt at reviving the vernacular tradition with a limited budget. In a way not dissimilar to several other architects interested in appropriating the Alpine vernacular for their contemporary designs, Sottsass published a series of drawings of "architettura minore e rustica trentina" (rustic and minor architecture of Trento).[72] These include examples of religious and domestic architecture located in urban and rural sites in which both vernacular and classical elements

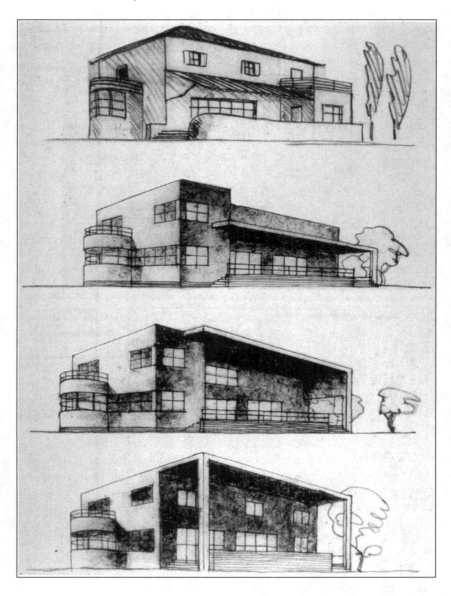

Fig. 4.10 Drawing by Ettore Sottsass, *Villino*, Turin, 1936–7.

Fig. 4.11 Drawing by Enrico Griffini, *Casone* (large house), in Enrico Griffini, "Case rustiche veneziane – I casoni," *Ingegneria* (1 July 1922): 18.

are employed. Sottsass's efforts were paralleled by a number of other architects of the period.

With Sottsass in Trento and Giorgio Wenter Marini (1890–1973) whose painting and design work also engaged the region's traditions, it was Enrico A. Griffini (1887–1952) who best exemplified an engineer's objective and empirical approach to the appropriation of vernacular models intended as a system that could inform contemporary design.[73] In 1922, the year Piacentini published his "Influssi" article that promoted the contemporary relevance of *architettura minore*, Griffini also published his first piece on Italian vernacular architecture in the newly founded Milan-based *Ingegneria*, the official journal of the Italian national association of engineers.[74] A first essay on the Venetian *casa rustica* or *casone*, a large barn-like dwelling constructed of reed, wood, and brick typical of the Lagoon and coastal Adriatic fishing communities, was followed by others on *architettura rustica* of the Italian Alps (1923) and the Valle Gardena (1925) (Fig. 4.11).[75]

Griffini alternated writing about the subject with design practice. Years earlier he and Paolo Mezzanotte had entered the 1919 Ercole Marelli competition on new housing for the war-torn areas of northern Italy.[76] Their project did not win, and Griffini later complained that the houses actually built in the Carnia and Friuli regions as a result of this initiative failed to include elements that were fundamental to the traditional houses of each region, such as loggias, the great *focolare* or hearth, and thus disrupted deep-rooted social traditions.[77] A drawing published in 1923 boldly claims – echoing the theories of Gottfried Semper: "The hearth is the soul of the Friulian family."[78]

Griffini presented numerous drawings of this central "moral" element of the home, as Mezzanotte had already done.[79] Griffini, like Ojetti before him, understood acutely the importance of the kitchen in the social and moral life of the Italian peasant family. In 1920, drawing upon local vernacular sources, Griffini proposed a *casa colonica* in the Carnia and Friuli regions. For his winning submission in a competition held by the Collegio degli Ingegneri e architetti di Milano, he and his brother Alberto designed a prominent hearth as part of the domestic environment.[80]

Griffini is an important figure for Italian modern architecture in between the two world wars because he and others of the Pagano milieu were instrumental in changing the perception held by a younger generation of Italian architects, mainly in Milan and other cities of northern Italy, who identified with the progressive rationalist strain. Thanks to Griffini's approach, he helped them recognize that the vernacular tradition could also be tapped as a source for contemporary rational design and building methods. It is no coincidence that Griffini's collaboration with younger architects like Giuseppe Ciribini (1913–1990) would lead to important research on rural architecture and the building industry from the 1940s during the Second World War and beyond.[81]

Griffini's interest in the vernacular was more practical than aesthetically motivated, and thus shared little with Giovannoni's and Piacentini's approach exemplified in the Mostra di arte rustica held in 1921. Griffini's early publications illustrated by his own drawings (often signed as Grifo, a nickname his classmates and later his students had playfully assigned to him) are particularly important in light of his influential 1932 publication *La costruzione razionale della casa*, in which he provides a brief introductory history of the house and numerous synthetic conceptual drawings; from this, one can deduce that his *existenz minimum* owes much to the rationality (and efficiency) that defines the rustic house. To the vernacular tradition, Griffini owes the understanding of the role that the climate and geology of different regions plays upon the characteristics of each design.

Within the European panorama, the engineer's appropriation of the vernacular during the late nineteenth and early twentieth centuries differed from that of the architects, especially in Austria, Germany, and England, insofar as it was substantially less aesthetically driven and more interested in extracting rational principles of building. Engineers, too, were less concerned with conceptualizing the vernacular in terms of identity politics. During the first decade of the twentieth century, the pioneering studies on the *Bauernhaus* (farmhouse) published by professional associations of architects and engineers in Austria, Germany, and Switzerland established a standard that the Italians never met with the same rigour and comprehensiveness.[32] The measured and drawn documents of these three pioneering publications, which were spearheaded by the associations of architects and engineers in these countries, provided a historic record that set an invaluable graphic standard. The assembly of technical drawings of plans, section, elevation, and the almost complete absence of any freehand sketches made them appear almost photographic in their documentary precision. The overlap between scientific inquiry and the typology interest of engineers like Griffini is evident through the insistence on such types as *casa* or *casoni* to describe the quality of the object of study, instead of a more conceptual approach implicit in Piacentini and Giovannoni's "minor architecture" and "contextualism."

In Italy, the first to take up the methods of the northern architect and engineer associations was not Griffini but Aristide Baragiola. In his *La casa villereccia delle colonie tedesche Veneto-Tridentine* (1908) Baragiola maps out the influence of German-Austrian vernacular upon Italian territories. Baragiola planned a trilogy, but only published a second volume in 1915, entitled *La casa villereccia delle colonie tedesche del gruppo carnico, Sappada, Sauris e Timau*. His term *casa villereccia* can be translated as pastoral, country, or rustic home. Baragiola was very careful about documenting not only the architecture but also the complex traditions associated with domestic architecture in these regions. Influenced by linguistics, he was especially interested in the terms used to describe different parts of the homes. Baragiola explicitly credited the German-speaking countries for having taken the lead in this type of study, as Renato Biasutti later did in his overview of 1926. It is important to note that Baragiola was the only expert on vernacular architecture to be invited to present a paper at the First Congress of Italian Ethnography in Rome, in 1911.[83] In the address he delivered on 20 October, Baragiola pointed out to his audience that it was the Society of Anthropology of Vienna and Berlin that, even before the engineers, had jump-started studies on rustic buildings.

The continued interest among rationalist architects in vernacular buildings was especially useful in the debate which ensued with the end of the First World War and into the early 1920s, as an urgent need for housing surfaced throughout Italy.[84] Griffini's was only one voice in a choir. In order to counteract the lagging Italian economy that followed the end of the war, agrarian reform measures were evoked as a way of boosting national productivity. During those years Benito Mussolini proclaimed that *"bisogna fare del fascisimo un fenomeno prevalentemente rurale"* ("we need to make of fascism a prevalently rural phenomenon"). Thus, rusticizing modern Italian society through the "promise of grain," later referred to in the 1925 legislation as the *"battaglia del grano"* ("the battle for grain"), insofar as it fostered a new relationship between city, town, and countryside, was also laced with consequences for the arts. Many propaganda paintings of the epoch aimed at promoting the healthy moral values of rural life indirectly celebrate the metaphysical qualities of haystacks and solitary farm houses. Combined, these economical and cultural incentives ensured that Italy's agrarian identity would remerge through a renewed interest in the vernacular tradition, which served to guide architects and engineers in the design of new homes for the working class and displaced peasant communities. In his promotion of a strongly agrarian component of the new fascist society based on timeless moral values, Mussolini laid the ideological foundations for the development of New Towns of the early 1930s.[85] An interesting example of this phenomenon is revealed in the remarks made by Luigi Piccinato (1899–1983), the urban planner and architect who designed Sabaudia, during the inauguration ceremony:

> With Sabaudia, the agricultural life of the Nation makes an enormous step forward toward a new reality. It is a gigantic step not only because of the quantity of the architectural works and the land which has been reclaimed for agriculture, but also, and most importantly, because it expresses in a concrete way, the acquisition of a new conscience of national rural values.[86]

The New Towns designed largely around work and vernacular models were not unprecedented. The late nineteenth-century *villaggi operai*, or workers' villages, such as Crespi d'Adda (1894–1925), also relied on vernacular models to convey this ethos.[87] In Italian company towns, the vernacular tradition developed into two distinct yet interrelated trends, which were later to find renewed vitality in fascist New Towns where the workers' residences were also standardized multiple units based on the *casa colonica* precedent. The other expression of country life informing the domestic architecture of Crespi D'Adda was to be found in the rusticated motifs for the exclusive single-family two-storey villas of the company administrators. Here, the vernacular tradition lived on as a rustic style and not for its economy of means. Thus, there was a double standard between vernacular working-class and upper-middle-class domestic architecture that selectively appropriated rustic elements.

Griffini was one of the first Italians to recognize that the time-less functional dimension of the vernacular tradition needed to pass through the eye of the needle of new hygiene standards in order to respond to contemporary needs of society, while still maintaining its intrinsic cultural identity. The New Towns were to become the most fertile experimentation ground for this "cleansing" or sanitization to occur. New standards relating to light and hygiene needed to be ful-filled, and this process eventually led to the transformation or modern-ization of original extant building types that were conceived prior to the twentieth century and therefore often lacking in indoor plumbing, for example. However, there was much disagreement over which type of substitution to provide, *casa colonica* or *casa rustica*. The *casa colonica* was totally void of ornament, whereas the *casa rustica* often incorporat-ed rustic motifs or accents. There is an abundance of before and after propagandistic literature which boasted the change from reed and ma-laria-bound hovels – which the fascist regime had actively eliminated in the interests of the disenfranchised poor, and as such ensured that these images circulated widely – to crisp and clean farmhouses made with bricks and mortar.

It was often the engineers who could synthesize the spatial and func-tional aspects of vernacular architecture and reconceptualize them for contemporary practice through serial repetition and modularity tuned to industrial materials and modes of production. This was certainly the case with Griffini, as well as Gaetano Ciocca.[88] It is no coincidence that Pagano would, alongside a volume celebrating vernacular architecture of the Italian peninsula (*Architettura rurale italiana*, 1936), publish a book on techniques of housing design entitled *Tecnica dell'abitazione* (1936). Thus, the vernacular was not viewed by Pagano and his followers as a source to merely simulate, but rather as a live tradition that could help to reform contemporary housing in Italy, public as well as private.

The interest in vernacular architectures of the Alps sets Griffini and Pagano (and Persico) aside from the rationalists who pursued *Mediterraneità*. In 1931, both Pagano and Persico moved from one hotbed of Italian modernism in Turin to another in Milan, in order to take up their positions as co-editors of *Casabella*. It was through this collaboration that Pagano could ensure that the journal provided a forum in which to discuss the vernacular tradition and its relationship to contemporary design. One of the first to win Pagano's interest was Carlo Mollino (1905–73), an architect trained and based in Turin.[89] Mollino's early drawings of rural architecture in the Valle D'Aosta (1930), which he planned on publishing (but never did), were attempts at understanding the construction methods of Alpine buildings such as the *rascard*, also referred to as a *fienile*, a type of wood storage shed built on stone piers in areas like Gressoney and Trinitè, which Jona had illustrated in his publication of 1920 (Fig. 4.9).The numerous construction details carefully drawn by Mollino, starting from the intersection of logs and including his drawings of the hearth, come across as analytical drawings and not as mere sketches. Writing in 1930 about the the upper Aosta Valley, Mollino stated:

> As for every building, Alpine houses have particular characteristics of their own: characteristics that originate from climatic and terrain conditions, from the quality of available materials, as well as from the economic and ethnic conditions of the inhabitants who built them ... Alpine houses were designed and built by their very same owners since skilled workers and contructors did not exist.[90]

In 1931, Pagano wrote to Carlo Mollino because he was interested in publishing some of his *"montagnini"* (designs for mountain settings) plans in *Casabella*. The competition launched in the journal in 1932 for a *"Casa in montagna"* (mountain house) gave him an early opportunity to determine how to recast the traditional technique of wood construction by applying a modernist approach to repetition and seriality for an Alpine setting. For the Italians, building in wood was only possible in the Alpine or mountain regions, where this material was more abundant.[91] Unlike the Mediterranean vernacular architecture of Italy's central and southern regions, which was perceived more in terms of sculptural mass due to the stucco which covered vaults and load bearing walls, variations of the log cabin, typical of the northern regions as well as England, Germany, and the Scandinavian countries seemed more compatible as prototypes for factory-produced serial buildings because they could be disassembled with greater ease than with stone and mortar buildings.

Mollino's studies during the interwar period provided the basis for much of his postwar work, in which he often combined traditional elements of Alpine buildings with new materials, such as reinforced concrete.[92] The overlap with the tourist industry, regionalism, nationalism, and the impulse to discover and document extant rural architecture in the Alps is perhaps best reflected in the work of Mollino. At the time, his unpublished drawings, and above all, Jona's study of 1920, did much to draw attention to the fact that the wood buildings of the north were also part of the Italian vernacular tradition. These buildings were found on a peninsula that boasted diverse topographic and climatic conditions (seaside, hill town, lowlands, lakeside, mountains). Despite his modest production prior to the Second World War, Mollino would later go on – thanks also to increased opportunities offered by an ever-expanding tourist and leisure industry in Italy – to become the architect of several important Alpine buildings, in which he would make great use of local building techniques in combination with more advanced reinforced concrete technology. Two significant postwar examples are his Stazione albergo at Lago Nero (Sauze d'Oulx, 1946–7) and the Casa del sole apartment block in Cervinia (1951–4).

Pagano's interest in the rural architecture of all of Italy extends beyond Mollino's world of leisure and excitement to Capri and the gulf of Naples, even though his specific approach goes against the grain of the concept of romanticizing *Mediterraneità*, as it was espoused by advocates of the *Quadrante* milieu, whose *Programma* of 1933 Pagano thoroughly criticized. Though several of the architects who signed the *Programma* identified with rationalism, many of them were original members of Gruppo 7, and looking to the vernacular, they took a decidedly more poetic approach. Bardi's efforts to support the appropriation of the Mediterranean vernacular as an expression of *Italianità*, as well as his manifest appreciation of Le Corbusier, led to his attempt to construct a strong ideological association with the vernacular. The polarization of the debate, with the Pagano camp versus the *Quadrante* milieu, has been observed by historians.[93] Fundamentally, Pagano was weary of the arbitrary qualities of poetic or lyrical architecture, espoused by Gruppo 7 and its followers.[94]

The subtle distinction between different approaches to the appropriation of the vernacular tradition by architects and engineers identifying with rationalism is seen in Pagano's endorsement of the Villa Oro (1934–7) built on a site looking out on the gulf of Naples and jointly designed by the Neapolitan engineer Luigi Cosenza (1905–84) and the Viennese émigré Bernard Rudofsky (1910–87) (Fig. 4.12).[95] The design was based on the appropriation of Ischian vernacular architecture, reconfigured as a series of interconnected whitewashed cubes mounted on a rusticated plinth. Thus what was achieved and shared among designers of the period was the desire to achieve a seamless continuity between the natural conditions and the man-made structures typical of modern architecture along the Gulf of Naples.[96] In 1936, Pagano compared "the serene geometries" of the houses of Torre del Greco, Positano, and Amalfi "the bold cubist abstractions of Boscotrecase" to the Villa Oro.[97] Here he drew attention to Cosenza's double identity as engineer and architect, as a sort of *antidote* to the "rustic" and "contextual" approach of exponents of the Roman milieu, who also had expressed interest in the vernacular builders of Capri, Ischia, Procida, and generally, the Neapolitan gulf.[98] Thanks to Pagano and Gio Ponti, at the helms of influential magazines like *Casabella* and *Domus*, Rudofsky's designs circulated in Italy and abroad during the 1930s.[99] Significant projects include his design for a house in Procida (1937). Rudofsky's collaborative work with Gio Ponti for Hotel San Michele in Capri (1938) is also significant.[100] His work and life experience in Italy during those years laid the foundation for the writing of his influential *Architecture without Architects* (1964). Recalling his learning experience with Rudofsky and the importance of "non-pedigreed" architecture Ponti thus wrote in his *In Praise of Architecture*: "Let us have regional architecture, an architecture *a paese*. This is organic architecture, and architecture not 'architected.'"[101]

During the 1930s when Villa Oro was realized, Capri and the surrounding area became a hotspot for villas that looked to both the classical and vernacular tradition in either mimetic-stylistic ways or highly inventive ones. Adalberto Libera's Casa Malaparte, Giuseppe Capponi's personal villa, and Edwin Cerio's various homes are the most significant examples. Even the German émigré Konrad Wachsmann (1901–80), who published his *Holzbauhaus* (1930), gave evidence of a brief interest in the Mediterranean vernacular in his design of the Tan-

Fig. 4.12 View of Luigi Cosenza and Bernard Rudofsky's Villa Oro (photographer unknown), Naples, 1934–7.

nenbaum villa for Capri (1932).[102] Wachsmann's friendship and collaboration with the other German émigré Wolfgang Frankl while he worked and lived in Rome until 1938 was significant. Frankl remained in Italy to work in collaboration with Mario Ridolfi; the two constantly looked to vernacular as a source of their gritty designs.[103]

Pagano's interest in economy of means and its relationship to the vernacular tradition were at the base of his appreciation for the work of Ignazio Gardella (1905–99). Pagano cites Alberti in the context of an article in which he comments on Gardella's design of 1936 for the chapel and altar at Varinella, which he describes as a "courageous lesson of modesty (Fig. 4.13)."[104] Only one year after his Architettura rurale italiana exhibition, Pagano openly commended Gardella's use of elements of *architettura rurale*. Gardella's design includes a brick screen that introduces the symbol of the cross as a means of achieving a work of modern art; the small yet thoughtful outdoor place of worship was at once rooted in the agrarian past of the area but also referenced contemporary materials and forms.

Fig. 4.13 Photograph by Ancillotti of Ignazio Gardella's chapel and altar, Vari-nella, 1936, in Giuseppe Mazzariol, "Umanismo di Gardella," *Zodiak – International Magazine of Contemporary Architecture* 2 (1958), 96.

The chapel project remained unrealized. However, Gardella used this type of screen solution in his Tuberculosis Sanatorium for Alessandria completed in 1938 in Alessandria, in northern Italy (Fig. 4.14). In this area, typically known for rice cultivation, the brick screens used to filter light and allow for continual air circulation called *gelosie* (screens) were quite common.[105] It is interesting to note, in terms of how education reflects approaches to the appropriation of the vernacular tradition, that Gardella had been trained as a civil engineer at the Milan Polytechnic, graduating in 1931. The brick screen was thus conceived as both functional and ornamental; this concept of beauty through utility was not appreciated by academic types who, rather than appreciating the use of the vernacular elements, described the building as looking inappropriately barn-like.[106] Here again we witness how the engineering link was especially appealing to Pagano, because he felt that engineers were most apt to use the vernacular tradition without falling into the trap of style and the picturesque. In numerous essays written during his tenure as co-editor of *Casabella* from 1931 to 1942, Pagano's only direct

Fig. 4.14 Photograph by G.E. Kidder Smith of Ignazio Gardella's Tuberculosis Sanatorium, Alessandria, 1938, in G.E. Kidder Smith, *Italy Builds Its Modern Architecture and Native Inheritance* (New York: Reinhold, 1955), 169.

reference to a treatise was to Book IX of Alberti's *De re aedificatoria* in his piece on Gardella. Quoting from the original Latin, Pagano's reference to the proper ornamentation of private dwellings points to his interest in Alberti's notion of ethics in relation to the art of building: "I notice that the most prudent and modest of our ancestors much preferred frugality and parsimony in building as in any other matter, public or private."[107] Frugality and modesty are fundamental pillars of the Lexicon Paganorum.

The term *modesty* had come to mean something very special for Pagano and *Casabella* readers since art historian Lionello Venturi, who had refused to swear an oath to fascism and was forced to emigrate to the United States as a result, published his 1933 essay *Per una nuova architettura*, linking "pride in modesty" with morality as he applied it to contemporary architecture. As early as 1926, Venturi's book *Il gusto dei primitivi* resonated as much among architects as it did among artists and architects because of its subversive ethical message.[108] Edoardo Persico described primitivism as the capacity to establish a new artistic tradition with universal qualities.[109] Persico, himself a fervent Catholic, also drew attention to the opinions of Maurice Denis and Jacques Maritain on primitivism that were in direct opposition to those of Venturi.[110] For Pagano and Persico, primitivism became more than a matter of artistic language or form; it became a matter of *process* and *method*. Persico was not as enthusiastic as Pagano about rural architecture, and yet the two managed to meet on the common ground of conviction about the moral undertones of primitivism.

In the same year that Giuseppe Pagano simply abandoned the fascist party, his last building, known as "una casetta in legno" (a small wooden house) built in the small town of Viggiù (Fig. 4.15), not too far from Milan, was published in *Domus*.[111] In the brief accompanying text to the plans and photographs illustrating the dwelling, Pagano explains how the design of the weekend home was motivated by the desire to make something which was truly "una cosa qualunque" ("just an ordinary thing"). He went on to claim that he hoped his design did not "offend the landscape."[112] Here again, Pagano continues to demonstrate adherence to the core tenets of the arguments he made during his Architettura rurale italiana exhibition; he continues to stress his commitment to the legacy of the anonymous builder, which he as an architect reinterpreted and offered as a new synthesis. He was weary of the arbitrary nature of poetics, and constantly downplays the lyricism celebrated by advocates of *Mediterraneità* like Terragni, whose Casa del Fascio he criticized with the following statement:

> If we wish that Italian architecture follows a path that allows for moral and aesthetic developments and if we want to express our world, we must act, think, and be poetic, not with an aristocratic and eccentric sensitivity. We must desire to be anonymous, to purify ourselves from rhetorical attitudes. We must not be enamored by rationalizing speculation. We must avoid imprisoning ourselves in an academy of forms and words ... I would like architects to work toward finding pride in modesty, in finding pride in great and anonymous heroism.[113]

Pagano's design was based on the use of local materials such as

Fig. 4.15 Giuseppe Pagano's Weekend House, Viggiù (Milan), 1942 (photographer unkown), "Una casetta in legno," *Domus* 177 (September 1942): 375.

wood, as components that could be assembled on a site, which were anchored to the stone foundation. The house is covered with only one large, inclined roof plain. In this last project, if one excludes the rusticated base, all the classical references in plan and elevation are completely eliminated. Even the choice of wood as a structural and not merely decorative element reinforces this self-conscious design understatement. Needless to say, this *ordinary thing* is in many respects extraordinary. Pagano was quick to understand that behind the rhetoric of *Italianità*, cities like Bergamo, Genoa, Milan, Naples, Rome, and Turin had become the object of aggressive real estate speculation. The activities of the Istituto Nazionale Assicurazioni (INA), which was assailing Italy and destroying parts of the existing historic fabric in the name of fascist "progress," were perhaps the most obvious manifestation of this trend. In light of these examples, Pagano's self-consciously modest designs resonate loudly as heroic resistance through understatement.

5 Continuity and Reality: The Vernacular Resumed in Postwar Architecture and Urbanism

Modern architecture in Italy, as elsewhere, is essentially a return to tradition – the tradition of the spirit against the false tradition of dogma. Therefore, what thus might be said of the essence of past architecture may also be translated into the terms of contemporary architecture.

Ernesto N. Rogers, "The Tradition of Modern
Architecture in Italy" (1955)[1]

The collapse of the fascist regime coupled with the destruction of Italian cities and its countryside during the Second World War created a backdrop of anxiety and poverty which challenged postwar efforts to rebuild. The spectre of the Holocaust and atomic bombs of Hiroshima and Nagasaki added to the mixture of anxiety and hope for renewal that permeated those years. Collaboration with the fascist regime had tarnished the reputations of many Italian architects both at home and abroad, despite mostly unsuccessful attempts of left-wing fascists to persuade the regime to adopt the progressive platform of the rationalist movement. Unlike progressive architects who fled Nazi Germany to go to England and America, almost all Italians remained.[2] During the postwar years, models drawn from Italy's vernacular tradition were used to design a number of urban-scale housing villages mostly on the periphery of large to mid-sized cities. The architectural and urban configurations of extant rural hamlets, villages, and towns of Italy thus helped shape the materiality and architectural types of the new single-family dwellings and housing estates that began to be slowly realized in the midst of hardship and hope.

The end of the Second World War prompted conscientious Italian architects to reassess their involvement with fascism and to think about how to restart their practices in the service of the complex task of mending the nation's broken spirit and physical environment. In the immediate postwar years, architect and critic Ernesto N. Rogers (1909–69) took a leading role after a brief stint as editor of *Domus* followed by his new appointment as the new editor of *Casabella-Continuità*. In these positions, he offered assessments of the physical and psychological reality of Italy and spoke openly about "catharsis," "continuity, and tradition."[3] In his opening editorial for *Casabella-Continuità*, Rogers promoted the notion that tradition (and not historicism) could play an integral role in shaping the phenomenon of modernism in postwar Italy.[4] The first issue featured a number of articles ranging from a piece about a Dogon village in Mali, Africa, to an essay by Giancarlo De Carlo comparing the recent domestic architecture in Italy by Mario Ridolfi and Wolfgang Frankl (Viale Etiopia towers, 1948–54) in Rome, and by Ignazio Gardella (namely, his Casa del Viticultore, House of a Vintner, realized near Pavia, 1944–7) (Fig. 5.1). Both of these examples of Italian architecture achieved poetic expression with frugal means.

Rogers' concepts of continuity and tradition implied selectively salvaging the lessons of fascist modernists like Giuseppe Pagano while thinking ahead to the responsibilities of architects and urbanists to mend the damaged fabric of existing cities. Writing about the urgency of housing, he encouraged architects to draw examples from the classical and vernacular traditions of the past: "With the exception of ancient Roman houses in Pompei and our very human and varied rural houses, where does one find other Italian examples [of houses] that are equally comforting?"[5]

Rogers and the *Casabella-Continuità* milieu he nurtured with his seductive intellectual leadership set the agenda that would shape Italian architecture and urbanism from the 1950s well into the 1970s. Kidder Smith's important book, *Italy Builds: Its Modern Architecture and Native Inheritance*, the first English-language publication to discuss modernism in relation to what he called "native inheritance," appeared at a difficult time for rationalism and modernism, with the disbanding of the CIAM (Congrès International d'Architecture Moderne) at Otterlo in 1959 after decades of collaboration between architects from a number of countries and of different generations. Guilio Carlo Argan was very vocal during those years in defence of rationalism.[6] It is precisely the continuity with tradition that Rogers used to justify Italy's "village" at

Fig. 5.1 Photograph by Gabrielle Basilico, Ignazio Gardella, Casa del Viticultore, House of a Vintner, Pavia, 1944–7, from Franco Buzzi Ceriani, ed., *Ignazio Gardella – progetti e architettura 1933 – 1990* (Venice: Marsilio, 1992), 88.

Expo 1958 in Brussels, the first world fair to be held after the end of the Second World War.[7] It was by way of the phenomenological teachings of Antonio Banfi and Enzo Paci that Rogers and others counteracted a technocentric vision of modernity.[8] The Italian pavilion designed collectively by architects Ignazio Gardella, Studio Architetti BBPR (Belgiojoso, Peressutti, and Rogers), Adolfo De Carlo, Giuseppe Perugini, and Ludovico Quaroni was an understated yet sophisticated reinterpretation of the Italian hill town that stood under the shadow of the bold scale of the Atomium by the Belgium engineer André Waterken. Citing this and other projects, Reyner Banham accused Italian architects of "infantile regression" in the name of neoliberty.[9] Banham openly questioned why Ernesto Rogers, "the hero-figure of European architecture in the late Forties and early Fifties," appeared to be abandoning rationalism and modernism for neoliberty. Yet, upon closer scrutiny, both Italy's interwar and postwar architectural identity was in some way or the other shaped by a dialogue with history; what changed was the nature of this dialogue. The interwar years were fraught with ideological interferences on behalf of the fascist regime whereas the postwar years left most architects free to interrogate history and the role of memory on their own terms.

Writing during the 1950s, architect and critic Paolo Portoghesi (1931) stated, "Appreciation for the spontaneous, the rustic, the anonymous, had already had a long period of success during the twentieth century in Italy. It was therefore, one could say, in the blood of the in-between generation that was at this time at the helm of architecture culture."[10] Portoghesi confirmed this opinion two decades later in a study entitled *After Modern Architecture* (1980), in which he discussed the "old passion" of Italian architects for "peasant culture": "The theme of memory emerged in the work of the Italian masters during the early years of reconstruction, and the first images were tied to an old passion, cultivated by Pagano, for the models of peasant culture."[11] Writing as the director of the 1980 Venice Architecture Biennale entitled "La presenza del passato (The Presence of the Past)," Portoghesi asserted that the "return of architecture to the womb of history and its recycling in new syntactic contexts of the traditional forms" characterized a series of designs in recent years.[12] Portoghesi also clarified that he wanted the title of the exhibition to explain "a phenomenon which has its symptoms in the 1950s."

During the 1950s and 1960s, Italian society moved from a primarily agrarian foundation to one that was increasingly more reliant upon industry. Rural dwellers of the South moved to cities of the North where they found employment in factories of industries like automobile manufacturer Fiat, whose famed Lingotto building in Turin had impressed Le Corbusier among others. This shift ushered in a renewed era of both *realist* and modernist architecture (and urbanism) that integrated the ethical, formal, and material qualities of the vernacular tradition within a new political framework of a democratic Italy focused upon providing the lower and middle classes a new voice after years of coercion, manipulation, and violence.[13] Although rebuilding and recovery were slow at first, the resources and incentives provided by the American-sponsored Marshall Plan soon set war-torn Italy on its path to what commentators described as an "economic miracle" and as a "metamorphosis."[14]

In state-sponsored buildings during the interwar years, the fascist regime championed the facile rhetoric of bombastic classicism, and to a lesser extent, expressions of neovernacular (which surfaced as the so-called *casa colonica* for tenant farmers in New Towns) were often used to design public housing estates. Large-scale public works that went against the grain of this trend were met with hostility by right-wing exponents of the regime who believed that engaging with *Italianità* meant imitating the past by way of banal mimesis: recall the hostility with which Gruppo Toscano's (Giovanni Michelucci et al.) Florence Train Station, inaugurated in 1934, was met despite its low-lying mass and *pietra-serena* surface that were both meant by the designers to engage creatively the context of historic Florence. When the regime did use neovernacular expressions for New Towns, it did so only within the sphere of domestic architecture and rarely as part of its public buildings programs that embodied a condescending message: neovernacular was appropriate for *the people* but not for the government, which wanted to express its authority through the nobility of classicism.

During the fascist years, a number of rationalist architects who appropriated classical and vernacular traditions managed to effectively integrate both of these within their designs for public buildings. Many of these continued to work after the fall of fascism. Ignazio Gardella incorporated a privacy screen made from brick for the rooftop terrace of his anti-tuberculosis sanatorium in Alessandria (1938–42); Giuseppe Pagano's Bocconi University in Milan (1938–42) echoed the loggia typical of Alpine dwellings found in the Alps not too far away from Milan. Yet the number of realizations by these architects was fairly limited. The majority of the experiments in the appropriation of cues from extant vernacular buildings and traditions were achieved with single-family residences such as the iconic Casa Malaparte in Capri (1938–42). Thus, during the postwar years the vernacular tradition went from functioning as a marginal yet important conduit of subversion if one compares it to the ubiquitous use of the classical tradition by interwar architects, to a new position of centrality within the design processes of public housing estates as well as a number of amenities for the leisure class such as hotels and ski lodges in the Alpine regions of northern Italy. While it was primarily domestic architecture, and still marginal insofar as the housing estates were found mainly in the peripheries of large cities or small Alpine resort towns where leisure buildings multiplied, the overall attitude changed towards the peasantry, and its rural traditions became increasingly diffuse among different social and economic brackets at a time that it was being threatened by incipient industrialization.

The urgent need for new housing to accommodate displaced urban dwellers as well as the newly urbanized former rural dwellers that had morphed into the working-class proletariat provided the socio-economic backdrop for the rekindling of intellectual debates in publications and exhibitions and within the domain of practice, which strategically employed the vernacular tradition as a vehicle with which to engage issues of popular, national, and regional identity. In order to resolve the housing shortage during the years following the end of the war, architects were invited by the newly elected government of Italy to design projects for the working class under the auspices of the state-sponsored Fanfani Plan (also referred to as the Piano INA-Casa) approved in 1949. Mario Ridolfi and Ludovico Quaroni's Tiburtino and Adalberto Libera's Tuscolano III housing estates in Rome (1950–4) were among the most compelling new neighbourhoods in the postwar city (Fig. 5.2). In Milan, the workers' neighbourhood of Cesate (1951–3), which was collaboratively designed by Franco Albini, Ignazio Gardella, and the Studio Architetti BBPR, was just one of the many interventions throughout the country developed and built under the auspices of the INA-Casa initiative. Bruno Zevi recognized the merits of modernizing *anonymous* architectural typologies, such as the patio house and the *casa colonica* and praised Libera's patio houses at Tuscolano III, which he likened to a "skyscraper lying down."[15] These were among the most emblematic experiments with appropriations of extant vernacular in postwar architecture in Italy's capital: the different types of buildings constructed in Tiburtino – for example, its *case in linea* (row houses) and *casa-torre* (tower houses), both designed by Mario Ridolfi – gave these neighbourhoods a sense of variety that avoided the image of the unrelenting, homogeneous building that constituted the Pruitt-Igoe housing project, designed for Minoru Yamasaki et al. for St Louis, Missouri, in 1954–5 and demolished in 1972 because it was no longer deemed an acceptable place to live.[16]

With their mixture of reinforced concrete and earth-tone bricks, and small, open-air personal as well as communal spaces, these housing estates embodied a mixture of urban and rural qualities that were intended to help ward off the anxiety of displacement many of the new inhabitants felt. While they echoed tenets of utopian modernism typical of interwar architecture and urban planning on a large scale, which had inspired some of the most interesting (if unrealized) projects during the 1920s and 1930s, they were much less homogeneous. Most architects realized that large-scale utopian projects for New Towns depended upon

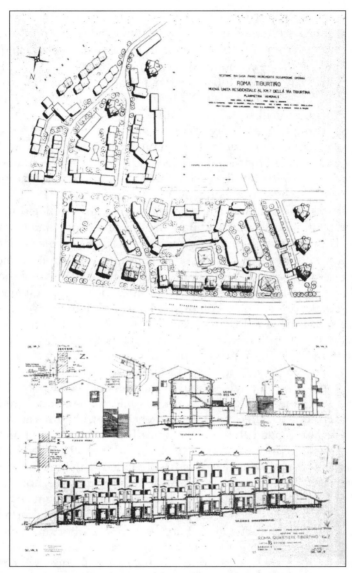

Fig. 5.2 Drawing by Mario Ridolfi, Tiburtino, INA-Casa Row houses with external corridor, Rome, 1950–4, from Vittorio Magnago Lampugnani, "Der Mythos der Wahrheit – Städtebau im Italien der Nach Kriegszeit," in *Die Architektur, die Tradition und der Ort – Regionalismen in der europäischen Stadt*, ed. Vittorio Magnago Lampugnani (Stuttgart–München: Deutsche Verlags-Anstalt, 2000), 381.

a centralized authority that was no longer viable or possible to imagine after the ravages of totalitarianism. A growing enthusiasm for projects on a smaller scale and greater architectural variety was in large measure also a function of the economic realities of postwar Italy. Not only did the Fanfani Plan strategically promote artisanal and craft approaches over more modern, industrialized technologies, it also encouraged the development of small-scale communities as villages.[17]

It was in this climate of renewed interest in "the people" that the Mostra di architettura spontanea (Exhibition of Spontaneous Architecture) was developed for the ninth Triennale in Milan in 1951, the second Triennale to be held after the end of the war (Fig. 5.3). The examples of spontaneous architecture were oddly out of place in the metaphysical geometries of Giovanni Muzio's Palazzo dell'Arte completed in 1933. Curated by architects Enzo Cerutti, Giancarlo De Carlo, and Giuseppe Samonà in conjunction with graphic designer Albe Steiner, this exhibition was *operative* insofar as it only focused upon extant vernacular buildings – architectural and urban expressions – which were thought to pose a viable model for contemporary urbanism.[18] Simultaneously, the Triennale presented a commemorative installation dedicated to architects who perished in the Second World War and who identified with rationalism in interwar modernism: Giuseppe Pagano, Edoardo Persico, Giuseppe Terragni, and the critic Raffaello Giolli, all of whom were considered to be victims of the fascist regime after it turned against them, even though several of them actually collaborated with it at different stages.[19] This exhibition was staged as an opportunity for Italian architects to reflect upon the currency of such figures as Pagano, who had championed the modesty and the virtues of rural architecture in his exhibition held at the Milan Triennale in 1936. Franco Albini coined the term *architettura spontanea* (spontaneous architecture), which although it shared elements with rural architecture was not charged with the negative associations of a disgraced political regime that had encouraged *ruralism*. Albini coined the term to describe "certain examples of urban planning and of spontaneous architecture which developed in strict coherence with their cultural, economic, social, and natural environment and not through external influences which were in turn imposed upon them."[20]

Albini's expression generated some controversy. Critic Gillo Dorfles complained that it was problematic because all forms of artistic creation are in some way or other spontaneous.[21] Liliana Grassi dedicated an entire chapter of her 1960 compendium *Storia e cultura dei monumenti*

Fig. 5.3 Giancarlo De Carlo et al.'s Exhibition of Spontaneous Architecture, Milan Triennale, 1951 (photographer unknown), *Catalogo Nona (ix) Triennale di Milan* (Milan: Triennale di Milano, 1951), 372

(History and Culture of Monuments) comparing those architects who gleaned cues from extant vernacular buildings for picturesque details such as accents or motifs rather than taking inspiration from the empirical as well as the practical quality of spontaneous architecture.[22] Grassi, in keeping with Albini's stance, rejected architects imposing external influences that were not really grass roots or in keeping with the sociocultural identity of the people for which they designed buildings:

> The risk with spontaneous architecture is that some designers might think it is possible to imitate spontaneity by simply repeating certain motifs of architecture they have already seen elsewhere, without worrying about the intrinsic value of such a transposition.[23]

In organizing the Mostra di architettura spontanea, De Carlo and collaborators engaged voices that had emerged during the years of the fascist regime. Such collaborations reinforced the perception of continuity of research agendas between prewar and postwar, although most historians of twentieth-century architecture and urbanism in Italy have been reluctant to acknowledge this fact. Roberto Pane, for example, was invited to contribute his photographs of rural architecture of southern Italy. His *Architettura rurale campana* was published in 1936 and had already received a considerable amount of attention. Art historian Renata Egle Trincanato (1910–88) was invited to contribute photographs and drawings from her book entitled *Venezia minore* (Minor Venice) published in 1948, which revived Giovannoni and Piacentini's term but did not subscribe to its nationalist thrust even though she carried out the research for the book at the height of the fascist regime (Fig. 5.4).[24] Trincanato describes minor architecture that "distinguishes itself for a lively participation with the general harmony of the whole."[25] Not long after the publication of Trincanato's study focusing on urban continuities and buildings that integrate rather than break this continuity, Gardella completed his Casa alle Zattere (1954–5), which reflected a growing concern of this Milanese architect for the extant "minor" buildings of Venice's architectural masterworks. The concept of *architettura minore* as it was recast in the 1950s was not burdened with issues of authorship and stylistic associations typical of the interwar years. Terms like *minor* and *major* echoed the redressing of differences between prose and poetry (vernacular versus architecture) delineated by Benedetto Croce in his seminal essay "Poesia popolare e poesia d'arte" (Folk Poetry and Poets' Poetry) (1929), to which Pane's essay "Architettura e letteratura" (Literature and Architecture) (1948) lent new currency just a couple of years prior to the Triennale exhibition.[26] While Trincanato's study echoed the interests of De Carlo by refocusing attention on minor architecture as an alternative to architect-designed buildings stressing context and *fabric* over one-off masterpieces, Bruno Zevi on the other hand, having just returned from the United States where he discovered Frank Lloyd Wright (as well as Walter Gropius), encouraged Italian architects to embrace organicism as a tonic against classicism and monumentality.[27] Since the vernacular tradition could easily be viewed as natural or organic buildings insofar as the materials and approach towards site and topography were also intuitive and spontaneous, it received Zevi's endorsement. The constitution of Bruno Zevi's APAO (Association for Organic Architecture) specifically targeted classically inspired architecture by stating:

> Organic architecture is thus the antithesis of the monumental architecture that serves myths of state. It opposes the major and minor axes of contem-

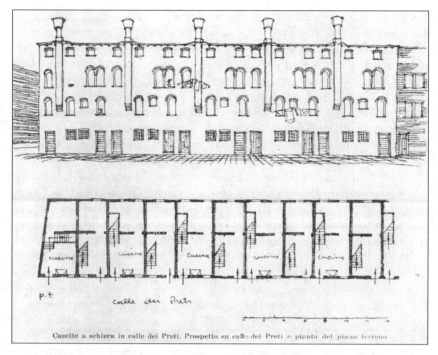

Casette a schiera in calle dei Preti. Prospetto su calle dei Preti e pianta del piano terreno

Fig. 5.4 Drawing by Egle Renata Trincanato of the row houses in Calle dei Preti, Venice, from Egle Renata Trincanato, *Venezia minore* (Venice: Filippi Editore, 1948), 156.

porary Neoclassicism – the vulgar Neoclassicism of arches and columns, and the false Neoclassicism that is born from the pseudomodern forms of contemporary monumental architecture.[28]

With the founding of the journal *Metron* and the Association for Organic Architecture (APAO) in 1944, Bruno Zevi and other proponents of organic architecture spearheaded a movement in opposition to classically inspired rationalism. If organicism sought to eliminate design solutions based on classical geometry, neorealism looked to activate the spontaneous poetics of everyday environments by echoing the countryside within new types of buildings. As the debate over spontaneous architecture and continuity with interwar rationalism surfaced among Milanese architects coming to terms with their own involvement with the fascist regime, similar and different discussions were taking place in

Rome. There were several causes for these. Rationalist modernism in Italy never successfully shed its associations with the classicism and nostalgia of the fascist regime. This was exaggerated in the Roman context, if not more understated in Milan and northern Italy in general. With the realization of monumental complexes like Esposizione Universale Roma (EUR), Città Universitaria (University of Rome – La Sapienza), and the Foro Mussolini (now Foro Italico), all in Rome, a new generation of architects (whether organic, spontaneous, or neorealist) began introducing into their practice more modest and less rhetorical references drawn from the diversity of vernacular forms.[29]

Most commentators were quick to point out the differences between nostalgia-driven appropriations of the vernacular tradition and progressive modernist approaches. Zevi opposed nationalist agendas of "picturesque folklore" and "Mediterranean tones" that thrived during the interwar years. In *Toward an Organic Architecture* (1945), Zevi wrote that

> the trend towards provincialism, which was the outcome of other pseudo-nationalist motives, became more marked as the reaction against the modern began. There was a pursuit of local color and the taste of the countryside, for decorative anecdotes, for a rancid sentimentalism with the suggestion of picturesque folklore; there was an attempt, through the so-called stylization of traditional forms, to achieve a modern version of the *atmosphere* of a particular place such as Venice or Capri. But in order to be able to deal with the evils of an equivocal position, it is necessary, as well as denouncing them, to be clear about their origin; and we must recognize that those architects who were willing to meet provincialism and the forms of *architettura minore* halfway, when they were not acting for merely tactical reasons, that is, when they were not consciously compromising *something* in order not to compromise *everything*, were animated by a sincere desire to humanize modern architecture and to bring it nearer to reality. Naturally, seeing that this reality had no existence in the concrete, in the content, so to speak, of architecture, the effort to *humanize* could only operate within the orbit of extraneous and stylistic elements, by seeking, for example, Mediterranean tones; and even these elements, to which the weariness with modern formalism had given birth, rapidly sank into the still more squalid weariness of an arbitrary romanticism.[30]

Even though Zevi elected Frank Lloyd Wright as his guiding light, his own version of organic architecture was based more on a social and cultural agenda than a linguistic or, *stricto senso*, folkloric one.[31] Zevi was both enthusiastic and cautious about endorsing the vernacular, perhaps because of its perceived vulnerability to nationalist ideology.[32] Quite revealing of his idiosyncratic interpretation of organicism and the role that the extant vernacular could play is the fact that Zevi cited the Villa Oro (1934–7) by Viennese émigré Bernard Rudofsky and Luigi Cosenza on the outskirts of Naples as the example of Italian architecture of the 1920s and 1930s that best exemplified the principles of organic architecture.[33]

During the 1950s, as editor of the popular journal *L'architettura – cronache e storia* he published a number of essays by Pier Luigi Giordani on the built environment of farming communities in the Po River Valley.[34] Giordani's 1958 book *I Contadini e l'urbanistica* (Peasants and Urban Planning) was hailed by Zevi for its contribution to the understanding of spontaneous planning as it was practised by peasants in rural Italy.[35] It is significant that Giordani combined research, writing, and practice, designing a number of rural hamlets or towns in the region in this same time period.[36] The Italian translation of Ebenezer Howard's *Garden Cities of To-morrow* by Giordani published in 1962 included an in-depth analysis and overview of Italian experiments with the English urban planning concepts, drawing new attention to the movement at a time when Gordon Cullen and Ivor De Wolfe published *Townscape* (1961) and *The Italian Townscape* (1963).[37]

Rather than taking up the picturesque cues of garden cities, Zevi's interest in the simple, functional character of rural architecture as opposed to rustic accents informed his collaboration with Mario Ridolfi, Pier Luigi Nervi, Mario Fiorentino, and Adalberto Libera on the publication of *Il Manuale dell'architetto* (1946), produced under the aegis of the Consiglio Nazionale della Ricerca (CNR) and the Information Office of the United States.[38] Much influenced by the American do-it-yourself spirit of self-reliance, the *Manuale* sought to merge the straightforwardness of the *Architectural Graphic Standards* (first published in 1932) with Italian know-how and was intended for amateur builders and artisans engaged in the production of neovernacular housing after the war when architects could not meet the overwhelming demands of the time.[39] As Tafuri observed,

> In reality, the tradition of construction extolled by the *Manuale* resulted from a cross-section of regional cultures that were not immune to intellectualism: the vernacular Esperanto taking on technological forms celebrates

regionalism in *folk* dress that had been one of the ideological ingredients of the New Deal. The manual, which became a reference text for architecture searching for the *national-popular*, served a conduit for political ideas imported from overseas.[40]

The *Manuale* was perhaps one of the most interesting postwar experiments with respect to neovernacular building per se, insofar as the authors demonstrated the degree to which extant vernacular forms could still be employed as models for affordable contemporary housing in semi-urban and rural contexts. Especially significant is the chapter dedicated to *costruzioni rurali* (rural buildings), presenting a brief history as well as an explanation of adaptive uses. The discussion about the elimination of multiple functions refers to the previous overlap of domestic, animal husbandry, and agricultural activities typical of vernacular building types of the past. Adaptation and change were thus part of the appropriation process

The overlap between the need for self-reliance and a desire to reignite the spontaneous quality of the modern design process was at the heart of De Carlo's strategies whose Mostra di architettura spontanea was an auspicious start for his architecture practice in Milan. De Carlo's growing interest in William Morris's Arts and Crafts Movement increased his awareness of the vernacular tradition and conditioned his architectural design during the postwar period.[41] Following the completion of De Carlo's first housing estate in Spine Bianche di Matera, 1956–7, in which his own brand of neorealism with an exposed structure, pitched roof, and simple massing was adumbrated, he was hired by the University of Urbino as a consulting architect. It was there, over a period of several decades, that De Carlo undertook the challenge of integrating contemporary architecture, vernacular forms, and ancient landscapes with simple and organic designs.[42] The crescent-shaped, two-storey housing complex for university employees (1955), executed in brick and terracotta tile, and the terraced Collegio del Colle (1965) were the first projects he realized under the direction of Carlo Bo, Catholic intellectual and rector of the university.[43] By the time De Carlo completed the construction of the student housing in 1987, his work covered the summit of an entire hill. He created a new hill town from scratch (Fig. 5.5).

During the years De Carlo spent building on the premises of his Spontaneous Architecture Exhibition, many architects and urban planners were turning to the study of *urbanistica minore* (minor urbanism).[44]

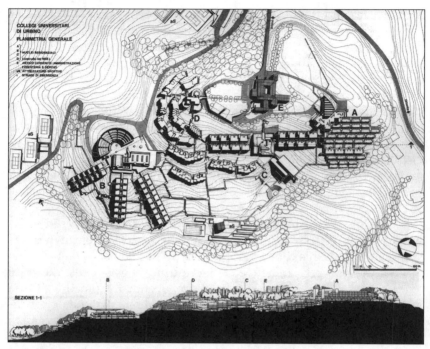

Fig. 5.5 Plan by Giancarlo De Carlo, Master Plan of the University of Urbino Colleges, 1965–87, from Lamberto Rossi, *Giancarlo De Carlo – Architetture* (Milan: Arnaldo Mondadori Editore, 1988), 167.

Responding to a movement to restore the historic centres and housing stock of the hill towns, especially after the end of the Second World War, a series of publications by architects and preservationists, including Edoardo Detti and others, established their importance as *minor centres* in relation to Florence and Rome and, in effect, strengthened Italy's cultural legacy with a more inclusive attitude towards centre and periphery, high and low art.[45] Unlike Renaissance urban projects and architecture, the built environment of hill towns was rarely designed by professional architects, and was instead produced by local builders' guilds. With its irregular topography, the hill town not only generated but also absorbed spontaneous forms adapted to the site that were integrated into the extant urban fabric.

For example, in his student housing projects for Urbino, rather than impose a rational grid on the highly irregular site on the outskirts of the city, De Carlo laid out cellular groupings or villages of dormitory buildings that fronted onto external paths that connected them. By doing so, he simultaneously embraced and facilitated communal student life by harmonizing the buildings with the topographical complexity of the site and offering open-air spaces for student interaction. Perhaps no other Italian university designed during the twentieth century received such endorsement from the international community. What made it more interesting, especially for non-Italian architects, was the fact that it was unquestioningly modernist and designed with great sensitivity to a historically charged site.[46] De Carlo alternated between using brick and reinforced concrete to evoke the rugged qualities of the hill town, and applied terracing strategies to ensure that the structures would not stick out like the proverbial sore thumb.

De Carlo's 1951 exhibition and the subsequent designs based on its premises were especially important if one considers his role in the moribund CIAM and his contribution to Team X, as one of the rebels who formed the group.[47] Architects he met during those years, like Aldo Van Eyck and Peter and Alison Smithson, eventually joined De Carlo in 1974 as participants in the ILA&UD (International Laboratory of Architecture & Urban Design), which conceived and functioned as an *in situ* design charrette, in which students and practising architects would meet annually to work collectively on thematic projects. In an unprecedented move, De Carlo installed a commemorative plaque honouring Astolfo Sartori, the master mason who worked on the colleges for Urbino, which in effect honoured all of the workers who served under him: "Astolfo Sartori. Master builder has participated in the building of these university colleges from 1965 to 1987." This plaque serves as a concrete reminder of Pagano's pioneering celebration of the vernacular tradition. It also attests to De Carlo's commitment to collaborative design, in no small part due to his appreciation of the vernacular tradition and his close engagement with end-users for his student housing in Urbino and for his Nuovo villaggio Matteotti (New Matteotti Village) built for workers in the industrial town of Terni between 1969 and 1974. De Carlo would later admit that his approach to designing both the colleges and the master plan for Urbino, followed by his founding in 1976 of the International ILA&UD, stemmed from Anglo-American debates about *participation*.[48]

Not far from Terni and Matera, the New Town of La Martella was completed in 1951, the same year that De Carlo's Mostra di architettura spontanea was installed. This was the first project of its kind that was inspired by the extant vernacular tradition. The harsh realities of a primarily agrarian and poor southern Italy inspired author Carlo Levi (1902–1975) to evoke the concept of godforsaken in his book *Christ Stopped at Eboli* (1945), which gives an account of his political exile from 1935–6 in a "primitive village" (Fig. 5.6). Levi wrote, "It had been hard at first. Grassano, like all the villages hereabouts, is a streak of white at the summit of a bare hill, a sort of miniature imaginary Jerusalem in the solitude of the desert."[49] His gripping tale of the year he spent among the unschooled, often illiterate peoples of southern Italy served to reignite interest in artisanal practices among book-fed intellectuals, artists, and architects. Levi's fascination with the natural and built environment of the South was captured in the ethereal palette of whites and pinks of his paintings, like *Aliano sul burrone* (1935).[50] As disparities between the industrial North and the agrarian South became more and more exaggerated, and as television exercised its capacity to diffuse information, the people of Italy became increasingly aware of the social inequities and, as a result, tensions increased. Even for those acting in good faith, this top-down paternalism was especially characteristic of architects and intellectuals from central and northern Italy attempting to address the so-called *Questione del sud* (the Southern Question) denounced by communist intellectual Antonio Gramsci, whose critique had been echoed after the war in the work of philosopher and anthropologist Ernesto De Martino (1908–1965) and by author Rocco Scotellaro (1923–53) whose *Peasants of the South* (*Contadini del Sud*, 1954) described the day-to-day hardships of southern Italy's peasantry.[51]

The "villaggio" of La Martella, designed by Ludovico Quaroni with Federico Gorio, Michele Valori, Piero Maria Lugli, and Michele Agati, was one of the first postwar experiments in which vernacular models like the *casa colonica* were used to create an autonomous village for peasants who formerly inhabited troglodyte dwellings referred to as *sassi* or caverns (Fig. 5.7).[52] Reviewing this contribution to Italian architectural culture, De Carlo openly praised the *realism* underlying the conception and realization of La Martella:

> The urban planners that designed this village did not think about realizing a dream of utopian ideal city. But rather, in front of the problem of having to build an organism that could provide housing for a group of peasants originally living in the *sassi* of Matera, they began their work thinking about the real limits of this problem.[53]

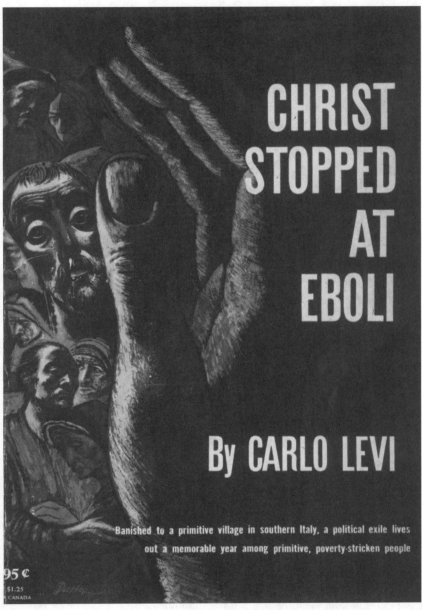

Fig. 5.6 Cover page, Carlo Levi, *Christ Stopped at Eboli*, trans. Frances Frenaye (New York: Farrar, Strauss, 1947).

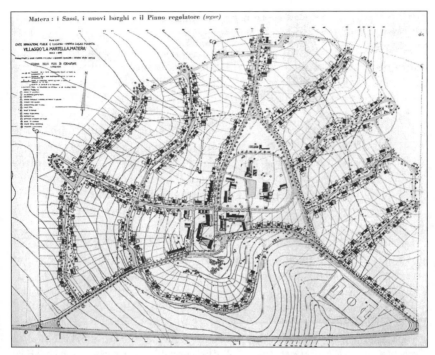

Fig. 5.7 Drawing by Ludovico Quaroni et al., plan for the "villaggio" (village) of La Martella, Matera, 1951, from Marida Talamona, "Dieci anni di politica dell'Unrra Casas: dalle case ai senzatetto ai borghi rurali nel mezzo giorno d'Italia (1945–1955). Il ruolo di Adriano Olivetti," in Carlo Olmo ed. *Costruire la città dell'uomo. Adriano Olivetti e l'urbanistica* (Milan: Edizioni di Comunità, 2001), 197.

Thus, for De Carlo, the strategic adoption of extant rural architectural models as part of a comprehensive idea of the town as village – in which domestic architecture coexisted with small artisanal *bottege* or workshops, a church, and other communal buildings to create an autonomous and self-sufficient community, not unlike Ebenezer Howard's Garden City – reflected a response to real conditions with concrete proposals that avoided abstract utopianism.

Although Quaroni's La Martella has some points in common with experiments conducted in the mid-1930s in the New Towns of the Roman littoral such as Sabaudia and Littoria (present-day Latina), the political and economical conditions that made these projects possible during the interwar years changed radically with the fall of fascism. While New Towns tended to fuse grid plans and winding streets, this postwar example steered completely away from any echo of orthogonality (Fig. 5.8). Despite the picturesque character of the winding streets, the serial quality of the homes recalled the overlap between extant vernacular and a machine-made vernacular. Much like the New Towns that embraced the *casa colonica* as a conventional typology, serially reproduced to house displaced rural peasants flooding into urban areas, the architects of La Martella also hoped to offer living conditions that were at once hygienic and with which the peasants could still identify culturally as a community. The elimination of those spaces associated with agrarian work was aimed at ensuring remediation of scarcely hygienic conditions of the *sassi*, in which residents and animals often shared living quarters.[54]

During the 1950s and 1960s, interest in Italian hill-town vernacular shifted to the United States, thanks to the presence of Italian émigré architect Paolo Soleri (1919).[55] His work is best exemplified by the self-built residential communities of Arizona, based entirely on principles of vernacular architecture of both Italy and the American Southwest. The pit-house-style Dome House of 1949 (built with Mark Mills) in Cave Creek, Arizona, which was included in the *Built in USA: Post-War Architecture Exhibition* catalogue of 1952, combines references to Native American pit-houses and rubble walls gleaned from apprenticing with Frank Lloyd Wright at Taliesin.[56] Soleri gravitated to an area of America in which he encountered a climate similar to that of central and southern Italy. In his work-in-progress communities of Cosanti (1955–) and Arco-Santi (1970–), Soleri's utopian spirit is deeply indebted to both the archaic imagery and pragmatics of hill-town planning (Fig. 5.9). While the social underpinning of his alternative off-the-grid living models of communes shared much with the hippie culture that produced Drop City in Colorado (1965) and other off-the-grid communities, his search for permanence distinguished his architecture and aligned it with Bernard Rudofsky's *Architecture without Architects* (1964).[57] In his *primitive* architecture and his production of objects like cast-iron bells, the archaic and futuristic artistic impulses happily coexist. Significantly, before settling in the United States and embarking on his American projects during the early 1950s, Soleri had experimented with subterranean, pod-like, terraced housing for the Amalfi coast (1952). With Soleri, utopian visions are firmly rooted in organic relationships that underlie the

Fig. 5.8 View of Matera, residential units, the "Villaggio" (Village) of La Martella, 1951, from Marida Talamona, "Dieci anri di poltica dell'Unrra Casas:
Dalle case ai senzatetto ai borghi rurali nel Mezzogiorno d'Italia (1945–1955):
Il ruolo di Adriano Olivettu," in *Costruire la città dell'uomo: Adriano Olivetti e
l'urbanistica*, ed. Carlo Olmo (Milan: Edizioni di Comunità, 2001), 195.

interaction between human beings and the environment they inhabit in
the vernacular tradition.[58]

Giovanni Michelucci, like Soleri, was somewhat of an outsider who
was also inspired by the principles of Wright's organic architecture.
Both Michelucci and Soleri drew upon the landscape and its relationship to certain forms of vernacular materiality. Interest in organic and
toned-down architecture defined Michelucci's design career early on.
Michelucci used the term *tono minore* (toned down) to describe Pompeian domestic architecture based on the courtyard.[59] Within the realm

Fig. 5.9 Photograph of the community of Arco-Santi, Paolo Soleri et al., Arizona, 1970 (photographer Michelangelo Sabatino).

of religious architecture, Michelucci employed vernacular and primitive materiality and types to counteract classical rhetoric and pomp and to produce spaces that were functional as well as mysterious.[60] Michelucci's Casa Pitigliani (1957) near Rome, in which he looks to the vernacular reed hut or *casone* typical of the Roman countryside, is the most literal translation of the type (Fig. 5.10).[61] The cave- and tent-like qualities of the Chiesa sul autostrada (1960–4) or his church for Longarone could not have been achieved without previous experiments like his Chiesa dei Santi Pietro e Gerolamo (Church of Saints Peter and Jerome) also near Pistoia (1946–53). Unlike these examples that were located in remote towns, Michelucci's Chiesa dell'autostrada, somewhere between a tent and a cave, was sited next to the so-called Autostrada del sole, a highway begun in the 1950s with the intent of linking fast-moving traffic from northern to southern Italy.[62] The contrast between the archetype of tent and the fast-moving automobile on the adjacent highways could not be more poignant.

Francesco Dal Co has observed how a "primitive religiosity" pervades Michelucci's Church of Saints Peter and Jerome, whose design is based upon local vernacular materials and building methods (Fig. 5.11).[63] Bruno Zevi commented on Michelucci's efforts: "The small and moving church of Collina is where he attempted to rescue the anonymous language and the continuity between cottage and land in the peasant world."[64] The architect Leonardo Ricci likened the nature of the church, described as "non-architecture," to anonymous Romanesque and Gothic works.[65] By firmly rooting the design of this and other churches within the vernacular tradition, Michelucci allowed concepts like *primitive* and *anonymous* to achieve poetic heights.

Along with housing and churches in central and southern Italy, the most significant experimentations with vernacular models during the postwar years were Alpine retreats and hotels in northern Italy, where increased wealth prompted the rise of a leisure industry and generated new demands for architects. While the stereotomic sculptural qualities of the Mediterranean's vernacular terraced buildings continued to fascinate architects of the *Mezzogiorno*, it was the post-and-beam, wood-and-stone constructions of the Alpine regions that inspired architects of industrial cities like Milan and Turin to take on projects for what Thorstein Veblen called the "leisure class," whose members could afford weekend retreats. For the most fortunate of wealthy Italians, skiing in the Alps occupied the winter months, and during the summer months, they flocked to the Mediterranean Sea; the architecture of

Fig. 5.10 Photograph of Giovanni Michelucci's Casa Pitigliani and extant *casone* (big house), Rome, 1957 (photographer unknown), from Antonio Albanese, "Una casa – capanna a Torre San Lorenzo," in *L'Architettura – Cronache e storia* 28 (1958), 656–9.

Fig. 5.11 Drawing by Serge Ambrose of Giovanni Michelucci, Chiesa dei Santi Pietro e Gerolamo (Church of Saints Peter and Jerome), Pistoia, 1946–53. Courtesy Fondazione Giovanni Michelucci (Pistoia).

luxury villas and resorts followed the vernacular traditions of these regions.

Among the designers of these highly sophisticated dwellings in Piedmont and Valle d'Aosta were Franco Albini, Mario Cereghini, Edoardo Gellner, Carlo Mollino, and Ettore Sottsass Senior.[56] Cereghini (1903–66) was the author of an important postwar study on extant vernacular buildings published in Italian, *Costruire in montagna* (*Building in the Mountains*) (1950), and subsequently translated into English.[67] Cereghini writes:

> I do not know if you have ever stopped wonderstruck at the amazing proportions of some of the humblest mountain huts … And, in this case, we fully agree with those who maintain that popular art often finds inspiration in the most significant expressions of the higher forms of learned art …[68]

Fig. 5.12 Photograph of Carlo Mollino's Stazione albergo al Lago Nero, Sauze d'Oulx, 1946–7 (photographer unknown), from Fulvio Ferrari and Napoleone Ferrari, eds., *Carlo Mollino – Arabeschi* (Milan: Electa 2006), 129

It is worth remembering that he was also one of the authors who identified with the rationalism of the *Quadrante* milieu and who co-wrote *Un programma d'architettura* (1933). Cereghini's design work in the Alps paralleled his historical investigations that were aimed at providing a backdrop and sustaining his practice.[69]

Carlo Mollino wrote less systematically about vernacular buildings of the Alps and designed more: his Stazione albergo al Lago Nero (Sauze d'Oulx, 1946–7) and Casa del sole (Cervinia, 1951–4) are key modernist buildings that attest to his interest in appropriating the extant vernacular architecture of the Alps (Fig. 5.12).[70] In Mollino's work, timeless tectonics and *genius loci* come together seamlessly.[71] Bruno Reichlin has written about how Mollino's analogical process was largely indebted to his discovery and use of Alpine vernacular architecture.[72] Mollino also demonstrated an interest in adapting materials and building types for new programs. In his Casa Garelli at Champoluc (1963–5), for exam-

Fig. 5.13 Photograph of Franco Albini's Pirovano Youth Hostel, Cervinia, 1949–51 (photographer unknown), from Franco Albini, "Albergo per ragazzi a Cervinia," *Edizioni Moderna* 47 (December 1951): 73.

ple, he adopted the *rascard*, a wood building traditionally used to store grain and house animals and that was usually raised from the ground on stone foundation pilasters that resemble the shape of a mushroom connecting the two parts. He also incorporated a loggia typical of Alpine vernacular architecture, which is not related to the *rascard*. Thus hybrid is embraced in the place of "coherence."

Franco Albini designed the Pirovano Youth Hostel in Cervinia between 1949 and 1951 (Fig. 5.13). The mountain location where it is located, north of Milan at the foot of the Alps, is also the town in which Mollino designed his residential tower, the Casa del sole.[73] The elongated pilotis of Albini's youth hostel resemble the mushroom supports typical of the *rascard*. Cervinia became one of Italy's most important centres for experimentation with the vernacular by Italian modernist architects. What is especially interesting about Albini and Mollino is how their architecture overlapped with the design of objects that reflect

Fig. 5.14 Design by Gio Ponti, *Superleggera*, Cassina, Milan, 1957, from Marco Romanell, Gio Ponti: A World (Milan: Abitare Segesta, 2002), 60.

similar interests in material and technique. Both Mollino and Albini admired organic materials typical of the vernacular tradition in ways that paralleled Gio Ponti's design of the lightweight *Leggera* of 1948 and the *Superleggera* chairs of 1957 (Fig. 5.14).[74] Ponti described it as a "chair without adjectives" to emphasize its ordinary quality.[75] Albini's wicker *Margherita* and *Gala* chairs (1950) are perhaps the most celebrated examples of the 1950s, when Italy struggled to hold onto its legacy of artisanal production in combination with new approaches to mass production.[76] Even Achille Castiglioni's *Mezzadro stool* (1957), a tractor seat mounted on a steel bar, celebrated the rural origins of Italian design. Vico Magistretti's *Carimate chair* (1960) was based on a traditional country chair made of wood and straw enlivened by glossy red paint.[77]

In parallel with the inventive and organic qualties of Mollino and Albini's Cervinia, Edoardo Gellner's vacation colony in Corte di Cadore, realized between 1954 and 1963, offered yet another site of experimentation with ordinary peasant things. At Corte di Cadore, a site near the fashionable vacation retreat of Cortina d'Ampezzo, Gellner adapted the local vernacular to create a formidable and diversified vacation community for the employees of Enrico Mattei's ENI (Ente Nazionale Idrocarburi) within the Alpine forest.[78] Gellner's engagement with vernacular architecture, which he referred to variously as *anonymous*, *rural*, and *spontaneous*, was not limited to his architectural projects and studies on the subject, but also included involvement in the preservation of the minor architecture of Alpine communities.[79]

During the years in which Italy followed the path of its "economic miracle" that made vacation communities economically possible, Pier Paolo Pasolini's cinematography celebrated the uncorrupted rugged vitality of the common people of a Calabrian hill town for his film *The Gospel According to Saint Matthew* (1964). Pasolini's classic tragedy *Madea* (1970) was filmed in between the reed huts of Marano Lagunare and the cave dwellings of Cappadocia, Turkey. In the same vein as Luchino Visconti's *The Earth Trembles* (1948), which depicted the existential difficulties of fishermen, Pasolini and several other film directors explored the rugged pre-industrial reality of the peasantry with the help of non-professional actors.[80] The daily struggles of peasantry became a favourite theme for film directors who matured in the wake of neorealist filmmakers like Bernardo Bertolucci whose epic film *Novecento (1900)*, released in 1976, took place in the Emilia Romagna region of the Po River Valley; the film traced the role of the peasantry in the birth of Italian socialism by recounting the lives of two men, one descended from landowners and the other a peasant born on the same day in the year 1900. Film directors Ermanno Olmi and the Taviani brothers have contributed to a growing body of films focused on rural landscapes and the hardships of the working class.[81] Recall Olmi's account of the struggles of a farming community in *The Tree of the Wooden Clogs* (1978) and Paolo and Vittorio Taviani's tale of a Sardinian shepherd and his son (Gavino Ledda) in *Padre Padrone* (1977).

It was the landscape of the Po River Valley and its vernacular farmhouses incorporated classical elements that fuelled the imagination of American photographer Paul Strand, whose collaboration with writer Cesare Zavattini produced the memorable photo essay entitled *Un paese* (A Village).[82] It was the Po River Valley, where a rural atmosphere prevailed in spite of the incursion of industry into the region, that inspired the Milanese architect Aldo Rossi (1931–97) to explore the role of memory in modernist architecture. Immediately before and after the

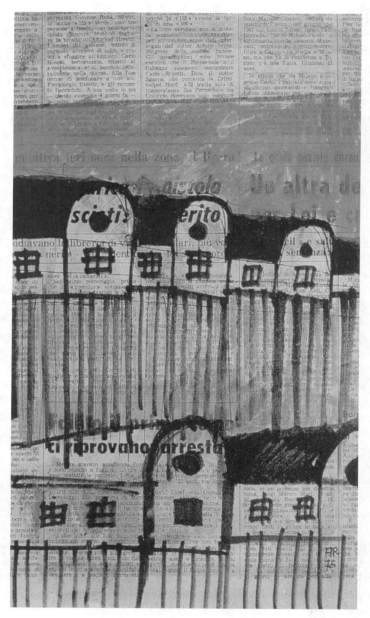

Fig. 5.15 Drawing by Aldo Rossi, Villa and pavilion (unbuilt), Borgo Ticino, 1973, from Alberto Ferlenga, *Aldo Rossi – Architetture* (Milan: Electa 1992), 92.

XV 1973 Triennale, Aldo Rossi made explicit use of both vernacular and classical models in a quest for the primitive or timeless domestic archetype and advanced his "critique of naïve functionalism."[83] Rossi's use of porticoes in his rational yet melancholic housing estate for Pegognaga near Mantova (1979) echoed the spirit of the Po River Valley, somewhere in between the mundane and the sacred.[84] In parallel to Rossi's poetic musings, the Milanese architect Giorgio Grassi (1935) also sought to merge vernacular and classical traditions: his student housing project for Chieti (1976–9) and numerous other public projects attest to his interest in both rationalism and primitivism.[85]

In his *Cabanas of Elba* (1975), Rossi celebrated ordinary maritime objects, redolent of archetype.[86] In a recent overview of contemporary theoretical anxieties and design strategies, Spanish architect Rafael Moneo stresses Rossi's "nostalgia of the rational construction of vernacular architecture," in relation to a 1973 project in Borgo Ticino (Fig. 5.15) influenced by indigenous housing built along the shores of lakes. Moneo goes on to discuss Rossi's interest in anonymous architecture, which led him to embrace urban spaces, ranging from a courtyard in Seville to houses on the Po River delta.[87] Significantly, the river dear to Rossi originates in Emilia Romagna and traverses the Veneto region, where Andrea Palladio's Renaissance villas combine "the portico and the farmyard," representing, respectively, the classical and vernacular traditions.[88] Rossi and contemporaries such as Grassi applied Palladio's synthesis of the mundane functions of a working farm and learned aspirations to civic representation in elements such as the covered entryway.[89] Rossi's use of the two-storey portico to span the facades of his low-cost housing estates in Pegognaga and Grassi's student housing at Chieti eloquently express an interest in the two traditions as filtered by rationalism. These projects, moreover, embody the creative tension between urban and rural types that characterizes so much of twentieth-century Italian architecture. In his attempt to circumvent *naïve functionalism*, Rossi, like Grassi, adapted pre-industrial urban environments to create new hybrid forms of architectural identity for a twentieth-century Italy struggling to redefine itself.[90] In a country with a long-standing rural reality like Italy, modernity and nostalgia are not necessarily at odds with each other. Rather than ignore the vestiges of an agrarian world threatened by dissolution in the wake of industrialization, Italian architects sought new forms of creative dialogue with the ordinary things of the city and the countryside. In so doing they created an architectural modernity of resistance.

Epilogue

Like an underground river that meanders through the crevices of the bedrock, only to surface occasionally and disappear once again, the ubiquitous presence of vernacular architecture was a continuous presence in Italian modernist architecture and design. In recent decades, the unregulated or *informal* building practices associated with *abusivismo* (illegal building activity) and the sprawling *città diffusa* (diffuse city) that has gradually filled in the territory between major Italian cities with its endless rows of *villini* and uninspired commercial vernacular cluttering the roadside has produced little of architectural interest. On the other hand, the timeless vernacular buildings of the different regions of Italy have been the object of intense study and debate as well as a vital source of inspiration for modernist designers since the 1920s. This interest and the research, publication, exhibitions, and architectural experiments it generated fostered two competing approaches to vernacular architecture. The first was a picturesque revival of rustic models, an approach grounded in historicism and fuelled by nationalist ideology with the rise of fascism. The second approach used rationalism to frame the appropriation of the vernacular tradition on the basis of its varied and rich types and materials.

In these two different approaches, tradition played fundamentally different roles. Whether the synthesis of extant vernacular buildings with modernist perspectives resulted in rationalist, organic, or neorealist approaches is less important than the fact that the phenomenon was deep and lasting for Italian architecture, arts, and culture. Moreover, not only did the vernacular tradition shape Italy's built environment but it also went well beyond national boundaries, thus demonstrating that it could negotiate different political regimes and cultural and architectural scenarios.

In America, the reception of an Italian modernist architecture inspired by vernacular traditions reached its height from the late 1950s through 1970s, when concepts like *critical regionalism* and *postmodernism* were challenging the orthodoxy of Nikolaus Pevsner's modern movement.[1] American interest during the 1960s in Italian and Mediterranean vernacular buildings was in no small part due to the work of Austrian *émigré* Bernard Rudofsky, even though architects like Irving Gill or George Washington Smith in California had begun to look to the anonymous architecture of the Mediterranean region.

Rudofsky had moved to Italy in the early 1930s following his training as an architect in Vienna, where he wrote a dissertation on the primitive dwellings of the Cycladic islands.[2] He remained there throughout the 1930s, and thus through the period in which interest in the vernacular tradition was at its height in Italy, and also its most politically charged with respect to the nationalist agendas of both right- and the left-wing factions. *Italianità* literally went both ways. His exposure to debates regarding the vernacular tradition set the groundwork for Rudofsky's exhibition and book *Architecture without Architects*, held at the Museum of Modern Art (MoMA) in New York between 9 November 1964 and 7 February 1965, which acquainted the American public with much more than just the Italian vernacular buildings and rural landscape. Architecture without Architects was not so much a historic exhibition on vernacular buildings of the world as it was an operative manifesto toward the rethinking of modernism from the point of view of context and climate.[3]

As late as 1949, as annotations in his personal notebooks attest, Rudofsky was not using his subversive expression 'Architecture without Architects' but still referred to vernacular buildings as *rural architecture*, an expression that had gained currency in Italy thanks to Giuseppe Pagano's Architettura rurale italiana exhibition at the Milan Triennale in 1936.[4] As Rudofsky became increasingly disenchanted with the architectural profession, he adopted an expression that would undermine its self-confidence and engender self-criticism. Rudofsky's tone was both moralizing and puritanical, a characteristic which aligns him with Pagano. Though it is unclear whether or not Rudofsky actually visited Pagano's exhibition, the impact of the Italian architectural debate, specifically the Mostra dell'architettura spontanea at the Milan Triennale of 1951, seems to have played an important role in shaping the MoMA exhibition.[5]

In 1954, a decade before Rudofsky's exhibition at the Museum of Modern Art, the Milanese architectural firm Studio Architetti BBPR introduced their version of the primitive and vernacular tradition to America. The Olivetti Showroom on Fifth Avenue in New York (later demolished) was replete with *cipollino,* marble stalagmites on which business machines and typewriters were displayed with a backdrop of primitive sand and concrete frescoes by the Italian *émigré* artist Costantino Nivola (also a close acquaintance and collaborator of Rudofsky), depicting female figures that were a cross between robots and mother earth. The relationship between these objects and the architecture of the Olivetti showroom announced that, on the threshold of the atomic age, primitivism and new technologies were capable of being fused.[6]

It was precisely this disagreement over the definition of *progress* and modernity that marked the reception of the Italian pavilion at Expo 58 in Brussels, designed by Ignazio Gardella, Studio Architetti BBPR (Belgiojoso, Peressutti, and Rogers), Adolfo De Carlo, Giuseppe Perugini, and Ludovico Quaroni (Fig. E.1). In opposition to the Atom Age aesthetic of André Waterkeyn's Atomium, the Italian architects expressed renewed interest in tradition by rethinking the hill-town vernacular model, as the Germans returned to high modernism of Mies van der Rohe (by way of Egon Eiermann's glass and steel pavilion design), who had fled the country and emigrated to the United States.

In the same year the Italian pavilion was completed only to generate mixed reviews, Eero Saarinen began his designs of the Ezra Stiles and Samuel Morse colleges for Yale University in New Haven, Connecticut, and completed them in 1962.[7] In close proximity to Roger Gamble's collegiate Gothic style, in which Beaux-Arts rationality met neomedievalism, Saarinen designed a modernist Italian hill town (Fig. E.2).[8] He commissioned Costantino Nivola to embed sculptures into the massive, rustic walls.[9] Nivola also added several large-scale statues recalling ancient maternal figures. In all, Nivola completed thirty-five sculptures. The scale and articulation of the central street that cuts across the grounds proposed a model for informal social interaction most appropriate for an academic community; yet the appearances of stereotomic, rubble-like walls must certainly have seemed somewhat exotic to a population still accustomed to quadrangles based on the English tradition of Oxford and Cambridge. Eero Saarinen wrote:

Fig. E.1 Photograph at inauguration of the Italian pavilion designed by Ignazio Gardella, Studio Architetti BBPR (Belgiojoso, Peressutti, and Rogers), Adolfo De Carlo, Giuseppe Perugini, and Ludovico Quaroni (photographer unknown), Brussels, Expo 1958, from *Ignazio Gardella – Progetti e architetture 1933–1990* (Venice: Marsilio, 1992), 171.

Dear Nivola: ... We have been working for some time on the design of two colleges for Yale University. The design is quite unique and special and does not follow the main copy-cat stream of modern architecture. The total conception of these colleges is quite a romantic one where actually masonry predominates and where the courts and quadrangles of the colleges are formed by polygonal shaped walls of a character that almost reminds one of the hill towns of Italy.[10]

Commenting on the colleges, Henry Russell Hitchcock described Nivola's sculptures as "rather pointless knots of sculpture," despite praising Saarinen's design:

The neo-medievalism is actually of an urbanistic nature, a rather successful attempt to recreate some of the spatial intimacy of a mediaeval Italian town, somewhat as Aalto attempted with much less plausibility at Säynatsälo or that architects of the Italian Pavilion at the Brussels Exposition in 1958. Although wholly different in scale and siting, the result compares

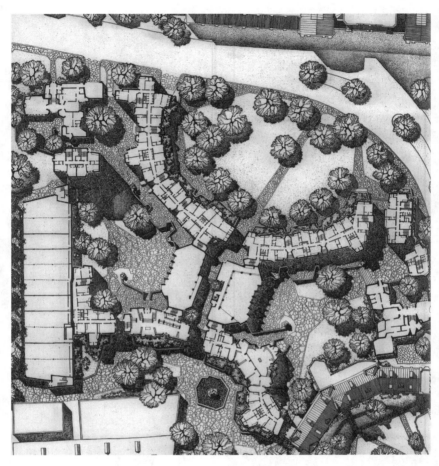

Fig. E.2 Plan by Eero Saarinen, Ezra Stiles and Samuel Morse Colleges, Yale University, New Haven, 1958–62, from Antonio Román, *Eero Saarinen – An Architecture of Multiplicity* (New York: Princeton Architectural Press, 2002), 78.

favourably with Utzon's development in Fredenborg. Only the rather pointless knots of sculpture by Nivola and the awkward subdivisions of the window sash seem serious blemishes. [11]

Hitchcock's appreciation of the traditionalist modernism of Utzon's Fredensborg for example is especially interesting in light of his mentorship of the Yale architectural historian Vincent Scully, whose *The Shingle and the Stick Style* (1955), followed by *The Shingle Style Today* (1974) and *Pueblo: Mountain, Village, Dance* (1975), did much to reignite interest in the vernacular (and the primitive) in both historiography and the contemporary practice of the 1970s and 1980s.[12] Although Scully did not start writing about Italian twentieth-century architecture until well into the 1970s, in his review of Kidder Smith's book *Italy Builds: Its Modern Architecture and Native Inheritance* (1955), he did distinguish between the *essential* and *romantic* approaches, Italian and otherwise, to vernacular architecture.[13]

Paralleling Saarinen's interest in *villages*, Paul Rudolph's 1961 residence for married students at Yale was based on vernacular models and designed a few years after the publication of his "Regionalism in Architecture" (1957).[14] The Italian *émigré* Pietro Belluschi, then dean of the architecture school at MIT, wrote in *Regionalism in Architecture* (1955):

> These were my Utopian thoughts as I was revisiting recently the exquisite little villages of the Aegean and Tyrrhenian Sea Islands, of Brittany and the Tyrol, and remembered how my generation was once somewhat ashamed to admit the delight in their simple spontaneous architecture lest it be tagged as romantic.[15]

Although De Carlo's first teaching appointment in America was at Yale, he spent a significant amount of time teaching at MIT, where he launched (ILA&UD).[16] As dean at Yale, Rudolph appointed Giancarlo De Carlo as a visiting professor. De Carlo recounted his experience as follows:

> My first visit to Yale in 1966 allowed me to discover America in years of extraordinary vitality. It was the moment of Vietnam, the youth protests, of pop-art, and of rock music. Paul Rudolph was dean of the school at the time he had invited me, a year earlier in 1965. By the time I arrived however in 1966, Rudolph had been replaced by Charles Moore. At the time there was great excitement in the schools of architecture and many young people were beginning to start their teaching careers. At the time at Yale, there were Bob Venturi, Chester Sprague, Hugh Hardy; others passed through like Hejduk, Stern, Eisenman and the inevitable Johnson. The students were background catalysts as were, in different ways, Vincent Scully and Serge Chermayeff.[17]

Significantly, Charles Moore's design-build program at Yale was

Fig. E.3 Photograph of Charles Moore's Kresge College (photographer un-known), Santa Cruz, California, 1964–74, from "P/A POE Kresge College," *Pro-gressive Architecture* (January 1987): 76.

launched in 1967, only a year after De Carlo arrived, and is likely an important model of his ILA&UD.[18] While he was a graduate student at Princeton, Moore was exposed to Italian modernism firsthand working as a teaching assistant for Enrico Peressutti, a member of the Studio Ar-chitetti BBPR, whose advocacy of tradition and continuity was part of a larger intellectual agenda spearheaded by Ernesto Rogers.[19] During his tenure as dean of the Yale School of Art and Architecture, Moore also ap-propriated the Italian (and Mediterranean) hill town as a model for his low-income Church Street housing complex, which was realized during the same years as Saarinen's colleges for Yale. Years later, the MLTW design (Moore, Lyndon, Turnbull, and Whitaker) for Kresge College at the University of California at Santa Cruz (1964–74) was based on a traditional Mediterranean townscape (Fig. E.3). Increasingly, the idea of

Fig. E.4 Cover page, Ivor De Wolfe (Hubert de Cronin Hastings), *The Italian Townscape* (London: The Architectural Press, 1963).

Fig. E.5 Photograph by Myron Goldfinger, view of steps of a *trullo* in Alberobello, from *Villages in the Sun: Mediterranean Community Architecture* (New York: Praeger, 1969), 88.

the *townscape* was galvanizing the interest of architects and urban planners in the Anglo-American world, thanks to the pioneering studies of Gordon Cullen and Ivor De Wolfe (Hubert de Cronin Hastings), who penned books on both *Townscape* (1961) and *The Italian Townscape* (1963) (Fig. E.4).[20] Cullen's study coincides with Jane Jacobs' *The Death and Life of Great American Cities*, published in the same year as an attempt to recall public attention to more traditional forms of urbanism at a time when heavy-handed urban renewal programs were behind the levelling of much of the nineteenth-century fabric of American cities.

A number of other studies published during those years attest to more widespread Anglo-American interest in the topic of vernacular buildings of Sibyl Moholy Nagy, *Native Genius in Architecture* (1957),

Fig. E.6 Louis I. Kahn, *View of Town*, no. 2, Positano, Italy (1929), Private Collection.

Daniel Paulk Branch's *Folk Architecture of the East Mediterranean* (1966), Edward Allen's *Stone Shelters* (1969), documenting the cone-shaped *trulli* of Apulia, as well as Myron Goldfinger's *Villages in the Sun: Mediterranean Community Architecture* (1969) (Fig. E.5) were based on the intentions of architects to draw formal inspiration from extant vernacular models for their contemporary design. Goldfinger's important publication drew attention not only to Italian vernacular models, but also, like Rudofsky, to vernacular architecture of the entire Mediterranean basin.

Thus, the interplay between American and European practice, criticism, and historiography played an important role in bringing to collective awareness the importance of the Italian (and Mediterranean) vernacular traditions within modernism. The discussion of Le Corbusier's Mediterranean-inspired Ronchamp (1954) and Maisons Jaoul (1954–6) spearheaded by James Stirling did much to expand the field of interest.[21] Israeli-born Moshe Safdie (1938) and collaborators designed Habitat as a housing exhibition for the 1967 Universal Exposition held in Montreal. For this scheme, Safdie combined Mediterranean vernacular hill-town models with metabolists' notions of capsule building. Safdie had worked for Louis Kahn (1901–1974), who produced a series of sketches of the Amalfi coast vernacular dwellings during his travels in Italy during the late 1920s (Fig. E.6). Kahn was simultaneously intrigued by monumental ancient Roman architecture and vernacular buildings.[22] In a rare written commentary on vernacular buildings, Kahn writes:

> To see these modest structures and see them again in the mind invokes wonder in what inspires the works of man … Later the Architect appears, admiring the work of the unschooled men, sensing in their work their integrity and psychological validity. They now stand in silence, yet stir the fairy tale and tell of life.[23]

In addition to Kahn's teachings, it was Rudofsky's *Architecture without Architects* that allowed Safdie to awaken his interest in the Mediterranean hill town.[24]

During the late 1970s, thanks to Kahn's impact and the endorsement of Peter Eisenman and Vincent Scully, the work of Aldo Rossi functioned as a stimulus for American architects seeking to establish a critical dialogue with history.[25] Both his *A Scientific Autobiography* (1981) and *The Architecture of the City* (1982) were published in English. Scully was best able to understand and appreciate Rossi's interest in various expressions of the vernacular as a source of inspiration for contemporary modern architecture. It was Scully, after all, who had written the introduction to Robert Venturi's *Complexity and Contradiction in Architecture* (1966), which in many ways laid the foundation for Rossi's re-

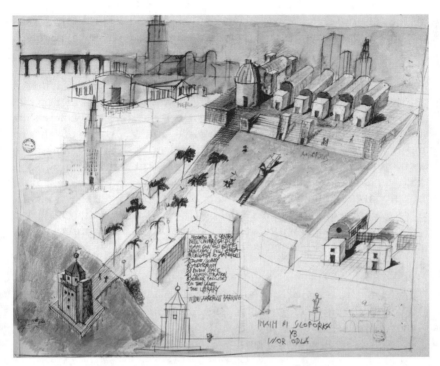

Fig. E.7 Drawing by Aldo Rossi, Proposal for University of Miami School of Architecture, 1986, Alberto Ferlenga, ed., *Aldo Rossi: The Life and Works of an Architect* (Cologne: Könemann, 2001), 157.

ception in America.[26] In an essay entitled *The End of the Century Finds a Poet*, Scully significantly celebrates Rossi not as an architect, but as an Italian builder, thereby using a title often associated with the vernacular tradition.[27] Not since Louis Kahn had Scully celebrated a contemporary architect with the same passion.

Rossi's work received equal endorsement from the neo-avant-garde and the neotraditionalists in America, ranging from Eisenman's Institute for Architecture and Urban Studies (IAUS) to Yale graduates Andrés Duany and Elizabeth Plater-Zyberk, founders of new urbanism. Rossi's numerous designs for Florida ranged from the unbuilt scheme for the epicentre of new urbanism, the University of Miami's School of Architecture (1986) (Fig. E.7) to the office complex for the Disney Development Company in Orlando (1991). Together with his house for the community of Seaside, master planned by DPZ in 1981, Rossi's work combined classical and vernacular influence to strike a note of gravitas among the levity of the surrounding tropics.[28]

Although the vernacular tradition has played an important role in tempering modernity with regionalist cues and infusing it with an anthropological dimension that was otherwise absent in functionalist practice, as well as reintroducing the role of nature, or *organicism*, its status remains uncertain and its true place among theories of modern and contemporary architecture and urbanism is elusive. It has have been influential in shaping architecture, urbanism, and design associated with a broad variety of historical and critical concepts as disparate as national romanticism, critical regionalism, postmodernism, new urbanism, and even glocalism. As late as the 1990s, the Italian historian and critic Bruno Zevi wrote a short treatise on "architectural dialects" (i.e., vernacular) and lamented that

> the topic is almost ignored from the point of view of critical analysis. Although there are many books on the topic of *minor* architecture, especially numerous those on the rural house, few of them deal with the phenomenon from the point of view of its urban scale and its relationship to the 100 or 500 monuments registered in the annals of history of art.[29]

One of the primary objectives of this book has been to trace an alternative genealogy of the spaces and places of Italian modernist architecture of the twentieth century. Why did contemporary architects, who were already acquainted with the classical language, appropriate the vernacular as an alternative source of inspiration when designing *case* (houses), villas, *villini* (small villas or cottages), weekend or vacation homes, *quartieri* (housing estates), student housing, seaside, mountain, and sun-therapy retreats or colonies? How did this collective and deep-seated interest in the rediscovery of the vernacular tradition, which spanned disparate generations and political agendas, distinguish itself from that of other contemporary architects in Europe and North America? By looking to vernacular models as a repository of uncorrupted moral values embodied in the Italian peasant's domestic environment, Italian architects built a common platform from which to *modernize rural life* and *ruralize modern life*. From the ethnographic buildings of 1911, where vernacular architecture intended to embody distinct regional identities, to the adoption of the hill town as a national model for the Italian pavilion at the Brussels Expo 1958, Italian designers and

Fig. E.8 Giorgio Morandi, *Natura morta*, 1956, Courtesy Museo Giorgio Morandi, Bologna.

intellectuals took on the challenge of engaging history. By simultaneously and selectively embracing urban and rural culture, artisanal craft and new manufacturing approaches, practical know-how and professional knowledge, Italian architectural culture produced a modern reformist project that was both utopian and nostalgic, subversive and anachronistic. In so doing, they ensured that a deep-seated tradition, which embodied the virtue of Venturi's "pride in modesty," would not be forgotten by future generations and would continue to offer a tonic against the frenetic cacophony of contemporary life. Like the ordinary things of Giorgio Morandi's still life paintings (Fig. E.8) that combine the political with "the art of silence," the best examples of modernist architecture inspired by extant buildings of the past offer silent (often overlooked) resistance to pompous formalism.[30]

Notes

Foreword

1 Gottfried Semper, "The Four Elements of Architecture: A Contribution to the Comparative Study of Architecure," in *The Four Elements of Architecture and Other Writings*, ed. by Harry Francis Mallgrave and Wolfgang Herrmann (Cambridge University Press, 1989), 74–129.

2 Gottfried Semper, Manuscript 129, fol. 1, Federal Institute of Technology, Zurich (ETH), Semper Archive.

3 See Kurt W. Forster, "L'abri du pauvre' im Kristallpalast," in *Grammatik der Kunstgeschichte. Oskar Baetschmann zum 65. Geburtstag*, ed. Peter Schneemann and Hubert Locher (Zurich: SIK-ISEA, 2008), 178–94.

4 A special issue of the *Du Magazin* 63 (March 1999) is dedicated to 'Gottfried Semper im Bergell' and details the ramified history of the villa and its client more fully than does the academic literature on Semper.

5 See Rebecca Bedell, "The History of the Earth: Darwin, Geology and Landscape Art," in *Endless Forms: Charles Darwin, Natural Science and the Visual Arts*, ed. by Diana Donald and Jane Munro (New Haven, CT: Yale University Press, 2009), 67.

6 Translated from *Grand dictionnaire universelle du XIX siècle* (Paris: Larousse, 1875): *"primitif qui a la simplicité des premiers ages."* See also Karlheinz Barck et al., *Aesthetische Grundbegriffe*, vol. 4 (Stuttgart-Weimar: Metzler, 2002), 368–77.

7 Cf. Myra N. Rosenfeld, *Sebastiano Serlio on Domestic Architecture: Different Dwellings from the Meanest Hovel to the Most Ornate Palace* (Cambridge, MA: MIT Press 1978), and Sebastiano Serlio, *The Sixteenth-Century Manuscript of Book VI in the Avery Library of Columbia University* (New York: Architectural History Foundation, 1978).

8 Kurt W. Forster, "Back to the Farm: Vernacular Architecture and the Development of the Renaissance Villa," *Architectura* 4:1 (1974): 1–12.
9 Alessia Borellini and Francesco Paolo Campione, eds., *Uomini e cose: Ugo Pellis Fotografie, Sardegna, 1932–1935* (Florence: Giunti, 2009).
10 Originally published in G 1:2 (September 1923): 1, reprinted and discussed in Fritz Neumeyer, *Mies van der Rohe. Das kunstlose Wort* (Berlin: Siedler, 1986), 130f.

Introduction

1 Marguerite Yourcenar, *Memoirs of Hadrian and Reflections on the Composition of Memoirs of Hadrian*, trans. Grace Frick in collaboration with author (New York: Farrar, Straus, and Giroux, 1999), 312; originally published as *Mémoires d'Hadrien* (Paris: Librairie Plon, 1951).
2 For an overview of Italy's political profile during the twentieth century, see Norberto Bobbio, *Ideological Profile of Twentieth-Century Italy*, trans. Lydia G. Cochrane (Princeton, NJ: Princeton University Press, 1995); originally published as *Profilo ideologico del Novecento* (Milan: Garzanti, 1990); see also Paul Ginsborg, *A History of Contemporary Italy: Society and Politics, 1943–1988* (New York: Penguin Books, 1990), and Martin Clark, *Modern Italy, 1871 to the Present* (New York: Pearson Longman, 2008).
3 Robert Venturi, Denise Scott Brown, and Steven Izenour, *Learning from Las Vegas: The Forgotten Symbolism of Architectural Form* (Cambridge, MA: MIT Press, 1977), 6.
4 On Italy's peasantry during the nineteenth and twentieth centuries, see Silvio Lanaro, "Da contadini a Italiani," in *Storia dell'agricoltura italiana in età contemporanea*, vol. 3, ed. Piero Bevilacqua (Venice: Marsilio Editori, 1991), 937–68. For the groundbreaking study on the topic outside of Italy, see Eugen Weber, *Peasants into Frenchmen: The Modernization of Rural France, 1870–1914* (Stanford, CA: Stanford University Press, 1976).
5 Two studies that simultaneously analysed interwar and postwar years are Ezio Bonfanti and Marco Porta, *Città, museo e architettura: Il Gruppo BBPR nella cultura architettonica italiana 1932–1970* (Florence: Vallecchi, 1973) (Reprint: Milan: Hoepli, 2009); and Manfredo Tafuri, *Ludovico Quaroni e lo sviluppo dell'architettura moderna in Italia* (Milan: Edizioni di Comunità, 1964). Most of the overviews published in recent decades have kept to the interwar and postwar subdivisions. See Giorgio Ciucci, *Gli architetti e il fascismo: Architettura e città, 1922–1944* (Turin: Einaudi, 1989) and Manfredo Tafuri, *History of Italian Architecture, 1944–1985*, trans. Jessica Levine (Cambridge, MA: MIT Press, 1989), which originally appeared in Italian as *Sto-*

ria dell'architettura italiana, 1944–1985 (Turin: Einaudi, 1986); and Amedeo Belluzzi and Claudia Conforti, *Architettura italiana: 1944–1994* (Rome: Laterza, 1994). The same approach persists in more recent studies, such as Giorgio Ciucci and Giorgio Muratore, eds., *Storia dell'architettura italiana – Il primo Novecento* (Milan: Electa, 2004); and Francesco Dal Co, ed., *Storia dell'architettura italiana – Il secondo Novecento* (Milan: Electa, 1997).

6 Parallel development occurred in other Europeans countries in which agrarian traditions were deep-seated; see, for example, Romy Golan, *Modernity and Nostalgia: Art and Politics in France between the Wars* (New Haven: Yale University Press, 1995), Matthew Afron and Mark Antliff, eds., *Fascist Visions: Art and Ideology in France and Italy* (Princeton, NJ: Princeton University Press, 1997).

7 Difficulties associated with translation complicate and enrich the story. Benedetto Croce quipped that a translator is a traitor because translation is impossible in his "Possibilità e impossibilità delle traduzioni," in *Conversazioni critiche*, vol. 4 (Bari: Laterza, 1951), 308–9. While Walter Benjamin declared, "If the kinship of larguages manifests itself in translations, this is not accomplished through a vague alikeness between adaptation and original. It stands to reason that kinship does not necessarily involve likeness." Walter Benjamin, "The Task of the Translator," in *Walter Benjamin: Illuminations*, ed. Hannah Arendt (New York: Schocken Books, 1968), 69–82. In his introduction entitled "Translation: The Art of Failure" in *Italian Literature in Translation*, ed. Leo B. Kneer (Glenview: Scott, Foresman and Company, 1970), 9, John Ciardi observed: "As soon as one begins to hunt the American-English language for words that are equivalent *in depth* to Italian words, he learns that whatever he does manage to get across the language boundary will not be got across by any simple one-for-one transliteration."

8 Lucien Febvre, "*Civilisation*: Evolution of a Word and a Group of Ideas," in *A New Kind of History and Other Essays*, ed. Peter Burke, trans. Keith Folca (New York: Harper and Row, 1973), 219–57.

9 George M. Foster, "What is a Peasant?" in *Peasant Society: A Reader*, ed. Jack M. Potter, May N. Diaz, and George M. Fosler (Boston: Little, Brown, 1967), 2–14 and Jules Michelet, *The People*, trans. John P. McKay (Urbana: University of Illinois Press, 1973).

10 For a definition of vernacular architecture from the point of view of a distinguished American folklorist, see Henry H. Glassie, *Vernacular Architecture* (Bloomington: Indiana University Press, 2000). Compare this with the definition in the Italian study by Enrico Guidoni, *L'architettura popolare italiana* (Rome: Laterza, 1980).

11 For an extended discussion on notions of the primitive, see my introduction "The Primitive in Modern Architecture and Urbanism," *Journal of Architecture* 13:4 (August 2008): 355–65.

12 John Michael Vlach, *Back of the Big House: The Architecture of Plantation Slavery* (Chapel Hill: University of North Carolina Press, 1993).

13 See Paul Oliver, "Vernacular Architecture," *Encyclopedia of Twentieth-Century Architecture*, vol. 3, ed. R. Stephen Sennott (New York: Fitzroy Dearborn, 2004), 1401–5; Paul Oliver, "Attitudes in the Modern Movement," in *Shelter and Society*, ed. Paul Oliver (New York: Praeger Publishers, 1969), 16–21. Influential books written from the perspective of practising architects include Myron Goldfinger, "Introduction," *Villages in the Sun: Mediterranean Community Architecture* (New York: Praeger Publishers, 1969), 9–24; Bernard Rudofsky, *Architecture without Architects: An Introduction to Non-Pedigreed Architecture* (New York: Museum of Modern Art, 1964).

14 For an explanation of operative criticism, see Manfredo Tafuri, *Theories and History of Architecture*, trans. Giorgio Verrecchia (New York: Harper and Row, 1980), 141–70; originally published as *Teorie e storia dell'architettura* (1968). See also Luca Monica, ed., *La critica operativa e l'architettura* (Milan: Unicopli, 2001). For an elaboration on the concept of misprision, see Harold Bloom, *The Anxiety of Influence: A Theory of Poetry* (New York: Oxford University Press, 1997), 17–45; and Harold Bloom, *A Map of Misreading* (New York: Oxford University Press, 2003).

15 George Kubler, *The Shape of Time: Remarks on the History of Things* (New Haven, CT: Yale University Press, 1962), 1.

16 Henri Focillon, "Introduction," in *Art Populaire: Travaux Artistiques et Scientifiques du 1er Congrès International des Arts Populaires Prague 1928*, vol. 1 (Paris: Éditions Duchartre, 1931), vii–xvi. (My translation.)

17 Sir George Gilbert Scott, *Remarks on Secular and Domestic Architecture, Present and Future* (London: John Murray, 1857), 7, where he writes, "I have for many years been strongly impressed with the following facts: First, that the vernacular Domestic architecture of our day is wholly unworthy of our state of civilization, and requires a thorough reformation."

18 The expression "relationship with history" was used by Tafuri in *History of Italian Architecture, 1944–1985*, 3–33; see also Henry A. Millon, "The Role of History of Architecture in Fascist Italy," *Journal of the Society of Architectural Historians* 24:1 (March 1965): 53–9.

19 Julien Benda, *La trahison des clercs*, trans. Richard Aldington (1927; reprint, New Brunswick: Transaction Publishers, 2007); Adriano Tilgher, *Julien Benda e il problema del "Tradimento dei Chierici"* (Rome: Libreria di scienze e lettere, 1930).

20 For an overview of the relationship between intellectuals and politics
    during the fascist years, see Philip V. Cannistraro, "Fascism and Culture,
    1919–1945," in *Italian Art in the Twentieth Century: Painting and Sculpture
    1900–1988,* ed. Emily Braun (Munich: Prestel, and London: Royal Acad-
    emy of Arts, 1989), 147–54; Marla Susan Stone, *The Patron State: Culture
    and Politics in Fascist Italy* (Princeton, NJ: Princeton University Press, 1998);
    Luisa Mangoni, *L'interventismo della cultura: Intellettuali e riviste del fascismo*
    (Rome: Laterza, 1974); Gabriele Turi, *Il fascismo e il consenso degli intellettuali*
    (Bologna: Il Mulino, 1980); and Renzo De Felice, *Intellettuali di fronte al fas-
    cismo: saggi e note documentarie* (Rome: Bonacci, 1985); Mario Isnenghi, *Intel-
    lectuali militant e intellettuali funzionari: Appunti sulla cultura fascista* (Turin:
    Einaudi, 1979).
21 Timothy J. Clark, *Image of the People: Gustave Courbet and the 1848 Revolution*
    (Berkeley: University of California Press, 1999); see also Linda Nochlin,
    Realism (Harmondsworth, UK: Penguin, 1971).
22 On the concept of realism (and neorealism) in modernist architecture,
    see Jorge Silvetti's erudite essay "On Realism in Architecture," *Beyond the
    Modern Movement, Special Issue, The Harvard Architecture Review* 1 (Spring
    1980): 10–31; and Manfredo Tafuri, "Architettura e Realismo," in *Architet-
    tura moderna. L'avventura delle idée, 1750–1980,* ed. Vittorio Magnago Lam-
    pugnani (Milan: Electa, 1985), 121–45. For an overview of neorealism in
    Italy, see Maristella Casciato, "Neorealism in Italian Architecture," in *Anx-
    ious Modernism: Experimentation in Postwar Architecture Culture,* ed. Sarah
    Goldhagen and Réjean Legault (Cambridge, MA: MIT Press, 2009), 25–53;
    *Bruno Reichlin, "Figures of Neorealism in Italian Architecture (Part 1),"
    Grey Room* 5 (Fall 2001): 78–101; Bruno Reichlin, "Figures of Neorealism in
    Italian Architecture (Part 2)," *Grey Room* 5 (Winter 2002): 110–33; and Vit-
    torio Magnago Lampugnani, "The Myth of Reality. Notes on Neorealism
    in Italy 1946–56," in *Architecture and Arts 1900/2004: A Century of Creative
    Projects in Building, Design, Cinema, Painting, Sculpture,* ed. Germano Celant
    (Milan: Skira, 2004), 75–9.
23 Emblematic of this shift was the publication by Charles Jencks, *Modern
    Movements in Architecture* (Garden City, NY: Anchor Press, 1973). Jencks'
    title targeted the lack of pluralism espoused in Nikolaus Pevsner, *Pioneers
    of the Modern Movement from William Morris to Walter Gropius* (London:
    Faber and Faber, 1936).
24 Two important overviews that use culture in their titles are Cesare De Seta,
    La cultura architettonica in Italia tra le due guerre (Bari: Laterza, 1972); and
    Bonfanti and Porta, *Città, museo e architettura: Il Gruppo BBPR nella cultura
    architettonica italiana 1932–1970.*

25 On the historiography of modern architecture, see the following: Renato De Fusco, *L'idea di architettura: storia della critica da Viollet-le-Duc a Persico* (Milan: Edizioni di Comunità, 1968); Maria Luisa Scalvini, *L'immagine storiografica dell'architettura contemporanea da Platz a Giedion* (Rome: Officina, 1984); Panayotis Tournikiotis, *The Historiography of Modern Architecture* (Cambridge, MA: MIT Press, 1999). For an overview of Italian criticism and historiography of modern architecture, see Giorgio Pigafetta, *Architettura moderna e ragione storica. La storiografia italiana sull'architettura moderna, 1928–1976* (Milan: Guerini Studio, 1993).

26 Leonardo Benevolo, *History of Modern Architecture*, vol. 2, *The Modern Movement* (Cambridge, MA: MIT Press, 1971), 561–76.

27 For an insightful overview of the reception of Italian architecture in the historiography of modern architecture, see Ciucci, *Gli architetti e il fasciso*, in particular, "Premessa," xvii–xxiv.

28 On Italian modernism's different voices, see Luca Somigli and Mario Moroni eds., *Italian Modernism: Italian Culture between Decadentism and Avant-Garde* (Toronto: University of Toronto Press, 2004); Emilio Gentile, *The Struggle for Modernity: Nationalism, Futurism, and Fascism* (Westport, CT: Praeger, 2003); Walter L. Adamson, *Avant-Garde Florence: From Modernism to Fascism* (Cambridge, MA: Harvard University Press, 1993); and Ruth Ben-Ghiat, *Fascist Modernities: Italy, 1922–45* (Berkeley: University of California Press, 2001).

29 On "Modern Architecture and the Eclipse of History," see Tafuri, *Theories and History of Architecture*, 11–77. On the use of history in fascist Italy, see Claudia Lazzaro and Roger J. Crum, eds., *Donatello among the Blackshirts: History and Modernity in the Visual Culture of Fascist Italy* (Ithaca, NY: Cornell University Press, 2005), in particular the essay by Claudio Fogu, "To Make History Present," 33–49.

30 For an overview of futurism, see Ezio Godoli, *Il Futurismo* (Rome: Laterza, 1983); and Iain Boyd Whyte, "The Architecture of Futurism," in *International Futurism in the Arts and Literature*, ed. Günter Berghaus (Berlin: De Gruyler, 2000), 353–72.

31 Alan Colquhoun, "From Rationalism to Revisionism: Architecture in Italy 1920–65," in Alan Colquhoun, *Modern Architecture* (New York: Oxford University Press, 2002), 183.

32 Palmiro Togliatti, *Lectures on Fascism* (New York: International Publishers, 1976), chap. 1, "The Basic Features of the Fascist Dictatorship," 1–12.

33 Giorgio Ciucci, "The Classicism of the E42: Between Modernity and Tradition," *Assemblage* 8 (February 1989), 79–87; Maurizio Calvesi, Enrico Guidoni, and Simonetta Lux, eds., *E42 Utopia e scenario del regime II Urbanistica, architettura, arte e decorazione* (Venice: Marsillio, 1987).

34 Aldo Rossi, *The Architecture of the City*, trans. Diane Ghirardo (Cambridge, MA: IAUS and MIT Press, 1982); in particular, see "Critique of Naive Functionalism," 46–8.

35 Vittorio Gregotti, *New Directions in Italian Architecture*, trans. Giuseppina Salvadori (New York: George Braziller, 1968), 54–6. For another view on this continuity, see Manfredo Tafuri, "Design and Technological Utopia," in *Italy: The New Domestic Landscape: Achievements and Problems of Italian Design*, ed. Emilio Ambasz (New York: Museum of Modern Art, and Florence: Centro Di, 1972), 388–404.

36 Stephanie Barron with Sabine Eckmann, *Exiles and Emigrés: The Flight of European Artists from Hitler* (New York: Harry N. Abrams, 1997), esp. 210–52. On German artists and intellectuals who emigrated from Germany to Italy, see Klaus Voigt and Wolfganz Henze, eds., *Rifugio Precario – Artisti e intellettuali tedeschi in Italia 1933–1945* (Milan: Mazzotta, 1995).

37 Terry Kirk, "Framing St. Peter's: Urban Planning in Fascist Rome," *The Art Bulletin* 88:4 (December 2006): 756–76.

38 Gavriel D. Rosenfeld, *Munich and Memory: Architecture, Monuments, and the Legacy of the Third Reich* (Berkeley: University of California Press, 2000).

39 Jeffrey T. Schnapp, "Fascism's Museum in Motion," *Journal of Architectural Education* 45:2 (February 1992): 87–97; Jeffrey T. Schnapp, *Anno X: La mostra della rivoluzione fascista del 1932* (Pisa: Istituti editoriali e poligrafici internazionali, 2003); Diane Ghirardo, "Architects, Exhibitions, and the Politics of Culture in Fascist Italy," *Journal of Architectural Education* 45:2 (February 1992): 67–75; and Antonella Russo, *Il fascismo in mostra* (Rome: Editori Riuniti, 1999). See my "Space of Criticism: Exhibitions and the Vernacular in Italian Modernism," *Journal of Architectural Education* 62:3 (February 2009): 35–52.

40 See Alberto Asor Rosa, *Scrittori e popolo: Saggio sulla letteratura populista in Italia* (Rome: Samonà e Savelli, 1965).

41 Arnold Hauser discussed the transition from folk art to popular art in "The Art of the People, the Masses, and the Educated," in *The Philosophy of Art History*, trans. Kenneth J. Northcott (Evanston: Northwestern University Press, 1985), 277–365.

42 Emilio Gentile, *Politics as Religion*, trans. George Staunton (Princeton, NJ: Princeton University Press, 2006).

43 Italo Calvino, *Fiabe italiane raccolte dalla tradizione popolare durante gli ultimi cento anni e trascritte in lingua dai vari dialetti da Italo Calvino* (Turin: Einaudi, 1956) and *Italian Folktales Selected and Retold by Italo Calvino*, trans. George Martin (New York: Harcourt, Brace, Jovanovich, 1980); Pier Paolo Pasolini, *La poesia popolare italiana* (Milan: Garzanti, 1960); Pier Paolo Pasolini, *Il canto popolare* (Milan: Meridiana, 1954); Mario dell'Arco and

Pier Paolo Pasolini, eds., *Poesia dialettale del Novecento* (Parma: Guanda, 1952).

44 Richard Weston, *Villa Mairea – Alvor Aalto* (London: Phaidon, 2002).

45 On tradition and nationalism, see Eric J. Hobsbawm and Terence Ranger, eds., *The Invention of Tradition* (Cambridge: Cambridge University Press, 2005). See also Eric J. Hobsbawn, *Nations and Nationalism since 1780: Programme, Myth, Reality* (Cambridge: Cambridge University Press, 1990).

46 Christian Norberg-Schulz, *Nightlands: Nordic Building* (Cambridge, MA: MIT Press, 1996) and *Architecture: Presence, Language, Place* (Milan: Skira, 2000). See also "Common Ground: An Interview with Juhani Pallasmaa," *Journal of Architectural Education* 63:1 (October 2009): 75–9.

47 Demetri Porphyrios, *Sources of Modern Eclecticism: Studies on Alvar Aalto* (London: Academy Editions, 1982).

48 See Alvar Aalto, "Karelian Architecture" (2 November 1941) published in *Alvar Aalto in His Own Words*, ed. Göran Schildt (New York: Rizzoli, 1998), 116–19; Marida Talamona, *Casa Malaparte* (New York: Princeton Architectural Press, 1992).

49 A succinct summary can be found in Franco Borsi, *L'architettura dell'unità d'Italia* (Florence: F. Le Monnier, 1966); see also Rosanna Pavoni, ed., *Reviving the Renaissance: The Use and Abuse of the Past in Nineteenth-Century Italian Art and Decoration*, trans. Adrian Belton (New York: Cambridge University Press, 1997).

50 Barbara Miller Lane, *National Romanticism and Modern Architecture in Germany and the Scandinavian Countries* (New York: Cambridge University Press, 2000), and *Architecture and Politics in Germany, 1919–1945* (Cambridge, MA: Harvard University Press, 1968); and Nicola Gordon Bowe, ed., *Art and the National Dream: The Search for Vernacular Expression in Turn-of-the-Century Design* (Dublin: Irish Academic Press, 1993).

51 Elias Canetti, *Crowds and Power* (New York: Farrar, Straus, and Giroux, 1998), 177–8.

52 Benito Mussolini, "Arte e civiltà" (1926), in *Opera Omnia di Benito Mussolini*, vol. 22, ed. Edoardo and Duilio Susmel, trans. Carol Stewart (Florence: La Fenice, 1957), 230. My translation. See also Umberto Silva, *Ideologia e arte del fascismo* (Milan: Mazzotta, 1973); and Laura Malvano, *Fascismo e politica dell'immagine* (Turin: Bollati Boringhieri, 1988).

53 In his pioneering study *Art under a Dictatorship* (New York: Oxford University Press, 1954), Hellmut Lehmann-Haupt declared, "Classicism is made to order for the purposed of the modern dictator" (xvii–xxii). See Luciano Canfora, "Classicismo e Fascismo," in *Matrici culturali del fascismo*, ed. Luciano Canfora (Rome: Laterza, 1977), 85–112. See also Giorgio Ciucci, "Lin-

guaggi classicist: negli anni trenta in Europa e in America," in *L'estetica della politica – Europa e America negli anni Trenta*, ed. Maurizio Vaudagna (Rome: Laterza, 1989), 45–58; Giorgio Ciucci, ed., *Classicismo – Classicismi: Architettura Europa – America 1920–1940* (Milan: Electa and Vicenza: Centro Internazionale di Studi di Architettura Andrea Palladio, 1995).

54 Spiro Kostof, *The Third Rome, 1870–1950: Traffic and Glory* (Berkeley, CA: University Art Museum, 1973). Simonetta Falasca-Zamponi, *Fascist Spectacle: The Aesthetics of Power in Mussolini's Italy* (Berkeley: University of California Press, 1997).

55 Henry A. Millon and Linda Nochlin, eds., *Art and Architecture in the Service of Politics* (Cambridge, MA: MIT Press, 1978); Jan Tabor, ed., *Kunst und Diktatur. Architektur, Bildhauerei und Malerei in Österreich, Deutschland, Italien und der Sowjetunion 1922–1956*, vol. 2. (Baden: Verlag Grasl, 1994), 610–717; Dawn Ades, Tim Benton, David Elliott, and Iain Boyd-Whyte, eds., *Art and Power: Europe under the Dictators, 1930–1945* (London: Thames and Hudson, 1995), 119–83; Richard Etlin, "Nationalism in Modern Italian Architecture, 1900–1940," in *Nationalism in the Visual Arts*, ed. Richard Etlin (Washington, DC: National Gallery of Art, 1991), 89–109.

56 Emily Braun, "Political Rhetoric and Poetic Irony: The Uses of Classicism in the Art of Fascist Italy," in *On Classic Ground: Picasso, Léger, de Chirico and the New Classicism 1910–1930*, ed. Elizabeth Cowling and Jennifer Mundy (London: Tate Gallery, 1990), 345–58; Annegret Burg, *Novecento Milanese: I novecentisti e il rinnovamento dell'architettura a Milano fra il 1920 e il 1940* (Milan: F. Motta, 1991); Emily Braun, *Mario Sironi and Italian Modernism: Art and Politics under Fascism* (New York: Cambridge University Press, 2000). Architectural studies include Carlo Cresti, *Architettura e fascismo* (Florence: Vallecchi Editore, 1986); Fabrizio Brunetti, *Architetti e fascismo* (Florence: Alinea Editrice, 1993); and Paolo Nicoloso, *Mussolini architetto: propaganda e paesaggio urbano nell'Italia fascista* (Turin: Einaudi, 2008).

57 See Gottfried Boehm, Ulrich Mosch, and Katharina Schmidt, eds., *Canto d'Amore: Classicism in Modern Art and Music, 1914–1935* (Basel: Kunstmuseum, 1996), esp. Wolf Tegethoff, "From 'Modern' Classicism to Classic Modernism: Methods and Objectives of Architecture in the First Half of the Twentieth Century," 442–51. See also Robert A.M. Stern with Raymond W. Gastil, *Modern Classicism* (New York: Rizzoli, 1988); Franco Borsi, *L'ordine monumentale in Europa 1929–1939* (Milan: Edizioni de Comunità, 1986); Lars Olof Larsson, "Classicism in the Architecture of the XXth Century," in *Albert Speer: Architecture 1932–1942*, ed. Léon Krier (Brussels: Archives d'architecture moderne, 1985), 233–45.

58 Luciano Patetta and Silvia Danesi, eds., *Il Razionalismo e l'architettura in*

Italia durante il Fascismo (Milan: Electa, 1976). More than a decade later an in-depth overview of the period was published: Riccardo Mariani, *Razionalismo e architettura moderna: Storia di una polemica* (Milan: Edizioni di Comunità, 1989).

59 See, for example, Peter Eisemann, *Giuseppe Terragni: Transformations, Decompositions, Critiques* (New York: Monacelli Press, 2003).

60 Mario Lupano, *Marcello Piacentini* (Rome: Laterza, 1991); Mario Pisani, ed., *Marcello Piacentini: Architettura moderna* (Venice: Marsilio, 1996); Sandro Scarrocchia, *Albert Speer e Marcello Piacentini: l'architettura del totalitarismo negli anni trenta* (Milan: Skira, 1999). For contemporary commentaries on Piacentini outside of Italy, see George Nelson, *Building a New Europe: Portraits of Modern Architects: Essays by George Nelson, 1935–36*, with an introduction by Kurt W. Forster (New Haven, CT: Yale University Press in association with Yale University School of Architecture, 2007).

61 Marco De Michelis, "Fascist Architectures in Italy," in *Back from Utopia: The Challenge of the Modern Movement*, ed. Hubert-Jan Henket and Hilde Heynen (Rotterdam: 010 Publishers, 2002), 86–91.

62 There are some notable exceptions. With regard to the decorative arts, see Penny Sparke, "The Straw Donkey: Tourist Kitsch or Proto-Design? Craft and Design in Italy, 1945–1960," *Journal of Design History* 11:1 (1998): 59–69; Maria Cristina Tonelli, "Il folclorismo," in *Artisti e cultura visiva del Novecento*, ed. Barbara Cinelli, Maria Cristina Tonelli, and Carlo Sisi (Pistoia: Comune di Pistoia, 1980), 49–51; Mario Quesada, "L'arte rustica," in *Le arti minori d'autore in Italia dal 1900 al 1930*, ed. Irene de Guttry, Maria Paola Maino, and Mario Quesada (Rome: Laterza, 1985), 58–60; Marianne Lamonaca, "A 'Return to Order': Issues of the Vernacular and the Classical in Italian Inter-War Design," in *Designing Modernity. The Arts of Reform and Persuasion 1885–1945*, ed. Wendy Kaplan (London: Thames and Hudson, 1995), 194–221. On architecture, see Michelangelo Sabatino, "Back to the Drawing Board? Revisiting the Vernacular Tradition in Italian Modern Architecture," *Annali di Architettura: Rivista del Centro Internazionale di studi di architettura Andrea Palladio* 16 (2004): 169–85; Carlo Cresti, "Mediterraneità e ruralità," *Architettura e fascismo* (Florence: Vallecchi, 1986), 95–144; Richard A. Etlin, "A Modern Vernacular Architecture," in *Modernism in Italian Architecture, 1890–1940* (Cambridge, MA: MIT Press, 1991), 129–61. Studies on the design and planning of Italian colonies, especially in Africa, have also provided an opportunity to reflect on the appropriation of the vernacular outside of Italy, see Brian L. McLaren, "The Italian Colonial Appropriation of Indigenous North African Architecture in the 1930s," *Muqarnas: An Annual on the Visual Culture of the Islamic World* 19, vol. 1, ed.,

Gülru Necipoglu (2002): 164–92; Giuliano Gresleri, P. G. Massaretti, and S. Zagnoni, eds., *Architettura italiana d'oltremare 1870–1940* (Venice: Marsilio, 1993); Giuliano Gresleri, "Classico e vernacolo nell'architettura dell' 'Italia d'oltremare,'" in *Classicismo – Classicismi: Architettura Europa/America 1920–1940*, ed. Giorgio Ciucci (Milan: Electa, and Venice: C.I.S.A. Andrea Palladio, 1995), 68–87. See also Brian L. McLaren, *Architecture and Tourism in Italian Colonial Libya: An Ambivalent Modernism* (Seattle: University of Washington Press, 2006), and Mia Fuller, *Moderns Abroad: Architecture, Cities and Italian Imperialism* (London: Routledge, 2007).

63 See Giorgio Ciucci, "Italian Architecture during the Fascist Period: Classicism between Neoclassicism and Rationalism: The Many Souls of the Classical," *The Harvard Architectural Review* 6 (1987): 76–87.

64 On the topic of *Mediterraneità* in architecture, see Silvia Danesi, "Aporie dell'architettura italiana in periodo fascista – mediterraneità e purismo," in *Il Razionalismo e l'architettura in Italia durante il Fascismo*, ed. Patetta and Danesi, 21–8; Benedetto Gravagnuolo, *Il mito mediterraneo nell'architettura contemporanea* (Naples: Electa, 1994). See also Vojtech Jirat-Wasiutynski, ed., *Modern Art and the Idea of the Mediterranean* (Toronto: University of Toronto Press, 2007), and Jean-François Lejeune and Michelangelo Sabatino, eds., *Modern Architecture and the Mediterranean: Vernacular Dialogues and Contested Identities* (London: Routledge, 2009); Fabrizio Brunetti, "L'idea di Mediterraneità negli scritti di Carlo Enrico Rava e del Gruppo di Quadrante," in *Architetti e fascismo* (Florence: Alinea, 1993), 203–16; Brian L. McLaren, "Die Konstruktion des mediterranen Mythos in der modernen italiensichen Architektur: Bezüge zwischen Italien und Wien," in *Das entfernte Dorf. Moderne Kunst und ethnischer Artefakt*, ed. Ákos Moravánszky (Vienna: Böhlau, 2002), 223–48

65 Manfredo Tafuri and Francesco Dal Co, *Modern Architecture*, vol. 2, trans. Robert Erich Wolf (New York: Harry N. Abrams, 1979), 259–61.

66 James Stirling, "Regionalism and Modern Architecture," *Architects' Year Book* 8 (1957): 62–8, republished in *Architecture Culture 1943–1968: A Documentary Anthology*, ed. Joan Ockman and Edward Eigen (New York: Rizzoli, 1993), 243–8. On English modernism and the place of tradition, see Alina A. Payne, "Rudolf Wittkower and Architectural Principles in the Age of Modernism," *Journal of the Society of Architectural Historians* 53:3 (September 1994): 322–42.

67 George Everard Kidder Smith, *Italy Builds: Its Modern Architecture and Native Inheritance* (New York: Reinhold Publishing Corporation, 1955).

68 James Stirling, "Ronchamp: Le Corbusier's Chapel and the Crisis of Rationalism," *The Architectural Review* 119:711 (March 1956): 161; republished

in Robert Maxwell, ed., *James Stirling: Writings on Architecture* (Milan: Skira, 1998), 44–9.

69 Caroline Maniaque Benton, *Le Corbusier and the Maisons Jaoul* (New York: Princeton Architectural Press, 2009).

70 Eeva-Liisa Pelkonen, *Alvar Aalto: Architecture, Modernity, and Geopolitics* (New Haven: Yale University Press, 2009); Thomas Da Costa Kaufmann and Elizabeth Pilliod, eds., *Time and Place: The Geohistory of Art* (Burlington, VT: Ashgate, 2005); Thomas Da Costa Kaufmann, *Toward a Geography of Art* (Chicago: University of Chicago Press, 2004); Néstor García Canclini, *Hybrid Cultures: Strategies for Entering and Leaving Modernity* (Minneapolis: University of Minnesota Press, 1995).

71 Edward W. Said, *Orientalism* (London: Routledge and Kegan Paul, 1978); Antonio Gramsci, *The Southern Question*, trans. Pasquale Verdicchio (Toronto: Guernica Editions, 2005); Rosario Villari, ed., *Il Sud nella storia d'Italia – Antologia della questione meridionale* (Rome: Laterza, 1988); Jane Schneider, ed., *Italy's "Southern Question": Orientalism in One Country* (Oxford: Berg, 1998).

72 Jared M. Diamond, *Guns, Germs, and Steel: The Fates of Human Societies* (New York: W.W. Norton, 1997).

73 John Ruskin, *Mornings in Florence: Being Simple Studies of Christian Art for English Travellers* (London: G. Allen, 1899), 59.

74 Neil Kent, *The Soul of the North: A Social, Architectural and Cultural History of the Nordic Countries, 1700–1940* (London: Reaktion, 2000); and Nils-Ole Lund, *Nordic Architecture* (Copenhagen: Danish Architectural Press, 2008).

75 Christian Norberg-Schulz, *Nightlands: Nordic Building* (Cambridge, MA: MIT Press, 1996), ix.

76 Lewis Mumford, *The South in Architecture: The Dancy Lectures, Alabama College 1941* (New York: Harcourt, Brace, 1941), 25.

77 Charles W. Moore, "Southernness: A Regional Dimension," *Perspecta* 15 (1975): 9–17; republished as "Southerners" in *Re-reading Perspecta: The First Fifty Years of the Yale Architectural Journal*, ed. Robert A. M. Stern, Peggy Deamer, and Alan Plattus (Cambridge, MA: MIT Press, 2004), 328–31.

78 Liane Lefaivre and Alexander Tzonis, *Critical Regionalism: Architecture and Identity in a Globalized World* (Munich: Prestel, 2003), 24–55.

79 For a discussion on Moore's interest in the vernacular tradition, see Michelangelo Sabatino, "The Poetics of the Ordinary: The American Places of Charles W. Moore," *Places: Forum of Design for the Public Realm* 19:2 (Summer 2007): 62–71.

80 See the introduction to Maiken Umbach and Bernd Hüppauf, eds., *Vernac-*

ular Modernism: Heimat, Globalization and the Build Environment (Stanford, CA: Stanford University Press, 2005), 1–23.

81 See Richard Pommer, "The Flat Roof: A Modernist Controversy in Germany," *Art Journal* 43:2 (Summer 1983): 158–69; Christian F. Otto and Richard Pommer, *Weissenhof 1927 and the Modern Movement in Architecture* (Chicago: University of Chicago Press, 1991), 140–4; and Karin Kirsch, *The Weissenhofsiedlung: Experimental Housing Built for the Deutscher Werkbund: Stuttgart 1927* (New York: Rizzoli, 1989).

82 Recent accounts of modern architecture have acknowledged the debt of regional vernacular traditions in Central Europe; see, for example, Ákos Moravánszky, *Competing Visions: Aesthetic Invention and Social Imagination in Central European Architecture, 1867–1918* (Cambridge, MA: MIT Press, 1998), and, more recently, Anthony Alofsin, *When Buildings Speak: Architecture as Language in the Habsburg Empire and Its Aftermath, 1867–1933* (Chicago: University of Chicago Press, 2006).

83 James Maude Richards, "The Condition of Architecture and the Principle of Anonymity," in *Circle: International Survey of Constructivist Art*, ed. Leslie Martin, Ben Nicholson, and Naum Gabo (New York: Praeger Publishers, 1971), 184–189.

84 William Morris, "The Revival of Handicraft," *Morris on Art & Design*, ed. Christine Poulson (Sheffield: Sheffield Academic Press, 1996), 192.

85 Frank Lloyd Wright, "The Sovereignty of the Individual," in *Frank Lloyd Wright: Writings and Buildings*, ed. Edgar Kaufmann and Ben Raeburn (Cleveland: Meridian Books, 1960), 85.

86 See Passanti, "The Vernacular, Modernism and Le Corbusier," 438–51.

87 Klaus Spechtenhauser and Arthur Rüegg, eds., *Maison Blanche: Charles-Edouard Jeanneret/Le Corbusier: History and Restoration of the Villa Jeanneret-Perret 1912–2005* (Basel: Birkhäuser, 2007).

88 Adolf Behne, "Art, Craft, Technology," in Francesco Dal Co, *Figures of Architecture and Thought: German Architecture Culture 1880–1920* (New York: Rizzoli, 1990), 338.

89 Marcel Breuer, "Where Do We Stand?" *The Architectural Review* 77/461 (April 1935): 133, and *Marcel Breuer: Buildings and Projects 1921–1962*, introduction and captions by Cranston Jones (New York: Frederick A. Praeger, 1962), 259–61. See Barry Bergdoll, "Encountering America: Marcel Breuer and the Discourses of the Vernacular from Budapest to Boston," in *Marcel Breuer: Design and Architecture*, ed. Alexander von Vegesack, and Mathias Remmele (Weil am Rhein: Vitra Design Museum, 2003), 260–307.

90 John Maas, "Where Architectural Historians Fear to Tread," *Journal of the Society of Architectural Historians* 28:1 (March 1969): 3–8.

91 See the author's preface, Bernard Rudofsky, *Architecture without Architects: A Short Introduction to Non-Pedigreed Architecture* (New York: Museum of Modern Art, 1964). *Rural* and *spontaneous* are terms that were specific to the Italian debate on the vernacular, with which Rudofsky had first-hand contact during the 1930s and later during his travels in Italy after the Second World War. His personal notebooks that reveal his experience in Italy are held with the Bernard Rudofsky Papers, Getty Research Institute, Getty Center, Los Angeles, and in the AWA Files, Museum of Modern Art Archive, New York, Department of Circulating Exhibitions Records, II.2/134 (5.1).

92 Henry-Russell Hitchcock and Philip Johnson, *The International Style: Architecture since 1922* (New York: W.W. Norton, 1932). See Terence Riley, *The International Style: Exhibition 15 and the Museum of Modern Art* (New York: Rizzoli/Columbia Books of Architecture, 1992).

93 Jean-Louis Cohen, *André Lurçat: 1894–1970: Autocritique d'un moderne* (Liège: Mardaga, 1995), 110–20.

94 Paolo Nicoloso, *Gli architetti di Mussolini: Scuole e sindacato, architetti e massoni, professori e politici negli anni del regime* (Milan: Franco Angeli, 1999).

95 Gianni Franzone, "Per un'analisi del 'ruralesimo' nella Collezione Wolfson. Da Cambellotti alla 'mistica rurale' fascista," in *La visione del prisma. La collezione Wolfson*, ed. Silvia Barisione, Matteo Fochessati, and Gianni Franzone (Milan: Mazzotta, 1999), 65–91.

96 The literature on the history of fascism is extensive. For an overview of different interpretations of fascism, see Renzo De Felice, *Interpretations of Fascism* (Cambridge, MA: Harvard University Press, 1977), and Emilio Gentile, *The Origins of Fascist ideology, 1918–1925* (New York: Enigma, 2005). See the monumental six-volume study on Mussolini by Renzo De Felice, vol. 1, *Mussolini il rivoluzionario, 1883–1920* (Turin: Einaudi, 1965); vol. 2, *Mussolini il fascista: La conquesta del potere, 1921–1925* (Turin: Einaudi, 1966); vol. 3, *Mussolini il fascista: L'organizzazione dello Stato fascista, 1925–1929* (Turin: Einaudi, 1968); vol. 4, *Mussolini il duce: Gli anni del consenso, 1929–1936* (Turin: Einaudi, 1974); vol. 5, *Mussolini il duce: Lo Stato totalitario, 1936–1940* (Turin: Einaudi, 1981); and vol. 6, *Mussolini l'alleato, 1940–1945* (Turin: Einaudi, 1990).

97 Giuseppe Pagano, "Una casetta in legno," *Domus* 177 (September 1942): 375–9.

1. In Search of *Italianità*

1 Camillo Boito, *Architettura del Medio Evo in Italia con una introduzione sullo stile futuro dell'architettura italiana* (Milan: Ulrico Hoepli, 1880), 26–7;

partially repubished in English as "On the Future Style of Italian Architecture," trans. Maria Pia Smargiasso, in *Architectural Theory*, ed. Harry Francis Mallgrave and Christina Contandriopoulos, vol. 2, *An Anthology from 1871–2005* (Malden: Blackwell Publishing 2008), 111–12. Boito's "Sullo stile futuro dell'architettura italiana," the introduction to *"Architettura del Medio Evo in Italia"* was republished in *Camillo Boito – Il nuovo e l'antico in architettura*, ed. Maria Antonietta Crippa (Milan: Jaca Book, 1989), 3–30.

2 For an overview of these changes as they relate to Italy, see Martin Clark, *Modern Italy, 1871 to the Present* (New York: Pearson Longman, 2008).

3 Hermann Muthesius, *Style-Architecture and Building Art: Transformations of Architecture in the Nineteenth Century and its Present Condition*, introduction and translation by Stanford Anderson (Santa Monica, CA: Getty Center for the History of Art and the Humanities, 1994), 1–43.

4 Harry Francis Mallgrave, *In What Style Should We Build? The German Debate on Architectural Style*, introduction and trans. Wolfgang Herrmann (Santa Monica, CA: Getty Center for the History of Art and the Humanities, 1992). For an overview of eighteenth-century through early-twentieth-century Italian architecture and urbanism, see Terry Kirk, *The Architecture of Modern Italy*, vol. 1, *The Challenge of Tradition, 1750–1900* (New York: Princeton Architectural Press, 2005); Carroll L.V. Meeks, *Italian Architecture, 1750–1914* (New Haven, CT: Yale University Press, 1966); Corrado Maltese, *Storia dell'arte in Italia, 1785–1943* (Turin: Einaudi, 1960).

5 Overviews of the topic can be found in Franco Borsi, *L'architettura dell'unità d'Italia* (Florence: F. Le Monnier, 1966); Renato De Fusco, *L'architettura dell'Ottocento* (Milan: Garzanti, 1992); and Rosanna Pavoni, ed., *Reviving the Renaissance: The Use and Abuse of the Past in Nineteenth-Century Italian Art and Decoration* (New York: Cambridge University Press, 1997).

6 Maria Cristina Buscioni, *Esposizioni e "Stile Nazionale" (1861–1925). Il linguaggio dell'architettura nei padiglioni italiani delle grandi kermesses nazionali ed internazionali* (Florence: Alinea Editrice, 1990); Mariantonietta P. Petrusa, Maria R. Pessolano, and Assunta Bianco Di, *Le Grandi Esposizioni in Italia 1861–1911: La competizione culturale con l'Europa e la ricerca dello Stile Nazionale* (Naples: Liguori, 1988). Cristina Della Coletta, *World's Fairs Italian Style: The Great Expositions in Turin and Their Narratives, 1860–1915* (Toronto: University of Toronto Press, 2006).

7 See Guido Zucconi, "Gli anni dieci tra riscoperte regionali e aperture internazionali," in *Storia dell'architettura italiana – Il primo Novecento*, ed. Giorgio Ciucci and Giorgio Muratore (Milan: Electa, 2004), 38–55.

8 On national romanticism, see Barry Bergdoll, *European Architecture 1750–1890* (Oxford: Oxford University Press, 2000), esp. Part II, "Nationalism, Historicism, Technology," 137–279. Barbara Miller Lane, *National Roman-*

ticism and Modern Architecture in Germany and the Scandinavian Countries (New York: Cambridge University Press, 2000); Nicola Gordon Bowe, ed., *Art and the National Dream: The Search for Vernacular Expression in Turn-of-the-Century Design* (Dublin: Irish Academic Press, 1993).

9 Camillo Boito, "Rassegna Artistica – Spavento delle grandezze di Roma. – Bestemmia politica intorno al loro carattere. L'architettura romana d'oggi, che è sgomentata. – Ricerca vana di un suo stile futuro," *Nuova Antologia – Rivista di scienze, lettere ed arti* 30 (September 1875): 184–97. My translation. For an insightful overview of Boito's multifaceted contribution to Italy's cultural life, see Guido Zucconi, *L'invenzione del passato: Camillo Boito e l'architettura neomedievale, 1855–1890* (Venice: Marsilio, 1997). See also Guido Zucconi and Francesca Castellani, eds., *Camillo Boito: Un architettura per l'Italia unita* (Venice: Marsilio, 2000).

10 Camillo Boito, "Vienna – L'architettura all'esposizione universale,"in *Camillo Boito – Gite di un artista*, ed. Maria Cecilia Mazzi (Rome: De Luca Edizioni d'Arte, 1990), 147. My translation. Originally published in *Gite di un artista* (Milan: Hoepli, Editore, 1884), 139–67.

11 For a stimulating discussion on regionalism in Italian Renaissance architecture, see James S. Ackerman, "The Regions of Italian Renaissance Architecture," in *The Renaissance from Brunelleschi to Michelangelo: The Representation of Architecture*, ed. Henry A. Millon and Vittorio Magnago Lampugnani (Milan: Bompiani, 1994), 319–47.

12 Emilio Bodrero, "Discorso di S. E. Il Prof. Emilio Bodrero," *Atti del III Congresso Nazionale di Arti e Tradizioni Popolari – Trento – Settembre 1934 XII* (Rome: Edizioni dell'O.N.D. – Comitato Nazionale Italiano per le arti popolari, 1936), 29–31.

13 Giovanni Crocioni, *Le regioni e la cultura nazionale* (Catania: Francesco Battiato Editore, 1914); Giovanni Crocioni, *Problemi fondamentali del folklore. Con due lezioni su il folklore e il D'Annunzio* (Bologna: Nicola Zanichelli, 1928); Giovanni Crocioni, *Folklore e letteratura* (Florence: L.S. Olschki, 1954).

14 On Crocioni and his contribution to Italian regionalism and folklore studies, see Luigi Ambrosoli, Giuseppe Anceschi, Carlo Dionisotti, and Enzo Santarelli, *Il Regionalismo di Giovanni Crocioni* (Florence: L.S. Olschki, 1972).

15 Paolo D'Ancona, "Artigianato regionale e arte decorativa in Italia," *Nuova Antologia – Rivista di lettere, scienze ed arti* 56:1187 (September 1921): 64–72. The impulse to promote regional and municipal identity in the arts is evident in a number of magazines and journals that flourished during those years, such as *Alba Trentina*, *Augusta Praetoria*, *Illustrazione toscana e dell'Etruria*, and *La Rivista di Bergamo*.

16 The "Regio Decreto 8.9.1921, n. 1319." See also "Profilo storico," in Livio

Paladin, *Diritto regionale* (Padua: Cedam, 1979), 3–33; and Carl Levy, ed., *Italian Regionalism: History, Identity and Politics* (Oxford: Berg Publishers, 1996).

17 Emilio Sereni, *History of the Italian Agricultural Landscape*, trans. R. Burr Litchfield (Princeton, NJ: Princeton University Press, 1997); originally published as *Storia del paesaggio agrario italiano* (Bari: Laterza, 1961). See also Piero Bevilacqua, *Il paesaggio italiano nelle fotografie dell'Istituto Luce* (Rome: Editori Riuniti – Istituto Luce, 2002); Pierluigi De Verchi and Graziano Alfredo Vergani, eds., *La natura e il paesaggio nella pittura italiana* (Verona: Unicredito italiano, 2002); Fabrizio D'Amico and Walter Guadagnini, *L'invenzione del paessagio – Pittura italiana da Morandi a Schifano* (Milan: Mazzotta, 1995).

18 Gianna Piantoni, ed., *Roma 1911* (Rome: De Luca Editore, 1980). For a specific account of the architecture, see the chapter by Paolo Marconi, "Roma 1911: L'architettura romana tra italianismo carducciano e tentazione 'etnografica,'" 224–8. See also Maria Cristina Buscioni, Roma 1911: L'esposizione del Cinquantenario. "Esposizione regionale ed etnografica" e "Esposizione internazionale di belle arti," in Buscioni, ed., *Esposizioni e "stile nazionale" (1861–1925)*, 223–40.

19 See "1911: Le esposizioni e le feste commemorative," *Rivista Marittima* (March 1911): 3–15. My translation.

20 See Rossana Bossaglia, "The Protagonists of the Italian Movement," in Pamela Johnson, ed., *Stile Floreale*, Special Issue, *The Journal of Decorative and Propaganda Arts 1875–1945*, 13 (Summer 1989): 32–51; Rossana Bossaglia, *Il Liberty – Storia e fortuna del liberty italiano* (Florence: G.C. Sansoni, 1974); Lara-Vinca Masini, *Art Nouveau* (London: The Promotional Reprint Co., 1995), esp. 308–43. On the 1902 exhibition in Turin, see Rossana Bossaglia, Ezio Godoli, and Marco Rosci, eds., *La Nascita del Liberty – Torino 1902: Le arti decorative internazionali del nuovo secolo* (Milan: Fabbri Editori, 1994).

21 Richard A. Etlin, "Turin 1902: The Search for a Modern Italian Architecture," in Johnson, ed., *Stile Floreale*, 94–109.

22 Sandra Puccini, *L'itala gente dalle molte vite – Lamberto Loria e la Mostra di Etnografia del 1911* (Rome: Meltemi, 2005).

23 Loria founded Italy's first ethnography museum in Florence in 1906, following his travels to areas under Italian colonial rule in Africa such as Eritrea, where he photographed, amongst other things, the vernacular huts of the indigenous population. See Lamberto Loria and Aldobrandino Mochi, *Museo de etnografia italiana in Firenze – Sulla raccolta de materiali per la etnografia italiana* (Milan: U. Marucelli, 1906). On Loria's contribution of

Lamberto Loria to Italian ethnography, see Arturo Lancellotti, "Le collezioni di Lamberto Loria," in *Le mostre romane del cinquantenario* (Rome: Fratelli Palombi, 1931), 55–7; Francesco Baldasseroni, "Lamberto Loria," *Lares* 1 (1913): 1–16; Silvia Barberani, "Tracce di campo – Antropologia di Lamberto Loria," in *Etno-grafie: Testi, oggetti, immagini,* ed. Setrag Manoukian (Rome: Meltemi, 2003), 41–60; Susan Weber, *Etnie: La Scuola antropologica fiorentina e la fotografia tra '800 e '900* (Florence: Alinari, 1996).

24 Marcello Piacentini, *Le vicende edilizie di Roma dal 1870 ad oggi* (Rome: Palombi Editori, 1952).

25 For a complete history, see Stefania Massari, *Arti e Tradizioni – Il Museo Nazionale dell'EUR* (Rome: De Luca Editori D-Arte, 2004).

26 Paolo Toschi, *Guida al Museo Nazionale delle Arti e Tradizioni Popolari d'Arte* (Terri: Edizioni Alterocca, 1956). On the difficulties surrounding the realization of the museum, see Raffaele Corso, "Per il Museo di Etnografia Italiana," *Il folklore italiano* (March 1927): 298–300; Roberta Del Negro, *Spazio e Tradizione: Il museo etnografico in Italia, 1906–1956* (Venice: Istituto Universitario di Architettura di Venezia, 1995–6).

27 See Francesco Baldasseroni, *Catalogo della Mostra di Etnografia Italiana in Piazza d'Armi* (Bergamo: Istituto Italiano d'Arti Grafiche, 1911).

28 For an anthology of writings on the *trullo,* see Carla Speciale Giorgi and Paolo Speciale, *La cultura del trullo: Antologia di scritti letterari e scientifici sui trulli* (Brindisi: Schena editore, 1989); Edward Allen, *Stone Shelters* (Cambridge, MA: MIT Press, 1969.

29 For an overview on Skansen and a history of the open-air museum, see Sten Rentzhog, *Open Air Museums: The History and Future of a Visionary Idea* (Stockholm: Carlssons, 2007); Edward P. Alexander, "Arthur Hazelius and Skansen: The Open Air Museum," in *Museum Masters: Their Museums and Their Influence,* ed. Edward P. Alexander (Nashville, TN: American Association for State and Local History, 1983), 239–75; and Ralph Edenheim et al., *Skansen: Traditional Swedish Style* (London: Scala Books, 1995).

30 In Luigi Angelini's favourable review of the Mostra di Etnografia, he refers to remarks regarding the objections made by some (without specifying whom) regarding the artificiality of the ethnography site. Luigi Angelini, "I padiglioni e gli edifici dell'esposizione di Roma – I padiglioni delle regioni d'Italia," *Emporium – Rivista mensile illustrata d'arte – letteratura – scienza e varietà* 35:205 (January 1912): 17–35.

31 Erik Mattie, *World's Fairs* (New York: Princeton Architectural Press, 1998); Edward N. Kaufman, "The Architectural Museum from World's Fair to Restoration Village," *Assemblage* 9 (June 1989): 20–39.

32 Arduino Colasanti, "Il bilancio delle esposizioni di Roma," *Il Marzocco* 16:49 (December 1911): 2. My translation.

33 Francesco Baldasseroni, "Il Museo di Etnografia Italiana – Ordinamento per regioni o per categorie di oggetti?" *Lares* 1 (1912): 39–55.

34 On the concept of material life and the role of the peasant houses in Europe, see Fernand Braudel, *Capitalism and Material Life, 1400–1800*, trans. Miriam Kochan (New York: Harper Colophon Books, 1973), 197–9; originally published as *Civilisation matérielle et capitalisme* (Paris: A. Colin, 1967). See also George Kubler, *The Shape of Time: Remarks on the History of Things* (New Haven, CT: Yale University Press, 1962).

35 The schematic plan drawings of the ethnographic buildings are located in the archives of the Museo Nazionale delle Arti e Tradizioni Popolari in Rome. My thanks go to the museum director Dottoressa Stefania Massari and research associate and curator Dottoressa Marisa Iori for assisting me and granting me access to the museum archives.

36 Renato Biasutti, "Per lo studio dell'abitazione rurale in Italia," *Rivista Geografica Italiana* 33:1–2 (January–February 1926): 1–24. My translation. This article gives a succinct and in-depth account of the history of Italian studies on the rural dwelling, with an ample bibliography; it was republished in Società di studi geografici, ed., *Renato Biasutti: Scritti minori con elenco delle pubblicazioni (1899–1963)* (Florence: Società di studi geografici, 1980), 63–82. Biasutti pioneered studies on Italian vernacular dwellings by promoting a 1924 inquiry that led to the extensive research published in the thirty-volume series. He wrote the first volume in the series: Renato Biasutti, *La casa rurale nella Toscana* (Bologna: Nicola Zanichelli Editore, 1938). On Biasutti's contribution, see Lucio Gambi, "Renato Biasutti e la ricerca sopra le dimore rurali in Italia," in *La casa rurale in Italia*, ed. Giuseppe Barbieri and Lucio Gambi (Florence: L.S. Olschki Editore, 1970), 3–14.

37 Francesco Baldasseroni, "L'etnografia italiana all'esposizione di Roma," *Emporium* 34:202 (October 1911): 305–19. My translation.

38 Francesco Baldasseroni, *Esposizione Internazionale di Roma 1911: Catalogo della Mostra di Etnografia Italiana in Piazza d'Armi* (Bergamo: Istituto Italiano d'Arti Grafiche, 1911), 5. Baldasseroni refers to *"popolo,"* which in my translation I have rendered as the "people," and *"arte popolare,"* which I take to mean vernacular art and architecture. My translation.

39 David Atkinson and Denis Cosgrove, "Urban Rhetoric and Embodied Identities: City Nation, and Empire at the Vittorio Emanuele II Monument in Rome, 1870–1945," *Annals of the Association of American Geographers* 88:1 (March 1998): 29–49. See Bruno Tobia, *L'altare della patria* (Bologna: Il Mulino, 1998).

40 On the work of Curri, see Fabio Mangone, ed., *Antonio Curri: Un architetto artista tra Alberobello e Napoli* (Naples: Electa, 1999). On Ongaro, see Liliana

Vazzoler, "Max Ongaro nella Venezia dei primi del '900" (Student thesis, Istituto Universitario di Architettura di Venezia, 1995–6).

41 Baldasseroni, "L'etnografia italiana all'esposizione di Roma," 308. My translation.

42 Angelini, "I padiglioni e gli edifici dell'esposizione di Roma – I padiglioni delle regioni d'Italia," 35. My translation. Luigi Angelini published a number of studies on the topic of vernacular buildings and objects. For a complete bibliography of his writings, see Piervaleriano Angelini, ed., *Luigi Angelini tra libri, riviste e giornali: Pubblicazioni 1905–1969 e bibliografia su Luigi Angelini* (Bergamo: Edizioni dell'Ateneo, 1999).

43 Walter Barbero, Giuseppe Gambirasio, and Vanni Zanella, eds., *Luigi Angelini – Ingegnere architetto* (Milan: Electa, 1984), esp. Enrico Guidoni, "Ambiente, architettura, arte popolare nell'opera del disegnatore dal vero," 140–3. Guidoni includes a list of texts that Angelini collected as part of his personal library on vernacular traditions. See also Enrico Guidoni, *L'architettura popolare italiana* (Rome: Laterza, 1980).

44 Robert L. Herbert, "Peasants and 'Primitivism,'" *From Millet to Léger: Essays in Social Art History* (New Haven, CT: Yale University Press, 2002), 49–65; E.H. Gombrich, *The Preference for the Primitive: Episodes in the History of Western Taste and Art* (London: Phaidon, 2002); Jack Flam and Miriam Deutch, eds., *Primitivism and Twentieth-Century Art: A Documentary History* (Berkeley: University of California Press, 2003); Robert Goldwater, *Primitivism in Modern Art* (Cambridge, MA: The Belknap Press of Harvard University Press, 1938).

45 Eric J. Hobsbawm, *Primitive Rebels: Studies in Archaic Forms of Social Movements in the Nineteenth and Twentieth Centuries* (Manchester: Manchester University Press, 1959); Eric J. Hobsbawm, "Peasants and Politics," in Eric J. Hobsbawn, *Uncommon People: Resistance, Rebellion, and Jazz* (New York: The New Press, 1998), 146–65.

46 Sally Price, *Primitive Art in Civilized Places* (Chicago: University of Chicago Press, 1989); Ivan Karp and Steven D. Lavine, *Exhibiting Cultures: The Poetics and Politics of Museum Display* (Washington, DC: Smithsonian Institution Press, 1991); Patricia A. Morton, *Hybrid Modernities: Architecture and Representation at the 1931 Colonial Exposition, Paris* (Cambridge, MA: MIT Press, 2000).

47 See Gauguin's comments on the Javanese village at the 1889 Universal Exhibition in Herschel B. Chipp, *Theories of Modern Art: A Source Book by Artists and Critics* (Berkeley: University of California Press, 1968), 78. For his collected writings, see Daniel Guérin, *Paul Gauguin: The Writings of a Savage* (New York: Viking Press, 1978), and Paul Gauguin, *Noa Noa: The*

Tahitian Journal of Paul Gauguin, trans. O.F. Theis (San Francisco: Chronicle Books, 1994).

48 Jean-Jacques Rousseau, *The First and Second Discourses*, trans. Roger D. and Judith R. Masters, with intro. and notes by Roger D. Masters (New York: St. Martin's Press, 1964), 37. Published in French as *Sur les Sciences et les arts: Premier discours, Préface au Narcisse Fiction*, with commentary by Gérald Allard (Sainte-Foy, QC: Éditions Le Griffon d argile, 1988), 11.

49 Petra ten-Doesschate Chu, ed. and trans., *Letters of Gustave Courbet* (Chicago: University of Chicago Press, 1992), 98–9.

50 Alexandre Labat, "Charles Garnier et L'Exposition de 1889. L'Histoire de L'Habitation," in *1889. La Tour Eiffel et L'exposition universelle*, ed. Renaud Piérard (Paris: Editions de la Réunion des Musées Nationaux, 1989), 130–61.

51 On Viollet-le-Duc and vernacular architecture, see Jacques Gubler, "Viollet-le-Duc et l'architecture rurale," in *Viollet-le-Duc Centenaire de la la mort à Lausanne*, ed. Jacques Gubler (Lausanne: Musée historique de l'Ancien-Evêché, 1979), 111–20; "Le programme ideal d'Eugene Viollet-le-Duc," in *Architectures de la vie privée: maisons et mentalités, XVIIe-XIXe siècles*, ed. Monique Eleb-Vidal and Anne Debarre-Blanchard (Brussels: Archives d'architecture moderne, 1989), 111–17.

52 For the first Italian translation of Viollet-le-Duc's history, see Viollet-le-Duc, *Storia dell'abitazione umana dai tempi preistorici fino ai nostri giorni*, (Milan: Tipografica Ed. Lombarda, 1877); Charles Garnier and Auguste Ammann, trans. Alfredo Melani, *L'abitazione umana* (Milan: Pubblicazione del Corriere della Sera, 1893).

53 See Maria Luisa Scalvini and Fabio Mangone, eds., *Alfredo Melani e l'architettura moderna in Italia – Antologia critica (1882–1910)* (Rome: Officina Edizioni, 1998).

54 On the storied history of the Roman countryside, see the comprehensive multivolume work of Giuseppe Tomassetti, *La campagna Romana antica, medioevale e moderna* (Rome: E. Loescher & C., 1910–26; reprint ed., Florence: L.S. Olschi, 1979–1980); Piero Becchetti, ed., *Immagini della campagna romana, 1853–1915* (Rome: Edizioni Quasar, 1983); Pier Andrea De Rosa and Paolo Emilio Trastulli, eds., *La campagna romana da Hackert a Balla* (Rome: Studio Ottocento – De Luca, 2001).

55 Giuseppe Pitrè, *Catalogo illustrato della mostra etnografica siciliana* (Palermo: Stabilimento Tipografico Virzì, 1892); Giuseppe Pitrè, *La famiglia, la casa, la vita del popolo siciliano* (Palermo: Libreria Internazionale A. Reber, 1913); Giuseppe Cocchiara, *La vita e l'arte del popolo Siciliano nel museo Pitrè* (Palermo: F. Ciuni Libraio Editore, 1938); Pasqualina Manzo, *Storia e folklore*

nell opera museografica di Giuseppe Pitrè (Frattamaggiore: Edizioni Istituo de Studi atellani, 1999).

56 Paolo Portoghesi et al., *Ernesto Basile Architetto* (Venice: Edizioni "La Biennale di Venezia," 1980); Ettore Sessa, *Ernesto Basile: Dall'Eclettismo Classicista al Modernismo* (Palermo: Novecento, 2002); Umberto di Cristina and Benito Li Vigni, eds., *La esposizione nazionale 1891–1892* (Palermo: Novecento, 1988), esp. "Il progetto di Ernesto Basile," 61–86.

57 The ethnographic collections of Africa that where shown were collected by Conte Antonelli, Dott. Traversici, and others. See *Esposizione nazionale, Palermo, 1891–1892, Catalogo generale* (Palermo: Virzì, 1892; reprint ed., Palermo: Accademia nazionale di scienze, lettere e arti già del buon gusto, 1991).

58 di Cristina and Li Vigni, *Palermo e le esposizione nazionale 1891–1892* 15 (1892), 1A.

59 Girolamo Ragusa-Moleti, "La mostra etnografica (Pt. 2)," *Palermo e l'Esposizione nazionale del 1891–92* 26 (1892): 203–6. My translation. See also Girolamo Ragusa-Moleti, "La mostra etnografica (Pt. 1)," *Palermo e l'Esposizione nazionale del 1891–92* 25 (1892): 193–4; Girolamo Ragusa-Moleti, *La poesia dei selvaggi* (Naples: Luigi Chiurazzi, 1897); see also Giuseppe Pipitone-Federico, "La mostra etnografica all'Esposizione Nazionale di Palermo," *Natura ed Arte – Rassegna Quindicinale Illustrata Italiana e Straniera di Scienze, Lettere ed Arti,* 19 (1 September 1892): 650–5; 20 (15 September 1892): 762–7; and 21 (1 October 1892): 845–52.

60 Italo Calvino, Introduction to *Italian Folktales Selected and Retold by Italo Calvino,* trans. George Martin (New York: Harcourt, Brace, Jovanovich, 1980), xv–xxxii; originally published as Italo Calvino, *Fiabe italiane: raccolte dalla tradizione popolare durante gli ultimi cento anni e trascritte in lingua dai vari dialetti* (Turin: Einaudi, 1956). A selection of Pitrè's work translated into English can be found in the recently published collection by Jack Zipes and Joseph Russo, eds., *The Collected Sicilian Folk and Fairy Tales of Giuseppe Pitrè* (New York: Routledge, 2009).

61 Giovanni Verga, *Cavalleria rusticana and Other Stories* (London: Penguin Books, 1999). This edition includes short stories published in both *Vita dei campi* (1880) and *Novelle rusticane* (1893). See also Giovanni Verga, *Life in the Country* (London: Hesperus, 2003). On Balzac's influence in Italy, see Giuseppe Gigli, *Balzac in Italia: Contributo alla biografia di Onorato di Balzac* (Milan: Fratelli Treves Editori, 1920).

62 Verga, *Cavalleria Rusticana and Other Stories* 27–33.

63 Aristide Baragiola, "Sulla casa villereccia," *Atti del Primo Congresso di Etnografia italiana,* ed. Società di etnografia italiana (Perugia: Unione tipografica cooperativa, 1912): 115–19; see Aristide Baragiola, *La casa villereccia*

delle colonie tedesche Veneto-Tridentine (Bergamo: Istituto Italiano D'Arte
Grafiche Editore, 1908) and Aristide Baragiola, *La casa villereccia delle colo-
nie tedesche del gruppo carnico, Sappada, Sauris e Timau* (Chiasso: Tipografia
Tettamanti, 1915). On Baragiola's contribution to vernacular studies, see
Patrizio Paganin, "Aristide Baragiola – Un piccolo Ulisse sulle Alpi,"
L'Alpe 12 (2006): 20–7.

64 Sidney John Alexander Churchill, "Introductory Note," in *Peasant Art in
Italy*, ed. Charles Holme (London: The Studio, 1913), 1–8. Charles Holme
(1848–1923) published a number of studies on peasant art on behalf of
the influential publisher The Studio, and was instrumental in promoting
peasant art of numerous countries throughout the 1910s and 1920s. These
include *Peasant Art in Sweden, Lapland and Iceland* (London: The Studio,
1910); *Peasant Art in Austria and Hungary* (London: The Studio, 1911); and
Peasant Art in Russia (London: The Studio, 1912). Even after Holme's death
in 1923, The Studio continued to publish sole-authored studies on the
topic, including Daniel Baud-Bovy, *Peasant Art in Switzerland* (London: The
Studio, 1924) and George Oprescu, *Peasant Art in Roumania* (London: The
Studio, 1929).

65 One could recall a similar phenomenon in America recounted by Leo Marx
in his study *The Machine in the Garden: Technology and the Pastoral Ideal in
America* (New York: Oxford University Press, 1967).

66 Guido Bogretti, "La prima 'rivista' del Touring," *Le vie d'Italia*, 36:1 (January 1930): 1–3.

67 Leonardo di Mauro, "L'Italia e le guide artistiche dall'Unità ad oggi," in
Storia d'Italia, Annali 5. Il Paesaggio, ed. Cesare De Seta (Turin: Einaudi,
1982), 369–428; Stefano Pivato, *Il Touring Club Italiano* (Bologna: Il Mulino,
2006).

68 *L'opera del Club Alpino Italiano nel primo suo cinquantennio: 1863–1913* (Turin:
Officine Grafiche della S.T.E.N., 1913), 91–103.

69 Marco Pozzetto, *Max Fabiani* (Trieste: MGS Press, 1998).

70 On Cambellotti, see Irene De Guttry, "Cambellotti architetto," in *Cambel-
lotti (1876–1960)*, ed. Giovanna Bonasegale, Anna Maria Damigella, and
Bruno Mantura (Rome: Edizioni De Luca, 2000), 39–42; see also Mario
Quesada, *Duilio Cambellotti, L'artista-artigiano negli scritti critici di Mario
Quesada* (Rome: Galleria Carlo Virgilio, 1998); Irene de Guttry, Maria Paola
Maino, and Gloria Raimondi, *Duilio Cambellotti: Arredi e decorazioni* (Rome:
Laterza, 2000); Eleonora Bairati, Rossana Bossaglia, and Marco Rosci,
L'Italia Liberty – Arredamento e arti decorative (Milan: Görlich Editore, 1973);
see, in particular, Marco Rosci, "Populismo e mito nell 'artigiano' Cambel-
lotti," 204–13.

71 Duilio Cambellotti, "La campagna romana ante bonifica," in *Duilio Cambellotti – Teatro – Storia – Arte*, ed. Mario Quesada (Palermo: Edizioni Novecento, 1982), 211. My translation. See also Mario Quasada, ed., *Natura e forma – La campagna romana e la palude pontina nell'opera di Duilio Cambellotti (1876–1960)* (Rome: Regione Lazio, 2004).

72 On Cambellotti's primitivism and contribution to the 1911 Roman celebrations, see Sabrina Spinazzé, "Cambellotti e la Mostra dell'Agro romano del 1911: Alle Radici dell'Espressione Artistica, tra Impegno Sociale e Primitivismo," in *Il Museo Duilio Cambellotti a Latina: Opere scelte dalla collezione* ed. Francesco Tetro (Rome: Palombi Editori, 2002), 118–32; "La Mostra dell'Agro Romano," De Guttry, Maino, and Raimondi, *Duilio Cambellotti: Arredi e decorazioni*, 22–4; Nicoletta Cardano, "La mostra dell'agro romano," *Roma 1911*, ed. Gianna Piantoni (Rome: De Luca Editore, 1980), 178–97.

73 Following the 1911 exhibition, Cambellotti designed several schools in collaboration with Cena and Marcucci as part of humanitarian initiatives aimed at providing basic education for the peasant children of the Agro Romano. See Vittorio Morpurgo, "Gli edifici scolastici e la Minerva," *Architettura e arti decorative* 1:2 (November–December 1921): 357–74; Mario De Angelis-Egidi, "Edilizia scolastica rurale," *Architettura e arti decorative* (December 1931): 853–64; Giovanna Alatri, "Le Scuole per i contadini dell'Agro romano," in *Le Capitali d'Italia – Torino – Roma – Arti – Produzione – Spettacolo*, ed. Marisa Vescovo and Netta Vespignani (Milan: Electa, 1997), 111–18; Alessando Marcucci, *La scuola di Giovanni Cena* (Turin: Paravia, 1948).

74 Lancellotti recounts his experience of viewing Balla's relief paintings in Arturo Lancellotti, *Le mostre romane del cinquantenario* (Rome: Palombi Editore, 1931), 50. Balla's daughter Elica recounted that "for this series of paintings Balla prepared a series of cartoons on which he spread red paint mixed with sand. With this use of materials he wanted to obtain the airy feeling of open-air paint ... These twelve paintings were displayed on the walls of the beautiful hut." Elica Balla, *Con Balla*, vol. 1 (Milan: Multhipla Edizioni, 1984), 224.

75 Anna Maria Damigella, "Idealismo e socialismo nella cultura figurative romana del primo '900: Duilio Cambellotti," *Cronache di archeologia e di storia dell'arte* 8 (1969): 119–73; Cecilia De Carli Sciumè, "Tematiche sociali nell'architettura," in *Arte e socialità in Italia: Dal Realismo al Simbolismo, 1865–1915*, ed. Rossana Bossaglia (Milan: La Società per le Belle Arti ed Esposizione Permanente, 1979), 591–601.

76 Leone Tolstoi, *Che cosa e l'arte?* (Milan: Fratelli Treves, 1900), 61–2. See the

English translation, *What Is Art?*, trans. Richard Pevear (London: Penguin Books, 1995), 41.

77 See John Russell Taylor, "Il divisionismo italiano," *L'Età del Divisionismo*, ed. Gabriella Belli and Franco Rella (Milan: Electa, 1990), 104–11; Renato Miracco, *Painting Light: Italian Divisionism, 1885–1910* (Milan: Mazzotta, 2003); and Vivien Greene, *Arcadia & Anarchy: Divisionism – Neo-Impressionism* (New York: Guggenheim Museum, 2007).

78 Gabriele D'Annunzio, *La figlia di Iorio – Tragedia pastorale in tre atti* (Milan: Fratelli Treves, 1902); Annamaria Andreoli, ed., *La figlia di Iorio, cent'anni di passione* (Rome: De Luca Editori d'Arte, 2004).

79 Gabriele D'Annunzio, *The Daughter of Jorio: A Pastoral Tragedy*, trans. Charlotte Porter, Pietro Isola, and Alice Henry (1907; reprint, New York: Greenwood Press, 1968), xi.

80 Piero Pacini, ed., *Galileo Chini: 1873–1956* (Florence: Pagnini and Martinelli, 2003). On the history of the poster in Italy, see Luigi Menegazzi, *Il manifesto italiano* (Milan: Arnoldo Mondadori Arte, 1989).

81 Manfredi Nicoletti, *L'architettura liberty in Italia* (Rome: Laterza, 1978), 344–6.

82 Arduino Colasanti, "Atti di amministrazione, Circolare n. 13, Raccolta di elementi decorative italiani di arte paesana," *Bollettino Ufficiale del Ministero Dell'Istruzione Pubblica* 1:6 (5 February 1920): 157–9.

83 Some time after its publication, an article in *Il folklore italiano*, the journal edited by Raffaele Corso, vehemently attacked Colasanti on the basis that the former had plagarized the text of his "Circolare" from *Catalogo della Mostra di Etnografia Italiana in Piazza d'Armi* (Bergamo: Istituto Italiano d'Arti Grafiche, 1911) by Francesco Baldasseroni. Though the article is not signed, it is likely by Corso; see "L'arte rustica e un articolo di Arduino Colasanti," *Il Folklore Italiano, Archivio per la raccolta e lo studio delle tradizioni popolari italiane* 1:1 (March 1925): 123–5.

84 Arduino Colasanti, "Una circolare della Direzione generale di Belle Arti," *La Fionda* 1 (August 1920): 55–7.

85 This quote is taken from Adolfo De Carolis, "L'arte popolare," *La Fionda* 1 (August 1920): 21; my translation; Adolfo de Carolis, "Arte tessile popolare I," *La Fionda* 6:7 (January–February 1921): 11–16. See also Adolfo de Carolis, "Arte tessile popolare. II," *La Fionda* 12–15 (July–October 1921): 209–13.

86 On D'Annunzio and his interest in folk traditions, see Giovanni Crocioni, *Problemi fondamentali del folkore – Con due lezioni su il folkore e il D'Annunzio* (Bologna: Nicola Zanichelli, 1928), 61–159; Paolo Toschi, "D'Annunzio e le tradizioni popolari," *L'Italia che scrive* 9–10 (September–October 1964): 177–8. See "D'Annunzio e l'arte popolare italiana (1920–1930)," in Alessia

Lenzi, *Adolfo De Carolis e il suo mondo (1892–1928). L'arte e la cultura attraverso i carteggi De Carolis, D'Annunzio, Maraini, Ojetti* (Ravagni: I.T.E.A. Editrice, 1999), 139–51.

87 Guido Tucci, ed., *Adolfo De Carolis: Xilografo e Illustratore* (Bologna: Sintesi, 1992).

88 Peg Weiss, *Kandinsky and Old Russia: The Artist as Ethnographer and Shaman* (New Haven, CT: Yale University Press, 1995); Doris Howard, "Kazimir Malevich's Paintings of Peasant Subjects" (MA thesis, Indiana University, 2004).

2. The Picturesque Revival

1 Gustavo Giovannoni, "Arte nuova ed arte popolare," *Bollettino della Società degli Ingegneri e degli Architetti Italiani* 12:20 (15 May 1904): 585–9. My translation.

2 Marcello Piacentini, "Arte artistocratica ed arte paesana," *La Tribuna* (3 April 1920): 3. My translation.

3 See *Catalogo illustrato – Prima biennale romana – Esposizione nazionale di belle arti nel cinquantenario della capitale Roma MCMXII* (Milan: Casa d'arte Bestetti and Tumminelli, 1921), 200–2.

4 Paolo Nicoloso, *Gli architetti di Mussolini – scuole e sindacato, architetti e massoni, professori e politici negli anni del regime* (Milan: Franco Angeli, 1999), esp. "Una scuola per l'architettura della nazione," 23–49.

5 Associazione artistica fra i cultori di architettura in *Architettura minore in Italia, Roma*, vol. 1 and vol. 2 (Turin: Società Italiana Edizioni Artistiche C. Crudo, 1926; reprint ed., Rome: Colombo Editore, 1990).

6 "Programma dell'opera," *Architettura minore in Italia, Roma*, vol. 1, i. My translation.

7 On the Associazione, see Elisabetta Pallottino, "I membri dell'Associazione artistica fra i cultori di architettura e la cultura tecnica romana tra la fine dell'Ottocento e i primi decenni del Novecento – Appunti per una ricerca," *Bollettino del Centro di Studi per la Storia dell'Architettura* 36 (1990): 67–8.

8 Centro nazionale di studi di storia dell'architettura, *Architettura minore in Italia, Lazio e suburbio di Roma*, vol. 3 (Rome: Max Bretschneider, 1940). Reviewed by Guglielmo De Angelis D'Ossat, "Bibliografia," *Palladio – Rivista bimestrale del centro nazionale di studi per la storia dell'architettura* 4 (1940): 89–91.

9 The relation between photography and architecture is the subject of Lindsay Harris's dissertation entitled "Reframing the Vernacular: Photography, Architecture and the Construction of Italian Modernism, 1911–1936" (PhD

dissertation, Institute of Fine Arts, New York University, in progress). On photography in Italy, see Italo Zannier, *Storia della fotografia italiana* (Rome: Laterza, 1986); Giovanni Fanelli and Barbara Mazza, *Storia della fotografia dell architettura* (Rome: Laterza, 2009). On photography and the Associazione, see Paolo Constantini, "Associazioni artistiche e raccolte fotografiche," in *Bollettino del Centro di Studi per la Storia dell'Architettura* 36 (1990): 75–7.

10 The designation "Scuola Romana" was introduced by Edgardo Negri at the First National Congress of Roman Studies; see his account in *Associazione artistica fra i cultori di architettura, Annuario, 1925–1928* (Rome: Tipografia Cooperativa Sociale, 1929), 7–14. For a history of the school, see Vittorio Franchetti Pardo, ed., *La Facoltà di architettura dell'università di Roma "La Sapienza" dalle origini al duemila – Discipline, docenti, studenti* (Rome: Gangemi Editore, 2001).

11 Duilio Cambellotti uses this expression to describe the marshlands surrounding Rome before they were reclaimed under the fascist regime. Duilio Cambellotti, "La campagna romana ante bonifica," in *Duilio Cambellotti – Teatro – Storia – Arte,* ed. Mario Quesada (Palermo: Edizioni Novecento, 1982), 211.

12 Ercole Metalli, *Usi e costumi della campagna romana – Seconda edizione riveduta e notevolmente ampliata con disegni orginali di Duilio Cambellotti* (Rome: Tipografia della Reale Accademic Nazionale dei Lincei, 1924; reprint ed., Rome: Edizioni NER, 1982).

13 Giulio Ferrari, *L'architettura rusticana nell'arte italiana – Dalle capanne alla casa medievale* (Milan: Hoepli Editore, 1925; reprint ed., Nendeln: Kraus Reprints, 1973).

14 Reviewed favourably by Gustavo Giovannoni, "Architettura minore di Roma e del Lazio," *Roma – Rivista di Studi e di Vita Romana* 18:7 (July 1940): 232–6.

15 See Giulio Ferrari, *Museo Artistico Industriale di Roma – Catalogo delle collezioni* (Rome: Bodoni, 1906); Luigi Serra, *Il Regio Museo artistico industriale di Roma* (Rome: La Libreria dello Stato, 1934); Vincenzo Golzio, *Il Regio museo artistico industriale di Roma* (Florence: Le Monnier, 1942); Maria Rita di Mino, ed., *Del M.A.I.: Storia del Museo artistico industriale di Roma* (Rome: Istituto Centrale per il Catalogo e la Documentazione, 2005).

16 Renato Biasutti, "Per lo studio dell'abitazione rurale in Italia," *Rivista Geografica Italiana* 33:1–2 (January–February 1926): 1–24. My translation. Republished in Società di studi geografici, ed., *Renato Biasutti – Scritti minori con elenco delle publicazioni (1899–1963)* (Florence: Società di studi geografici, 1980), 63–82.

17 In an article Biasutti published some twenty years later, he added the following names to this list, thus demonstrating the continued interest in the
subject matter: Giuseppe Pagano, Mario Tinti, Roberto Pane, Vincenzo
Fasolo, Luigi Epifanio, and Giuseppe Ciribini. Renato Biasutti, "Orientamento ed organizzazione delle ricerche sull'abitato e l'architettura rurale
in Italia," *La ricerca scientifica* 18 (October 1948): 1235–42.

18 Antonio Maraini, "L'architettura rustica alla cinquantenale romana," *Architettura e arti decorative* 1:4 (November–December 1921): 379–85.

19 Ibid., 379. My translation.

20 See Raffele Corso, "Il volto di Napoleone: L'arte rustica alla Prima Biennale Romana," *La Fionda* 10:11 (May–June 1921): 189–91.

21 See Arturo Lancellotti, *La prima biennale romana d'arte, 1921* (Rome: Edizio-
ni la Fiamma, 1922), 59–60. On the Roman biennales, see Federica Pirani,
"Le biennali romane," in *Il palazzo delle Esposizioni,* ed. Rosella Siligato and
Maria Elisi Tittoni (Rome: Edizioni Carte Segrete, 1990), 183–97.

22 On Piacentini's early career, "La prima stagione," see Mario Lupano, *Marcello Piacentini* (Rome: Laterza, 1991), in chap. 2, 25–72.

23 "Villa Nobili al quartiere dei Parioli in Roma," *L'architettura italiana* 14
(February 1919), 12–16. On Piacentini's early career and the Villa Nobili, see
Arianna Sara De Rose, *Marcello Piacentini, Opere 1903–1923* (Modena: Franco Cosimo Panini, 1995), 137–8. On the *casale,* see Carla Tagliaferri, *I casali
della campagna romana* (Rome: Pieraldo Editore and Regione Lazio, 1991).

24 Bruno Zevi, "Marcello Piacentini: Morì nel 1925," *L'architettura, cronache
e storia* 6/4 (August 1960), 220; republished in Bruno Zevi, *Cronache di architettura,* vol. 3 (Bari: Laterza, 1971), 541–3.

25 Benito Mussolini, "Arte e civiltà," in *Opera omnia di Benito Mussolini,* ed.
Edoardo and Duilio Susmel, vol. 22 (Florence: La Fenice, 1957), 230.

26 Marcello Piacentini, "Influssi d'Arte Italiana nel Nord America," *Architettura e arti decorative* 1:6 (March–April 1922): 536–55; republished without
the original thirty illustrations in Mario Pisani, ed., *Marcello Piacentini:
Architettura moderna* (Venice: Marsilio Editori, 1996), 110–12.

27 Piacentini, "Influssi d'Arte Italiana nel Nord America," 536–7. My translation.

28 See, for example, Austin Whittlesey, *The Minor Ecclesiastical, Domestic,
and Garden Architecture of Southern Spain* (New York: Architectural Book
Publishing Company, 1917); Winsor Soule, *Spanish Farm Houses and Minor Public Buildings* (New York: Architectural Book Publishing Company,
1923); Arthur Byne and Mildred Stapley, *Provincial Houses in Spain* (New
York: H. Helburn, 1925); and Samuel Chamberlain *Domestic Architecture in
Rural France* (New York: Architectural Publishing Company, 1928). All of

these publications fuelled a substantial romance with the Mediterranean in America, especially on the West and East Coasts, which lasted from the 1920s well into the 1940s. See David Gebhard, "The Mediterranean Villa in America: Three Episodes," in *Ah Mediterranean! Twentieth Century Classicism in America*, vol. 2, ed. Charles W. Moore and Wayne Attoe (New York: Rizzoli, 1986), 41–50; Beth Dunlop, "Inventing Antiquity: The Art and Craft of Mediterranean Revival Architecture," *Journal of Decorative and Propaganda Arts 1875–1945* 23 (May 1998): 190–207; Marc Appleton, *California Mediterranean* (New York: Rizzoli, 2007).

29 Piacentini, "Influssi d'Arte Italiana nel Nord America," 537–8. My translation.

30 Gustavo Giovannoni, "Arte nuova ed arte popolare," *Bollettino della Società degli ingegneri e degli Architetti Italiani* 12:20 (May 1904): 585–9; and "Vecchie città ed edilizia nuova," *Nuova Antologia di lettere, scienze ed arti* 5 (May–June 1913): 449–72.

31 Gustavo Giovannoni, *Vecchie città ed edilizia nuova* (Turin: UTET, 1931); it was republished as Francesco Ventura, ed., *Gustavo Giovannoni: Vecchie città ed edilizia nuova* (Milan: Città Studi Edizioni, 1995); then published in French with an introduction by Françoise Choay as *L'urbanisme face aux villes anciennes*, trans. Jean-Marc Mandosio, Amélie Petita, and Claire Tandille (Paris: Editions du Seuil, 1998).

32 Published as Marcello Piacentini, "Nuovi orizzonti dell'edilizia cittadina," *Nuova Antologia* 57:1199 (March 1922): 60–72; partially reprinted in Giorgio Ciucci and Francesco Dal Co, eds., *Architettura italiana del '900* (Milan: Electa, 1993), 91–2.

33 Piacentini, "Nuovi orizzonti dell'edilizia cittadina," 65. My translation.

34 Quoted in David Gebhard, *George Washington Smith, 1876–1930: The Spanish Colonial Revival in California* (Santa Barbara, CA: Santa Barbara Art Gallery, 1964), n.p. See also David Gebhard, "The Spanish Colonial Revival in Southern California (1895–1930)," *Journal of the Society of Architectural Historians* 26:2 (1967): 131–47; Marc Appleton, ed., *George Washington Smith: An Architect's Scrapbook* (Los Angeles: Tailwater Press, 2001); Patricia Gebhard, *George Washington Smith: Architect of the Spanish Colonial Revival* (Salt Lake City: Gibbs Smith, 2005).

35 Carlo Enrico Rava, "Spirito Latino," *Domus* 38 (February 1931): 24–9; Carlo Enrico Rava, "Giovani architetti nordamericani," *Domus* 43 (July 1931): 33–6. Both articles were republished in Carlo Enrico Rava, *Nove anni di architettura vissuta, 1926 IV–1935 XIII* (Rome: Cremonese, 1935), 85–97 and 113–15, respectively.

36 Both the catalogue of the 1911 exhibition written by Francesco Baldasse-

roni and *Peasant Art in Italy* (1913) edited by Charles Holme gave cursory treatments of peasant architecture which was seen in holistic terms in relationship to the domestic realm in which arts and crafts also played an important and complementary role. See Camillo Jona, *L'architettura rusticana in Valle D'Aosta* (Turin: Società di edizioni artistiche C. Crudo & C., 1920); and Camillo Jona, *L'architettura rusticana nella costiera d'Amalfi* (Turin: Società di edizioni artistiche C. Crudo & C., 1920).

37 Lowell was a Harvard graduate and Diplomé of the Ecole des Beaux-Arts. His achievements include Boston's Museum of Fine Arts (1907–15), Emerson Memorial Hall and Lowell House on the Harvard campus, as well as the Carrie Memorial Tower at Brown University. Despite the significant output of this architect, there is surprisingly little scholarship on him. See the entry by Marjorie Pearson on "Guy Lowell," in *MacMillan Encyclopedia of Architects*, vol. 3, ed. Adolf K. Placzek (New York: The Free Press, 1982), 34–5.

38 Guy Lowell, *Smaller Italian Villas and Farmhouses* (New York: The Architectural Book Publishing Co., 1916;reprint ed., New York: The Architectural Book Publishing Co., 1922); Guy Lowell, *More Small Italian Villas and Farmhouses* (New York: The Architectural Book Publishing Co., 1920).

39 Cited in Biasutti, "Per lo studio dell'abitazione rurale in Italia."

40 Anne Blecksmith, "'Raccolte di vedute': Early Twentieth Century Architects' Books and the Making of a Landscape for California," *Art Documentation* 21:2 (November 2002): 14–17.

41 Elsewhere, in North America, during those same years, Eric Arthur, the architect and historian trained in Liverpool under Charles Reilly, was using "small" as the adjective to describe the local vernacular of the province of Ontario, Canada. See Eric Ross Arthur, *Small Houses of the Late Eighteenth and Early Nineteenth Century in Ontario* (Toronto: University of Toronto Press, 1926). On Arthur, see Michelangelo Sabatino, "Eric Arthur: Practical Visions," *Journal of the Society for the Study of Architecture in Canada* 26:1–2 (December 2001): 33–42.

42 Katharine Hooker and Myron Hunt, *Farmhouses and Small Provincial Buildings in Southern Italy* (New York: Architectural Book Publishing Co., 1925). On Myron Hunt's work, see *The Search for a Regional Architecture* (Santa Monica, CA: Hennessey and Ingalls, 1984).

43 Rexford Newcomb, *Mediterranean Domestic Architecture in the United States* (Cleveland: J.H. Jansen, 1928; reprint ed. with new introduction by Marc Appleton, New York: Acanthus Press, 1999); Rexford Newcomb, *Spanish-Colonial Architecture in the United States* (New York: Augustin, 1937; reprint ed. New York: Dover, 1990); Rexford Newcomb, "On Regionalism in

American Architecture," in Merrill Jensen, *Regionalism in America* (Madison: University of Wisconsin Press, 1965), 273–95. Recently reprinted in Vincent Canizaro, ed., *Architectural Regionalism: Collected Writings on Place, Identity, Modernity, and Tradition* (New York: Princeton Architectural Press, 2007), 80–95.

44 Whittlesey, *The Minor Ecclesiastical, Domestic, and Garden Architecture of Southern Spain*; Baxter Sylvester, *Spanish-Colonial Architecture in Mexico* (Boston: J. B. Millet, 1901); Bertram Grosvenor Goodhue, *Mexican Memories: The Record of a Slight Sojourn Below the Yellow Rio Grande* (New York: G.M. Allen, 1892). On Goodhue's architecture, see Romy Wyllie, *Bertram Goodhue: His Life and Residential Architecture* (New York: W.W. Norton, 2007).

45 Addison Mizner, *Florida Architecture of Addison Mizner* (New York: William Helburn, 1928; reprint ed. with introduction by Donald Curl, New York: Dover Publications, 1992); Donald Curl, *Mizner's Florida* (New York: The Architectural History Foundation and Cambridge, MA: MIT Press, 1984); Roberto M. Behar and Maurice G. Culot, eds., *Coral Gables: An American Garden City* (Paris: Norma Editions, 1997).

46 Gustavo Giovannoni, "Resoconto Morale per l'anno 1911," *Associazione Artistica fra i cultori di architettura, Annuario – Roma dall'anno XXI–MCMXI – All'anno XXV–MCMXV* (Rome: Tipografia Innocenzo Artero, 1916), 3. My translation. For an anthology of Giovannoni's writings, see Guido Zucconi, ed., *Gustavo Giovannoni: Dal Capitello alla Città* (Milan: Editoriale Jaca Book SpA, 1997); Guglielmo de Angelis d'Ossat, *Gustavo Giovannoni. Storico e critico dell'architettura* (Rome: Istituto di Studi Romani, 1949).

47 On the Garbatella neighbourhood, see Innocenzo Costantini, "Le nuove costruzioni dell'istituto per le case popolari di Roma: La borgata giardino 'Garbatella'," *Architettura e arti decorative* 2 (November 1922): 119–37; Monica Sinatra, *La Garbatella a Roma* (Milan: Franco Angeli, 2006); and Romano Stabile, "La borgata giardino 'Garbatella' 1920–1929," in *Architettura moderna a Roma e nel Lazio 1920–1945*, ed. Luigi Prisco (Rome: Edilstampa, 1996), 151–2. On the garden city tradition in Italy, see Alberto Corlaita, "La città giardino in Italia. Un futuro possibile?" in Gabriele Tagliaventi, ed., *Città giardino: cento anni di teorie, modelli, esperienze* (Roma: Gangemi, 1994), 279–307.

48 Gustavo Giovannoni, "Case del quattrocento in Roma," in Gustavo Giovannoni, *Saggi sulla architettura del rinascimento* (Milan: Fratelli Treves editori, 1931), 28–47.

49 Guido Marangoni, "Lettera aperta a Emilio Caldara," *Bollettino municipale di Milano* (January 1918): 17. My translation. See Anty Pansera, *Storia e cronaca della Triennale* (Milan: Longanesi, 1978), esp. 13–21.

50 Carlo Carrà, *L'arte decorative contemporanea alla prima Biennale internazionale di Monza* (Milan: Edizioni "Alpes," 1923).

51 Società Amatori e Cultori di Belle Arti, *XCI Esposizione di Belle Arti* (Rome: Alfieri and Lacroix, 1923).

52 Roberto Papini, "Le Arti a Monza nel 1925; Dagli architetti ai pastori," *Emporium* 62:369 (September 1925): 139–60. On the Monza exhibitions and their impact on Italian design, see Vittorio Magnago Lampugnani, "Architecture, Painting and the Decorative Arts in Italy 1923–1940, from the First Biennale to the Seventh Triennale," in *Italian Art 1900–1945*, ed. Germano Celant and Pontus Hulten (Milan: Bompiani, 1989), 69–76.

53 See the Swedish catalogue of the exhibition: *Italienska utställningen: November–December 1920* (Stockholm: Liljevalchs konsthall, Katalog no. 27, 1920). An Italian translation of this catalogue was not produced, nor was any other Italian catalogue for the exhibition. On Paulsson, see Gunnela Ivanov, "Gregor Paulsson and the Swedish Society of Arts and Crafts 1915–1925" (PhD diss., Umea University, 2004).

54 For a summary description of the exhibition, see Guido Balsamo-Stella, "Esposizione italiana d'arte industriale e decorative a Stoccolma," *Architettura e arti decorative* 1 (May–June 1921): 93–9. See also Remigio Strinati, "L'esposizione italiana di arte decorativa a Stoccolma," *Rassegna D'Arte Antica e Moderna* 4 (April 1921): 134–9; and Strinati, "L'arte rustica italiana e l'esposizione di Stoccolma," *La Fionda* 5 (December 1920): 48.

55 For a brief description of the Liljevalchs Art Gallery, see Claes Caldenby, Jöran Lindvall, and Wilfried Wang, eds., *Twentieth Century Architecture – Sweden* (Munich: Prestel, 1998), 260–1.

56 Emilio Bodrero, "La cenerentola italiana," *La Fionda* 16/17 (November–December, 1921): 255–65.

57 The first of the series was actually dedicated to Sweden. See Charles Holme, ed., *Peasant Art in Sweden, Iceland and Lapland* (London: The Studio Ltd., 1910).

58 Balsamo spent several years living in Stockholm before the exhibition. Stella likely met Barbantini while he was a resident artist at the Fondazione Bevilacqua La Masa in Venice. See *Guido Balsamo-Stella – Opera grafica e vetraria* (Milan: Galleria Philippe Daverio, 1977); *Guido Balsamo-Stella (1882–1941) Opera incisoria e vetraria* (Bassano del Grappa: Istituto nazionale per la grafica, 1988); Valentina Conedera, *I vetri della SALIR (Studio ARS Labor Industrie Riunite) a Murano, 1923–1985* (Venice: Università di Ca' Foscari, Venezia, 1987). Also see the entry on Guido Maria Balsamo Stella,

in *Le arti minori d'autore in Italia dal 1900 al 1930*, ed. Irene De Guttry, Maria Paola Maino, and Mario Quesada (Bari: Laterza, 1985), 78–83.

59 Strinati, "L'arte rustica italiana e l'esposizione di Stoccolma," 48.

60 Albert Sautier, *Tappeti rustici italiani* (Milan: Carlo Valcarenghi, 1922), 9. My translation. It was published in as *Italian Peasant Rugs* (Milan: Gli Editori Piantanida-Valcarenghi, 1923), and in French as *Tapis rustiques italiens* (Milan: Bottega di Poesia, 1924).

61 Antonio Maraini, "Esposizione," *Enciclopedia italiana di scienze, lettere ed arti* (Rome: Istituto della enciclopedia italiana fondata da Giovanni Treccani, 1951), 361–6. The reference to Stockholm is dated 13 November 1920 and reads: *"Tra le principali esposizioni del dopoguerra meritano ricordo quella d'arte decorative italiana a Stoccolma* (13 novembre 1920)" ("Among the principal exhibitions during the post-war period worthy of note is the exhibition of Italian decorative art in Stockholm") (366).

62 The displays included sections devoted to lighting, books and book binding, ivory, photographs, glass, gold and silver, household crafts, ceramics, coral objects, puppets, carved marble objects, metal works, furniture, toys, leather works, paper objects, jewellery, sculpture, lace, and textiles, as well as wagons and harnesses.

63 Vittorio Pica, *Vittorio Zecchin* (Milan: Publisher, 1925); Guido Perocco, ed., *Vittorio Zecchin* (Milan: Electa, 1981); Marino Barovier, Marco Mondi, and Carlo Sonego, eds., *Vittorio Zecchin, 1878-1947: Pittura, vetro, arti decorative* (Venice: Marsilio, 2002). See Giudo Perocco, *Le origini dell'arte moderna a Venezia* (Treviso: Canova, 1972), 309–23.

64 Jesurum was an important Venetian lace producer based in Venice. Michelangelo Jesurum had founded a school of lace in 1870 which revived the artisanal important tradition and offered work for young women from economically disadvantaged backgrounds. An important exhibition was held in London in 1908; see Waring and Gillow, Ltd., *Exhibition of the Jesurum Collection of Venetian Real Lace* (London: Waring and Gillow Ltd., 1908). Elisa Ricci, *Merletti e recami della Aemilia Ars* (Milan: Bestetti and Tumminelli, 1929); Carla Bernardini, Doretta Davanzo Poli, and Orsola Ghetti Baldi, eds., *Aemilia Ars 1898–1903: Arts and Crafts in Bologna* (Milan: A+G edizioni, 2001).

65 Anty Pansera and Tiziana Occleppo, eds., *Dal merletto alla motocicletta: Artigiane/artiste e designer nell'Italia del Novecento* (Milan: Silvana Editoriale, 2002). For a general framing of the issue, see Rozsika Parker and Griselda Pollock, "Crafty Women and the Hierarchy of the Arts," in *Old Mistresses: Women, Art and Ideology*, ed. Rozsika Parker and Griselda Pollock (London:

Routledge and Kegan Paul, 1981), 50–81. See Linda Nochlin's ground-breaking essay, "Why Have There Been No Great Women Artists?" in Linda Nochlin, *Women, Art, and Power and Other Essays* (New York: Harper and Row, 1988), 145–78.

66 While Ricci published numerous books in Italian on lace and women's crafts in the 1910s throughout the 1920s and early 1930s, her only book published in English was the rather luxurious two-volume publication entitled *Old Italian Lace* (London: William Heinemann, and Philadelphia: J.B. Lippincott Co., 1913); this translation is based on the 1908 Italian version by Elisa Ricci, *Antiche trine italiane raccolte e ordinate* (Bergamo: Istituto Italiano d'arti grafiche, 1908).

67 Eleonora Gallo, *Arte rustica italiana* (Florence: G. Giannini and Figlio, 1929). Published in English as *Peasant Art in Italy*, trans. C. Danyell Tassinari (Florence: G. Giannini and Figlio, 1929).

68 Emma Calderini, *Il costume popolare in Italia* (Milan: Hoepli Editore, 1934).

69 Marcello Piacentini, "Arte aristocratica ed arte paesana," *La Tribuna* 3 (April 1920): 3.

70 Despite this disagreement, the two still remained on good terms. In April, a cordial letter from Maraini to Ojetti dated November 1920, he wrote: "Peasant art is a good teacher because it teaches me to find not so much abstract beauty but to understand how beauty can be generated naturally" (My translation.) See Alessia Lenzi, *Adolfo De Carolis e il suo mondo (1892–1928). L'arte e la cultura attraverso i carteggi De Carolis, D'Annunzio, Maraini, Ojetti* (Ravagni: I.T.E.A., 1999), 117.

71 Antonio Maraini, "Il concetto di arte popolare," *Enciclopedia Italiana di Scienze, Lettere ed Arti* (Rome: Istituto Italiano della Enciclopedia Giovanni Treccani, 1929), 634–5.

72 Antonio Maraini, "L'arte paesana come materia d'insegnamento e di studio," *Atti del Iv Congresso Nazionale di Arti e Tradizioni Popolari – Venezia – Settembre 1940 XVIII* (Rome: Edizione dell'O.N.D., 1942), 113–15.

73 Plinio Marconi, "Architettura rustica," *Enciclopedia italiana di scienze, lettere ed arti*, vol. 30 (Rome: Istituto dell'Enciclopedia Giovanni Treccani, 1936), 344–6. See also "Architettura minime mediterranee e architettura moderna," *Architettura e arti decorative* (1929): 27–44; "Capri," *Enciclopedia italiana di scienze, lettere ed arti*, vol. 9 (Rome: Istituto dell'Enciclopedia Giovanni Treccani, 1931), 905–7. On Marconi as critic and advocate of vernacular architecture, see Giuseppe Torresi, ed., "Dibattiti e ricerche: Plinio Marconi e l'estetica dell'architettiro," in *Bolleltino della Biblioteca della Facoltà di Architettura dell'Università degli Studi di Roma 'La Sapienza,'* 59 (1996), esp. Paolo Marconi, "Architettura minore, Architetture minime

– Architettura moderna – Plinio Marconi e l'Associazione Artistica dei Cultori d'Architettura," 15–24; and Danilo De Vito, "Plinio Marconi itinerario critic," 31–44.

74 Marcello Piacentini, "Arte aristocratica ed arte paesana," *La Tribuna* 3 (April 1920): 3. My translation.

75 Wille received his architectural education in his native Berlin, and lived there until he moved to Rome in 1897 at the age of thirty-seven. On the work of Wille in Rome, see Roberto Papini, "Edilizia Moderna: L'Architetto Ernesto Wille," *Emporium* 40:236 (August 1914): 97–111; republished in Rosario De Simone, ed., *Cronache di architetura, 1914–1957: Antologia degli scritti di Roberto Papini* (Florence: Edifir Edizioni Firenze, 1998), 3–7. See Friedrich Noack, *Das Deutschtum in Rom seit dem Ausgang des Mittelalters* (Stuttgart: Deutsche Verlangsanstalt, 1927; reprint ed., Aalen: Scientia, 1974), vol. 1, 617, and vol. 2, 647; see also the entry on Ernest Wille in *Allgemeines Lexicon der Bildenden Künstler*, ed. Hans Vollmer (Leipzig: Von E.A. Seemann, 1947), 11.

76 See comments in Ezio Garroni, "Commemorazione del socio Ernesto Wille" *Associazione artistica fra i cultori di architettura Roma, Annuario, Dall'anno XXI-MCMXI – all'anno XXV–MCMXV* (Rome: Tipografia Innocenzo Artero, 1916), 183–5, in which the author mentions plans to publish a collection of drawings of the vernacular architecture of Ischia.

77 For a history of this neighborhood, see Carlo Cecere, "Il quartiere Villa Patrizi nella costruzione di Roma capitale," in Rinaldo Capomolla and Rosalia Vittorini, eds., *Studi sull'edilizia in Italia tra ottocento e novecento* (Rome: Edilstampa, 1999), 14-35. On this history of the *villino* in Roman neighbourhoods, see Irene De Guttry, *Il villino a Roma: Prati di Castello, Delle Vittorie* (Rome: Palombi and Italia Nostra, 2001).

78 Paolo Cavallari, "Aspetti del linguaggio neomedievale a Roma: architetture di Antonio Ventura, Ernesto Wille e Carlo Busiri Vici nel quartiere Villa Patrizi," in *Studi sull'edilizia in Italia tra ottocento e novecento*, ed. Rinaldo Capomolla and Rosalia Vittorini (Rome: Edil Stampa, 1999), 60–85.

79 Luigi-Federico Babini, *Ville moderne in Italia – Ville di Roma – Facciate – Particolari – Piante – Raccolte* (Turin: C. Crudo, 1915), 14-15 and 26-27.

80 Bruno Zevi's *Storia dell'architettura moderna* (1950) mentioned Wille briefly and deemed him worthy of critical attention he had not yet received. Bruno Zevi, *Storia dell'architettura moderna* (Turin: Einaudi, 1950), 220–1. Art and architecture critic Roberto Papini, who a year after Wille's death published a text that remained for years the only substantial account in Italian of his work, echoed Piacentini's cautious appreciation. Like Piacentini, he claimed in a somewhat resentful tone that foreigners often used Italian

sources as the basis of a *modernismo conquistatore* (conquering modernism), which they claimed as their own. See Roberto Papini, "Architetture di Capri," *Emporium* 404 (August 1928): 117–25. In his review of Giambattista Ceas's book, Papini refers to his *Emporium* article of 1914 on Ernest Wille: "Foreigners come to Italy and study the spirit and not the exterior forms of our architectural glories ... they study the most healthy expressions of our race, and then create the most unusual deformations which bear their stamp and not ours," reprinted in *Cronache di Architettura 1914–1957 Antologia degli scritti di Roberto Papini*, ed. Rosario De Simone (Florence: Edifir Edizioni Firenze, 1998), 154–5. My translation.

81 Ugo Ojetti, "L'arte di Lorenzo il Magnifico e l'arte di Nenciozza," *La Tribuna* (11 March 1920): 8; Ugo Ojetti, "L'arte in campagna," in *Raffaello e altri leggi* (Milan: Fratelli Treves, 1921), 32–42; Ugo Ojetti, "Commenti," *Dedalo* (December 1920): 485–6.

82 In 1933, more than a decade later, Ojetti antagonized Italian architects with his accusations regarding the design of the new University of Rome for which the master planner was Marcello Piacentini who brought together several architects like Giovanni Michelucci, Giuseppe Pagano, and Gio Ponti to design the various buildings. In the first of his two letters in 1933, after the unveiling of the plan and designs of the single buildings, Ojetti objected to the lack of *"Italianità."* He felt these designs lacked columns and arches (*"le colonne e gli archi"*). Piacentini responded to Ojetti and argued in defence of his scheme by claiming that to be Italian today was not only to employ columns and arches. As late as 1933, Piacentini wasn't interested in literal or archaeological citations of columns and arches. Yet he does express regret for what he perceived as the "fashionable" approach of some Italian architects for *"certe forme contrarie al nostro clima,"* thus drawing attention to the relationship to site that included climate. Clearly, Piacentini was alluding to the wave of perceived references to recent examples of German or Russian architecture, especially by the younger rationalist architects like Giuseppe Terragni and other members of Gruppo 7.

83 Piero Jahier, "Arte alpina," *Dedalo* 1:2 (July 1920): 87–103; republished as part of a more indepth study entitled *Arte alpina* (Milan: Vanni Scheiwiller, 1958) and in Piero Jahier, *Arte alpina* (Florence: Vallecchi, 1961). The first of the footnotes in the 1958 edition reads: "Ojetti fell in love with them after my return from the war and he had several pieces photographed that I later showed for the Dedalo piece." In his footnotes, Jahier goes on to add, "In the catalogue of the 1911 *Italian Exhibition of Ethnography*, Alpine art is virtually absent." My translation.

84 Sandra Barbieri, *Jules Brocherel: Alpinismo, etnografia, fotografia e vita cul-*

turale in Valle D'Aosta fra Ottocento e Novecento (Ivrea: Priuli & Verlucca, 1992).

85 See a comment on his 1920 article published in note 1, page 25 of *Arte Alpina* 1961, where he wrote: "If I could I would have included some examples of Alpine architecture on our side of the border." He also mentioned that the Nordiska Museet of Stockholm had approached him for copies of his photographs of Alpine folk art.

86 Though Antonio Gramsci acknowledged the presence of "some interesting things in the work of Piero Jahier," he denounced the "writer's biblical and Claudellian style" as less effective, and claimed that this style "masks a snobbish form of rhetoric." The article was republished in *Antonio Gramsci: Selections from Cultural Writings*, ed. David Forgacs and Geoffrey Nowell-Smith, trans. William Boelhower (Cambridge, MA: Harvard University Press, 1985), 212, 216. See also Maura Del Serra, *L'uomo Comune – Claudellismo e passione ascetica in Jahier* (Bologna: Pàtron Editiore, 1986).

87 Jahier, "Arte Alpina," 90. My translation.

88 Bruno Taut, *Glass Architecture and Alpine Architecture*, ed. Dennis Sharp, trans. James Palmes (New York: Praeger, 1972); Matthias Schirren, *Bruno Taut: Alpine Architecture: A Utopia* (Munich: Prestel, 2004); Iain Boyd Whyte, *Bruno Taut and the Architecture of Activism* (New York: Cambridge University Press, 1982); and Iain Boyd Whyte, ed., *The Crystal Chain Letters: Architectural Fantasies by Bruno Taut and His Circle* (Cambridge, MA: The MIT Press, 1985). See Bernhard Mendes Bürgi, *Ernst Ludwig Kirchner – Mountain Life: The Early Years in Davos 1917–1926* (Ostfildern-Ruit: Hatje Cantz Verlag, 2003).

89 Ugo Ojetti, "Commenti," 485–6. On the topic of war-time destruction, see also Ugo Ojetti, "Bellezze perdute (March 1919)," in *I nani tra le colonne* (Milan: Fratelli Treves, 1920), 41–6.

90 Despite D'Annunzio's interest in peasant art, when he commissioned a house on the Lake of Garda by Giancarlo Maroni, it was designed in a stripped-down classicism, which reflected a bias for Novecento. However, Sardinian peasant rugs were prominently displayed in the main entranceway. See Annamaria Andreoli, "Gabriele D'Annunzio e il suo architetto," in *L'architetto del lago: Giancarlo Maroni e il Garda*, ed. Fulvio Irace (Milan: Electa, 1993), 95–118. See also Carlo Cresti, *Gabriele D'Annunzio –"architetto imaginifico"* (Florence: Angelo Pontecorboli Editore, 2005).

91 Unsigned, but likely authored by Raffaele Corso, "La prima bottega d'arte popolare italiano" in *La Fionda* 3 (October 1920), 42.

92 Letter from Bernard Berenson to Salvatore Lauro, *La Fionda* (August 1920): 44–5. My translation.

93 See Le Corbusier's map, which lists places of interest for culture, folkore, and industry, *L'Art Decoratif d'Aujourd Hui* (Paris: G. Cres, 1925); published in English as *The Decorative Art of Today*, trans. James I. Dunnett (Cambridge, MA: MIT Press, 1987), 212.

94 Raffaele Corso's "L'arte dei pastori" was originally published in *La Fionda* 3 (October 1920): 13–29, and subsequently as a pamphlet (1920), but never as a book. Corso went on to publish his seminal text *Folklore – Storia – Obbietto – Metodo – Bibliografia* (Rome: Casa Editrice Leonardo Da Vinci, 1923). He published a number of essays, but none specifically on architecture. For a study of Corso's contribution, see Ricciotti Mileto, *Etnografia e folklore nelle opere in Raffaele Corso* (Soveria Mannelli: Rubbettino Editore, 1985), in which Corso's essays published on peasant arts and crafts are listed and which includes an exhaustive bibliography.

95 Emilio Gentile, "The Myth of National Regeneration in Italy: From Modernist Avant-Garde to Fascism," in *Fascist Visions: Art and Ideology in France and Italy*, ed. Matthew Affron and Mark Antliff (Princeton, NJ: Princeton University Press, 1997), 25–45.

96 Lionello Balestrieri, Guido Biagi, Giovanni Bordiga, Arduino Colasanti, Adolfo De Carolis, Melchiorre Zagarese, Ettore Ferrari, Augusto Osimo, and Ugo Ojetti, "Per la riforma dell'insegnamento artistico," in Ugo Ojetti, *Raffaello e altre leggi* (Milan: Fratelli Treves Editori, 1921), 231–51.

97 Ugo Ojetti, *La Università delle Arti decorative in Monza. Discorso inaugurale* (Milan: Coi Tipi della Scuola del Libro di Milano, 1922). On the history of the school, see Rosanna Bossaglia, *L'ISIA a Monza: Una Scuola d'Arte Europea* (Milan: Silvana Editoriale, 1986).

98 Giulio Ulisse Arata, "Arte rustica sarda 1. Gioielli e utensili intagliati," *Dedalo* 1:3 (April 1921): 698.

99 Giulio Ulisse Arata and Giuseppe Biasi, *Arte sarda* (Milan: Fratelli Treves, 1935; reprint ed., Sassari: Carlo Delfino, 1983).

100 Giuliana Altea and Marco Magnani, *Giuseppe Biasi* (Nuoro: Illisso, 1998).

101 August Sander, *Eine Reise nach Sardinien: Fotografien 1927 Landeshauptstadt* (Hannover: Sprengel Museum, 1995). Sander came to Italy shortly after the inauguration of the Museum für Völkerkunde in Hamburg, which featured an installation devoted to Sardinia. See H. Glenn Penny, *Ethnology and Ethnographic Museums in Imperial Germany* (Chapell Hill: University of North Carolina Press, 2002). Raffaele Corso's "Note e Commenti" on the Regio Museo di Etnografia Italiana mentions Byham searching for ethnographic materials from Sardinia for the Hamburg museum. Raffaele Corso, "Note e commenti," *Il folklore italiano* (March 1927): 298–300.

102 D.H. Lawrence, *Sea and Sardinia* (New York: T. Seltzer, 1921); reprinted in
     D.H. Lawrence and Italy (London: Penguin Books, 1997), 53–69.
103 Giulio Ulisse Arata, "Arte rustica sarda 1," 698. My translation.
104 Guilio Ulisse Arata, "Arte rustica Sarda I," 698. My translation.
105 Giulio Ulisse Arata, *Costruzioni e progetti con alcune note sull'architettura
     contemporanea* (Milan: Hoepli Editore, 1942); Fabio Mangone, *Giulio Ulisse
     Arata – Opera completa* (Naples: Electa, 1993).
106 Mangone, *Giulio Ulisse Arata*, 32–3.
107 Alfredo Melani, *L'architettura di Giulio Ulisse Arata*, vol. 1, *Ville* (Milan: Be-
     stetti and Tumminelli, 1913). See "Case e ville moderne in Italia," *Natura
     e Arte* 19 (September 1909): 435–41; republished in Maria Luisa Scalvini
     and Fabio Mangone, eds., *Melani e l'architettura moderna in Italia: Antologia
     critica (1882–1910)* (Rome: Officina Edizioni, 1998), 163–8; see also Carroll
     L. Meeks, *Italian Architecture, 1750–1914* (New Haven: Yale University
     Press, 1966).
108 Giulio Ulisse Arata, "L'arte paesana alla prima biennale di Monza," *Le arti
     Decorative* (May 1923): 16–22.
109 On Melis, see Antonello Cuccu, ed., *Studio Artistico Melkiorre Melis* (Bosa:
     Regiona Autonoma della Sardegna, 1989). See also Melis entry in Irene
     de Guttry, Maria Paola Maino, and Mario Quesada, eds., *Le arti minore
     d'autore in Italia dal 1900 al 1930* (Bari: Laterza, 1985): 242–5. For an early
     essay on his ceramic work, see Dionigi Scano, "La bottega d'arte ceramica
     in Cagliari," in *Mediterranea: Rivista mensile di cultura di problemi isolani*
     1:11–12 (November–December, 1927): 66–72.
110 Paolo Mezzanotte, "La prima mostra internazionale delle arti decorative
     a Monza – I, " *Architettura e arti decorative* (February 1923): 391-404; "La
     prima mostra internazionale delle arti decorative a Monza – II," *Architet-
     tura e arti decorative* (March 1923): 429-57; "La prima mostra internazionale
     delle arti decorative a Monza – III," *Architettura e arti decorative* (April
     1923): 481–95.
111 See Paolo Mezzanotte, "Il focolare friulano," *L'Edilizia Moderna – Periodico
     mersile di architettura e costruzione* 26:12 (December 1917): 66–8. Mezza-
     notte had also participated with some of his drawings in the Rome exhi-
     bition of 1921.
112 Ezio Antonini, *La Borsa di Milano: Da origini a Palazzo Mezzanotte* (Milan:
     Federico Motta, 1993).
113 Terry Kirk, "Framing St. Peter's: Urban Planning in Fascist Rome," *The
     Art Bulletin* 88:4 (December 2006): 756–76.
114 Mario Pisani, *L'onta di Parigi – Il padiglione italiano di Armando Brasini
     all'expo di Parigi del 1925* (Melfi: Libria, 1996).

3. *Tabula rasa* and Tradition

1 *Godard on Godard: Critical Writings by Jean-Luc Godard*, ed. Jean Narboni and Tom Milne (New York: Viking Press, 1972), 200.
2 In *Futurist Manifestoes*, ed. Umbro Apollonio, trans. Robert Brain, R. W. Flint, J. C. Higgitt, and Caroline Tisdall (New York: Viking Press, 1973), 27–30.
3 On the role of nature and vernacular architecture in modernism, see Tim Benton, "Modernism and Nature," in *Modernism: Designing a New World*, ed. Christopher Wilk (London: V&A Publications, 2006), 310–26.
4 See notes 53, 56, and 57 in the introduction to this volume.
5 For an overview of classicism in Italian architecture during fascism, see Giorgio Ciucci, "Italian Architecture during the Fascist Period: Classicism between Neoclassicism and Rationalism: The Many Souls of the Classical," *The Harvard Architectural Review* 5 (Spring 1987): 76–87. For a complete bibliography of classicism in twentieth-century architecture, see note 57 in the introduction to this volume.
6 Annegret Burg, *Novecento Milanese. I novecentisti e il rinnovamento dell'architettura a Milano fra il 1920 e il 1940* (Milan: Federico Motta Editore, 1991); Rossana Bossaglia, *Il Novecento Italiano* (Milan: Edizioni Charta, 1995).
7 See *F.T. Marinetti Critical Writings*, ed. Günter Berghaus (New York: Farrar, Straus, and Giroux, 2006), 11–17. On futurism and nationalist politics, see Maria Elena Versari, "International Futurism Goes National: The Ambivalent Identity of a National/International Avant-garde," in *Nation – Style – Modernism*, ed. Jacek Purchla and Wolf Tegethoff (Cracow: International Cultural Centre, and Munich: Zentralinstitut für Kunstgeschicte, 2006), 171–84; and Christine Poggi, *Inventing Futurism: The Art and Politics of Artificial Optimism* (Princeton, NJ: Princeton University Press, 2009).
8 See Reyner Banham, *Theory and Design in the First Machine Age* (Cambridge, MA: MIT Press, 1960), 127–37.
9 Theo van Doesburg published an article on Sant'Elia's manifesto entitled "Futurism between Whim and Revelation: The Manifesto of Sant'Elia," in *Het Bouwbedrijf* 6:9 (April 1929): 179–81; republished in Theo Van Doesburg, *On European Architecture: Complete Essays from Het Bouwbedrijf 1924–1931* (Basel: Birkhäuser, 1990), 224–9.
10 Carlo Olmo et al., *Le metafore e il cantiere: Lingotto 1982–2003* (Turin: U. Allemandi, 2003).
11 Le Corbusier, *Vers une architecture* (Paris: Crés, 1923. Published in English as *Toward an Architecture*, trans. John Goodman, with an introduction by Jean-Louis Cohen (Los Angeles, CA: Getty Research Institute, 2007).

12 Sigfried Giedion, "Situation de l'architecture contemporaine en Italie" *Cahiers d'art* 9–10 (1931): 442–9.

13 Ezio Godoli, *Guide all'architettura moderna: Il futurismo* (Rome: Laterza, 1983); Iain Boyd Whyte, "The Architecture of Futurism," in *International Futurism in Arts and Literature*, ed. Günter Berghaus (Berlin: De Gruyter, 2000), 353–72.

14 Lea Vergine, *Capri 1905–1940: Frammenti postumi* (Milan: Skira, 2003); Enrico Crispolti, ed., *Futurismo e Meridione* (Naples: Electa, 1996); Claudio Fogu, "Futurist *mediterraneità* between *Emporium* and *Imperium*," *Modernism/Modernity* 15:1 (2008): 25–43.

15 Giulio Carlo Argan, ed., *Dopo Sant'Elia: Con il manifesto dell'architettura futurista di Antonio Sant'Elia* (Milan: Editoriale Domus, 1935).

16 Apollonio, *Futurist Manifestos*, 160–72.

17 Alberto Longati, "Il caso Sant'Elia," *Nuove Tendenze: Milano e l'atro futurismo* (Milan: Electa, 1980), 14–20.

18 Adalberto Libera, "Arte e razionalismo," *La rassegna italiana* (March 1928); republished in *L'architettura in Italia 1919–1943 – Le polemiche*, ed. Luciano Patetta (Milan: Clup, 1972), 149–51. My translation.

19 Edoardo Persico, "Punto ed a capo per l'architettura" *Domos* (November 1934); reprinted in *Edoardo Persico – Scritti d'architettura (1927–1935)*, ed. Giulia Veronesi (Florence: Vallecchi Editore, 1968), 153–68; cited in Bruno Zevi, "The Italian Rationalists," in *The Rationalists: Theory and Design in the Modern Movement*, ed. Dennis Sharp (London: Architectural Press, 1978), 118–29. For an overview on Persico, see Cesare De Seta, *Il destino dell'architettura – Persico – Giolli – Pagano* (Rome: Laterza, 1985); and Cesare De Seta, ed., *Edoardo Persico* (Naples: Electa, 1987).

20 Fabio Mangone, *Viaggi a Sud: Gli architetti nordici e l'Italia 1850–1925* (Naples: Electa Napoli, 2002).

21 Eduard F. Sekler, *Josef Hoffmann: Monograph and Catalogue of Works* (Princeton, NJ: Princeton University Press, 1985), 486–92.

22 Franco Borsi and Ezio Godoli, "The Mediterranean Myth and Rediscovery of the Popular," in Franco Borsi and Ezio Godoli, ed., *Vienna 1900: Architecture and Design* (New York: Rizzoli, 1986), 177–205.

23 Gaetana Cantone and Italo Prozzillo, *Case di Capri: Ville, palazzi, grandi dimore* (Naples: Electa 1994).

24 Filippo Tomaso Marinetti, "Lo stile pratico," in *Il convegno del paesaggio*, ed. Edwin Cerio (Naples: Gaspare Casella, 1923), 66–8; reprinted in Giuseppe Galasso, Alberto G. White, and Valeria Mazzarelli, eds., *1923–1993: Contributi a settanta anni dalla pubblicazione degli atti del Convegno del Paesaggio* (Capri: Edizioni La Conchiglia, 1993).

25 "Il Discorso di Marinetti," in Cerio, ed., *Il convegno del paesaggio*, 38. My translation.

26 Filippo Tommaso Marinetti, "The Founding and Manifesto of Futurism" (1909), originally published in *Le Figaro* (Paris), 20 February 1909, 19–24.

27 Filippo Tommaso Marinetti, "Elogio di Capri," *Natura* 1:1 (January 1928): 41–8. My translation.

28 Francesco Cangiullio, *Marinetti a Capri* (Naples: Gaspare Casella Editore, 1922).

29 Alessandro Del Puppo, *"Lacerba" 1913–1915 Arte e critica d'arte* (Bergamo: Lubrina, 2000), 211–19.

30 Pia Vivarelli, "Classicism and Tradition in Italian Art of the 1920s," in *On Classic Ground: Picasso, Léger, de Chirico and the New Classicism 1910–1930*, ed. Elizabeth Cowling and Jennifer Mundy (London: Tate Gallery, 1990), 371–82. Vivarelli stresses classicism in the work of De Chirico and primitivism in the work of Carrà.

31 Carlo Carrà, "Parlata su Giotto" (originally published in *La Voce*, 31 March 1916), and Carlo Carrà, "Il doganiere Rousseau e la tradizione italiana" (originally published in *Magazine of Art* [November 1951]), in *Carlo Carrà. Tutti gli scritti*, ed. Massimo Carrà (Milan: Feltrinelli, 1978), 63–71 and 594–602, respectively.

32 On the contribution of futurists (primarily Balla and Depero) to the applied arts, see Filiberto Menna, "Il Futurismo e le arti applicate: La 'Casa d'arte Italiana,'" in *Studi in onore di Vittorio Viale*, ed. Association internationale des critiques d'art (Turin: Edizioni d'arte Fratelli Pozzo, 1967), 91–7.

33 On primitivism and expressionism, see Jill Lloyd, *German Expressionism: Primitivism and Modernity* (New Haven, CT: Yale University Press, 1991).

34 Carlo Anti, "Mostra di Scultura Negra," *Catalogo della XIII Esposizione Internationale d'arte della città di Venezia* (Milan: Bestetti and Tumminelli, 1922), 41–4; Carlo Anti, "Scultura negra," *Dedalo: Rassegna d'arte* 1:3 (1921): 592–621; published in English as "The Sculpture of the African Negroes," *Art in America and Elsewhere* 12:1 (December 1923): 14–26. Anti's essay is included in Jack Flam and Miriam Deutch, eds., *Primitivism and Twentieth-Century Art: A Documentary History* (Berkeley: University of California Press, 2003), 180–3. On Anti's contribution to the debate on arte in Italy, see Giuseppina Dal Canton, "Anti e l'arte contemporanea," in *Carlo Anti – giornate di studio nel centenario della nascita*, ed. Regione Veneto (Trieste: Edizioni Lint, 1992), 317–46.

35 Ezio Bassani, "Italian Painting," in *"Primitivism" in Twentieth-Century Art: Affinity of the Tribal and Modern*, vol. 2, ed. William Rubin (New York: Mu-

seum of Modern Art, 1988), 405–15; Ardengo Soffici published a number
of articles on the topic in the right-wing journal *Il Selvaggio*: "Di vari primitivismi," *Il Selvaggio* (20 January 1938), in *Selva Arte* (Florence: Vallecchi,
1943), 218–19; and "Neoprimitivismo," *Il Selvaggio* (4 October 1941), in *Selva Arte* (Florence: Vallecchi, 1943), 323–6. On Modigliani, see Emily Braun,
"The Faces of Modigliani: Identity Politics under Fascism," in *Modern Art
and the Idea of the Mediterranean*, ed. Vojtech Jirat-Wasiutynski (Toronto:
University of Toronto Press, 2007), 181–205.

36 Romain H. Rainero, "Eurocentrismo e rifiuto dell'arte dell'Africa Nera
nell'Italia fascista," in *Arte in Africa: Realtà e prospettive nello studio della storia delle arti africane*, ed. Ezio Bassani (Modena: Edizioni Panini, 1986), 61–3.
On African art in public and private collections in Italy, see Nicola La-
banca, ed., *L'africa in vetrina – storie di musei e di esposizioni coloniali in Italia*
(Treviso: Pagus Edizioni, 1992); Vittorio Carini, *A Hidden Heritage: Sculture
africane in collezioni private italiane* (Milan: Galleria Dalton – Somaré, 2004).
See Brian McLaren, *Architecture and Tourism in Italian Colonial Libya* (Seattle:
University of Washington Press, 2006).

37 See Massimiliano Savorra, "La legge e la natura – Strategie istituzionali
per la salvaguardia del panorama (1922–1939)," *Bollettino d'Arte* 113 (2002):
101–12.

38 Giuseppe Basile, Sabino Cassese, and Vincenzo Cazzato, eds., *Istituzioni
e politiche culturali in Italia negli anni Trenta* (Rome: Istituto poligrafico e
Zecca dello Stato, 2001); Tommaso Alibrandi and Piergiorgio Ferri, *I beni
culturali e ambientali* (Milan: Giuffrè, 2001).

39 Luigi Parpagliolo, *La difesa delle bellezze naturali dell'Italia* (Rome: Società
editrice d'arte illustrata, 1923), 201-3; see "Annesso A" for the integral version of new law.

40 "Il Convegno di Capri per la bellezza paessistica," *Architettura e arti decorative* 1:2 (1922): n.p. My translation.

41 Edwin Cerio, "L'architettura minima nella contrada delle Sirene," *Architettura e arti decorative* 4:2 (August 1922): 156–76. See also Alberto Micciche,
"L'architettura minore a Capri," *La vie d'italia* 45:10 (October 1939): 1368–74.

42 Paolo Marconi, "Architettura minore, architetture minime, architettura
moderna – Plinio Marconi e l'associazione artistica dei cultori d'architettura," in Dibattiti e ricerche: Plinio Marconi e l'estetica dell'architettura,
Bollettino della Biblioteca della Facoltà di Architettura dell'Università
degli studi di Roma "La Sapienza," 54–5 (1996): 15–24.

43 Axel Munthe, *The Story of San Michele* (New York: E.P. Dutton, 1929), 313.
See also Bengt Jangfeldt, *Munthes Capri: En bildberättelse* (Stockholm: Wahl-
ström and Widstrand, 2004).

44 See Renato Paoli, "Amalfi I," *The Architect* 54:2689 (2 July 1920): 4–6. Renato Paoli, "Ravello – II," *The Architect* 55:2719 (28 January 1921): 70–1. Renato Paoli, "Capri and Amalfi, III" *The Architect* (4 March 1921): 158–61. See also in Italian, Renato Paoli, "Bellezze d'Italia: Amalfi," *Emporium* 55:325 (January 1922): 41–51.

45 Edwin Cerio, "Una casa a Capri di Giuseppe Capponi," *Architettura* 12:2 (February 1934): 102–6.

46 Paolo Cortese and Isabella Sacco, *Giuseppe Capponi: 1893–1936* (Rome: Gangemi, 1991); Giuseppe Capponi, "Motivi di architettura ischiana," *Architettura e arti decorative* 4:11 (July 1927): 481–94.

47 Marida Talamona, *Casa Malaparte* (New York: Princeton Architectural Press, 1992).

48 Bruce Chatwin, "Among the Ruins," in *Bruce Chatwin – Anatomy of Restlessness: Selected Writings 1969–1989*, ed. Jan Borm and Matthew Graves (New York: Viking, 1996), 151–69.

49 Umberto Boccioni, Carlo Carrà, Luigi Russolo, Giacomo Balla, and Gino Severini, "Futurist Paintings: Technical Manifesto (1910)," in *Futurist Manifestoes*, ed. Umbro Apollonio, trans. Robert Brain, R. W. Flint, J. C. Higgitt, and Caroline Tisdall (New York: Viking Press, 1973), 27–31.

50 Quoted in *Godard on Godard: Critical Writings*, ed. Jean Narboni and Tom Milne (New York: Viking Press, 1972), 200.

51 Talamona, *Casa Malaparte*, 49.

52 Fabrizio Brunetti, *Architetti e fascismo* (Florence: Alinea Editrice, 1993), in particular, see the chapter entitled "La polemica di Strapaese," 217–37.

53 Curzio Malaparte, *Italia barbara* (Turin: Piero Gobetti Editore, 1925), 39. My translation.

54 Virgilio Marchi, *Architettura futurista* (Foligno: Franco Campitelli Editore, 1924); and *Italia nuova architettura nuova* (Foligno: Franco Campitelli Editore, 1931).

55 Elena Vitas, ed., *Depero, Capri, il teatro* (Naples: Electa, 1988); Gabriella Belli, *La Casa del Mago: Le Arti applicate nell'opera di Fortunato Depero, 1920–1942* (Milan: Edizioni Charta, 1992); Gabriella Belli, "Fonti del racconto popolare di Depero," in *Depero*, ed. Maurizio Fagiolo dell'Arco (Milan: Electa, 1988), 206–9.

56 Fortunato Depero, *Fortunato Depero nelle opere e nella vita* (Trento: Tipografia Editrice Mutilati e Invalidi, 1940), 207–8. My translation.

57 See Anty Pansera and Tiziana Occleppo, eds., *Dal merletto alla motocicletta: Artigiane/artiste e designer nell'Italia del Novecento* (Milan: Silvana Editoriale, 2002)

58 For a discussion on Kandinsky and folk art, see Alison Hilton, "The Peas-

ant House and Its Furnishings: Decorative Principles in Russian Folk Art," *Journal of Decorative and Propaganda Arts* 11 (Winter 1989): 10–29; Alison Hunter, *Russian Folk Art* (Bloomington: Indiana University Press, 1995).

59 See "Reminiscences/Three Pictures (1912–1913)," in *Kandinsky: Complete Writings on Art*, ed. Kenneth C. Lindsay and Peter Vergo (New York: Da Capo, 1994), 368–9. See also Peg Weiss, "Kandinsky and 'Old Russia': An Ethnographic Exhibition Exploration," in *The Documented Image: Visions in Art History*, ed. G. Weisberg, L. Dixon, and A. Lemke (Syracuse: Syracuse University Press, 1988), 187–222; Peg Weiss, *Kandinsky and Old Russia: The Artist as Ethnographer and Shaman* (New Haven, CT: Yale University Press, 1995).

60 E. F. Kovtun, "Kazimir Malevich," *Art Journal* (Fall 1981): 234–41.

61 Alison Hunter, *Kazimir Malevich* (New York: Rizzoli, 1992).

62 See Edith Balas, *Brancusi and Rumanian Folk Traditions* (Boulder, CO: East European Monographs, 1987).

63 Enrico Prampolini, "The Futurist 'Atmosphere-Structure': Basis for an Architecture 1914–15," in *Futurist Manifestoes*, ed. Apollonio Umbro, trans. R. W. Flint, J. C. Higgitt, and Caroline Tisdall (New York: Viking Press, 1972), 181–3.

64 Enrico Crispolti, *Prampolini: dal futurismo all'informale* (Rome: Carte Segrete, 1992), 278. See also Ezio Godoli *Il futuriso* (Rome: Laterza, 1983), 52–8.

65 J.L. Locher, ed., *Escher: His Life and Complete Graphic Work* (New York: Harry N. Abrams, 1982), esp. "Italy and Spain 1922–1924," 21–30, and "Rome, 1924–1935," 31–46.

66 Cited in Silvia Danesi, "Aporie dell'architettura italiana in periodo fascista – mediterraneità e purismo," in *Il razionalismo e l'architettura in Italia durante il fascismo*, ed. Silvia Danesi and Luciano Patetta (Milan: Electa, 1976), 21–8. My translation.

67 Gian Carlo Jocteau, ed., *Ai monti e al mare – Cento anni di colonie per l'infanzia* (Milan: Fabbri Editori, 1990).

68 On Lurçat, see Jean-Louis Cohen, *André Lurçat: 1894–1970: Autocritique d'un moderne* (Liège: Mardaga, 1995), 110–20.

69 Gio Ponti, "Esempi da fuori per le case da Riviera – una interessante costruzione mediterranea a Calvi in Corsica," *Domus* (November 1932): 654-5. My translation.

70 Josep Lluis Sert, "San Pol de Mar," *AC – Revista Trimestral – Publicación del "G.A.T.E.P.A.C. 1* (1931): 25. My translation. On Sert and the Mediterranean, see also Jan Birksted, *Modernism and the Mediterranean: The Maeght Foundation* (Burlington, VT: Ashgate, 2004).

71 Enrico Peressutti, "Architettura mediterranea," *Quadrante* 21 (1935): 40–1; republished as "Mediterranean Architecture," in *Cities of Childhood: Italian Colonies of the 1930s*, ed. Stefano de Martino and Alex Wall (London: Architectural Association, 1988), 78.

72 Richard Pommer, "The Flat Roof: A Modernist Controversy in Germany," *Art Journal* (Summer 1983): 158–69; Christian F. Otto and Richard Pommer, *Weissenhof 1927 and the Modern Movement in Architecture* (Chicago: University of Chicago Press, 1991), 140–4; Karin Kirsch, *The Weissenhofsiedlung: Experimental Housing Built for the Deutscher Werkbund, Stuttgart 1927* (New York: Rizzoli, 1989).

73 Gio Ponti, "Facciamoci una coscienza nazionale della architettura mediterranea," *Stile* 7:19 (July 1941): 2–12.

74 Werner Blaser, *Patios: 5,000 Años de evolución* (Barcelona: Editorial Gustavo Gili, 2004).

75 Giovanni Michelucci and Roberto Papi, "Lezione di Pompei," *Arte mediterranea: Rivista bimestrale di arte, letteratura, e musica* 1:1 (1934): 23–32. My translation.

76 On Pompeian revivalism in fascist Italy, see Marilena Pasquali, ed., *Pompei e il recupero del classico* (Ancona: Galleria d'Arte Moderna, 1980), esp. Carlo Cresti, "Segni e soggezioni di paternità Latina nell'architettura italiana degli anni venti e Trenta," 120–35.

77 Cherubino Gambardella, *Il sogno bianco – Architettura e "mito mediterraneo" nell'Italia degli anni '30* (Naples: Clean, 1989), 94–100; Benedetto Gravagnuolo, *Il mito mediterraneo nell'architettura contemporanea* (Naples: Electa, 1994).

78 Vittorio Savi, *Figini e Pollini: Architetture 1927–1989* (Milan: Electa, 1990), 2–3.

79 Paul Overy, *Light, Air and Openness: Modern Architecture between the Wars* (London: Thames and Hudson, 2007).

80 Luigi Figini, "Architettura naturale ad Ischia," *Comunità* 3:3 (May–June 1949): 36–9; Luigi Figini, "Architettura naturale a Ibiza," *Comunità* 8 (May–June 1950): 40–3.

81 Figini, "Architettura naturale a Ibiza," 42. My translation.

82 Gio Ponti, "Un villa all a Pompeiana," *Domus* 79 (July 1934): 19.

83 Maristella Casciato, "The 'Casa all'Italiana' and the Idea of Modern Dwellings in Fascist Italy," *The Journal of Architecture* 5:4 (Winter 2000): 335–53; Annalisa Avon, "La casa all'italiana," in *Storia dell'architettura italiana – Il primo Novecento*, ed. Giorgio Ciucci and Giorgio Muratore (Milan: Electa, 2004), 162–79.

84 Republished in Gio Ponti, *La casa all'italiana* (Milan: Edizioni Domus, 1933), 7. My translation.

85 Pierre Pinon, "Calcestruzzo e Mediterraneo," *Tony Garnier 1869–1948* (Milan: Mazzotta, 1990), 102–35.

86 Le Corbusier, *Toward an Architecture* trans. John Goodman, with an introduction by Jean-Louis Cohen (Los Angeles: Getty Research Institute, 2007), 218–19. See also Maria Salerno, "Mare e memoria: la casa mediterranea nell'opera di Le Corbusier," in *Le Corbusier e l'Antico – Viaggi nel Mediterraneo*, ed. Benedetto Gravagnuolo (Naples: Electa, 2000), 107–13.

87 Marida Talamona, "Primi passi verso l'Europa (1927–33)," in *Luigi Figini. Gino Polllini. Opera Completa*, ed. Vittorio Gregotti and Giovanni Marzari (Milan: Electa 1996), 55–81.

88 Kurt W. Forster, "Antiquity and Modernity in the La Roche-Jeanneret Houses of 1923," *Oppositions* 15–16 (Winter/Spring 1979): 131–53.

89 Gruppo 7, "Architettura (I)," *La Rassegna italiana* 19:103 (December 1926): 849–54; trans. Ellen R. Shapiro, *Oppositions* 6 (Fall 1976): 92. The other articles followed: Gruppo 7, "Architettura (II): Gli Stranieri," *La Rassegna italiana* 9:105 (February 1927): 129–37 ; "Architettura (III): Impreparazione, Incomprensione, Pregiudizi," *La Rassegna italiana* 9:106 (February 1927): 247–52; and "Architettura (IV): Una nuova epoca arcaica," *La Rassegna italiana* 19:108 (May 1927): 467–72. "Architettura" and "Architettura II" were published in English as "Architecture" and "Architecture II: The Foreigners," trans. Ellen R. Shapiro, *Oppositions* 6 (Fall 1976): 89–92 and 93–102, respectively; "Architettura III" and "Architettura IV" were published in English as "Architecture III: Unpreparedness-Incomprehension-Prejudices" and "Architecture IV: A New Archaic Era," trans. Ellen R. Shapiro, *Oppositions* 12 (Spring 1978): 91–5 and 96–8, respectively.

90 Franco Biscossa, "'Quadrante': Il dibattito e la polemica," in *La costruzione dell'utopia – architetti e urbanisti nell'Italia fascista*, ed. Giulio Ernesti (Rome: Edizioni Lavoro, 1988), 67–89.

91 Patetta, ed., *L'architettura in Italia 1919–1943*, 227–9. My translation.

92 On CIAM, see Eric Mumford, *Defining Urban Design: CIAM Architects and the Formation of a Discipline* (New Haven, CT: Yale University Press, 2009).

93 Talamona, "Primi passi verso l'Europa (1927–1933)," 57.

94 Luisa Martina Colli, *Arte artigianato e tecnica nella poetica di Le Corbuiser* (Bari: Laterza, 1982). Gerard Monnier, "L'architecture vernaculaire, Le Corbusier et les autres," in *La Méditerranée de Le Corbusier* (Aix-en-Provence: Publications de l'Université de Provence, 1991), 139–55.

95 Giorgio Frisoni, Elisabetta Gavazza, Mariagrazia Orsolini, and Massimo Simini, "Origins and History of the Colonies," in *Cities of Childhood: Italian Colonies of the 1930s*, ed. De Martino and Wall, 6–9.

96 The BBPR colony was published in Alfred Roth, *The New Architecture*

(Zurich: H. Girsberger, 1940), 131–5. Daneri's colony was published in Sigfried Giedion, ed., *A Decade of New Architecture* (Zurich: Editions Girsberger, 1951).

97 Mario Labò, "Seaside, Mountain, and Sun-Therapy Colonies," in *Cities of Childhood*, ed. De Martino and Wall, 78–82, originally published as Mario Labò and Attilio Podestà, *Colonie: Marine, montane, elioterapiche* (Milan: Editoriale S.A. Domus, 1942), 115.

98 Labò, "Seaside, Mountain, and Sun-Therapy Colonies," 81.

4. Engineering versus Architecture

1 Adolf Loos, "Rules for Building in the Mountains," in *Trotzdem, 1900–1930* (Innsbruck: Brenner Verlag, 1931), 131–2; republished in *Adolf Loos on Architecture*, trans. Michael Mitchell (Riverside, CA: Ariadne Press, 2002), 122–3.

2 For an overview of Pagano's life, work, and writings see Franco Albini, Giancarlo Palanti, and Anna Castelli, eds., *Giuseppe Pagano Pogatschnig: Architettura e scritti* (Milan: Edizioni Domus, 1947); Carlo Melograni, *Giuseppe Pagano* (Milan: Il Balcone, 1953); Cesare De Seta, ed., *Giuseppe Pagano: Architettura e Città Durante il Fascismo* (Bari: Laterza, 1990); Antonio Saggio, *L'opera di Giuseppe Pagano tra politica e architettura* (Bari: Edizioni Dedalo, 1984); Cesare De Seta, *Il destino dell'architettura – Perisco – Giolli – Pagano* (Rome: Editori Laterza, 1985); Alberto Bassi, Laura Castagno, *Giuseppe Pagano* (Rome: Laterza, 1994).

3 On the history of the term in Italy, see Paolo Nicoloso, "Le parole dell'architettura: Il dibattito terminologico 1929–1931," in *La Costruzione dell'Utopia. Architetti e urbanisti nell'Italia fascista*, ed. Giulio Ernesti (Rome: Edizioni Lavoro, 1988), 31–45.

4 Mario Isnenghi, "Il ruralismo nella cultura italiana," in *Storia dell'agricoltura italiana in età contemporanea*, ed. Piero Bevilacqua, vol. 3 (Venice: Marsilio, 1991), 877–910. Benito Mussolini, "Fascist Agrarian Program," speech delivered in January 1921, published in Charles F. Delzell, trans. and ed., *Mediterranean Fascism 1919–1945* (New York: Walker and Company, 1970), 18–22; originally published in Renzo De Felice, ed., *Mussolini il fascista*, vol. 1, *La conquista del potere, 1921–1925* (Turin: Einaudi, 1966), 736–40. See also Benito Mussolini, "Il fascismo e i rurali," in *Scritti e discorsi di Benito Mussolini: La Rivoluzione Fascista (23 marzo 1919–28 ottobre 1922)* (Palermo: Edizioni Librarie Siciliane, 1992), 281–90; originally published in *Gerarchia* (25 May 1922).

5 On architectural education in Italy during and immediately before fascism,

see Paolo Nicoloso, *Gli architetti di Mussolini – Scuole e sindacato, architetti e massoni, professori e politici negli anni del regime* (Milan: Franco Angeli, 1999).

6 On the relationship between morality and rural architecture, see Marida Talamona, "Modernité et Fascisme: Illusions croisées," in *Annes 30. L'architecture et les arts de l'espace entre industrie et nostalgie*, ed. Jean-Louis Cohen (Paris: Editions du Patrimoine, 1997), 126–43.

7 For Pagano's comment on primitivism, see Giuseppe Pagano, "Documenti di architettura rurale," *Casabella* 95 (November 1935): 18–19. My translation.

8 Lionello Venturi, "Per la nuova architettura," *Casabella* 6:1 (January 1933): 2–3.

9 Ernesto N. Rogers, "Catarsi," *Casabella-Costruzioni* 195–198 (December 1946): 40–2; republished in Ernesto N. Rogers, *Esperienza dell'architettura*, ed. Luca Molinari (Milan: Skira, 1997), 62–71. One might also be temped to compare Pagano with Marie-Alain Couturier, the Dominican who promoted the "magnificence of poverty" as an antidote to postwar nihilism. See Marie-Alain Couturier, "The Magnificence of Poverty" and "The Modesty of the Past," in *M.-A. Couturier: Sacred Art*, ed. Dominique de Menil (Austin: University of Texas Press, 1989), 40–5 and 111–17.

10 "Moralizing impulse" is the expression that Rogers, following Pagano, used to refer to Adolf Loos. See Ernesto Rogers, "Attualità di Adolf Loos," *Casabella-Continuità* 233 (November 1959): 3.

11 David Watkin, *Morality and Architecture: The Development of a Theme in Architectural History and Theory from the Gothic Revival to the Modern Movement* (Oxford: Clarendon Press, 1977).

12 For a discussion on the contribution of Laugier's theories to Italian architecture, see Carroll L. Meeks, *Italian Architecture, 1750–1914* (New Haven: Yale University Press, 1966) esp. 13, 25, 33–6, 38. Liliana Grassi, *Razionalismo architettonico, dal Lodoli a Giuseppe Pagano* (Milan: Edizioni Bignami, 1966); and Alan Colquhoun, "Vernacular Classicism," in *Modernity and the Classical Tradition: Architectural Essays 1980–1987* (Cambridge, MA: MIT Press, 1989): 21–31. Colquhoun writes: "Laugier was no more concerned with the 'real' Mediterranean vernacular than was Rousseau with a historical primitive society. He was concerned with a distillation of classical doctrine. He was not seeking to return to the earliest hours of man, but to the pure sources of classical architecture This process entailed, not the discovery of vernacular building, but the *revernacularization* of classicism with which to substantiate a myth of origins," 30.

13 Antonio La Stella, "Architettura rurale," in *Giuseppe Pagano Fotografo*, ed. Cesare De Seta (Milan: Electa, 1979), 12–21.

14　On the history of Italian exhibitions, see Sergio Polano, *Mostrare: Exhibition Design in Italy from the Twenties to the Eighties* (Milan: Edizioni Lybra Immagine, 1988); see also Michelangelo Sabatino, "Space of Criticism: Exhibitions and the Vernacular in Italian Modernism," *Journal of Architectural Education* 62:3 (February 2009): 35–52; Diane Ghirardo, "Architects, Exhibitions, and the Politics of Culture in Italy," *Journal of Architectural Education* 45:2 (February 1992): 67–75; and Paolo Morello, "Esposizioni e mostre: 1932–36," in *Storia dell architettura italiana: Il primo Novecento*, ed. Giorgio Ciucci and Giorgio Muratore (Milan: Electa, 2004), 306–23.

15　Sandro Scarrocchia, *Albert Speer e Marcello Piacentini: l'architettura del totalitarismo negli anni trenta* (Milan: Skira, 1999); Enrico Crispolti, ed., *Arte e fascismo in Italia e in Germania* (Milan: Feltrinelli, 1974).

16　Giuseppe Pagano and Werner Daniel, *Architettura rurale italiana* (Milan: Hoepli Editore, 1936).

17　Giulio Ferrari, *L'architettura rusticana nell'arte italiana* (Milan: Hoepli Editore, 1925).

18　The examples of this regionalist phenomenon are numerous: Capri's mayor, Edwin Cerio, wrote about the island's vernacular tradition; Venice architect Egle Renata Trincanato wrote about minor architecture in the lagoon city; native of Valle D'Aosta, folklorist Jules (Giulio) Brocherel, also wrote about the vernacular arts and architecture of his region; architect Luigi Angelini wrote about Bergamo and surroundings; in Tuscany, Mario Tinti addressed the study of extant farmers cottages; in Sicily, folklorist Giuseppe Pitrè's work was key for folk studies; in Campania, architect Roberto Pane produced a number of studies on "rural architecture"; architects Mario Cereghini, Giorgio Wenter Marini, and Edoardo Gellner all wrote about the Alpine regions of northern Italy.

19　Guglielmo De Angelis D'Ossat, "Recensioni," *Palladio* 1:2 (1938): n.p.

20　Gustavo Giovannoni, "Architettura minore di Roma e del Lazio," *Roma – Rivista di Studi e di Vita Romana* 18:7 (1940): 232: "la più ampia e nota è quella del Ferrari." My translation.

21　Pagano and Daniel, *Architettura rurale italiana*, 15. My translation.

22　Giorgio Ciucci, *Gli architetti e il fascismo: Architettura e città, 1922–1944* (Turin: Einaudi, 1989), 160–4.

23　Cesare De Seta points out that Pagano was one of the only Italian modernist architects to demonstrate a sustained interest for peasant arts and crafts, "*le arti 'minori' popolari*," alongside his interest for in rural architecture. See the introduction to Cesare De Seta, ed., *Giuseppe Pagano: Architettura e città durante il fascismo* (Bari: Laterza, 1990), xv.

24　Arturo Carlo Quintavalle, *Gli Alinari* (Florence: Alinari, 2003).

25 See Daria De Seta, *Giuseppe Pagano: Vocabulario de imágines* (Madrid: Lampreave & Millán, 2008). For a history of documentary photography, see Olivier Lugon, *Le style documentaire. D'August Sander à Walker Evans, 1920–1945* (Paris: Macula, 2001).

26 For a more recent overview of vernacular architecture of the Campana region, see Roberto Pane, *Architettura rurale campana* (Florence: Rinascimento del libro, 1936): Adriana Baculo Giusti, ed., *La casa contadina – La casa nobile – La casa artigiana e mercantile – I caratteri* (Naples: Liguori Editore, 1979).

27 The 1940 Congresso nazionale followed the meeting of 1929, which was the first after 1911 to collectively take up the theme of *tradizioni populari* (folk traditions or folklore). Guglielmo De Angelis D'Ossat, "Notizie e commenti, Il IV Congresso Nazionale di Arti e Tradizioni Popolari," *Palladio: Rivista bimestrale del centro nazionale di studi per la storia dell'architettura* 4:5 (1940): 238–9. See also *Atti del IV Congresso Nazionale di Arti e Tradizioni Popolari* (Rome: Edizione dell'O.N.D., 1942).

28 For a sample of the discussions and addresses, see Giovanni Sacchi, "Architettura rustica di oggi e di ieri," *Atti dei sindacati provinciali fascisti ingegneri di Lombardia* (October 1940): 207–12.

29 The exhibition was to be hosted in a neoclassical building in proximity to the Piazza Imperiale, now Piazza Marconi. Tullio Gregory and Achille Tartaro, eds., *E 42 Utopia e scenario del regime, I: Ideologia e programma dell'Olimpiade delle Civiltà* (Venice: Marsilio Editori, 1987), 108–9; Maurizio Calvesi, Enrico Guidoni, and Simonetta Lux, eds., *E 42 Utopia e scenario del regime, II: Urbanistica, architettura, arte e decorazion* (Venice: Marsilio Editori, 1987), 371–3.

30 See Pagano's letters "A Giuseppe Bottai" (Milan, 6 February, 1942) republished in Cesare De Seta, ed., *Giuseppe Pagano: Architettura e città durante il fascismo* (Bari: Laterza, 1990), 304–7; see the "Risposta di Giuseppe Bottai" (Rome, 25 February 1942), republished in De Seta, ed., *Giuseppe Pagano: Architettura e città durante il fascismo*, 307–8.

31 Giuseppe Bottai, "Le arti popolari nell'educazione del ministero dell'educazione nazionale," *Le Arti* 3:1 (October–November 1940): 35–8; republished in Alessandro Masi, ed., *Giuseppe Bottai: La politica delle arti scritti 1918–1943* (Rome: Editalia, 1992), 243–9.

32 William E. Simeone, "Fascists and Folklorists in Italy," *The Journal of American Folklore* 91:359 (January–March 1978): 543–57; William E. Simeone, "Italian Folklore Scholars," *The Journal of American Folklore* 74:294 (October–December 1961): 344–53.

33 Achille Starace, *Opera nazionale dopolavoro* (Milan: A. Mondadori, 1938); Opera Nazionale Dopolavoro, *The National Dopolavoro Foundation in Italy*

(Rome: Società editrice di novissima, 1938). On the use (and abuse) of folklore by the fascist regime, see the work of Stefano Cavazza, "La folkloristica italiana e il fascismo: Il Comitato Nazionale per le Arti Popolari," *La ricerca folklorica – contributi allo studio della cultura delle classi popolari* 15 (April 1987): 109–22; Stefano Cavazza, "Tradizioni regionali e riesumazioni demologiche durante il fascismo," *Studi Storici – Rivista trimestrale dell'istituto gramsci* 2–3:34 (April–September 1993): 625–55; Stefano Cavazza, *Piccole patrie: Feste popolari tra regione e nazione durante il fascismo* (Bologna: Il Mulino, 1997). On the role of leisure in fascist Italy, see Victoria De Grazia, *The Culture of Consent: Mass Organization of Leisure in Fascist Italy* (New York: Cambridge University Press, 1981). On festivals and spectacle, see also Medina Lasansky, *The Renaissance Perfected: Architecture, Spectacle, and Tourism in Fascist Italy* (University Park, PA: Pennsylvania State University, 2004).

34   *Atti del I Congresso Nazionale di Arti e Tradizioni Popolari* (Florence: Rinascimento del libro, 1930); *Atti del III Congresso Nazionale di Arti e Tradizioni Popolari* (Rome: Edizione dell'O.N.D., 1936); *Atti del IV Congresso Nazionale di Arti e Tradizioni Popolari* (Rome: Edizione dell'O.N.D., 1942).

35   On the role of kitsch and right-wing ideology, see the classic study by Clement Greenberg, "The Avant-garde and Kitsch," in *Kitsch: The World of Bad Taste*, ed. Gillo Dorfles (1939; reprint, New York: Bell Publishing, 1969), 116–26.

36   See Giuseppe Pagano, "La Villa," *Casabella* 5:7 (July 1933): 2–3. My translation.

37   For a discussion on this topic, see "North versus South" in Jean-François Lejeune and Michelangelo Sabatino, *Modern Architecture and the Mediterranean: Vernacular Dialogues and Contested Identities* (London: Routledge, 2009), 1–12.

38   Mario Tinti, *L'architettura delle case coloniche in Toscana* (Florence: Rinascimento del Libro, 1934). See also Luigi Cavallo, ed., *Ottone Rosai* (Milan: Mazzotta, 1995); Luigi Cavallo, *Cinquanta dipinti di Ottone Rosai a 50 anni dopo la Scomparsa* (Florence: Pananti, 2008).

39   Tinti, *L'architettura delle case coloniche in Toscana*, 14. My translation.

40   Mario Tinti, "L'equivoco dell'arte rustica," *Casabella* 49 (January 1932): 51–2.

41   Giuseppe Pagano, "Case rurali," *Casabella* 86 (February 1935): 9–15.

42   My translation. The expression *"colore locale"* was later used by Raffaello Giolli as the title of an essay published in *Casabella* 108 (December 1936): 26–7. During the 1930s, Giolli published several articles in praise of vernacular architecture as well as a review of Pagano and Daniel's *Architettura Rurale Italiana* of 1936. See his "Architettura vivente," *Casabella* 10:30 (Oc-

tober 1938): 2C–1; republished in *Raffello Giolli. L'architettura razionale*, ed. Cesare De Seta (Bari: Laterza, 1972), 249–50. See also Raffaello Giolli, "Per una ricognizicne dell'arte popolare italiana," *Domus* 134 (February 1939): 47.

43 Pagano, "Case rurali," 9. My translation.

44 Mario Castelli, *Fabbricati rurali* (Turin: UTET, 1938); Carlo Manetti, *La casa dell'uomo in ca·npagna: progetti e realizzazioni moderne di case rurali* (Florence: Marzocco, 1940); Amos Edallo, *Ruralistica: urbanistica rurale con particolare riferimento alla valle padana* (Milan: Hoepli Editore, 1946); in English, see Amos Edallo, "What Is Ruralism?" *Landscape: Magazine of Human Geography* 3:1 (Summer 1953): 12–19.

45 This is also the case in English-speaking countries; see, for example, Henry Stephens and Robert Scott Burn, *The Book of Farm Buildings: Their Arrangement and Construction* (Edinburgh: William Blackwood and Sons, 1861).

46 Archimede Sacchi, *Le abitazioni: Alberghi, case operaie, fabbriche rurali, case civili, palazzi e ville* (Milan: Hoepli Editore, 1886); Isidoro Andreani, *Case coloniche* (Milan: Hoepli Editore, 1919). On Hoepli manuals, see Elena Svalduz, "Aggiornare la professione: L'Editoria tecnico-scientifica, Ulrico Hoepli e i manuali per l'architetto," *Richerche Storiche* 29:2 (May–August 1999): 299–329; Clementina Barucci, *Strumenti e cultura del progetto: Manualistica e letteratura tecnica in Italia 1860–1920* (Rome: Officina Edizioni, 1984); and Carlo Guenzi, ed., *L'arte di edificare – Manuali in Italia 1750–1950* (Milan: Be-Ma Editrice, 1993).

47 Giuseppe Pagano, "Le case coloniche nella pianura lombarda," *Casabella-Costruzioni* 146 (February 1940): 25–6. My translation. Cited in Cino Zucchi, Francesca Cadeo, and Monica Lattuada, *Asnago e Vender: L'astrazione quotidiana. Architetture e progetti 1925–1970* (Milan: Skira, 1999), 76–9.

48 On the relationship between politics, propaganda, and rural culture pursued by the fascist regime, see Laura Malvano, *Fascismo e politica dell'immagine* (Turin: Bollati Boringhieri, 1988), 144–51.

49 Guido Biffoli and Guido Ferrara, *La casa colonica in Toscana* (Florence: Vallecchi, 1966); Francesco Gurrieri and Gianluca Belli, *La casa colonica in Italia* (Florence: Ponte alle Grazie, 1994).

50 Walter L. Adamson, *Avant-garde Florence: From Modernism to Fascism* (Cambridge, MA: Harvard University Press, 1993); Walter L. Adamson, "The Culture of Italian Fascism and the Fascist Crisis of Modernity: The Case of Il Selvaggio," *Journal of Contemporary History* 30:4 (October 1995): 555–75. An anthology of the journal was published as Carlo Ludovico Ragghianti, *Il Selvaggio di Mino Maccari* (Vicenza: Neri Pozza, 1994); see also Luciano Troisio, ed., *Le riviste di Strapaese e Stracittà – Il Selvaggio – L'italiano* (Tre-

viso: Canova, 1975); Emily Braun, "Speaking Volumes: Giorgio Morandi's Still Lifes and the Cultural Politics of Strapaese," *Modernism/Modernity* 2:3 (1995): 89–116.

51 Ardengo Soffici, "Architettura rustica," *Il Selvaggio* (22 June 1939); republished in *Selva Arte* (Florence: Vallecchi, 1943), 285–8.

52 See Luigi Cavallo, ed., *Ardengo Soffici* (Milan: Mazzotta, 1992).

53 When in 1936 Pagano gathered images of Tuscan farmhouses for the *Architettura Rurale Italiana Exhibition*, he sought the help of local architect Pier Niccolò Berardi, who had already spent years studying and documenting examples. These photographs are published in Giovanni Fanelli and Barbara Mazza, *La casa colonica in Toscana: Le fotografie di Pier Niccolò Berardi alla Triennale del 1936* (Florence: Octavo, 1999).

54 Corrado Pavolini, "Case toscane," *Illustrazione toscana e dell'Etruria* 2:12 (December 1933): 22. My translation.

55 Pavolini, "Case toscane," 24; Luigi Parpagliolo and Giovanni Battista Ceas, *Capri – Visioni architettoniche di Gio. Batt. Ceas* (Rome: Biblioteca d'Arte Editrice, 1930).

56 Giovanni Michelucci, "Contatti fra architetture antiche e moderne," *Domus* 50 (February 1932): 70–1; Giovanni Michelucci, "Contatti fra architetture antiche e moderne (II)," *Domus* 51 (March 1932): 134–6; Giovanni Michelucci, "Fonti della moderna architettura italiana," *Domus* 56 (August 1932): 460–1.

57 Edoardo Persico, "Un 'cottage' nel Canavese," *Casabella* 45 (September 1931): 16–27; republished in Giulia Veronesi, ed., *Edoardo Persico: Tutte le opere (1923–1935)*, vol. 2 (Milan: Edizioni di Comunità, 1964), 50. On Levi-Montalcini's work, see Emanuele Levi-Montalcini, ed., *Gino Levi-Montalcini: Architetture, disegni e scritti* (Turin: Società degli ingegneri e degli architetti in Torino, 2003).

58 For a discussion of the vernacular and classical dimension to Palladio, see Howard Burns, in collaboration with Lynda Fairbairn and Bruce Boucher, *Andrea Palladio, 1508–1580: The Portico and the Farmyard* (London: Arts Council of Great Britain, 1975), and Kurt W. Forster, "Back to the Farm: Vernacular Architecture and the Development of the Renaissance Villa," *Architectura* 4:15 (1974): 1–12.

59 Edwin Cerio, "L'architettura minima nella contrada delle serene," *Architettura e arti decorative* 4:2 (August 1922): 156–76.

60 Carlo Melograni, *Giuseppe Pagano* (Milan: Il Balcone, 1955).

61 Jules (Giulio) Brocherel, ed., *Arte Popolare Valdostana*, (Rome: Edizione dell'Opera Nazionale Dopolavoro, 1937). On Brocherel, see Sandra Barberi, *Jules Brocherel: Alpinismo, etnografia, fotografia e vita culturale in Valle D'Aosta*

fra Ottocento e Novocento (Ivrea: Priuli & Verlucca, 1992). On his personal collection of peasant art, see *Arte popolare valdostana. La collezione Jules Brocherel dei Musei Civici di Torino* (Turin: GAM, 2000). Important writings by Brocherel on architecture-related matters include his review of Jona's book "Camillo Jona, L'architettura rusticana in Valle d'Aosta," *Augusta-Praetoria* (January–February 1921): 37–9; "La casa rustica valdostana," *Atti del III Congresso Nazionale di arti e tradizioni popolari* (Rome: Edizione dell'O.N.D., 1936), 197–99; "Tipi di case rustiche valdostane," *Le alpi – rivista mensile del centro alpinistico italiano* (January–February 1940–1941): 41–3.

62 During the interwar period, Bruno Moretti was perhaps the most dedicated publicist of residential architecture. Over the course of two decades, he published several anthologies on the subject. Moretti's first sourcebook was *Ville* (Milan: Hoepli Editore, 1934), which focused on the villa within the international context. In 1939 he followed this up with *Case d'abitazione in Italia* (Milan: Hoepli Editore, 1939), an anthology dedicated to the *casa*, or house.

63 John Ruskin, *The Poetry of Architecture or The Architecture of the Nations of Europe Considered in its Association with Natural Scenery and National Character* (New York: D.D. Merrill Co., 1893), 30–1; published in Italian as *La poesia dell'architettura*, trans. Dora Prunetti (Milan: Editore A. Solmi, 1909), esp., "Il 'cottage' della pianura italiana," 39.

64 Giuseppe Pagano, "Architecttura rurale in Italia," *Casabella* 96 (December 1935): 16–23.

65 On the cosmopolitan leanings of one of Italy's leading architects, see Michelangelo Sabatino, "Ernesto N. Rogers as Student: His Education, Books and Writing," *Casabella* 688 (April 2001): 76–83.

66 See Markus Kristan, ed., *Adolf Loos Villen* (Vienna: Album, 2001).

67 This project was published in an early study of Loos by Heinrich Kulka, *Adolf Loos: Das Werk des Architekten* (Vienna: A. Schroll, 1931), which Pagano had discussed in the pages of *Casabella*. Loos was also the subject of a retrospective exhibition at the V Triennale in Milan in 1933.

68 Armando Melis, "L'esposizione di Torino del 1928," *Architettura e arti decorative* 4:10 (April 1928): 372–81. My translation.

69 Valeria Garuzzo, *Torino 1928: L'architettura all'Esposizione Nazionale Italiana* (Turin: Testo & Immagine, 2002).

70 Gianni Pettena and Milco Carboni, eds., *Ettore Sottsass senior, Architetto* (Milan: Electa, 1991), 70–81.

71 Heinz P. Adamek, "Armoniosa dissonanza. L'architettura a Vienna intorno al 1912," in Pettena and Carboni, eds., *Ettore Sottsass senior, Architetto*, 50–9.

72 Giuseppe Gerola, "Architettura minore e rustica trentina," *Architettura e arti decorative* 6:8 (March 1929): 291–301.

73 Massimiliano Savorra, *Enrico Agostino Griffini – la casa, il monumento, la città* (Naples: Electa, 2000); Maurizio Scudiero, *Giorgio Wenter Marini: Pittura, Architettura, Grafica* (Trent: L'Editore, 1991).

74 The journal *Ingegneria* published by Hoepli in Milan was transformed in 1927 to become *L'ingegnere: Rivista tecnica del sindacato nazionale fascista ingegneri*; its editorial offices were relocated to Rome, a move consistent with a gradual transfer of administrative and legislative offices to the nation's capital during the fascist period. See M.C. Colleoni, *L'associazionismo professionale degli ingegneri italiani: dai Collegi di fine Ottocento al sindacato fascista*, in *Il Politecnico di Milano nella storia italiana (1914–1963)*, vol. 1 (Bari: Laterza, 1988), 161–4.

75 Enrico Griffini's essays are as follows: "Case rustiche veneziane: I casoni," *Ingegneria* 1:1 (July 1922): 17–18; "La casa rustica delle Alpi Italiane," *Ingegneria* 3:2 (March 1923): 66–9; "La casa rustica della Valle Gardena," *Architettura e arti decorative* 7:4 (1925): 291–8.

76 See *Concorso "Ercole Marelli" per progetti di ricostruzione di piccole case rurali nei territori devastati dalla Guerra* (Milan: Touring Club Italian, 1920), 4–17; Raffaello Giolli, "In attesa del concorso Marelli. Osservazioni di Valle Strona," *Le vie d'Italia* (January 1919): 27–33.

77 Cited in Paolo Toschi, *Saggi sull'arte popolare* (Rome: Edizioni Iitaliane, 1944), 36–7.

78 Griffini, "La casa rustica delle alpi italiane," 66.

79 Paolo Mezzanotte, "Il focolare Friulano," *L'Edilizia Moderna* 26:12 (December 1917): 66–8; on the domestic architecture of the Friuli region, see the pioneering study by Giovanni Del Puppo, *La casa in Friuli: Appunti e note* (Udine: Tipografia Domenico Del Bianco, 1907).

80 See Enrico Griffini, "Progetto di una casa colonica per la carnia e l'alto friuli," *L'architettura italiana* 15:11 (November 1920): 85–7; also published as "La casa rustica delle Alpi Italiane," *Ingegneria* 3:2 (March 1923): 66–9. On the professional overlap and competition between engineers and architects, see Guido Zucconi, *La città contesa. Dagli ingegneri sanitari agli urbanisti, 1885–1942* (Milan: Jaca Book, 1989).

81 See Griffini's preface to Giuseppe Ciribini, *Per un metodo nelle ricerche sulla architettura rustica* (Milan: Polver Stampa, 1942), 9–12; see also, Giuseppe Cirbini, "Genesi e suiluppi dell'abitazione rustica italiana nel quadro dell'architettura rustica mediterranea," in *Atti dei sindacati provinciali fascisti ingegnero: Di Lombardia*, 16 (1940): 189–206; Giuseppe Ciribini, *Architettura e industria: lineamenti di tecnica della produzione edilizia* (Milan: Libreria Editrice Politecnica Tamburini, 1958).

82 Österreichischer Ingenieur und Architekten-Verein, *Das Bauernhaus in Österreich-Ungarn und in seinen Grenzgebieten* (Vienna: Verlag des Oslerr, 1901–6); Schweizerischer Ingenieur und Architekten-Verein, *Das Bauernhaus in der Schweiz* (Zurich: Hofer and Co., 1903); Verband Deutscher Architekten und Ingenieur Vereine, *Das Bauernhaus im Deutschen Reiche und in seinen Grenzgebieten* (Dresden: Küthmann, 1906; reprint ed., Hannover: Vincentz, 1974).

83 Aristide Baragiola, "Sulla casa villereccia," *Atti del Primo Congresso di Etnografia Italiana, Roma 19–24 Ottobre 1911*, ed. Società di etnografia italiana (Perugia: Unione Tipografica Cooperativa, 1912), 115–19.

84 See Lando Bortolotti, *Storia della politica edilizia in Italia* (Rome: Editori Riuniti, 1978).

85 Riccardo Mariani, *Città e campagna in Italia 1917–1943* (Milan: Edizioni di Comunità, 1986). Riccardo Mariani, *Fascismo e "città nuove"* (Milan: Feltrinelli Editore, 1976); Diane Ghirardo, *Building New Communities: New Deal America and Fascist Italy* (Princeton, NJ: Princeton University Press, 1989); Renato Besana, Carlo Fabrizio Carli, Leonardo Devoti, and Luigi Prisco, eds., *Metafisica costruita: Le città di fondazione degli anni Trenta dall'Italia all'Oltremare* (Milan: Touring Club Italiano, 2002).

86 Luigi Piccinato, "Il significato urbanistico di Sabaudia," *Urbanistica* 1 (January–February 1934): 10; republished in Federico Malusardi, *Luigi Piccinato e l'urbanistica moderna* (Rome: Officina Edizioni, 1993), 363. My translation.

87 Roberto Gabetti, ed., *Villaggi operai in Italia: La Val Padana e Crespi d'Adda* (Turin: Einaudi, 1981), 111–26; Luigi Cortesi, *Crespi d'Adda, Villaggio ideale del lavoro* (Bergamo: Grafica e Arte, 1995).

88 Jeffrey T. Schnapp, ed., *Gaetano Ciocca: Costruttore, inventore, agricoltore, scultore* (Milan: Skira, 2000). See also Jeffrey T. Schnapp, *Building Fascism, Communism, Liberal Democracy: Gaetano Ciocca—Architect, Inventor, Farmer, Writer, Engineer* (Stanford, CA: Stanford University Press, 2003).

89 Giovanni Brino, *Carlo Mollino: Architecture as Autobiography* (London: Thames and Hudson, 2005). See also Sergio Pace, ed., *Carlo Mollino architetto, 1905–1973* (Milan: Electa, 2006).

90 Napoleone Ferrari, *Mollino Casa del Sole* (Turin: Museo Casa Mollino, 2007), 115, which includes Mollino's previously unpublished article "Country Architecture in the Upper Aosta Valley." For a recent anthology of his writings, see Michela Comba, ed., *Carlo Mollino – Architettura di parole* (Turin: Bollati Boringhieri, 2007).

91 Luciano Bolzoni, *Architettura moderna nelle Alpi italiane dal 1900 alla fine degli anni Cinquanta* (Turin: Priuli & Verlucca, 2000); Luciano Bolzoni, *Architettura moderna nelle Alpi italiane dagli anni Sessanta alla fine del XX secolo*

(Turin: Priuli & Verlucca, 2001); Luca Moretto, *Architettura moderna alpina in Valle d'Aosta: Albini, BBPR, Cereghini, Figini e Pollini, Melis, Mollino, Muzio, Ponti, Sottsass Senior, Sottsass Junior* (Aosta: Musumeci, 2003).

92 Renato Biasetti, *L'opera architettonica di Carlo Mollino – L'architettura montana* (Turin: Facoltà di Architettura, 1981).

93 Franco Biscossa, "'Quadrante': Il dibattito e la polemica, in *La Costruzione dell'Utopia. Architetti e urbanisti nell'Italia fascista*, ed. Giulio Ernesti (Rome: Edizioni Lavoro, 1988), 67–89.

94 Giuseppe Pagano, "Tre anni di architettura in Italia," *Casabella* 10:110 (1937): 2–5; republished in De Seta, *Giuseppe Pagano: Architettura e città durante il fascismo*, 155–65.

95 Giuseppe Pagano, "Un architetto: Luigi Cosenza," *Casabella* 100 (April 1936): 6–17. On Rudofsky, see Andrea Bocco-Guarneri, *Bernard Rudofsky: A Humane Designer* (Vienna: Springer, 2003); and Architekturzentrum Wien, ed., *Lessons from Bernard Rudofsky: Life as a Voyage* (Boston-Basel: Birkhäuser, 2007). On Cosenza, see Giorgio Ciucci, "Un sognatore razionale," in *Luigi Cosenza: Scritti e progetti di architettura*, ed. Francesco Domenico Moccia (Naples: Clean, 1994), 17–19.

96 Cherubino Gambardella, *Case sul Golfo: Abitare lungo la costa Napoletana 1930–1945* (Naples: Electa, 1993); Jean-Louis Cohen, "La Villa Oro, o tre miti moderni," in *Luigi Cosenza oggi 1905/2005*, ed. Alfredo Buccaro and Giancarlo Mainini (Naples: Clean, 2006), 116–17.

97 Pagano, "Un architetto: Luigi Cosenza," 6.

98 See the interview with mason master Alberto in Giancarlo Cosenza and Mimmo Jodice, *Procida: A Mediterranean Architecture* (Naples: Clean, 2007), 216–19.

99 Bernard Rudofsky wrote several articles for *Domus* under the direction of Gio Ponti, including "Non ci vuole un nuovo mode di costruire – Ci vuole un modo di vivere," *Domus* 123 (March 1938): 2–3.

100 Felicity Scott, "Allegories of Nomadism and Dwelling," in *Anxious Modernisms: Experimentation in Postwar Architectural Culture*, ed. Sarah Williams Goldhagen and Réjean Legaut (Cambridge, MA: MIT Press, 2000), 215–37, and Felicity Scott, review of *Architecture without Architects*, by Bernard Rudofsky, *Harvard Design Magazine* (Fall 1998): 69–72.

101 Gio Ponti, *In Praise of Architecture*, trans. Giuseppina and Mario Salvadori (New York: F.W. Dodge, 1960), 211.

102 See the brief essay by Michael Grüning and Rowena Lanfermann, "Entwerfen und Bauen in Rom – Konrad Wachsmanns italienische Jahre," *Zuflucht auf Widerruf. Deutsche Künstler und Wissenschaftler in Italien 1933–1944* (Milan: Mazzotta, 1995), 235–48; Michael Grüning, *Der Architekt Konrad Wachsmann – Erinnerungen und Selbstauskünfte* (Vienna: Löcker, 1986);

Wachsmann published his photographs of travels to Italy in Konrad Wachsmann, *Aspekte* (Wiesbaden: Krausskopf, 1961).

103 Francesco Cellini, *Le architetture di Ridolfi e Frankl* (Milan: Electa, 2005).

104 Giuseppe Pagano, "Una lezione di modestia," *Casabella* 11 (March 1937): 2–5. My translation.

105 Stefano Guidarini, *Ignazio Gardella nell'architettura italiana. Opere 1929– 1999* (Milan: Skira, 2002), 32–45; Marco Casamonti, ed., *Ignazio Gardella, architetto (1905–1999): Costruire la modernità* (Milan: Electra, 2006). For Gardella's personal commentary on the use of the brick screen, see Ignazio Gardella, "Materiale e immateriale," *Materia – Rivista di architettura* 5 (1990): 22–33.

106 See Raffaello Giolli, "Il dispensario antitubercolare d'Alessandria," *Casabella-Costruzioni* 128 (August 1938): 4–9; republised in *L'architettura razionale*, ed. Cesare De Seta (Bari: Laterza, 1972), 245–8.

107 Leon Battista Alberti, *On the Art of Building in Ten Books*, trans. and ed. Joseph Rykwert, Robert Tavernor, and Neil Leach (Cambridge, MA: MIT Press, 1988), 291.

108 Ernst Gombrich cited Venturi's pioneering study in his *The Preference for the Primitive* (London: Phaidon, 2002).

109 Edoardo Persico, "Primitivi," *Casabella* (February 1935): 6; republished in Giulia Veronesi, ed., *Edoardo Persico. Scritti d'architettura (1927–1935)* (Florence: Vallecchi Editore, 1968), 87–8.

110 Edoardo Persico, "Punto e a capo per l'architettura," *Domus* (November 1934); republished in Veronesi, ed., *Edoardo Persico: Scritti d'architettura (1927–1935)*, 153–68.

111 Giuseppe Pagano, "Una casetta in legno," *Domus* 177 (September 1942): 375–9.

112 Ibid., 375. My translation.

113 Giuseppe Pagano, "Tre anni di architettura italiana," *Casabella* 110 (February 1937): 2–5; republished in De Seta, *Giuseppe Pagano: Architettura e città durante il fascismo*, 160–1. My translation.

5. Continuity and Reality

1 Ernesto N. Rogers, "The Tradition of Modern Architecture in Italy," in *Italy Builds: Its Modern Architecture and Native Inheritance*, ed. George Everard Kidder Smith, trans. Giuliana Baracco (New York: Reinhold Publishing Corporation, 1955), 10; originally published as "La tradizione dell'architettura moderna italiana," *Casabella-Continuità* 206 (July–August 1955): 1–7.

2 Although a number of individuals left Italy (including Lionello Venturi

and Ernesto N. Rogers), they ultimately returned to Italy. See Renata Brog-gini, *Terra d'Asilo – I rifugiati Italiani in Svizzera 1943–1945* (Bologna: Mulino, 1993). Pier Maria Bardi, an outspoken critic, moved to Brazil in 1946 with his wife, architect Lina Bo Bardi. Olivia de Oliveira, *The Architecture of Lina Bo Bardi: Subtle Substances* (Barcelona: Editorial Gustavo Gili, 2006).

3 See Ernesto N. Rogers, "Catarsi," in *Casabella-Construzioni* 195–198 (December 1946): 40; "Continuità," *Casabella-Continuità* 199 (December–January 1953–4): 2; both are republished in Luca Molinari, ed., *Ernesto N. Rogers – Esperienza dell'architettura* (Milan: Skira, 1997), 62–71, 92–5.

4 On Rogers' role as an editor and the history of this important journal and its postwar reconfiguration as *Casabella – Continuità,* see the recent overview by Chiara Baglione, *Casabella, 1928–2008* (Milan: Electa, 2008).

5 Ernesto N. Rogers, "Una casa a ciascuno," *Il Politecnico* 4 (20 October 1945): 4; republished in Rogers, *Esperienze dell'architettura,* 72. See also Dennis Doordan, "Rebuilding the House of Man," in *The Italian Metamorphosis, 1943–1968,* ed. Germano Celant (New York: Harry N. Abrams, 1994), 586–95.

6 See Guilio Carlo Argan, "Architecture and Ideology," *Zodiac* 1 (1957): 45–52; republished in Giulio Carlo Argan, *Progetto e destino: saggi di arte e letteratura* (Milan: Il Saggiatore, 1965), 82–90.

7 For an analysis of the Italian pavilion, see Geert Bekaert, "'Un volto sincero' – Le Pavillon Italien," in *L'architecture moderne à l'Expo 58,* ed. Rita Devos and Mil de Kooning (Brussels: Fonds Mercator et Dexia Banque, 2006), 131–43. For an overview of the exhibition, see Karel Velle, ed. *Expo 58: Between Utopia and Reality: Under the Leadership of Gonzague Pluvinage* (Brussels: Editions Racine, 2008).

8 Ernesto N. Rogers, "All'Expo 58 il futuro (dell'architettura) non è cominciato," *Casabella-Continuità* 221 (September 1958): 3–5; published in English as "The Future Was Not to Be Seen at Brussels," *Architects Yearbook* 9 (1959): 132–9.

9 Reyner Banham, "Neoliberty: The Italian Retreat from Modern Architecture," *The Architectural Review* 125:747 (April 1959): 231–5.

10 Paolo Portoghesi, "Dal neorealismo al neoliberty," *Comunità* 12:65 (December 1958): 73. My translation.

11 Paolo Portoghesi, "Italy in Retreat," *After Modern Architecture,* trans. Meg Shore (New York: Rizzoli, 1982), 36; originally published in Italian as *Dopo l'architettura moderna* (Bari: Laterza, 1980).

12 Paolo Portoghesi, ed., *The Presence of the Past* (London: Academy, 1980), 9–14; originally published in Italian as *La presenza del passato* (Venice: La Biennale di Venezia, 1980).

13 On the concepts of *realism* and *neorealism* in modernist architecture, see Jorge Silvetti's erudite essay, "On Realism in Architecture," *The Harvard Architecture Review* 1 (Spring 1980): 11–31, and Manfredo Tafuri, "Architettur e realismo," *Architettura moderna. L'avventura delle idée 1750–1980*, ed. Vittorio Magnago Lampugnani (Milan: Electa, 1985), 123–45. On neorealism in Italy, see Bruno Reichlin, "Figures of Neorealism in Italian Architecture (Part 1)," *Grey Room* 5 (Fall 2001): 78–101; "Figures of Neorealism in Italian Architecture (Part 2)," *Grey Room* 6 (Winter 2002): 110–33; Vittorio Magnago Lampugnani, "The Myth of Reality: Notes on Neorealism in Italy 1946–56," *Architecture & Arts 1900–2004: A Century of Creative Projects in Building, Design, Cinema, Painting, Sculpture*, ed. Germano Celant (Milan: Skira, 2004), 75–9; Maristella Casciato, "Neorealism in Italian Architecture," in *Anxious Modernism: Experimentation in Postwar Architecture Culture*, ed. Sarah Williams Goldhagen and Réjean Legault (Cambridge, MA: MIT Press, 2000), 25–53.

14 Germano Celant, ed., *The Italian Metamorphosis, 1943–1968* (New York: Harry N. Abrams, 1994).

15 Bruno Zevi, "Il grattacielo sdraiato," *L'Espresso* 8 (22 February 1955): 28–9; republished in Bruno Zevi, *Cronache di Architettura*, vol. 1 (Bari: Laterza, 1971), 300.

16 Carlo Aymonino, "Storia e cronaca del quartiere Tiburtino," *Casabella-Continuità* 215 (April–May 1957): 18–43. See also Margherita Guccione, *Guida ai quartieri romani INA Casa*, ed. Maria Margarita Segarra Lagunes and Rosalia Vittorini (Rome: Gangemi Editore, 2002).

17 Paolo Nicoloso, "Genealogie del piano Fanfani 1939–1950," in *La grande ricostruzione. Il piano Ina-Casa e l'Italia degli anni 50*, ed. Paola Di Biagi (Rome: Donzelli, 2001), 33–62.

18 For a detailed discussion of the nature of architect-designed exhibitions and the notion of *operative* practice, see Michelangelo Sabatino, "Space of Criticism: Exhibitions and the Vernacular in Italian Modernism," *Journal of Architectural Education* 62:3 (February 2009): 35–52.

19 See Giulia Veronesi, *Difficoltà politiche dell'architettura in Italia 1920–1940* (Milan: Libreria Editrice Politecnica Tamburini, 1953; reprinted, Milan: C. Marinotti, 2008).

20 Franco Albini, "Nota per il coordinamento degli studi regionali per la Mostra di Architettura spontanea alla IX Triennale" (ca. 1950–1), Archivio Progetti, Fondo Giuseppe Alberto Samonà, IUAV, Samonà 2, fascicle 058. My translation.

21 Gillo Dorfles, "Architettura 'spontanea' e tutela del paesaggio," *Domus* 305 (April 1955): 8, 64.

22 Liliana Grassi, *Storia e cultura dei monumenti* (Milan: Società editrice libraria, 1960).
23 Ibid., 46. My translation.
24 Egle Renata Trincanato, *Venezia minore* (Venice: Filippi Editore, 1948). For an overview of Trincanato, see Maddalena Scimemi and Anna Tonicello, eds., *Egle Renata Trincanato: 1910–1988* (Venice: Marsilio and IUAV, 2008); Egle Trincanato, *A Guide to Venetian Domestic Architecture: "Venezia Minore"* (Venice: Canal and Stamperia Editrice, 1995).
25 Egle Renata Trincanato, *Venezia minore* (Venice: Filippi Editore, 1948), 51.
26 Roberto Pane, "Architettura e letteratura," in Roberto Pane, *Architettura e arti figurative* (Venice: Neri Pozza Editore, 1948), 63–73. Pane's discussion was largely based on the work of Benedetto Croce, who published a study on the impact of folk traditions on poetry. See Benedetto Croce, *Poesia popolare e poesia d'arte* (Rome: Laterza, 1930), published in English as "Folk Poetry and Poets' Poetry," in *Philosophy, Poetry, History: An Anthology of Essays by Benedetto Croce*, trans. Cecil Sprigge (London: Oxford University Press, 1966): 382–96. Worthy of note is the translation of the Italian word *popolare* into *folk* rather than *popular* or *of the people*.
27 See, for example, Fabrizio Brunetti, "L'architettura organica secondo Bruno Zevi e la *riscoperta* di Wright in Italia," in *L'architettura in Italia negli anni della ricostruzione* (Florence: Alinea Editrice, 1986), 125–42.
28 Bruno Zevi, "Constitution of the Association for Organic Architecture in Rome," in *Architecture Culture 1943–1968: A Documentary Anthology*, ed. Joan Ockman and Edward Eigen (New York: Columbia Books of Architecture – Rizzoli, 1993), 68–9; originally published as Bruno Zevi et al., "La Costituzione dell'Associazione per l'Architettura Organica a Roma," *Metron* 2 (September 1945): 75–6. Maristella Casciato, "Gli esordi della rivista 'Metron': eventi e protagonisti," *Rassegna di Architettura e Urbanistica* 117 (September–December 2005): 45–55.
29 On the Foro Mussolini's reception after the fall of fascism, see Michelangelo Sabatino, "The *Foro Italico* and the *Stadio dei marmi*: Monuments and Monumentality," in *Foro Italico*, ed. Giorgio Armani, Luigi Ballerini, and Michelangelo Sabatino (New York: PowerHouse Books, 2003), i–viii.
30 Bruno Zevi, *Towards an Organic Architecture* (London: Faber and Faber, 1950), 51–2; originally published as *Verso un'architettura organica* (Turin: Giulio Einaudi Editore, 1945).
31 Frank Lloyd Wright expressed interest in the vernacular on several occasions, most explicitly in his "The Sovereignty of the Individual" (1910), in *Frank Lloyd Wright: Writings and Buildings*, ed. Edgar Kaufmann and Ben Raeburn (New York: Horizon Press, 1960), 84–106. Wright's essay was

originally published as the preface to his *Ausgeführte Bauten und Entwürfe* (Berlin: Wasmuth, 1910); and was reprinted on the occasion of the 1951 exhibition *Mostra di Frank Lloyd Wright* as the Introduction to *Sixty Years of Living Architecture* (Florence: Studio Italiano di Storia dell'Arte, 1951). In this essay, Wright wrote: "No really Italian building seems ill at ease in Italy. All are happily content with what ornament and color they carry naturally. The native rocks and trees and garden slopes are at one with them. Wherever the cypresses rise, there, like the touch of a magician's wand, all resolves into composition harmonious and complete" (86).

32 See the last publication of Bruno Zevi, entirely dedicated to the vernacular, in which he still offers cautious support for this tradition: *Controstoria dell'architettura in Italia: Dialetti architettonici* (Rome: Newton and Compton Editori, 1996).

33 For the complete text of this interview, see Emanuele Carreri, *Architettura italiana, 1940–1959* (Naples: Electa, 1998), 34. See also Roberto Dulio, *Introduzione a Bruno Zevi* (Rome: Laterza, 2008).

34 See Pierluigi Giordani, "Vocazione degli abitanti del Delta: I 'casoni' del Polesine," *L'architettura – cronache e storia* 7 (May 1956): 58–61; "Vocazione degli abitanti del Delta: Misure dell'uomo e della produttività," *L'architettura – cronache e storia* 9 (July 1956): 208–13; "Vocazione degli abitanti del Delta: Paesi di bonifica," *L'architettura – cronache e storia* 10 (August 1956): 284–90; "Vocazione degli abitanti del Delta: Comunità autonome," *L'architettura – cronache e storia* 11 (September 1956): 370–3; "Vocazione degli abitanti del Delta: Le città storiche: Comacchio e Chioggia," *L'architettura – cronache e storia* 13 (November 1956): 526–31.

35 Bruno Zevi, "Contadini e urbanistica – Cafoni spossessano miserabili," *Cronache di architettura* 6:258–320 (1958): 265.

36 Errico Ascione, "Nuove opere dell'architetto Pierluigi Giordani nella Delta Padano: Borgata rurale San Romualdo," *L'architettura – cronache e storia* 47 (September 1959): 304–23.

37 Pierluigi Giordani, "Considerazioni intorno a 'Garden Cities of To-Morrow,'" in *L'idea della città-giardino di Ebenezer Howard* (Bologna: Calderini, 1962), 147–309.

38 Giorgio Muratore, "L'esperienza del manuale," *Controspazio* 6:1 (1974): 82–92.

39 George Barnett Johnston, *Drafting Culture: A Social History of Architectural Graphic Standards* (Cambridge, MA: MIT Press, 2008).

40 Manfredo Tafuri, *History of Italian Architecture, 1944–1985* (Cambridge, MA: MIT Press, 1989), 13.

41 Giancarlo De Carlo, *William Morris* (Milan: Il Balcone, 1947).

42 See Giancarlo De Carlo, *Urbino: The History of a City and Plans for its Development*, trans. Loretta Schaeffer Guarda (Cambridge, MA: MIT Press, 1970); originally published as *Urbino: La storia di una città e il piano della sua evoluzione urbanistica* (Padua: Marsilio, 1966).

43 It is especially interesting that an anarchist sympathizer like De Carlo and a Catholic intellectual like Bo could find a common ground by looking to the hill town as a model of and a resource for contemporary design. See Lamberto Rossi, *Giancarlo De Carlo, Architetture* (Milan: Arnoldo Mondadori Editore, 1988); Benedict Zucchi, *Giancarlo De Carlo* (Oxford: Butterworth Architecture, 1992); John McKean, *Giancarlo De Carlo: Layered Places* (Stuttgart: Edition Axel Menges, 2004).

44 Edoardo Detti, "Urbanistica medievale minore," *Critica d'arte* 24 (November–December 1957): 489–504; "Urbanistica medieval minore, n. 2," *Critica d'arte* 25–26 (January–April 1958): 73–101.

45 Not by coincidence, this initiative was spearheaded by Federico Zeri, who had been instrumental decades earlier in re-evaluating *minor* artists. See Enrico Guidoni's introduction to *Storia dell'arte italiana, Parte terza. Situazioni momenti indagini*, ed. Federico Zeri, vol. 1 (Turin: Einaudi, 1980), 3–33.

46 Peter Blake, "Urbino: From the Past Emerge Some Significant Principles to Nourish the Present," *The Architectural Forum* 122:1 (April 1965): 44–51.

47 Sara Protasoni, "Il Gruppo Italiano e la tradizione del moderno," *Rassegna* 52 (December 1992): 28–39. For an overview on the CIAM, see Eric Mumford, *The CIAM Discourse on Urbanism, 1928–1960* (Cambridge, MA: MIT Press, 2000). See also Hermann Schlimme, "The Mediterranean Hill Town: A Travel Paradigm," in *Travel, Space, Architecture*, ed. Jilly Traganov and Miodrag Mitrasinovic (Burlington, VT: Ashgate, 2009), 148–66.

48 Giancarlo De Carlo, "Il pubblico dell'architettura," *Parametro* 3:4 (1970): 4–12; partially republished in English as "Architecture's Public," in *Theories and Manifestoes*, ed. Charles Jencks and Karl Kropf (London: Academy Editions, 1997), 47–8, and as "An Architecture of Participation," *Perspecta* 17 (1980): 74–9.

49 Carlo Levi, *Christ Stopped at Eboli*, trans. Frances Frenaye (New York: Farrar, Strauss, 1947), 5; originally published as *Cristo si è fermato a Eboli* (Turin: Einaudi, 1945).

50 On Levi as painter during his period of exile, see Pia Vaverelli, ed., *Carlo Levi e la Lucania: Dipinti del confino 1935–1936* (Rome: De Luca Edizioni d'Arte, 1990).

51 Ernesto De Martino, *Sud e magia* (Milan: Feltrinelli, 1959); Claudio Barbati, Gianfranco Mingozzi, and Annabella Rossi, eds., *Profondo sud: viaggio nei luoghi di Ernesto De Martino a vent'anni da Sud e magia* (Milan: Feltrinelli,

1978); Ernesto De Martino, *The Land of Remorse: A Study of Southern Italian Tarantism* (London: Free Association, 2005); originally published as *La terra del remorse* (Milan: Saggiatore, 1961). A number of works by Scotellaro have been translated into English. See Rocco Scotellaro, *The Garden of the Poor: Selections*, trans. Ruth Feldman and Brian Swann (Merrick, NY: Cross-Cultural Communications, 1993), and Rocco Scotellaro, *The Dawn Is Always New: Selected Poetry of Rocco Scotellaro*, trans. Ruth Feldman (Princeton, NJ: Princeton University Press, 1980).

52 Marida Talamona, "Dieci anni di politica dell'Unrra Casas: Dalle case ai senzatetto ai borghi rurali nel Mezzoogiorno d'Italia (1945–1955): Il ruolo di Adriano Olivetti," in *Costruire la città dell'uomo: Adriano Olivetti e l'urbanistica*, ed. Carlo Olmo (Milan: Edizioni di Comunità, 2001), 173–204.

53 Giancarlo De Carlo, "A proposito di La Martella," *Casabella-Continuità* 200 (February–March 1954): v–viii. My translation.

54 See Amerigo Restucci, *Matera: I sassi* (Turin: Einaudi, 1991).

55 Antonietta Iolanda Lima, *Soleri, Architecture as Human Ecology* (New York: Monacelli Press, 2003).

56 Henry-Russell Hitchcock and Arthur Drexler, eds., *Built in USA: Post-war Architecture* (New York: Thames and Hudson, 1952), 106–7. The authors refer to it as the Desert House and date its completion as 1951. Hitchcock and Drexler's book was the sequel to Elizabeth Mock, *Built in USA: 1932–1944* (New York: The Museum of Modern Art, 1945).

57 Soleri's model of self-sustainable and self-built communities influenced the hippie generation of the 1960s and 1970s that looked to do-it yourself vernacular approaches promoted in publications such as *Shelter* (1973) and *Shelter 2* (1978).

58 Paolo Soleri, "Utopia and/or Revolution," *Perspecta* 13–14 (1971): 281–5.

59 Giovanni Michelucci and Roberto Papi, "Lezione di Pompei," *Arte mediterranea. Rivista bimestrale di arte, letteratura e musica* 1:1 (1934): 23–33.

60 Amedeo Belluzzi and Claudia Conforti, *Lo spazio sacro nell'architettura di Giovanni Michelucci* (Turin: Allemandi, 1987).

61 Antonio Albanese, "Una casa-capanna a Torre San Lorenzo," *L'architettura – Croniche e storia* 28 (1958): 656–9.

62 On the *architecture* of caves, see Manfredi Nicoletti, *L'architettura delle caverne* (Rome: Laterza and Figli Spa, 1980).

63 Francesco Dal Co, "Giovanni Michelucci: A Life One Century Long," *Perspecta* 27 (1992): 99–115.

64 Bruno Zevi, "The Italian Rationalists," in *The Rationalists. Theory and Design in the Modern Movement*, ed. Dennis Sharp (London: Architectural Press, 1978), 124. The essay is also published in Andrea Oppenheimer

Dean, ed., *Bruno Zevi on Modern Architecture* (New York: Rizzoli, 1983), 107–13.

65 Leonardo Ricci, "Michelucci attraverso un suo lavoro," *Architetti* 18–19 (1953): 13–18.

66 Luca Moretto, ed., *Architettura moderna Alpina in Valle d'Aosta – Albini, BBPR, Cereghini, Figini e Pollini, Melis, Mollino, Muzio, Ponti, Sottsass Senior, Sottsass Junior* (Quart: Musumeci, 2003); Antonio De Rossi, *Modern Alpine Architecture in Piedmont and Valle d'Aosta* (Turin: Umberto Allemandi, 2006).

67 Mario Cereghini, *Costruire in montagna*, 2nd ed. (Milan: Edizioni del Milione, 1956). An English summary was published as *Building in the Alps: An Introduction* (Milan: Edizioni del Milione, 1953); it was first published in a complete English version as *Building in the Mountains: Architecture and History*, trans. Lucia Krasnik (Milan: Edizioni del Milione, 1957).

68 Mario Cereghini, *Architecture in the Alps: An Introduction* (Milan: Edizioni del Milione, 1953), xi.

69 Luigi Dell'Oro, ed., *Mario Cereghini - L'architettura, la grafica, il design, l'opera letteraria* (Lecco: Stefanoni, 1987).

70 Carlo Mollino, "Tabù e tradizione nella costruzione Montana," *Atti e rassegna tecnica della Società degli Ingegneri e degli Architetti in Torino* 4 (April 1954): 151–4.

71 For an overview of his oeuvre, see Giovanni Brino, *Carlo Mollino: Architecture as Autobiography* (London: Thames and Hudson, 2005).

72 Bruno Reichlin, "Mollino, écrits au pied du mur," *Faces* 19 (Spring 1991): 36–47. See also Bruno Reichlin and Adolphe Stiller, eds., *Carlo Mollino baut in den Bergen* (Basel: Basel Architekturmusuem, 1991).

73 Franco Albini, "Albergo per ragazzi a Cervinia," *Edilizia Moderna* 47 (December 1951): 67–74; Vittorio Prina, *Franco Albini: Albergo rifugio Pirovano a Cervinia* (Florence: Alinea Editrice, 2005).

74 Giampiero Bosoni, ed., *Made in Cassina* (Milan: Skira, 2009).

75 Giovanni Ponti, "Senza aggettivi," *Domus* 268 (March 1952): 1; published in English in *Il Design Italiano degli anni '50*, ed. Andrea Branzi and Michele De Lucchi (Milan: IGIS Edizioni, 1981), 296. See Marco Romanelli, ed., *Giò Ponti: A World* (Milan: Abitare Segesta, 2002); and Laura Falconi, *Gio Ponti: Interni, Oggetti, Disegni, 1920–1976* (Milan: Electa, 2004).

76 Penny Sparke, "The Straw Donkey: Tourist Kitsch or Proto-Design? Craft and Design in Italy, 1945–1960," *Journal of Design History* 11:1 (1998): 58–69.

77 Vanni Pasca, *Vico Magistretti: Designer* (New York: Rizzoli, 1991), 58–9.

78 Friedrich Achleitner, Paolo Biadene, Edoardo Gellner, and Michele Merlo, *Edoardo Gellner - Corte di Cadore* (Milan: Skira, 2002). See Franco Mancuso, *Edoardo Gellner: Il mestiere di architetto* (Milan: Electa, 1996).

79 See the following works by Edoardo Gellner: *Architettura anonima ampez-*

zana nel paesaggio storico di Cortina (Padua: Franco Muzzio and C. Editore, 1981); *Architettura rurale nelle dolomiti venete* (Cortina: Edizioni Dolomiti, 1988); "L'architettura spontanea," in *Atti del VI Convegno Nazionale di Urbanistica, Difesa e valorizzazione del paesagio urbano e rurale* (Rome: Istituto Nazionale di Urbanistica, 1958), 449–57.

80 Gian Piero Brunetta, *Cent'anni di cinema italiano* (Bari: Laterza, 1991), 489–536.

81 Stefano Socci, *Bernardo Bertolucci* (Milan: Il castoro, 1996). Among films by the Taviani Brothers, *Padre Padrone* (1977) focused on the life of a Sardinian peasant who lives in isolation, and their *The Night of the Shooting Stars* (1983) explored the lives of peasants in Tuscany. For more about their work, see Marcia Landy, "Language, Folklore, and Politics in the Films of the Taviani Brothers," in *Film Politics, and Gramsci*, ed. Marcia Landy (Minneapolis: University of Minnesota Press, 1994), 155–84. For an interesting analysis of the agrarian myth in film, see Tom Brass, "Reel Images of the Land (Beyond the Forest): Film and the Agrarian Myth," *The Journal of Peasant Studies* 28:4 (July 2001): 1–56.

82 Paul Strand and Cesare Zavattini, *Un Paese: Portrait of an Italian Village* (New York: Aperture, 1997); originally published in Italian as *Un paese* (Turin: Einaudi, 1955).

83 Aldo Rossi, *The Architecture of the City*, trans. Diane Ghirardo (Cambridge, MA: MIT Press, 1981), 46–8; originally published in Italian as *L'architettura della città* (Padua: Marsilio, 1966).

84 His housing estates for Mozzo near Bergamo (1977) and Goito (1979) also draw upon local vernacular forms, which he codified as recurring types. See "Architetture padane," in *Aldo Rossi: Architetture padane* (Modena: Edizioni Panini, 1984): 11–14; Aldo Rossi et al., *Vivere lungo il Po* (Bologna: Zanichelli, 1982); Paolo Costantini, *Luigi Ghirri – Aldo Rossi – Things Which Are Only Themselves* (Montreal: Canadian Centre for Architecture, and Milan: Electa, 1996).

85 Giovanna Crespi, ed., *Giorgio Grassi. I progetti, le opere e gli scritti* (Milan: Electa, 1996).

86 Morris Adjmi and Giovanni Bertolotto, eds., *Aldo Rossi: Drawings and Paintings* (New York: Princeton Architectural Press, 1993), 145–59. In the preface, the authors wrote that, "Rossi continues to use both vernacular and universal imagery throughout his oeuvre."

87 Rafael Moneo, *Theoretical Anxiety and Design Strategies in the Work of Eight Contemporary Architects* (Cambridge, MA: MIT Press, 2004), 102–43.

88 See Howard Burns, in collaboration with Lynda Fairbairn and Bruce Boucher, *Andrea Palladio, 1508–1580: The Portico and the Farmyard* (London: Arts Council of Great Britain, 1975).

89 See Giorgio Grassi, "La licenza dell'ovvio, nota sull'architettura rurale," *Lotus* 15 (1977): 22–29, republished in Giorgio Grassi, *L'architettura come mestiere e altri scritti* (Milan: Franco Angeli, 1980), 197–9; see also his "'Rurale' e 'urbano' nell'architettura," in *L'architettura come mestiere e altri scritti*, 140–56.
90 See Aldo Rossi, "Critique of Naïve Functionalism," in *The Architecture of the City*, 46–8.

Epilogue

1 One of the numerous important texts of the period because it targeted Pevsner's modernity was Charles Jencks, *Modern Movements in Architecture* (Garden City, NY: Anchor Press, 1973).
2 Bernard Rudofsky, *Eine primitive Betonbauweise auf den südlichen Kykladen, nebst dem versuch einer Datierung derselben* (Vienna: Technische Hochschule, 1931).
3 Felicity Scott, "Architecture without Architects: A Short Introduction to Non-Pedigreed Architecture," *Harvard Design Magazine* (Fall 1998): 69–72; and Felicity Scott, "Bernard Rudofsky: Allegories of Nomadism and Dwelling," in *Anxious Modernisms: Experimentation in Postwar Architectural Culture*, ed. Sarah Williams Goldhagen and Réjean Legault (Cambridge, MA: MIT Press, 2000), 215–37.
4 While preparing the exhibition, Rudofsky consulted several Italian critics, architects, and industrial designers who had already expressed interest in the vernacular; these included Pietro Belluschi, Giovanni Ponti, Bruno Munari, Bruno Zevi, Roberto Pane, and Werner Daniel. His correspondence with these figures is held in the Museum of Modern Art Archive, New York, Department of Circulating Exhibitions Records, II, 2:134 (5.1).
5 Though Rudofsky's notebooks attest to the fact that he was in Italy in 1951 when the exhibition was on view in Milan, he does not mention seeing it. However, he eventually became aware of it, because he wrote to Giancarlo De Carlo in the early 1960s, asking to borrow materials for his exhibition at MoMA. In fact, none of the panels displayed in Milan were loaned to the MoMA exhibition. See the Museum of Modern Art Archive, New York, Department of Circulating Exhibitions Records, II.2/134 (5.1).
6 Lewis Mumford, "Typewriter Palazzo in New York," *The Architectural Forum* 102 (August 1954): 98–103; "Charivari and Confetti," *The New Yorker* (19 June 1954): 114–19.
7 Antonio Romàn, *Eero Saarinen: An Architecture of Multiplicity* (New York: Princeton Architectural Press, 2003), 78–91.

8 Aaron Betsky, *James Gamble Rogers and the Architecture of Pragmatism* (Cambridge, MA: MIT Press, 1994).

9 Fred Licht, Antonello Satta, and Richard Ingersoll, *Nivola Sculture* (Milan: Jaca Book, 1991).

10 Eero Saarinen, "Letter to Mr. Costantino Nivola," *Art in America* 1 (1963): 88.

11 Henry-Russell Hitchcock, "Connecticut, U.S.A. in 1963," *Zodiac* (1964), 8.

12 For a recent assessment of Scully's contribution, see Neil Levine, ed., *Vincent Scully: Modern Architecture and Other Essays* (Princeton, NJ: Princeton University Press, 2003). One of Scully's former students went on to produce several photographic essays on vernacular architecture of different countries; see, for example, Norman F. Carver Jr., *Italian Hilltowns* (Kalamazoo, MI: Documan Press, 1979).

13 See Vincent Scully, "Architecture and Ancestor Worship," *Art News* 10 (1956): 26, 56–7.

14 Paul Rudolph, "Regionalism in Architecture," *Perspecta* 4 (1957): 12–19; republished in *Writings on Architecture: Paul Rudolph*, ed. Robert A.M. Stern (New Haven, CT: Yale School of Architecture, 2008), 30–8.

15 Pietro Belluschi, "The Meaning of Regionalism in Architecture," *The Architectural Record* (December 1955): 132; republished in Vincent Canizaro, ed., *Architectural Regionalism: Collected Writings on Place, Identity, Mondernity and Tradition* (New York: Princeton Architectural Press, 2007), 321–5. See Meredith L. Clausen, *Pietro Belluschi. Modern American Architect* (Cambridge, MA: MIT Press, 1994), esp. the chapter dedicated to "Regional Modernism: The Houses," 80–133.

16 Donlyn Lyndon, "Giancarlo De Carlo in the US," in *Giancarlo de Carlo: Archivio Progetti*, ed. Francesco Samassa (Padova: Il Poligrafo, 2004), 245–57.

17 Lamberto Rossi, *Giancarlo De Carlo: Architettura* (Milan: Arnoldo Mondadori Editore, 1988), 240. My translation.

18 On Yale in the 1960s, see Eve Blau, ed., *Architecture or Revolution: Charles Moore and Yale in the Late 1960s* (New Haven, CT: Yale University School of Architecture, 2001). Richard W. Hayes, *The Yale Building Project: The First 40 Years* (New Haven, CT: Yale University School of Architecture, 2002).

19 Kevin P. Keim, ed., *An Architectural Life: Memoirs and Memories of Charles W. Moore* (Boston: A Bulfinch Press Book, Little, Brown, 1996), 58.

20 Gordon Cullen, *Townscape* (London: The Architectural Press, 1961); Ivor de Wolfe [Hubert de Cronin Hastings], *The Italian Townscape* (London: The Architectural Press, 1963).

21 James Stirling, "Ronchamp: Le Corbusier's Chapel and the Crisis of Rationalism," *The Architectural Review* 119:711 (March 1956): 155–61.

22 On Kahn and his travel sketches, see Vincent Scully, "Marvelous Fountainheads: Louis I. Kahn: Travel Drawings," *Lotus international* 68 (1991): 48–63; see also Jan Hochstim, *The Paintings and Sketches of Louis I. Kahn*, intro. Vincent Scully (New York: Rizzoli, 1991).

23 Louis I. Kahn, "Foreword," in Clovis Heimsath, *Pioneer Texas Buildings: A Geometry Lesson* (Austin: University of Texas Press, 1968), n.p.

24 John Kettle ed., *Moshe Safdie: Beyond Habitat* (Montreal: Tundra Books, 1970), 167–72. Safdie acknowledged that he shared Christopher Alexander's interest in Rudofsky's *Architecture without Architects: A Short Introduction to Non-Pedigreed Architecture* (New York: Museum of Modern Art, 1964), published only three years prior to the opening of Habitat. Safdie claims to have submitted drawings for Habitat in May 1965, giving him enough time to see Rudofsky's book and exhibition. See also John Kettle, ed., "The Indigenous Builders," in *Moshe Safdie, Form and Purpose* (Boston: Houghton Mifflin, 1982), 21–48. Christopher Alexander wrote *Community and Privacy* (1963), *Notes on the Synthesis of Form* (1964), *A Pattern Language* (1977), and *The Timeless Way of Building* (1979) to stimulate neovernacular practices. See also Blake Gopnick and Michael Sorkin, *Moshe Safdie: Habitat '67, Montreal* (Turin: Testo and Immagine, 1998).

25 Kenneth Frampton, ed., *Aldo Rossi in America, 1976 to 1979* (New York: Institute for Architecture and Urban Studies, 1979).

26 The Yale School of Architecture is especially significant in the development of a dialogue with history. While teaching at Yale from 1967 to 1970, Robert Venturi and Denise Scott Brown's studio focused on the vernacular architecture of Las Vegas and Levittown, leading to the publication of Robert Venturi, Denise Scott Brown, and Steven Izenour, *Learning from Las Vegas* (Cambridge, MA: MIT Press, 1972).

27 See his introduction to Peter Arnell and Ted Bickford eds., *Aldo Rossi, Buildings and Projects* (New York: Rizzoli, 1985). Scully also wrote the postscript to Aldo Rossi, *A Scientific Autobiography* (Cambridge, MA: MIT Press, 1981).

28 See Maurice Culot and Jean-François Lejeune, eds., *Miami: Architecture of the Tropics* (New York: Princeton Architectural Press, 1993); Vincent Scully, *Between Two Towers: The Drawings of the School of Miami* (New York: Monacelli Press, 1996). See *Seaside: Making a Town in America*, ed. David Mohney and Keller Easterling (New York: Princeton Architectural Press, 1991).

29 Bruno Zevi, *Controstoria dell'architettura italiana – Dialetti architettonici* (Rome: Newton and Compton, 1996), 9.

30 See Janet Abramowicz, *Giorgio Morandi: The Art of Silence* (New Haven, CT: Yale University Press, 2004).

Selected Bibliography

Primary Sources

Albini, Franco. "Note per il coordinamento degli studi regionali per la Mostra di Architettura spontanea alla IX Triennale." Undated, ca.1950–1. IUAV. Archivio Progetti, Fondo Giuseppe Alberto Samonà, IUAV, Samonà 2, fascicle 058.
– "Albergo per ragazzi a Cervinia." *Edilizia Moderna* 47 (December 1951): 67–74.
Andreani, Isidoro. *Case coloniche*. Milan: Ulrico Hoepli, 1919.
Angelini, Luigi. "I padiglioni e gli edifici dell'esposizione di Roma: I padiglioni delle regioni d'Italia." *Emporium* 35:205 (January 1912): 17–35.
– "Criteri di bellezza nell'arte rustica nostra." *Pagine d'arte* (January 1915): 13–14.
– "Caraterri e schemi dell'architettura rustica bergamasca. I." *La Rivista di Bergamo* (August 1932): 329–37.
– "Caratteri e schemi dell'architettura rustica bergamasca. II." *La Rivista di Bergamo* (September 1932): 370–8.
– "Aspetti della architettura rustica nelle valli bergamasche." *Lares* (December 1932): 79–82.
– *Architettura delle case rurali del bergamasco*. Bergamo: Conti, 1941.
– *Arte minore bergamasca*. Bergamo: Istituto Italiano d'Arti Grafiche, 1947.
Anti, Carlo. "Dedalo. Rassegna d'arte diretta da Ugo Ojetti." *Scultura negra* (1921): 592–621.
– "Mostra di Scultura Negra." In *Catalogo della XIII Esposizione Internazionale d'arte della città di Venezia*, 41–4. Milan: Bestetti and Tumminelli, 1922.
– "The Sculpture of the African Negroes." *Art in America and Elsewhere*

(December 1923): 14–26. Republished in *Primitivism and Twentieth-Century Art: A Documentary History*, edited by Jack Flam and Miriam Deutch, 180–3. Berkeley: University of California Press, 2003.

Arata, Giulio Ulisse. "La prima mostra di architettura promossa dall'associazione degli architetti Lombardi." *Vita d'arte* (March 1914): 66–72.

– "L'architettura futurista." *Pagine d'arte* (August 1914): 160–72.

– "I morti per la patria. Antonio Sant'Elia." *Pagine d'arte* (November 1916): 139–40.

– "Arte rustica sarda. I. Gioielli e utensili intagliati." *Dedalo* 1:3 (April 1921): 698–722.

– "Arte rustica sarda. II. Tappeti e trine." *Dedalo* 1:2 (May 1921): 777–802.

– "Arte rustica sarda. III. Mobili e arredi domestici." *Dedalo* 1:3 (July 1921): 130–46

– "L'arte paesana alla prima biennale di Monza." *Le arti decorative* (May 1923): 16–22.

– "L'arte decorative alla prima biennale di Monza I." *L'illustrazione italiana* (October 1923): 476–9

– *Arte sarda*. (With Giuseppe Biasi). Milan: Fratelli Treves editori, 1935. Reprint Sassari: Carlo Delfino, 1983.

Argan, Giulio Carlo. "Architettura e ideologia." *Zodiac* 1 (1958): 47–52. Republished in *Progetto e destino: Saggi di arte e di letteratura*, edited by Giulio Carlo Argan, 82–90. Milan: Il Saggiatore, 1965; and in *Architecture Culture 1943–1968: A Documentary Anthology*, edited by Joan Ockman and Edward Eigen, 254–9. New York: Columbia Books of Architecture – Rizzoli.

– "L'arte popolare con particolare riguardo ai fenomeni europei." In *Enciclopedia universale dell'arte*, 802–6. Venice-Rome: Istituto per la collaborazione culturale, 1963.

– "Arte moderna come arte popolare." *Civiltà delle machine* (July–August 1966): 45–8.

Associazione artistica fra i cultori di architettura in Roma. *Architettura minore in Italia, Roma.*Vol. 1. Turin: Società italiana edizioni artistiche C. Crudo and Co, 1926. Reprint Rome: Colombo editore, 1990.

– *Architettura minore in Italia, Roma*. Vol. 2. Turin: Società italiana edizioni artistiche C. Crudo and Co., 1926. Reprint Rome: Colombo editore, 1990.

– *Architettura minore in Italia, Roma*. Vol. 3. Rome: Max Bretschneider, 1940.

Aymonino, Carlo. "Storia e cronaca del quartiere Tiburtino." *Casabella-Continuità* 215 (April–May 1957): 18–43.

Baldasseroni, Francesco. "Della Società di Etnografia Italiana e di alcuni scopi cui deve mirare." *Rassegna Contemporanea* 7 (1910): 15–24. Reprint Loria Lamberto, Francesco Baldasseroni. *Per la etnografia italiana: Del modo di promuovere gli studi di etnografia italiana.* Rome: Cooperativa tipografica Manunzio, 1910.

– *Esposizione Internazionale di Roma 1911: Catalogo della Mostra di Etnografia Italiana in Piazza d'Armi.* Bergamo: Istituto Italiano d'Arti Grafiche, 1911.

– "L'etnografia italiana all'esposizione di Roma" *Emporium* 34: 202 (October 1911): 305–19.

– *Il Museo di Etnografia Italiana e la Esposizione del 1911 in Roma. Archivio per l'antropologia e l'etnologia* (1911): 457–60.

– "Il Museo di Etnografia Italiana – Ordinamento per regioni o per categorie di oggetti?" *Lares* 1 (1912): 39–55.

– "Lamberto Loria" *Lares* 1 (1913): 1–16.

Balsamo-Stella, Guido. "Esposizione italiana d'arte industriale e decorative a Stoccolma." *Architettura e arti decorative* (May–June 1921): 93–9.

Banham, Reyner. "Neoliberty: The Italian Retreat from Modern Architecture." *The Architectural Review* 125:747 (April 1959): 231–5.

– *Theory and Design in the First Machine Age.* Cambridge, MA: MIT Press, 1960.

Baragiola, Aristide. *La casa villereccia delle colonie tedesche Veneto–Tridentine con raffronti.* Bergamo: Istituto Italiano D'Art Grafiche Editore, 1908.

– "Sulla casa villereccia." In *Atti del primo congresso di etnografia italiana*, edited by Società di etnografia italiana, 115–19. Perugia: Unione tipografica co-operativa, 1912.

– *Folklore di Val Formazza.* Rome: E. Loescher and C., 1914. Reprint Sala Bolognese: A. Forni, 1981. Republished as *Folklore di Val Formazza e Bosco Gurin*, edited by Enrico Rizzi. Verbania: Fondazione Enrico Monti, 2003.

– *La casa villereccia delle colonie tedesche del gruppo carnico Sappada, Sauris e Timau con raffonti delle zone contermini italiana ed austriaca Carnia, Cadore, Zoldano, Agordino, Carintia e Tirolo.* Chiasso: Tipografia Tettamanti, 1915. Reprint Verona: Taucias garëida, 1989.

Biasutti, Renato. "Per lo studio dell'abitazione rurale in Italia." *Rivista Geografica italiana* 33:1–2 (January–February 1926): 1–24. Republished in Società di studi geografici, ed., *Renato Biasutti – Scritti minori con elenco delle publicazioni (1899–1963)*, 63–82. Florence: Società di studi geografici, 1980.

– "Abitazione." In *Enciclopedia italiana di scienze, lettere ed arti.* Vol. 1, 79–89. Rome: Istituto Giovanni Treccani, 1929.

– "Capanna (Le forme odierne)." In *Enciclopedia italiana di scienze, lettere ed arti.* Vol. 8, 827–9. Rome: Istituto Giovanni Treccani, 1929.

– *La casa rurale nella Toscana.* Bologna: Nicola Zanichelli Editore, 1938.

– "Orientamento ed organizzazione delle ricerche sull'abitato e l'architettura rurale in Italia." *La ricerca scientifica* 18 (October 1948): 1235–42.

– "Lo studio della casa rurale." *La ricerca scientifica* (October 1952): 1884–92.

Bodrero, Emilio. "La cenerentola italiana." *La Fionda* 16–17 (November–December 1921): 255–65.

– "Discorso di S. E. Il Prof. Emilio Bodrero." In *Atti del III Congresso Nazionale di Arti e Tradizioni Popolari*, 29–31. Rome: Edizioni dell'Opera Nazionale Dopolavoro (O.N.D.), 1936.

Boito, Camillo. "Vienna – L'architettura all'esposizione universale." In *Camillo Boito: Gite di un artista*, edited by Maria Cecilia Mazzi, 139–67. Rome: De Luca Edizioni d'Arte, 1990. Originally published in *Gite di un artista*. Milan: Ulrico Hoepli, 1884.

Bono, Francesco. "Architettura 'spontanea' o 'popolare.'" *Prospettive* 7 (September–December 1953): 47–51.

Borrelli, Nicola. "L'architettura rustica in Campania." *Lares* (August 1941): 293–304.

Bottai, Giuseppe. "Le arti popolari nell'azione del ministero dell'educazione nazionale." *Le arti* (October–November 1940): 35–8. Also published in *Il Primato* (September 1940): 1–2.

Brocherel, Jules. "Review of Camillo Jona, L'architettura rusticana in Valle d'Aosta." *Augusta-Praetoria* (January–February 1921): 37–9.

– "La casa rustica valdostana." In *Atti del III Congresso Nazionale di arti e tradizioni popolari*, 197–9. Rome: Edizione dell'O.N.D., 1936

– "La mostra valdostana di arte popolare." *Lares* (September 1936): 145–53.

– ed. *Arte popolare Valdostana, Catalogo generale della Mostra di Arte Popolare.* Rome: Edizione dell'O.N.D., 1937.

– "Tipi di case rustiche valdostane." *Le alpi, rivista mensile del centro alpinistico italiano* (January–February 1940–41): 41–3.

Buttitta, Antonio. "Caratteri, momenti e motivi della pittura del carro siciliano." *Annali del Museo Pitrè* 5–7 (1954–56): 92–101.

Byne, Arthur, and Mildred Stapley. *Provincial Houses in Spain.* New York: H. Helburn Inc., 1925.

Calderini, Emma. *Il costume popolare in Italia.* Milan: Sperling & Kupfer, 1934.

Cambellotti, Duilio. "La campagna romana ante bonifica," (1948), in *Duilio Cambellotti – Teatro – Storia – Arte*, edited by Mario Quesada, 211–19. Palermo: Edizioni Novecento, 1982.

Capitò, Giuseppe. *Il Carretto Siciliano.* Milan: Editori Piantanida Valcarenghi, 1923.

Capponi, Giuseppe. "Motivi di architettura ischiana." *Architettura e arti decorative* (July 1927): 481–94.

– "Architettura ed accademia a Capri – Il 'Rosaio' di Edwin Cerio." *Architettura e arti decorative* (December 1929): 177–88.

- "Per una architettura italiana moderna. L'architettura è l'espressione istin-
  tiva e originale di un ambiente spirituale e materiale, o non è architettura."
  La Tribuna (March 1931): 3.
Carli, Enzo. "Il 'genere' architettura rurale e il funzionalismo." *Casabella* 107
  (November 1936): 6–7.
Carrà, Carlo. *L'Arte decorative contemporanea alla prima Biennale internazionale di
  Monza*. Milan: Edizioni "Alpes", 1923.
Castelli, Mario. *Fabbricati rurali*. Turin: UTET, 1938.
Ceas, Giovanni Battista, with Edwin Cerio and Luigi Parpagliolo. *Capri – Vi-
  sioni architettoniche di Giovanni Battista Ceas*. Rome: Biblioteca d'arte editrice,
  1930.
Cecchi, Emilio. "La Mostra dell'Agro." *Il Marzocco* (29 October, 1911): 3–4.
Cena, Giovanni. *Pensieri e frammenti inediti*. Turin: Edizioni "L'Impronta," 1928.
- *Lettere scelte*. Turin: Edizioni "L'Impronta," 1929.
- *Opere complete*. Turin: Edizioni "L'Impronta," 1928–9.
- *Saggi critici*. Turin: Edizioni "L'Impronta," 1929.
Cereghini, Mario. *Costruire in montagna*. Milan: Edizioni del Milione, 1950.
  English translation, *Building in the Mountains. Architecture and History*. Trans-
  lated by Lucia Krasnik. Milan: Edizioni del Milione, 1957.
- *Prima mostra di architettura alpine*. Catalogo mostra al Circolo Artistico
  Cortina d'Ampezzo. Lecco: ti. F.lli Grassi, 1951.
- "Particolarità dell'architettura alpine." *Spazio* (December 1951–April 1952):
  51–8.
- *Architecture in the Alps: An Introduction*. Milan: Edizioni del Milione, 1953.
- *Mostra delle architetture tipiche alpine*. Catalogo X Triennale di Milano. Lecco:
  Arte Grafica Valsecchi, 1954.
- "Il montanaro va, senza architetto – L'edilizia della razza alpine." *L'architet-
  tura* 15 (January 1957): 678–81.
- "Il montanaro va, senza architetto – Dalle grotte ai fienili." *L'architettura* 16
  (February 1957): 752–5.
- "Il montanaro va senza archiettto – Genti nomadi cercano casa." *L'architet-
  tura* 17 (March 1957): 822–5.
- *Architettura tipiche del Trentino*. Trento: G.B. Monauni, 1966.
Cerio, Edwin. *Le pagine dell'isola di Capri*. Naples: Ed. Casella, 1921.
- "La casa nel paesaggio di Capri." *Rassegna d'arte antica e moderna* 7 (July
  1921): 233–45.
- *La casa nel paesaggio di Capri*. Rome: Editori Alfieri & Lacroix, 1922.
- "Aspetti pittoreschi di Capri." *Emporium* 335 (November 1922): 290–300.
- "L'architettura minima nella contrada delle Sirene." *Architettura e arti decora-
  tive* 4:2 (August 1922): 156–76.

- Introduction to Mario Hyerace, ed., *Catalogo delle opere – Interpretazione futurista del paesaggi di Capri del pittore futurista Enrico Prampolini,* by Premiata tipografia Italo-Americana Raffaello. Salerno: R. Beraglia, 1922.
- "L'Architettura rurale della contrada delle Sirene," in *Il Convegno del Paesaggio,* 55–64. Capri: Edizione delle "Pagine dell'Isola," 1923.
- *Il giardino e la pergola nel paesaggio di Capri.* Rome: Editori Alfieri and Lacroix, 1923.
- ed. *Il convegno del paesaggio.* Naples: Gaspare Casella, 1923. Republished in *1923–1993 – Contributi a settanta anni dalla pubblicazione degli atti del Convegno del Paesaggio* by G. Galasso, A.G. White, and V. Mazzarelli. Capri: Edizioni la conchiglia, 1993.
- *Aria di Capri.* Naples: Casella, 1927.
- "Una casa a Capri di Giuseppe Capponi." *Architettura* 12:2 (February, 1934): 102–6.
Ciribini, Giuseppe. "Genesi e sviluppi dell'abitazione rustica italiana nel quadro dell'architettura rustica mediterranea." *Atti dei Sindacati provinciali ingegneri di Lombardia* (October 1940): 189–206.
- *Per un metodo nelle ricerche sull'architettura rustica.* Milan: Polver Stampa, 1942.
- *L'analisi tecnica delle dimore rurali.* Como-Milan: Marzorati Editore, 1946.
- *Architettura e industria; lineamenti di tecnica della produzione edilizia.* Milan: Libreria Editrice Politecnica Tamburini, 1958.
- "Architettura e industria." In *Cento Anni di Edilizia,* edited by Agnoldomenico Pica, 115–47. Rome: Emilio Pifferi, 1963.
Cocchiara, Giuseppe. *Folklore.* Milan: Ulrico Hoepli, 1927.
- *Storia degli studi delle tradizioni popolari in Italia.* Palermo: G.B. Palumbo, 1947.
- *Storia del folklore in Europa.* Turin: Einaudi, 1952. English translation, *The History of Folklore in Europe.* Philadelphia: Institute for the Study of Human Issues, 1981.
- "Presenza dell'etnologia e del folklore nella cultura moderna." *Annali del Museo Pitrè* 11–13 (1960–62): 1–9.
- "Popolare." In *Enciclopedia universale dell'arte.* 783–802. Rome: Istituto per la collaborazione culturale, 1963.
Colasanti, Arduino. "Il bilancio delle esposizioni di Roma." *Il Marzocco* 16:49 (December 1911): 2.
- "Circolare n. 13. Raccolta di elementi decorative italiani di arte paesana." *Bollettino Ufficiale del Ministero dell'Istruzione pubblica* 1:6 (February 1920): 157–9.
- Preface to *La difesa delle bellezze naturali d'Italia,* by Luigi Parpagliola. Rome: Società d'arte illustrata, 1923.

Corso, Raffaele. "L'arte dei pastori." *La Fionda* 3 (October 1920): 29.

– "L'arte popolare italiana – Rustica Ars." In *XCI Esposizione di Belle Arti*, by Società degli amatori e cultori di belle arti in Roma, 32–9. Rome: Alfieri and Lacroix, 1923.

– *Folklore – Storia – Obbietto – Metodo – Bibliografia*. Rome: Casa Editrice Leonardo Da Vinci, 1923.

– "L'arte rustica e un articolo di Arduino Colasanti." *Il Folklore Italiano* 1:1 (March 1925): 123–5.

– "Per il Museo di Etnografia Italiana." *Il folklore italiano* (March 1927): 298–300.

– "Folklore." In *Enciclopedia italiana di scienze, lettere ed arti*. Vol. 15, 606–8. Rome: Istituto Giovanni Treccani, 1932.

Costantini, Innocenzo. "Le nuove costruzioni dell'istituto per le case popolari di Roma – La borgata giardino 'Garbatella.'" *Architettura e arti decorative* 2 (November 1922): 119–37.

Croce, Benedetto. *Poesia popolare e poesia d'arte*. Rome: Gius. Laterza and Figli, 1930. Published in English as "Folk Poetry and Poets' Poetry." In *Philosophy, Poetry, History: An Anthology of Essays by Benedetto Croce*, 382–96. Translated and introduced by Cecil Sprigge. London: Oxford University Press, 1966.

Crocioni, Giovanni. *Le regioni e la cultura nazionale*. Catania: Francesco Battiato Editore, 1914.

– *Problemi fondamentali del folklore – Con due lezioni su il folklore e il D'Annunzio*. Bologna: Nicola Zanichelli, 1928.

– *Folklore e letteratura*. Florence: L.S. Olschki, 1954.

Cullen, Gordon. *Townscape*. London: The Architectural Press, 1961.

– *The Concise Townscape*. New York: Van Nostrand Reinhold Company, 1971.

D'Ancona, Paolo. "Artigianato regionale e arte decorativa in Italia." *Nuova Antologia – Rivista di lettere, scienze ed arti* (September 1921): 64–72.

D'Annunzio, Gabriele. *Laudi del cielo, del mare, della terra e degli eroi*. Roma: Tipografia dello Stato, 1899.

– *La figlia di Iorio – Tragedia pastorale in tre atti*. Milan: Fratelli Treves, 1902. First English translation, Boston: Little, Brown, and Company, 1907.

De Angelis D'Ossat, Guglielmo. "Il IV Congresso Nazionale di arti e tradizioni popolari." *Palladio* (1940): 238–9

– "Recensioni" (*Architettura rurale italiana* – Giuseppe Pagano and Werner Daniel), *Palladio-Rivista di Storia dell'Architettura* 1:2 (1938): n.p.

De Angelis-Egidi, Mario. "Edilizia scolastica rurale." *Architettura e arti decorative* (December 1931): 853–64.

De Carlo, Giancarlo. *William Morris*. Milan: Il Balcone, 1947.

– "A proposito di La Martella." *Casabella-Continuità* 200 (February–March 1954): v–viii.

288　Selected Bibliography

- *Urbino: The History of a City and Plans for Its Development*. Translated by Loretta Schaeffer Guarda. Cambridge, MA: MIT Press, 1970. Originally published as *Urbino: La storia di una città e il piano della sua evoluzione urbanistica*. Padua: Marsilio, 1966.
- "Il pubblico dell'architettura." *Parametro* 3:4 (1970): 4–12.
- "An Architecture of Participation." *Perspecta* 17 (1980): 74–9.
De Carolis, Adolfo. "L'arte popolare." *La Fionda* (August 1920): 13–21.
- "Arte tessile popolare I." *La Fionda* (January–February 1921): 11–16.
- "Arte tessile popolare II." *La Fionda* (July–October 1921): 209–13.
- "L'arte rustica italiana e l'esposizione di Stoccolma." *La Fionda* (December 1920): 48.
- "L'arte rustica alla prima biennale romana." *La Fionda* (May–June 1921): 189–91.
De Mandato, Mario. *La primitività nell'abitare umano*. Turin: Fratelli Bocca, 1933.
De Rocchi Storai, Tina. *Guida bibliografica allo studio dell'abitazione rurale in Italia*. Florence: L.S. Olschki, 1950.
- *Bibliografia degli studi sulla casa rurale italiana*. Florence: L.S. Olschki, 1968.
De Wolfe, Ivor [Hubert de Cronin Hastings]. *The Italian Townscape*. Centro di studi per la geografica etnologica. London: The Architectural Press, 1963.
Depero, Fortunato. *Fortunato Depero nelle opere e nella vita*. Trent: Tipografia Editrice Mutilati e Invalidi, 1940.
Del Puppo, Giovanni. *La casa in Friuli: Appunti e note*. Udine: Tipografia G.B. Doretti, 1912.
Detti, Edoardo. "Urbanistica medievale minore." *Critica d'arte* 24 (November–December 1957): 489–504.
- "Urbanistica medieval minore, n. 2." *Critica d'arte* 25–26 (January–April 1958): 73–101.
Dorfles, Gillo. "Architettura 'spontanea' e tutela del paesaggio." *Domus* 305 (April 1955): 8, 64.
Edallo, Amos. *Ruralistica: urbanistica rurale con particolare riferimento alla valle padana*. Milan: Hoepli Editore, 1946.
- "What is Ruralism?" *Landscape: Magazine of Human Geography* 3: 1 (1953): 12–19.
Ente Nazionale Industrie Turistiche (ENIT). *Agro Pontino. Anno IX–XV*. Milan-Rome: Pizzi and Pizio, 1938.
Epifanio, Luigi. *L'architettura rustica in Sicilia*. Palermo: G.B. Palumbo Editore, 1939.
Fanelli, Giuseppe Attilio. *L'artigianto – Sintesi di una economia corporative*. Rome: Spes Editrice, 1929.

Ferrari, Giulio. *Museo Artistico Industriale di Roma – Catalogo delle collezioni.* Rome: Bodoni, 1906.

– *L'architettura rusticana nell'arte italiana – Dalle capanne alla casa medievale.* Milan: Hoepli Editore, 1925. Reprint Nendeln: Kraus Reprints, 1973.

Figini, Luigi. "Architettura naturale ad Ischia." *Comunità* 3 (May–June 1949): 36–9.

– *L'elemento "verde" e l'abitazione.* Milan: Editore Ulrico Hoepli, 1950.

– "Architettura naturale a Ibiza." *Comunità* 8 (May–June 1950): 40–3.

Gallo, Eleonora. *Arte rustica italiana.* Florence: Giulio Giannini e Figlio, 1929. English translation, *Peasant Art in Italy.* Florence: Giulio Giannini e Figlio, 1929.

Gambi, Lucio. "Per una storia della abitazione rurale in Italia." *Rivista storica italiana* (June 1964): 427–54.

– *La casa rurale in Italia.* Edited by Lucio Gambi, and Giuseppe Barbieri. Florence: L.S. Olschki Editore, 1970.

– "La casa Contadina." In *Storia d'Italia.* Vol. 6, 479–504. Turin: Einaudi, 1976.

Garnier, Charles, and Auguste Ammann. *L'habitation humaine.* Paris: Hachette et Co., 1892. Italian translation, *L'abitazione umana.* Milan: Pubblicazione del Corriere della sera, 1893.

Garroni, Ezio. "Commemorazione del socio Ernesto Wille." In Associazione artistica fra I cultori di architettura, *Annuario, Dall'anno XXI-MCMXI – all'anno XXV-MCMXV,* 183–5. Rome: Tipografia Innocenzo Artero, 1916.

Gellner, Edoardo. "L'architettura spontanea." In *Atti del VI Convegno Nazionale di Urbanistica, Difesa e valorizzazione del paesagio urbano e rurale,* 449–57. Rome: Istituto Nazionale di Urbanistica, 1958.

– *Architettura anonima ampezzana nel paesaggio storico di Cortina.* Padua: Franco Muzio and C. Editore, 1981.

– *Architettura rurale nelle dolomiti venete.* Cortina: Edizioni Dolomiti, 1988.

Gerola, Giuseppe. "Architettura minore e rustica trentina." *Architettura e arti decorative* 6:8 (March 1929): 291–301.

Giedion, Sigfried. "Situation de l'architecture contemporaine en Italie." *Cahiers d'art* 9–10 (1931): 442–9.

Giolli, Raffaello. "In attesa del concorso Marelli – Osservazini di Valle Strona." *Le vie d'Italia* (January 1919): 27–33.

– "L'arte popolare." *Il primato artistico italiano* 1 (1920): n.p.

– "Colore locale." *Casabella* (December 1936): 26–7.

– "Architettura vivente." *Casabella-Costruzioni* (October 1938): 20–1.

– "Per una ricognizione dell'arte popolare italiana." *Domus* 10:30 (February 1939): 47.

Giordani, Pierluigi. "Vocazione degli abitanti del Delta: I 'casoni' del Poles-ine." *L'architettura* 7 (May 1956): 58–61.

– "Vocazione degli abitanti del Delta: Misure dell'uomo e della produttività." *L'architettura* 9 (July 1956): 208–13.

– "Vocazione degli abitanti del Delta: Paesi di bonifica." *L'architettura – Cro-nache e storia* 10 (August 1956): 284–90.

– "Vocazione degli abitanti del Delta: Comunità autonome." *L'architettura – Cronache e storia* 11 (September 1956): 370–3.

– "Vocazione degli abitanti del Delta: Le città storiche: Comacchio e Chiog-gia." *L'architettura – Cronache e storia* 13 (November 1956): 526–31.

– *I contadini e l'urbanistica.* Bologna: Edizioni agricole, 1958.

– "Considerazioni intorno a 'Garden Cities of To-Morrow.'" In *L'idea della città-giardino di Ebenezer Howard*, 147–309. Bologna: Calderini, 1962.

– *L'idea della città giardino.* Bologna: Calderini, 1972.

Giovannoni, Gustavo. "Arte nuova ed arte popolare." *Bollettino della Società degli Ingegneri e degli Architetti Italiani* 12:20 (May 1904): 585–9.

– "Resoconto Morale per l'anno 1911." In *Associazione Artistica fra I cultori di architettura, Annuario*, 3. Rome: Tipografia Innocenzo Artero, 1916.

– "Vecchie Città ed Edilizia Nuova." *Nuova Antologia di Lettere, Scienze ed Arti* 5 (May–June 1913): 449–72.

– *Vecchie città ed edilizia nuova.* Turin: UTET, 1931. Reprint Milan: Città Studi Edizioni, 1995.

– "Architettura minore di Roma e del Lazio." *Roma – Rivista di Studi e di Vita Romana* 18: 7 (July 1940): 232–6.

Gori-Montanelli, Lorenzo. "Difesa dell'architettura colonica." *Italia nostra* (January–February 1961): n.p.

– "Problemi di difesa dell'architettura rurale." *Antichità viva* (May–June 1962): 46–53.

– *Architettura rurale in Toscana.* Florence: Edam Editrice, 1964.

Gorio, Federico. "Il villaggio La Martella - Autocritica di Federico Gorio." *Casabella-Continuità* 200 (February–March, 1954): 31–8.

Gramsci, Antonio. "Observations on Folklore: Giovanni Crocioni." In *Antonio Gramsci, Selections from Cultural Writings*, edited by David Forgacs, 188–91. Cambridge: Harvard University Press, 1985.

– "Observations on Folklore: 'Natural Law' and Folklore." In *Antonio Gram-sci, Selections from Cultural Writings*, edited by David Forgacs, 192–4. Cam-bridge: Harvard University Press, 1985.

– "Folklore: ['Contemporary Pre-history']." In *Antonio Gramsci, Selections from Cultural Writings*, edited by David Forgacs, 194–5. Cambridge: Harvard University Press, 1985.

Grassi, Giorgio. "Nota sull'architettura rurale." In *L'architettura come mestiere e altri scritti*, 197–9. Milan: Franco Angeli, 1980.

– "'Rurale' e 'Urbano' nell'architettura." In *L'architettura come mestiere e altri scritti*, 140–56. Milan: Franco Angeli, 1980.

Grassi, Liliana. *Storia e cultura dei monumenti*. Milan: Società editrice libraria, 1960.

– *Razionalismo architettonico, dal Lodoli a Giuseppe Pagano*. Milan: Edizioni Bignami, 1966.

Griffini, Enrico Agostino. "Case rustiche veneziane: I casoni." *Ingegneria* 1:1 (July 1922): 17–18.

– "La casa rustica delle Alpi Italiane." *Ingegneria* 3:2 (March 1923): 66–9.

– "La casa rustica della Valle Gardena." *Architettura e arti decorative* (March 1925): 291–8.

– *Costruzione razionale della casa*. Milan: Hoepli Editore, 1931.

– Preface to *Per un metodo nelle ricerche sull'architettura rustica*, by Giuseppe Ciribini, 9–12. Milan: Ed. Tecniche Polver, 1942.

– *Progetti e realizzazioni – MCMXX–MCML*. Milan: Hoepli, 1950.

– "Progetto di una casa colonica per la Carnia e l'alto Friuli." *L'architettura italiana* 15:11 (November 1920): 85–7.

Gruppo 7 (Ubaldo Castagnoli, Gino Figini, Guido Frette, Sebastiano Larco, [Adalberto Libera] Gino Pollini, Carlo Enrico Rava, Giuseppe Terragni). "Architettura I." *La Rassegna italiana* 19:103 (December 1926): 849–54. Reprinted in *Oppositions* 6 (Fall 1976): 89–92.

– "Architettura II: Gli Stranieri." (Trans. Ellen R. Shapiro). *La Rassegna italiana* 9:105 (February 1927): 129–37. Reprinted in *Oppositions* 6 (Fall 1976): 93–102.

– "Architettura III: Impreparazione, Incomprensione, Pregiudizi." *La Rassegna italiana* 19:106 (February 1927): 247–52. Reprinted in *Oppositions* 12 (Spring 1978): 91–5. (Trans. Ellen R. Shapiro).

– "Architettura IV: Una nuova epoca archaic." *La Rassegna italiana* 19:108 (May 1927): 467–72. Reprinted in *Oppositions* 12 (Spring 1978): 96–8. (Trans. Ellen R. Shapiro).

Hoffmann, Josef. "Architektonisches von der Insel Capri – Ein Beitrag für malerische Architekturempfindungen." *Der Architekt* 3 (1897): 13–14. English translation, "Architectural Matters from the Island of Capri." In *Josef Hoffmann – Monograph and Catalogue of Works*, edited by Eduard F. Sekler, 479. Princeton, NJ: Princeton University Press, 1935.

– "Meine Arbeit." Lecture given on 22 February 1911. English translation, "My Work." In *Josef Hoffmann, the architectural work: monograph and catalogue of works*, edited by Eduard F. Sekler, 486–92. Princeton, NJ: Princeton University Press, 1985.

Holme, Charles, ed. *Peasant Art in Italy.* London: The Studio Ltd., 1913.

Hooker, Katharine, and Myron Hunt. *Farmhouses and Small Provincial Buildings in Southern Italy.* New York: Architectural Book Publishing Co., 1925.

Istituto Nazionale L.U.C.E. *L'Italia Fascista in Cammino.* Rome: Istituto Poligrafico dello Stato, 1932.

Jahier, Piero. "Arte alpine." *Dedalo* 1:2 (July 1920): 87–103.

– *Arte alpina.* Milan: Vanni Scheiwiller, 1958.

– *Arte alpina.* Florence: Vallecchi, 1961.

Jona, Camillo. *L'architettura rusticana in Valle D'Aosta.* Turin: Società di Edizioni Artistiche C. Crudo and Co., 1920.

– *L'architettura rusticana nella costiera d'Amalfi.* Turin: Società di Edizioni Artistiche C. Crudo & C., 1920.

Kidder Smith, George Everard. *Italy Builds: Its Modern Architecture and Native Inheritance.* New York: Reinhold Publishing Corporation, 1955.

Labò, Mario. "Arte rustica nell'alto appennino modenese." *Emporium* (September 1920): 143–56.

– "Gusto dell'Ottocento nelle Esposizioni." *Costruzioni-Casabella* 159–60 (March–April 1941): 4–29.

Labò, Mario, and Attilio Podestà. *Colonie: marine, montane, elioterapiche.* Milan: Editoriale S. A. Domus, 1942.

– "L'architettura delle colonie marine italiane." *Casabella* 167 (November 1942): 2–35.

– "Le colonie montane." *Casabella* 168 (December 1942): 2–23.

– "Le colonie elioterapiche." *Casabella* 168 (December 1942): 23–39.

Lancellotti, Arturo. *La prima biennale romana d'arte, 1921.* Rome: Edizioni La Fiamma, 1922.

– "Il museo etnografico italiano." *Nuova Antologia* (October 1926): 481–9.

– *Le mostre romane del cinquantenario.* Rome: Fratelli Palombi, 1931.

Lawrence, D.H. *Sea and Sardinia.* New York: T. Selzer, 1921. Reprinted in *D.H. Lawrence and Italy* (London: Penguin, 1997).

Lanza, V.P. Airoldi, and E. Caracciolo. *Rilievi di edilizia minore siciliana.* Palermo, 1938.

Levi, Carlo. *Cristo si è fermato a Eboli.* Turin: Einaudi, 1947. English translation, *Christ Stopped at Eboli.* Translated by Frances Frenaye. New York: Farrar, Straus, 1947.

Loos, Adolf. "Rules for Building in the Mountains." In *Trotzdem, 1900–1930.* Innsbruck: Brenner Verlag, 1931), 131–2. Republished in *Adolf Loos on Architecture*, trans. Michael Mitchell, 122–3. Riverside, CA: Ariadne Press, 2002.

Loria, Lamberto, and Aldobrandini Mochi. *Sulla raccolta di materiali per la etnografia italiana.* Florence: Museo di Etnografia Italiana, 1906.

Loria, Lamberto. "L'Etnografia italiana – Dal Museo all'Esposizione." *Il Marzocco* 31 (August 1908): 1–2.

– "Dal modo di promuovere gli studi di Etnografia italiana." *Rassegna Contemporanea* (1910): 3–13.

Lowell, Guy. *Smaller Italian Villas & Farmhouses*. New York: The Architectural Book Publishing Co., 1916.

– *More Small Italian Villas & Farmhouses*. New York: The Architectural Book Publishing Co., 1920.

Luzzato, Gino. "L'artigianato." In *Enciclopedia italiana di scienze, lettere, ed arti*. 703–5. Rome: Istituto Giovanni Treccani, 1929.

Malaparte, Curzio. *Italia barbara*. Turin: Piero Gobetti, 1925.

Manetti, Carlo. *La casa dell'uomo in campagna: progetti e realizzazioni moderne di case rurali*. Florence: Marzocco, 1940.

Maraini, Antonio. "L'arte popolare." *La Tribuna* (April 1918): 3.

– "Arte popolare e stile decorativo nazionale." *La Tribuna* (February 1920): 8.

– "L'Architettura rustica alla cinquantenale romana." *Architettura e arti decorative* 1:4 (November–December, 1921): 379–85.

– "Adolfo de Carolis silografo." *Dedalus* (October 1921): 332–51.

– "Il concetto di arte popolare." In *Enciclopedia italiana di scienze, lettere ed arti*, 634–5. Rome: Istituto della Enciclopedia Giovanni Treccani, 1929.

– "Radici paesane nell'arte italiana." In *Atti del I Congresso Nazionale delle Tradizioni Popolari*, 158–161. Florence: Rinascimento del Libro, 1930.

– "L'arte paesana come materiale d'insegnamento e di studio." In *Atti del IV Congresso Nazionale di Arti e Tradizioni Popolari*, 113–15. Rome: Edizione dell'O.N.D, 1942.

Marchi, Virgilio. "Primitivismi capresi." *Cronache d'attualità* 6–10 (1922): 49–51.

– "Architettura futurista." In *Il Convegno del Paesaggio*, edited by Edwin Cerio, 68–9. Naples: Gaspare Casella, 1923.

– *Architettura futurista*. Foligno: Franco Campitelli Editore, 1924.

– *Italia nuova architettura nuova*. Rome-Foligno: Franco Campitelli Editore, 1931.

Marconi, Plinio. "Architettura minime mediterranee e architettura moderna." *Architettura e arti decorative* (September 1929): 27–44.

– "Casette modello costruite dall'istituto per le case popolari di Roma alla borgata-giardino 'Garbatella.'" *Architettura e arti decorative* (May 1929): 254–75.

– "Architettura rustica." In *Enciclopedia italiana di scienze, lettere ed arti*. Vol. 30, 344–6. Rome: Istituto dell'Enciclopedia Giovanni Treccani, 1936.

– "Casa." In *Enciclopedia italiana di scienze, lettere ed arti*. Vol. 9, 255–76. Rome: Istituto dell'Enciclopedia Giovanni Treccani, 1931.

- "Capri." In *Enciclopedia italiana di scienze, lettere ed arti*. Vol. 9, 905–7. Rome: Istituto dell'Enciclopedia Giovanni Treccani, 1931.

Marescotti, Francesco, and Irenio Diotallevi. *Ordine e destino della casa popolare: risultati e anticipi*. Milan: Editoriale Domus, 1941.

- *Il problema sociale, costruttivo ed economico dell'abitazione*. Milan: Poligono, 1948. Republished in *Scritti di Franco Marescotti*, edited by Maristella Casciato. Rome: Officina, 1984.

Marinetti, Filippo Tommaso. "Lo stile pratico," In *Il convegno del paesaggio*, edited by Edwin Cerio, 66–8. Naples: Gaspare Casella, 1923.

- "Il discorso." In *Il convegno del paesaggio*, edited by Edwin Cerio, 37–41. Naples: Gaspare Casella, 1923. Republished in *1923–1993: Contributi a settanta anni dalla pubblicazione degli atti del Convegno del Paesaggio*, edited by G. Galasso, A.G. White, and V. Mazzarelli. Capri: Edizioni la conchiglia, 1993.

- "Elogio di Capri." *Natura* 1 (January 1928): 41–8.

Marini, Giorgio Wenter. "L'italianità dell'arte trentina." *Alba trentina* (October 1918): n.p.

- "Architetti trentini." *Architettura e arti decorative* (1922–23):377–90.

Melani, Alfredo. Italian translation-adaptation, *L'abitazione umana*, by Charles Garnier and Auguste Ammann. Milan: Pubblicazione del *Corriere della Sera*, 1893.

- "Folklorismo d'arte." *Vita d'Arte* (May 1911):182–5.

- *L'architettura di Giulio Ulisse Arata*. Vol. 1, *Ville*. Milan: Bestetti & Tumminelli, 1913.

Melis, Armando. "L'esposizione di Torino del 1928." *Architettura e arti decorative* 4:10 (April 1928): 372–81.

Metalli, Ercole. *Usi e costumi della campagna romana*. Rome: Tipografia della Reale Accademic Nazionale dei Lincei, 1924. Reprint Rome: Edizioni NER, 1982.

Mezzanotte, Paolo. "Il focolare friulano." *L'edilizia moderna* 26:12 (December 1917): 66–8.

- "La prima mostra internazionale delle arti decorative a Monza I." *Architettura e arti decorative* (February 1923): 391–404.

- "La prima mostra internazionale delle arti decorative a Monza II." *Architettura e arti decorative* (March 1923): 429–57.

- "La prima mostra internazionale delle arti decorative a Monza III." *Architettura e arti decorative* (April 1923): 481–95.

Michelucci, Giovanni. "'Contatti' fra architettura antiche e moderne (I)." *Domus* 50 (February 1932): 70–1.

- "'Contatti' fra architettura antiche e moderne (II)." *Domus* 51 (March 1932): 134–6.

- "Fonti della moderna architettura italiana." *Domus* 56 (August 1932): 460–1.
- "Lezione di Pompei." (with Roberto Papi) *Arte Mediterranea* 1:1 (1934): 23–33.
- "Tradizione della casa italiana." *Illustrazione Toscana e dell'Etruria* (May 1941): 5–10.

Mochi, Aldobrandino. "Il primo congresso d'etnografia italiana." *Lares* 1 (1912): 25–38.

Mollino, Carlo. "La casa e l'ideale: casa in collina." *Domus* (February 1941): 50–4.
- "Disegno di una casa sull'altura." *Stile* 40 (April 1944): 2–11.
- "Gusto dell'architettura organica." *Tendenza* 1 (April 1946): 26–8.
- "Una costruzione di oggi a Cervinia, che deve entusiasmare gli sciatori." *Domus* 226 (1948): n.p.
- "Casa per sciatori." *Domus* 238 (1948): n.p.
- "Dalla funzionalità all'utopia nell'ambientazione." *Atti e Rassegna Tecnica della Società degli Ingegneri e degli Architetti in Torino* (January 1949): 59–70.
- "Utopia e ambientazione (I)." *Domus* 237 (1949): 14–19.
- "Utopia e ambientazione (II)." *Domus* 238 (1949): 20–25.
- "La stazione della funivia del Fürggen." *Prospettive* 1 (December 1951): 32–7.
- "La stazione della funivia del Fürggen." *Atti e Rassegna Tecnica della Società degli Ingegneri e degli Architetti in Torino* (March 1953): 89–90.
- "Tabù e tradizione nella costruzione Montana." *Atti e Rassegna Tecnica della Società degli Ingegneri e degli Architetti in Torino* (April 1954): 151–4.

Moretti, Luigi. "Tradizione muraria ad Ibiza." *Spazio* 5 (July–August. 1951).

Moretti, Bruno. *Ville – Eesempi di ville, piccole case private di abitazione scelti fra le opere più recenti degli artisti di tutto il mondo.* Milan: Hoepli Editore, 1934.
- *Ville.* Milan: Hoepli Editore, 1939.
- *Case d'abitazione in Italia.* Milan: Hoepli Editore, 1939.

Morpurgo, Vittorio. "Gli edifici scolastici e la Minerva." *Architettura e arti decorative* 1:2 (November–December, 1921): 357–74.

Mossa, Vico. *Architettura domestica in Sardegna. Contributi per una storia della casa mediterranea.* Cagliari: Edizioni della Zattera, 1957.

Munthe, Axel *The Story of San Michele.* New York: E.P. Dutton, 1929. First Italian translation, *La storia di San Michele.* Milan-Rome: Fratelli Treves, 1932.

Nangeroni, Giuseppe. *Geografia delle dimore e degli insediamenti rurali.* Como-Milan: Marzorati Editore, 1946.

Naselli, Carmelina. "Costumi, tradizioni e unificazione." *Civiltà delle machine* (October 1961): 36–41.

Newcomb, Rexford. *Mediterranean Domestic Architecture in the United States.*

Cleveland: J.H. Jansen, 1928. Reprint with new introduction by Marc Appleton, New York: Acanthus Press, 1999.

– *Spanish-Colonial Architecture in the United States*. New York: Augustin, 1937. Reprint New York: Dover, 1990.

Ojetti, Ugo. "Bellezze perdute." In *I nani tra le colonne*, 41–46. Milan: Fratelli Treves, 1920.

– "L'arte di Lorenzo il Magnifico e l'arte di Nenciozza." *La Tribuna* (11 March 1920).

– "L'arte in campagna." In *Raffaello e altre leggi*, 32–42. Milan: Fratelli Treves Editore, 1921.

– "Commenti." *Dedalo* (December 1920): 485–6.

– "Per la riforma dell'insegnamento artistico." In *Raffaello e altre leggi*, 231–51. Milan: Fratelli Treves Editore, 1921.

– "Arte sarda." In *Ottocento novecento e via dicendo*, September 1933, 225–31. Milan: A. Mondadori, 1936.

Opera Nazionale Dopolavoro. *The National Dopolavoro Foundation in Italy*. Rome: Società editrice di novissima, 1938.

Ortensi, Dagoberto. *Edilizia rurale – Urbanistica di centri comunali e di borgate rurali*. Rome: Casa editrice Mediterranean, 1941.

Pagano, Giuseppe. "Case rurali." *Casabella* 86 (February 1935): 9–15. Also in *Giuseppe Pagano: Architettura e città durante il fascismo*, edited by Cesare De Seta, 32–41. Bari: Laterza, 1976, 1990.

– "Documenti di architettura rurale." *Casabella* 95 (1935): 18–19.

– "Architettura rurale in Italia." *Casabella* 96 (December 1935): 16–23. Also in *Giuseppe Pagano: Architettura e città durante il fascismo*, edited by Cesare De Seta, 124–7. Bari: Laterza, 1976, 1990.

– "Un architetto: Luigi Cosenza." *Casabella* 100 (April 1936): 6–17.

– "Una lezione di modestia." *Casabella* 111 (March 1937): 2–5.

– "Una casetta in legno." *Domus* 177 (September 1942): 375–9.

Pagano, Giuseppe, and Daniel Werner. *Architettura Rurale Italiana*. Milan: Hoepli Editore, 1936.

Pane, Roberto. "Tipi di architettura rustica in Napoli e nei campi flegrei." *Architettura e arti decorative*. (August 1928): 529–43.

– *Architettura rurale campana*. Florence: Rinascimento del libro, 1936.

– *Architettura e letteratura*, in *Architettura e arti figurative*. Venice: Neri Pozza Editore, 1948: 63–73.

– *Capri*. Venice: Neri Pozza Editore, 1954.

Paoli, Renato. Amalfi I. *The Architect* (July 1920): 4–6.

– "Ravello – II." *The Architect* (January 1921): 70–1.

– "Capri and Amalfi – III." *The Architect* (March 1921): 158–61.

– "Il casale romano." *Circeo* (November 1921): n.p.
– "Bellezze d'Italia: Amalfi." *Emporium* (January 1922): 41–51.
– *Estetica e ragione dell'urbanistica.* Rome: Biblioteca d'arte editrice, 1934.
Papini, Roberto. "Edilizia moderna: l'architetto Ernesto Wille." *Emporium* 40:236 (August 1914): 97–111.
– "La mostra delle arti decorative a Monza. 1. Architettura e decorazione." *Emporium* (May 1923): 275–90.
– "Le arti a Monza nel 1925; Dagli architetti ai pastori," *Emporium* 62:369 (September 1925): 139–60.
– "Cronache Romane – Architettura di Capri." *Emporium* 4 (August 1928): 117–25.
– *Le arti d'oggi – Architettura e arti decorative in Europa.* Milan: Bestetti e Tuminelli, 1930.
Parpagliolo, Luigi. *La difesa delle bellezze naturali d'Italia.* Rome: Società d'arte editrice illustrata, 1923.
Pasolini, Pier Paolo. *La poesia popolare italiana.* Milan: Garzanti, 1960.
Pavolini, Corrado. "Case toscane." *Illustrazione Toscana e dell'etruria* 2:12 (December 1933): 20–4.
Peressutti, Enrico. "Architettura mediterranea." *Quadrante* 21 (1935): 40–1.
Persico, Edoardo. "Un 'cottage' nel Canavese." *Casabella* 45 (September 1931): 16–27.
Piacentini, Marcello. "Nuovi orizzonti dell'edilizia cittadina." *Nuova Antologia* 57:1199 (March 1922): 60–72.
– "Arte artistocratica ed arte paesana." *La Tribuna* 3 (April 1920): 3.
– "Il momento architettonico all'estero." *Architettura e arti decorative* (May–June, 1921): 32–76.
– "Influssi d'Arte Italiana nel Nord-America." *Architettura e arti decorative* (March–April, 1922): 536–55. Republished in Mario Pisani ed., *Marcello Piacentini – Architettura moderna*, 110–12. Venice: Marsilio Editori, 1996.
– "La Casa nel Paesaggio di Capri." *Architettura e arti decorative* (March–April, 1922): 595–6.
– *Architettura d'oggi.* Rome: Paolo Cremonese Editore, 1930. Reprint Mario Pisani ed., Melfi: Libria Editore, 1994.
– *Le vicende edilizie di Roma dal 1870 ad oggi.* Rome: Palombi, 1952.
Pica, Agnoldomenico. "Recensione alla VI Triennale di Milano." *Rassegna di Architettura* (August–September 1936): 267–70.
– "Sapor di Venezia." Introduction to *Venezia Minor,* 11–28, by Egle Renata Trincanato. Venice: Filippi Editore, 1948.
– *Storia della Triennale, 1918 – 1957.* Milan: Edizione del Milione, 1957.
Piccinato, Luigi. "Case popolari – Il nuovo quartiere della garbatella in

Roma dell'Istituto delle case popolari di Roma" *Domus* (February 1930): 10–31.

**Pipitone-Federico, Giuseppe. "La mostra etnografica all'Esposizione Nazionale di Palermo." In *Natura ed Arte – Rassegna Quindicinale Illustrata Italiana e Straniera di Scienze, Lettere ed Arti.* 1892 19 (1 September 1892): 650–5; 20 (15 September 1892): 762–7; 21 (1 October 1892): 845–52.

Pitrè, Giuseppe. *Catalogo illustrato della mostra etnografica siciliana.* Palermo: Stabilimento Tipografico Virzì, 1892.

– *La Famiglia, la Casa, la Vita del Popolo Siciliano.* Palermo: Libreria Internazionale A. Reber, 1913.

Podestà, Attilio. "Una casa di Procida dell'arch – Bernard Rudofsky." *Casabella* (September 1937): 12–17.

Ponti, Giovanni. *La casa all'italiana.* Milan: Edizioni Domus, 1933.

– "Facciamoci una coscienza nazionale della architettura mediterranea." *Stile* 7:19 (July 1941): 2–12.

– "Senza aggettivi." *Domus* 268 (March 1952): 1. English translation published in *Il Design Italiano degli anni '50*, edited by Andrea Branzi and Michele De Lucchi, 296. Milan: IGIS Edizioni, 1981.

– "Invito a considerare tutta l'architettura come 'spontanea.'" *Domus* (March 1955): n.p.

Portoghesi, Paolo. "Si leggano i paesi." *Civiltà delle machine* 3:5 (September–October 1955): 44–8.

– "L'esperimento la Martella," *Civiltà delle machine* 3:6 (November–December 1955): 16–20.

– "Dal neorealismo al neoliberty." *Comunità* 12:65 (December 1958): 69–79.

– ed. *The Presence of the Past.* London: Academy, 1980.

– *After Modern Architecture.* Translated by Meg Shore. New York: Rizzoli, 1982.

Quaroni, Ludovico. *La Torre di Babele.* Padua: Marsilio Editori, 1967.

Ragusa-Moleti, Girolamo. "La mostra etnografica." Pt. 1 of *Palermo e l'Esposizione nazionale del 1891–92.* 25: 193–4.

– "La mostra etnografica." Pt. 2 of *Palermo e l'Esposizione nazionale del 1891–92.* 26: 203–6.

Rava, Carlo Enrico. "Spirito Latino." *Domus* 38 (February 1931): 24–9.

– "Giovani architetti nordamericani." *Domus* 43 (July 1931): 33–6.

– *Nove anni di architettura vissuta, 1926 IV–1935 XIII.* Rome: Cremonese Editore, 1935.

– "Bilancio della IX Triennale." *Propsettive* 2 (1951): 33–40.

Ricci, Elisa. *Antiche trine italiane.* Bergamo: Istituto Italiano d'arti grafiche,

1908. English Translation, *Old Italian Lace*. Vol. 2. London: William Heinemann, 1913.

- "Industrie femminili: I lavori delle nostre contadine." *Emporium* (February 1914): 120–32.
- "Industrie femminili: I lavori delle nostre contadine: ricami, paglie." *Emporium* (April 1914): 280–90.

Ricci, Leonardo. "Michelucci attraverso un suo lavoro." *Architetti* 18–19 (1953): 13–18.

Rogers, Ernesto Nathan. "Catarsi." *Casabella-Costruzioni* (December 1946): 40.
- Editorial. *Casabella-Continuità* (December–January, 1953–4): 2
- "La tradizione dell'architettura moderna italiana." *Casabella-Continuità* (July–August 1955): 1–7. Also published in *Italy Builds: Its Modern Architecture and Native Inheritance*, by George Everard Kidder Smith, 9–14. New York: Reinhold Publishing Corporation, 1955.
- *Esperienza dell'architettura*. Turin: Einaudi, 1958.
- "The Future Was Not to Be Seen at Brussels." *Architects Yearbook* (1959): 132–9.

Rogers, Meyric R. *Italy at Work – Her Renaissance in Design Today*. Rome: Istituto Poligrafico dello Stato, 1950.

Rossi, Aldo. *The Architecture of the City*. Translated by Diane Ghirardo. Cambridge, MA: MIT Press, 1981. Padua: Marsilio, 1966.
- "Il concetto di tradizione nell'architettura neoclassica Milanese." *Società* (June 1956) 474–93. Also in *Aldo Rossi Scritti scelti sull'architettura e la città, 1956–1972*, edited by Rosaldo Bonicalzi. Milan: Cooperativa libraria universitaria del politecnico, 1975.
- "Architetture padane." In *Aldo Rossi: Architetture Padane*, 11–14. Modena: Edizioni Panin, 1984.

Rudofsky, Bernard. *Eine primitive Betonbauweise auf den südlichen Kykladen, nebst dem versuch einer Datierung derselben*. Vienna, Technische Hochschule, 1931.
- "Capresisches, Anacapresisches." *Montashefte für Baukunst und Städtebau* (January 1934): 22–4.
- "Non ci vuole un nuovo modo di costuire – Ci vuole un nuovo modo di vivere." *Domus* 123 (March 1938): 2–3.
- "The Cradle of Architecture in the Mediterranean and Unit Architecture in the Mediterranean." *The Architectural Review* (March 1941): n.p.
- *Architecture without Architects: A Short Introduction to Non-Pedigreed Architecture*. New York: Museum of Modern Art, 1964.
- *The Prodigious Builders: Notes Toward a Natural History of Architecture with*

Special Regard to Those Species That Are Traditionally Neglected or Downright Ignored. New York: Harcourt Brace Jovanovich, 1977.

Rudolph, Paul. "Regionalism in Architecture." *Perspecta* 4 (1957): 12–19. Republished in *Writings on Architecture: Paul Rudolph,* ed. Robert A.M. Stern (New Haven, CT: Yale School of Architecture, 2008), 30–8.

Ruskin, John. *The Poetry of Architecture or The Architecture of the Nations of Europe Considered in its Association with Natural Scenery and National Character.* New York: D.D. Merrill Co., 1873. Italian translation by Dora Prunetti, *La poesia dell'architettura.* Milan: A. Solmi, 1909.

– ed. Francesca Alexander. *Christ's Folk in the Apennine – Reminiscences of Her Friends Among the Tuscan Peasantry.* Sunnyside: George Allen, 1887.

Sacchi, Giovanni. "*Architettura rustica di oggi e di ieri.*" *Atti dei sindacati provinciali fascisti ingegneri di Lombardia* (October 1940): 207–12.

Samonà, Giuseppe. "Tradizionalismo ed internazionalismo architettonico." *Rassegna d'architettura* (1929): 97–104.

– *La Casa Popolare.* Naples, 1935. Reprint in Mario Manieri Elia, ed., *La casa popolare degli anni '30.* Venice: Marsilio, 1972.

– "Architettura spontanea: documento di edilizia fuori della storia." *Urbanistica* (1954): 6–10.

Sant'Elia, Antonio. "Messaggo." *Catalogo Nuove Tendenze.* Milan, 1914.

– "L'architettura futurista – Manifesto." *Lacerba* 1 and 14 (August 1914): 228–31.

Sanminiatelli, Bino. "Case Coloniche in Toscana." *Civiltà – Rivista Trimestrale della Esposizione Universale di Roma* (January 1942): 85–93.

Sapori, Francesco. "La prima mostra biennale d'arte in Roma. II. Architettura, scultura, decorazione, bianco e nero." *Emporium* (June 1921): 303–19.

Sarfatti, Margherita. *L'Italia alla Esposizione Internazionale di Arti Decorative e Industriali Moderne.* Paris: 1924.

– "Le arti decorative a Monza." *La Rivista illustrata del popolo d'Italia.* (July 1925): 41–5.

Sartoris, Alberto. *Gli elementi dell'architettura funzionale.* Milan: Hoepli Editore, 1932.

– "Architettura rurale moderna." *Natura* 3 (1932): 47–9.

– *Encyclopédie de l'architecture nouvelle.* Vol. 1, *Ordre et climat méditerranees,* 1948. Vol. 2, *Ordre et climat Nordiques,* 1957. Vol. 3, *Ordre et climat américains,* 1954. Milan: Hoepli Editore, 1948.

Sautier, Albert. *Tappeti rustici italiani.* Milan: Gli Editori Piantanida – Valcarenghi, 1922.

Scano, Dionigi. "La bottega d'arte ceramica in Cagliari." *Mediterranea – Rivista mensile di cultura di problemi isolani* (November–December 1927): 66–72.

Schinkel, Karl Friedrich. *Reisen nach Italien: Tagebücher, Briefe, Zeichnungen, Acquarelle.* Berlin: Aufbau Verlag, 1994. Italian translation *Viaggio in Sicilia*, edited by Michele Cometa, and Gottfried Riemann. Messina: Sicania, 1990.

Sestini, Aldo. *Il paessagio.* Vol. 7, *Conosci l'Italia.* Milan: Touring Club Italiano, 1963.

Società amatori e cultori di belle arti. *XCI – Esposizione di belle arti.* Rome: Alfieri and Lacroix, 1923.

Soffici, Ardengo. "Di vari primitivismi (1938)." In Ardengo Soffici, ed., *Selva Arte*, 218–19. Florence: Vallecchi, 1943.

– "Architettura rustica (1939)." In Ardengo Soffici, ed., *Selva Arte*, 285–8. Florence: Vallecchi, 1943.

– "Neoprimitivismo (1941)." In Ardengo Soffici, ed., *Selva Arte*, 323–6. Florence: Vallecchi, 1943.

Soleri, Paolo. *The Bridge Between Matter Becoming Spirit – The Arcology of Paolo Soleri.* New York: Anchor Books, 1973.

– "Utopia and/or Revolution." *Perspecta* 13–14 (1971): 281–5.

Soule, Winsor. *Spanish Farm Houses and Minor Public Buildings.* New York: Architectural Book Publishing Co., 1923.

Starace, Achille. *Opera nazionale dopolavoro.* Milan: A. Mondadori, 1938.

Strand, Paul, and Cesare Zavattini. *Un paese: Portrait of an Italian Village.* New York: Aperture, 1997. Originally published as *Un paese.* Turin: Einaudi, 1955.

Strinati, Remigio. "L'esposizione italiana di arte decorative a Stoccolma." *Rassegna d'Arte antica e moderna* 4 (April 1921): 134–9.

Tinti, Mario. "L'equivoco dell'arte rustica." *Casabella* (1932): 51–2.

– *L'architettura delle case coloniche in Toscana.* Florence: Rinascimento del Libro, 1934.

Togliatti, Palmiro. *Lectures on Fascism.* New York: International Publishers Co. Inc., 1976.

Tolstoy, Leo. *What Is Art?* Translated by Richard Pevear. London: Walter Scott, 1898.

– *Che cosa e l'arte?* Milan: Fratelli Treves, 1900.

Torres, Duilio. *La casa veneta: raccolta di tipi preminenti delle case costruite nella regione veneta dal secolo IX al secolo XVI.* Venice, 1933.

Toschi, Paolo. *Saggi sull'arte popolare.* Rome: Edizioni italiane, 1944.

– *Guida al Museo Nazionale delle Arti e Tradizioni Popolari.* Terni: Edizioni Alterocca, 1956.

– *Il folklore.* Rome: Universale Studium, 1951.

– *Arte popolare italiana.* Rome, 1951.

– *Il folklore: Tradizioni, vita e arti popolari.* Milan: Touring Club Italiano, 1967.

Trincanato, Egle Renata. *Venezia Minore*. Venice: Filippi Editore, 1948.
– *A Guide to Venetian Domestic Architecture* – "Venezia Minore." Edited by Renzo Salvadori. Venice: Canal and Stamperia Editore, 1995.
– *La Casa Veneziana delle Origini ed altri scritti sulla casa veneziana*, edited by Corrado Balistreri-Trincanato, and Emiliano Balistreri. Venice: Edizioni Stamperia Cetid, 1999.
Venturi, Lionello. *Il gusto dei primitivi*. Turin: Einaudi, 1926.
– "Per la nuova architettura." *Casabella* (January 1933): 2–3.
Verga, Giovanni. *Cavalleria rusticana and Other Stories*. London: Penguin Books, 1999.
Whittlesey, Austin. *The Minor Ecclesiastical, Domestic, and Garden Architecture of Southern Spain*. New York: Architetural Book Pub. Co., 1917.
Wright, Frank Lloyd. "The Sovereignty of the Individual." In *Frank Lloyd Wright: Writings and Buildings*, edited by Edgar Kaufmann, and Ben Raeburn, 84–106. New York: Horizon Press, 1960.
Zavattini, Cesare. *Un paese vent'anni dopo*. Turin: Einaudi, 1976.
Zevi, Bruno. *Verso un'architettura organica*. Turin: Einaudi, 1945. English translation, *Towards an Organic Architecture*. London: Faber and Faber, 1950.
– "Urbanistica e architettura minore." *Urbanistica* (April–June 1950): 68–9.
– *Il linguaggio moderno dell'architettura*. Turin: Einaudi, 1973. In English, *The Modern Language of Architecture*. Seattle: University of Washington Press, 1977.
– "The Italian Rationalists." In *The Rationalist: Theory and Design in the Modern Movement*, edited by Dennis Sharp, 118–29. London: Architectural Press, 1978. Also in Andrea Oppenheimer Dean, *Bruno Zevi on Modern Architecture*, 107–113. New York: Rizzoli, 1983.
– *Controstoria dell'architettura italiana – Dialetti architettonici*. Rome: Newton and Compton, 1996.

Secondary Sources

Achleitner, Friedrich. "Edoardo Gellner und ein 'Gründungsdorf' im Cadore." In *Die Architektur, die Tradition und der Ort. Regionalismen in der europäischen Stadt*, edited by Vittorio Magnago Lampugnani, 399–415. Stuttgart-München: Deutsche Verlags-Anstalt, 2000. Also in *Edoardo Gellner: Corte di Cadore*, edited by Friedrich Achleitner, Paolo Biadene, Edoardo Gellner, and Michele Merlo, 7–19. Milan: Skira, 2002.
Ackerman, James, S. "The Regions of Italian Renaissance Architecture." In *The Renaissance from Brunelleschi to Michelangelo: The Representation of Architecture*, edited by Henry A. Millon, and Vittorio Magnago Lampugnani, 319–47. Milan: Bompiani, 1994.

Adamson, L. Walter. *Avant-Garde Florence: From Modernism to Fascism.* Cambridge, MA: Harvard University Press, 1993.

– "The Culture of Italian Fascism and the Fascist Crisis of Modernity: The Case of Il Selvaggio." *Journal of Contemporary History* 20 (1995): 555–75.

– "Ardengo Soffici and the Religion of Art." In *Fascist Visions: Art and Ideology in France and Italy,* edited by Matthew Affron and Mark Antliff, 46–72. Princeton, NJ: Princeton University Press, 1997.

Affron, Matthew, and Mark Antliff, eds. *Fascist Visions: Art and Ideology in France and Italy.* Princeton, NJ: Princeton University Press, 1997

Allen, Edward. *Stone Shelters.* Cambridge, MA: MIT Press, 1969.

Asor Rosa, Alberto. *Scrittori e popolo – Saggio sulla letteratura populista in Italia.* Rome: Samonà e Savelli, 1965.

Baculo Giusti, Adriana. *La casa contadina – La casa nobile – La casa artigiana e mercantile – I caratteri.* Naples: Liguori Editore, 1979.

Barilli, Renato, and Franco Solmi, eds. *"La Metafisica": gli Anni Venti.* Bologna: Galleria d'arte moderna, 1980.

Barilli, Renato, ed. *Gli Anni Trenta: Arte e Cultura in Italia.* Milan: Mazzotta, 1982.

Barucci, Clementina. *Strumenti e cultura del progetto: Manualistica e letteratura tecnica in Italia 1860–1920.* Rome: Officina Edizioni, 1984.

Bassani, Ezio. *Scultura Africana nei musei italiani.* Bologna: Calderini, 1977.

– "Italian Painting." In *Primitivism in Twentieth-Century Art: Affinity of the Tribal and the Modern,* vol. 2, edited by William Rubin, 405–15. New York: The Museum of Modern Art, 1984.

Belli, Carlo. *Il volto del secolo – La prima cellula dell'architettura razionalista italiana.* Bergamo: P. Lubrina, 1988.

Belli, Gabriella. *La Casa del Mago – Le Arti applicate nell'opera di Fortunato Depero 1920–1942.* Florence: Edizioni Charta, 1992.

Belluzzi, Amedeo and Claudia Conforti. *Architettura italiana: 1944–1994.* Bari: Laterza, 1985.

Ben-Ghiat, Ruth. *Fascist Modernities: Italy, 1922–45.* Berkeley: University of California Press, 2001.

– ed., with Mia Fuller. *Italian Colonialism.* New York: Palgrave Macmillan, 2005.

Benton, Tim "Rome Reclaims its Empire – Architecture." In *Art and Power: Europe Under the Dictators, 1930–1945,* edited by Dawn Ades, 121–9. London: The Southbank Centre, 1995.

– "Italian Architecture and Design." In *Art deco 1910 – 1939,* edited by Charlotte Benton, Tim Benton, and Chislaine Wood, 219–29. New York: Bulfinch Press, 2003.

Besana, Renato, Carlo Fabrizio Carli, Leonardo Devoti, and Luigi Prisco. *Metafisica costruita – Le città di fondazione degli anni Trenta dall'Italia all'Oltremare.* Milan: Touring Editore, 2002.

Bevilacqua, Piero. *Il paesaggio italiano nelle fotografie dell'Istituto Luce*. Rome: Editori Riuniti, 2002.

Biscossa, Franco. "'Quadrante': Il dibattito e la polemica." In *La Costruzione dell'Utopia: Architetti e urbanisti nell'Italia fascista*, edited by Giulio Ernesti, 67–89. Rome: Edizioni lavoro, 1988.

Blecksmith, Anne. "'Raccolte di vedute': Early Twentieth Century Architect Books and the Making of a Landscape for California." *Art Documentation* (November 2002): 14–17.

Bobbio, Norberto. *Profilo ideological del Novecento*. Milan: Garzanti, 1990. English translation, *Ideological Profile of Twentieth-Century Italy*. Princeton, NJ: Princeton University Press, 1995.

Bocco-Guarneri, Andrea. *Bernard Rudofsky: A Humane Designer*. New York: Springer, 2003.

Bolzoni, Luciano. *Architettura moderna nelle Alpi italiane: dal 1900 alla fine degli anni cinquanta*. Turin: Priuli and Verlucca Editore, 2000.

– *Architettura moderna nelle Alpi italiane: dagli anni Sessanta alla fne del XX secolo*. Turin: Priuli and Verlucca Editore, 2001.

Borsi, Franco, and Ezio Godoli. "The Mediterranean Myth and the Rediscovery of the Popular." In *Vienna 1900: Architecture and Design*, 177–205. New York: Rizzoli, 1986.

Bossaglia, Rossana. *Il liberty in Italia*. Milan: Mondadori, 1968.

– *Il liberty – Storia e fortuna del liberty italiano*. Florence: G.C. Sansoni, 1974.

– *L'ISIA a Monza: Una scuola d'arte europea*. Milan: Silvana Editoriale, 1986.

– "The Protagonists of the Italian Liberty Movement." *Journal of Decorative and Propaganda Arts* 13 (Summer 1989): 32–51.

Bosoni, Giampiero, ed. *Italy: Contemporary Domestic Landscapes 1945–2000*. Milan: Skira Editore, 2001.

Braun, Emily, ed. *Italian Art in the 20th Century: Painting and Sculpture 1900–1988*. Munich: Prestel Verlag – Royal Academy of Arts, 1989.

– "Political Rhetoric and Poetic Irony: The Uses of Classicism in the Art of Fascist Italy." In *On Classic Ground: Picasso, Léger, de Chirico and the New Classicism, 1910–1930*, edited by Elizabeth Cowling and Jennifer Mundy, 345–58. London: Tate Gallery, 1990.

– "Speaking Volumes: Giorgio Morandi's Still Lifes and the Cultural Politics of Strapaese." *Modernism/Modernity* 2: 3 (1995) 89–116.

– "Expressionism as Fascist Aesthetic." *Journal of Contemporary History* 31 (1996): 273–92.

– *Mario Sironi and Italian Modernism: Art and Politics under Fascism*. New York: Cambridge Unviersity Press, 2000.

Brunetti, Fabrizio. *Architetti e fascismo*. Florence: Alinea Editrice, 1993.

Burdett, Richard, ed. *Sabaudia – Città Nuova Fascista*. London: Architectural Association, 1981.

Buscioni, Maria Cristina. *Esposizioni e "Stile Nazionale" (1861–1925) – Il linguaggio dell'architettura nei padiglioni italiani delle grandi kermesses nazionali ed einternazionali*. Florence: Alinea Editrice, 1990.

Calvino, Italo. *Italian Folktales: Selected and Retold by Italo Calvino*. Translated by George Martin. San Diego: Harcourt, 1980.

Canfora, Luciano. "Classicismo e Fascismo." In *Matrici culturali del Fascismo*, edited by Luciano Canfora, 85–112. Bari: Laterza, 1977.

– *Ideologie del classicismo*. Turin: Einaudi, 1980.

Cannistraro, Philip V. *La fabbrica del consenso: Fascismo e mass media*. Bari: Laterza, 1975.

– "Fascism and Culture, 1919–1945." In *Italian Art in the Twentieth Century: Painting and Sculpture 1900–1988*, edited by Emily Bruan, 147–54. Munich: Prestel Verlag – Royal Academy of Arts, 1989.

Cantone, Gaetana, and Italo Prozillo. *Case di Capri – ville, palazzi, grandi dimore*. Naples: Electa, 1994.

Cardini, Franco, ed. *La cultura folklorica*. Busto Arsizio: Bramante Editrice, 1988.

Carver Jr., Norman F. *Italian Hilltowns*. Kalamazoo: Documan Press, 1979.

Casciato, Maristella. "L'abitazione e gli spazi domestici." In *La famiglia italiana dall'Ottocento a oggi*, edited by Piero Melograni, 525–87. Bari: Laterza, 1988.

– "Wright and Italy: The Promise of Organic Architecture." In *Frank Lloyd Wright: Europe and Beyond*, edited by Anthony Alofsin, 76–99. Berkeley: University of California Press, 1999.

– "Neorealism in Italian Architecture." In *Anxious Modernisms: Experimentation in Postwar Architectural Culture*, edited by Sarah William Goldhagen and Rejean Legault, 25–53. Cambridge: CCA – MIT, 2000.

– "The 'Casa all'Italiana' and the Idea of Modern Dwelling in Fascist Italy." *The Journal of Architecture* 5:4 (2000): 335–53.

Castellano, Aldo. *La casa rurale in Italia*. Milan: Electa, 1986.

Cavazza, Stefano. "La folkloristica italiana e il fascismo. Il Comitato Nazionale per le Arti Popolari." In *La ricerca folklorica – contributi allo studio della cultura delle classi popolari* 15 (April 1987): 109–22.

– "Tradizioni regionali e riesumazioni demologiche durante il fascismo." In *Studi Storici – rivista trimestrale dell'istituto gramsci* 2–3 (April–September 1993): 625–55.

– *Piccole patrie: Feste popolari tra regione e nazione durante il fascism*. Bologna: Il Mulino, 1997.

Celant, Germano, ed. *The Italian Metamorphosis, 1943–1968*. New York: Harry N. Abrams, 1994.

Cennamo, Michele ed. *Materiali per l'analisi dell'architettura moderna. La prima Esposizione Italiana di Architettura Razionale*. Naples: Fauto Fiorentino Editore, 1973.

– *Materiali per l'analisi dell'architettura moderna – Il Miar*. Naples: Società Editrice Napoletana, 1976.

Ciucci, Giorgio. "Italian Architecture during the Fascist Period: Classicism between Neoclassicism and Rationalism: The Many Souls of the Classical." *The Harvard Architectural Review* 6 (1987): 76–87.

– "Linguaggi classicisti negli anni trenta in Europa e in America." In *L'estetica della politica – Europa e America negli anni Trenta*, edited by Maurizio Vaudagna, 45–58. Rome: Laterza, 1989.

– *Gli architetti e il fascismo – Architettura e città, 1922–1944*. Turin: Einaudi, 1989.

– Introduction to *Casa Malaparte*, by Marida Talamona, 21–6. New York: Princeton Architectural Press, 1992.

– ed. *Classicismo, classicismo: Architettura Europa/America 1920–1940*. Milan: Electa, and Venice: C.I.S.A. Andrea Palladio, 1995.

Ciucci, Giorgio, and Francesco Dal Co, eds. *Architettura italiana del '900*. Milan: Electa, 1993.

Ciucci, Giorgio, and Maristella Casciato. *Franco Marescotti e la casa civile, 1934–1956*. Rome: Officina, 1980.

Clausen, Meredith L. *Pietro Belluschi – Modern American Architect*. Cambridge, MA: MIT Press, 1994.

Clemente, Pietro, Maria Luisa Meoni, and Massimo Squillacciotti. *Il dibattito sul folklore in Italia*. Milan: Edizioni di cultura popolare, 1976.

Clemente, Pietro, and Luisa Orrú. "Sondaggi sull'arte popolare." In *Storia dell'arte italiana*. Vol. 4, 239–341. Turin: Einaudi, 1982.

Cohen, Jean-Louis, ed. *Annes 30. L'architecture et les arts de l'espace entre industrie et nostalgie*. Paris: Edition du Patrimoine, 1997.

Colquhoun, Alan. "Vernacular Classicism." In Alan Colquhoun, *Modernity and the Classical Tradition, Architectural Essays 1980–1987*, 21–31. Cambridge: MIT Press, 1989.

– "The Concept of Regionalism." In *Postcolonial space(s)*, edited by Gülsüm Baydar Nalbantoglu and Wong Chong Thai. New York: Princeton Architectural Press, 1997.

– *Modern Architecture*. Oxford and New York: Oxford University Press, 2002. 183–92.

Cresti, Carlo. "Segni e soggezioni di paternità Latina nell'architettra italiana degli anni Venti e Trenta." In *Pompei e il recupero del classico*, edited by Marilena Pasquali, 20–35. Ancona: Galleria d'arte moderna, 1980.

– *Architettura e fascismo*. Florence: Vallecchi, 1986.

Crispolti, Enrico. *Il mito della macchina e altri temi del futurism*. Trapani: Editore Celebes, 1971.

– ed. *Arte e fascismo in Italia e in Germania*. Milan: Feltrinelli, 1974.

– *Attraverso architettura futurista*. Modena: Galleria Fonte d'Abisso Edizioni, 1984.

– *Storia e critica del Futurismo*. Bari: Laterza, 1987.

Cuccu, Antonello. *Studio Artistico Melkiorre Melis*. Bosa: Amm. Comunale di Bosa, 1989.

Dal Co, Francesco. "Giovanni Michelucci: A Life One Century Long." *Persepecta* 27 (1992): 99–115.

Danesi, Silvia, and Luciano Patetta, eds. *Il Razionalismo e l'archiettura in Italia durante il Fascismo*. Milan: Electa, 1976.

Della Coletta, Cristina. *World's Fairs Italian Style: The Great Expositions in Turin and their Narratives, 1860–1915*. Toronto: University of Toronto, 2006.

De Michelis, Marco. "Fascist Architectures in Italy." In *Back from Utopia: The Challenge of the Modern Movement*, edited by Hubert-Jan Henket, Hilde Heynen, 86–91. Rotterdam: 010 Publishers, 2002.

De Guttry, Irene. "Cambellotti architetto." In *Cambellotti (1876–1960)*, edited by Giovanna Bonasegale, Anna Maria Damigella, and Bruno Mantura. Rome: Edizioni De Luca, 2000.

– "The Design Reform Movement in Rome at the Beginning of the Century." *Journal of Decorative and Propaganda Arts* 13 (Summer 1989): 52–75.

De Guttry, Irene, Maria Paola Maino, and Mario Quesada. *Le arti minore d'autore in Italia dal 1900 al 1930*. Bari: Laterza, 1985.

De Guttry, Irene, Maria Paola Maino, and Gloria Raimondi. *Duilio Cambellotti – Arredi e decorazioni*. Bari: Laterza, 2000.

Denti, Giovanni, Andrea Savio, and Calzà Gianni. *Le Corbusier in Italia*. Milan: Clup, 1988.

De Felice, Renzo. *Mussolini il rivoluzionario 1883–1920*. Vol. 1. Turin: Einaudi, 1965.

– Vol. 2: *Mussolini il fascista: La conquista del potere, 1921–1925*. Turin: Einaudi, 1966.

– Vol. 3: *Mussolini il fascista: L'organizzazione dello Stato fascista, 1925–1929*. Turin: Einaudi, 1968.

– Vol. 4: *Mussolini il duce: Gli anni del consenso, 1929–1936*. Turin: Einaudi, 1974.

– Vol. 5: *Mussolini il duce: Lo Stato totalitario 1936–1940*. Turin: Einaudi, 1981.

– Vol. 6: *Mussolini: L'alleato, 1940–1945*. Turin: Einaudi, 1990.

De Fusco, Renato. *L'idea di architettura: storia della critica da Viollet-le-Duc a Persico*. Milan: Garzanti, 1968.

De Grand. J. Alexander. *Bottai e la cultura fascista*. Rome: Laterza, 1978.

De Grazia, Victoria. *The Culture of Consent: Mass Organization of Leisure in Fascist Italy*. New York: Cambridge University Press, 1981.

De Seta, Cesare. *La cultura architettonica in Italia tra le due guerre*. (Bari: Laterza, 1972.

De Seta, Cesare, ed. *Raffaello Giolli – L'architettura razionale*. Bari: Laterza, 1972.

– *Giuseppe Pagano. Architettura e città durante il fascismo*. Bari: Laterza, 1976.

– *Giuseppe Pagano Fotografo*. Milan: Electa, 1979.

Di Biagi, Paola, ed. *La grande ricostruzione. Il piano Ina-Casa e l'Italia degli anni 50*. Rome: Donzelli, 2001.

Doordan, Dennis. "The Political Content in Italian Architecture During the Fascist Era." *Art Journal* 2 (Summer 1983): 121–31.

– *Building Modern Italy – Italian Architecture 1914 – 1936*. New York: Princeton Architectural Press, 1988.

– "Changing Agendas: Architecture and Politics in Contemporary Italy." *Assemblage* 8 (1989): 61–77.

– "Rebuilding the House of Man." In *The Italian Metamorphosis, 1943–1968*, edited by Germano Celant, 586–95. New York: Harry N. Abrams, 1994.

Eisenman, Peter. "From Object to Relationship II: Giuseppe Terragni's Casa Giuliani Frigerio." In *Perspecta* 13–14 (1971) 36–65.

– *Giuseppe Terragni: Transformations, Decompositions, Critiques*. New York: Monacelli Press, 2003.

Ernesti. Giulio, ed. *La Costruzione dell"Utopia – Architetti e urbanisti nell'Italia fascista*. Rome: Edizioni lavoro, 1988.

Etlin, Richard. *Modernism in Italian Architecture, 1890–1940*. Cambridge, MA: MIT Press, 1991.

– "Nationalism in Modern Italian Architecture, 1900–1940." In *Nationalism in the Visual Arts*, edited by Richard Etlin, 89–109. Washington, DC: National Gallery of Art, 1991.

Falasca-Zamponi, Simonetta. *Fascist Spectacle: The Aesthetics of Power in Mussolini's Italy*. Berkeley: University of California Press, 1997.

Fanelli, Giovanni, and Barbara Mazza. *La casa colonica in Toscana: Le fotografie di Pier Niccolò Berardi alla Triennale del 1936*. Florence: Octavo, 1999.

Farnetti, Fauzia, ed. "Italian peninsula." In *Encyclopedia of Vernacular Architecture of the World*, edited by Paul Oliver, 1564–79 and 2282–92. New York: Cambridge University Press, 1997.

Finelli, Luciana, and Bonalda Stringher. "Architettura e urbanistica popolare." In *Dizionario enciclopedico di architettura e urbanistica*, edited by Paolo Portoghesi, 496–503. Rome: Istituto Editoriale Romano, 1968–69.

Folchi, Annibale. *I contadini del Duce – Agro Pontino – 1932–1941*. Rome: Pieraldo Editore, 2000.

Fogu, Claudio. *The Historic Imaginary: Politics of History in Fascist Italy*. Toronto: University of Toronto Press, 2003.

Forster, Kurt W. "Back to the Farm – Vernacular Architecture and the Development of the Renaissance Villa." *Architectura. Zeitschrift für Geschicte der Architektur* 1 (1974): 1–12.

Franzone, Gianni. "Per un'analisi del 'ruralesimo' nella Collezione Wolfson – Da Cambellotti alla 'mistica rurale' fascista." In *La visione del prisma. La collezione Wolfson*, edited by Silvia Barisione, Matteo Fochessati, and Gianni Franzone, 65–91. Milan: Mazzotta 1999.

Fuller, Mia, with Ruth Ben-Ghiat. *Italian Colonialism*. New York: Palgrave Macmillan, 2005.

– *Moderns Abroad: Architecture, Cities and Italian Imperialism*. London: Routledge, 2007.

Gambardella, Cherubino. *Il sogno bianco – Architettura e mito mediterraneo nell'Italia degli anni '30*. Naples: Clean, 1988.

– *Case sul Golfo – Abitare lungo la costa Napoletana 1930–1945*. Naples: Electa, 1993.

Gambi, Lucio. "Per una storia dell'abitazione rurale in Italia." *Rivista Storica Italiana* (June 1964): 427–54.

– "La casa contadina." *Storia d'Italia*. Vol. 6, 479–505. Turin: Einaudi, 1976.

Gambi, Lucio, and Giuseppe Barbieri. *La casa rurale in Italia*. Florence: L.S. Olshki, 1970.

Gebhard, David. *George Washington Smith, 1876–1930: The Spanish Colonial Revival in California*. Santa Barbara: Santa Barbara Art Gallery, 1964.

– "The Spanish Colonial Revival in Southern California (1895–1930)." *Journal of the Society of Architectural Historians* 2 (1967): 131–47.

– "The Mediterranean Villa in America: Three Episodes." In *Ah Mediterranean! Twentieth Century Classicism in America*, edited by Charles W. Moore and Wayne Attoe, 41–50. New York: Rizzoli, 1985.

Gentile, Emilio. *Le origini dell'ideologia fascista, 1918–1925*. Bari: Laterza, 1975.

– *The Sacralization of Politics in Fascist Italy*. Cambridge: Harvard University Press, 1996. Published in Italian as *Il culto del littorio: la sacralizzazione della politica nell'Italia fascista*. Rome: Laterza, 1993.

– *The Struggle for Modernity: Nationalism, Futurism, and Fascism*. Westport: Praeger, 2003.

Ghirardo, Diane. *Building New Communities: New Deal America and Fascist Italy.* Princeton, NJ: Princeton University Press, 1989.

Godoli, Ezio, and Milva Giacomelli, eds. *Virgilio Marchi – Scritti di Architettura.* 2 vols. Florence: Octavo, 1997.

Godoli, Ezio. "Liberty Architecture in Italy." In *Art Nouveau Architecture,* edited by Frank Russell, 197–217. Rizzoli: New York 1979.

Goldfinger, Myron. *Villages in the Sun: Mediterranean Community Architecture.* New York: Praeger, 1969; reprint ed., New York: Rizzoli, 1993.

Gravagnuolo, Benedetto. *Il mito mediterraneo nell'architettura contemporanea.* Naples: Electa, 1994.

– ed. *Le Corbusier e l'Antico – Viaggi nel Mediterraneo.* Naples: Electa, 1997.

Gresleri, Giuliano, ed. *Architettura italiana d'oltremare 1870–1949.* Venice: Marsilio, 1993.

– "Classico e vernacolo nell'architettura dell'Italia d'oltremare.'" In *Classicismo – Classicismi, Architettura. Europa-America 1920–1940,* edited by Giorgio Ciucci, 69–87. Milan: Electa-C.I.S.A. Andrea Palladio, 1995.

Gregotti, Vittorio. *New Directions in Italian Architecture.* New York: Braziller, 1968.

Gregotti, Vittorio, Giovanni Marzari, eds. *Luigi Figini – Gino Pollini – Opera Completa.* Milan: Electa, 1996.

Grüning, Michael, and Rowena Lanfermann. "Progettare e costruire a Roma: gli anni italiani di Konrad Wachsmann." In *Rifugio Precario: Artist e intellettuali tedeschi in Italia 1933–1945,* 235–44. Milan: Edizioni Gabriele Mazzotta, 1995.

Guccione, Margherita, Maria Lagunes, Margarita Segarra, Rosalia Vittorini, eds. *Guida ai quartieri romani INA Casa.* Rome: Gangemi Editore, 2002.

Guenzi, Carlo. *L'arte di edificare – Manuali in Italia 1750–1950.* Milan: Be-Ma Editrice, 1993.

Guidoni, Enrico. *Architettura primitive.* Milan, Electa, 1975. English translation, *Primitive Architecture.* New York: Harry N. Abrams, 1978.

– *L'architettura popolare italiana.* Rome: Laterza, 1980.

– Introduction to *Storia dell'arte italiana, Parte terza. Situazioni momenti indagini.* Edited by Walter Barbero, Giuseppe Gambirasio, and Vanni Zanella. 3–33. Turin: Giulio Einaudi editore, 1980.

– "Ambiente, architettura, arte popolare nell'opera del disegnatore dal vero." In *Luigi Angelini. Ingegnere architetto,* 140–3. Milan: Electa, 1984.

Hitchcock, Henry-Russell. "Connecticut, U.S.A. in 1963." *Zodiac* (1964): 8.

Hitchcock, Henry-Russell, and Arthur Drexler, eds. *Built in USA: Post-war Architecture.* New York: Thames and Hudson, 1952.

Hulten, Pontus, and Germano Celant, eds. *Italian Art – 1900–1945*. New York: Rizzoli, 1989.

Jocteau, Gian Carlo, ed. *Ai monti e al mare – Cento anni di colonie per l'infanzia*. Milan: Fabbri Editori, 1990.

Kirk, Terry. *The Architecture of Modern Italy*. Vols. 1–2. New York: Princeton Architectural Press, 2005.

Kostof, Spiro. *The Third Rome, 1870–1950: Traffic and Glory*. Berkeley: University Art Museum, 1973.

La Regina, Francesco. *Architettura rurale – Problemi di storia e conservazione della civiltà edilizia contadina in Italia*. Bologna: Calderini, 1980.

Lamonaca, Marianne. "Tradition as Transformation: Gio Ponti's Program for the Modern Italian Home, 1928–1933." *Studies in the Decorative Arts* (Fall–Winter 1997–1998), 52–82.

– "A 'Return to Order': Issues of the Classical and Vernacular in Italian Inter-War Design." In *Designing Modernity: The Arts of Reform and Persuasion 1885–1945*, edited by Wendy Kaplan, 195–221. London: Thames and Hudson, 1995.

Lampugnani, Vittorio Magnago. "Architecture, Painting and the Decorative Arts in Italy 1923–1940 from the First Biennale to the Seventh Triennale." In *Italian Art 1900–1945*, edited by Pontus Hulten and Germano Celant, 69–76. New York: Rizzoli, 1989.

– "Razionalismo e Italianità – L'architettura italiana moderna tra cosmopolitismo e nazionalismo (1926–1936)." In *L'Europa e l'arte italiana*, edited by Max Seidel, 563–73. Venice: Marsilio Editore, 2000.

– ed. *Die Architektur, die Tradition und der Ort – Regionalismen in der europäischen Stadt*. Stuttgart-München: Deutsche Verlags-Anstalt, 2000.

– "The Myth of Reality: Notes on Neorealism in Italy 1946–56." In *Architecture & Arts 1900–2004: A Century of Creative Projects in Building, Design, Cinema, Painting, Sculpture*, edited by Germano Celant, 75–9. Milan: Skira 2004.

Lasansky, D. Medina. *The Renaissance Perfected: Architecture, Spectacle, and Tourism in Fascist Italy*. University Park, PA.: Pennsylvania State University Press, 2004.

Lazzaro, Claudia. "Rustic Country Houses to Refined Farmhouse: The Evolution and Migration of an Architectural Form." *Journal of the Society of Architectural Historians* 4 (December 1985): 346–67.

– "Forging a Visible Fascist Nation: Strategies for Fusing Past and Present." In *Donatello Among the Blackshirts: History and Modernity in the Visual Culture of Fascist Italy*, edited by Claudia Lazzaro and Roger J. Crum. Ithaca, NY: Cornell University Press, 2005.

Lima, Antonietta Iolanda. *Soleri, Architecture as Human Ecology*. New York: Monacelli Press, 2003.

Lobsinger, Mary Louise. "Antinomies of Realism in Postwar Italian Architecture." PhD disseration, Harvard University, 2004.

McDonough, Michael, ed. *Malaparte: A House Like Me*. New York: Clarkson Potter Publishers, 1999.

McLaren, Brian Lloyd. "Mediterraneità and Modernità: Architecture and Culture during the Period of Italian Colonization of North Africa." PhD dissertation, MIT, 2001.

– "Die Konstruktion des mediterranen Mythos in der modernen italienischen Architektur: Bezüge zwischen Italien und Wien." In *Das entfernte Dorf – Moderne Kunst und ethnischer Artefakt*, edited by Akos Moravánszky, 223–48. Vienna: Böhlau Verlag, 2002.

– "The Italian Colonial Appropriation of Indigenous North African Archtiecture in the 1930's." In *Muqarnas: An Annual on the Visual Culture of the Islamic World*, edited by Gülru Necipolglu. 19 (2002): 164–92.

– *Architecture and Tourism in Italian Colonial Libya: An Ambivalent Modernism*. Seattle: University of Washington Press, 2006.

Malvano, Laura. *Fascismo e politica dell'immagine*. Turin: Bollati Bollinghieri, 1988.

Mangone, Fabio. *Giulio Ulisse Arata – Opera complete*. Naples: Electa, 1993.

– *Viaggi a sud – Architetti nordici in Italia, 1850–1925*. Naples: Electa, 2002.

– *Capri e gli architetti*. Naples: Massa, 2004.

Mariani, Riccardo. *Fascismo e "città nuove."* Milan: Feltrinelli Editore, 1976.

– *Città e campagna in Italia 1917 1943*. Milan: Edizioni di Comunità, 1986.

– *Razionalismo e architettura moderna. Storia di una polemica*. Milan: Edizioni di Comunità, 1989.

Marconi, Paolo. "Roma 1911: L'architettura romana tra italianismo carducciano e tentazione 'etnografica.'" In *Roma 1911*, edited by Gianna Piantoni, 223–8. Rome: De Luca Editore, 1980.

– "Il regionalismo italiano degli anni '20 e '30 e la borgata giardino 'La Garbatella' a Roma." In *Architettura moderna a Roma e nel Lazio, 1920–1945*, edited by Luigi Prisco, 43–9. Rome: Edil Stampa, 1996.

Masi, Alessandro, ed. *Giuseppe Bottai. La politica delle arti – Scritti 1918–1943*. Rome: Editalia, 1992.

Massari, Stefania. *Guida – Museo nazionale delle arti e tradizioni popolari*. Venice: Marsilio Editori, 2000.

– *Arte e tradizioni – Il Museo Nazionale dell'EUR*. Rome: De Luca editore, 2004.

Miller Lane, Barbara. *Architecture and Politics in Germany, 1918–1945*. Cambridge, MA: Harvard University Press, 1968.

– "National Romanticism and Modern German Architecture." In *Nationalism in the Visual Arts*, edited by Richard Etlin, 111–39. Washington, DC: National Gallery of Art, 1991.

– *National Romanticism and Modern Architecture in Germany and the Scandinavian Countries*. New York: Cambridge University Press, 2000.

Millon, Henry A. "The Role of History of Architecture in Fascist Italy." *Journal of the Society of Architectural Historians* 24:1 (March 1965): 53–9.

Millon, Henry, A., and Linda Nochlin, eds. *Art and Architecture in the Service of Politics*. Cambridge and London: MIT Press, 1978.

Moravánszky, Akos, ed. *Das entfernte Dorf. Moderne Kunst und ethnischer Artefakt*. Vienna: Böhlau, 2002.

Moretto, Luca, ed. *Architettura moderna alpina in Valle d'Aosta: Albini, BBPR, Cereghini, Figini e Pollini, Melis, Mollino, Muzio, Ponti, Sottsass Senior, Sottsass Junior*. Quart: Musumeci, 2003.

Nicoloso, Paolo. "Le parole dell'architettura. Il dibattito terminologico. 1929–1931." In *La Costruzione dell'Utopia. Architetti e urbanisti nell'Italia fascista*, edited by Giulio Ernesti, 31–45. Rome: Edizioni Lavoro, 1988.

– *Gli architetti di Mussolini – Scuole e sindacato, architetti e massoni, professori e politici negli anni del regime*. Milan: Franco Angeli, 1999.

– "Genealogie del piano Fanfani 1939–1950." In *La grande ricostruzione: Il piano Ina-Casa e l'Italia degli anni 50*, edited by Paola Di Biagi, 33–62. Rome: Donzelli Editore, 2001.

– *Mussolini architetto: Propaganda e paesaggio urbano nell'Italia fascista*. Turin: Einaudi, 2008.

Oliver, Paul. "Vernacular Architecture." In *Encyclopedia of Twentieth-Century Architecture*, 1401–5. New York: Cambridge University Press, 2004.

– "Primitive Dwelling and Vernacular Architecture." In *Shelter and Society*, 7–29. New York: Frederick A. Praeger, 1969.

– "Attitudes in the Modern Movement." In *Shelter and Society*, 16–22. New York: Frederick A. Praeger, 1969.

Pansera, Anty. *Storia e cronaca della Triennale*. Milan: Longanesi, 1978.

Pasquali, Marilena, ed. *Pompei e il recupero del classico*. Ancona: Galleria d'arte moderna, 1980.

Patetta, Luciano, ed. *L'architettura in Italia 1919–1943 – Le polemiche*. Milan: Clup, 1972.

Pettena, Gianni. *Casa Malaparte – Capri*. Florence: Le lettere, 1999.

Piantoni, Gianna, ed. *Roma 1911*. Rome: De Luca Editore, 1980.

Pigafetta, Giorgio. *Architettura moderna e ragione storica – La storiografia italiana sull'architettura moderna, 1928–1976.* Milan: Guerini, 1993.

Pirani, Federica. "Le Biennali Romane." In *Il Palazzo delle Esposizioni,* edited by Rosella Siligato, and Maria Elisi Tittoni, 183–97. Rome: Edizioni Carte Segrete, 1990.

Pirillo, Paolo. *Le forrme delle dimore e degli insediamenti.* In *La Cultura Folklorica,* edited by Cardini, Franco, 341–69. Busto Arsizio: Bramante Editrice, 1988.

Pontiggia, Elena, and Mario Quesada, eds. *L'idea del classico 1916–1932. Temi classsici nell'arte italiana degli anni Venti.* Milan: Electa, 1992.

Prina, Vittorio. *Franco Albini: Albergo Rifugio Pirovano a Cervinia.* Florence: Alinea Editrice, 2005.

Quesada, Mario. "L'arte rustica." In *Le arti minori d'autore in Italia dal 1900 al 1930,* edited by Irene De Guttry, Maria Paola Maino, and Mario Quesada, 58–60. Bari: Laterza, 1985.

Reichlin, Bruno. "Mollino, écrits au pied du mur." *Faces* 19 (Spring 1991): 36–47.

– *Carlo Mollino baut in den Bergen.* Edited by Bruno Reichlin, and Adolphe Stiller. Basel: Basel Architekturmusuem, 1991.

– "Figures of Neorealism in Italian Architecture (Part 1)." *Grey Room* 5 (Fall 2001): 78–101.

– "Figures of Neorealism in Italian Architecture (Part 2)." *Grey Room* 6 (Winter 2002): 110–33.

Saarinen, Eero. "Letter to Mr Costantino Nivola." *Art in America* 1 (1963): 88–90.

Saraceno, Chiara. "The Italian Family: Paradoxes of Privacy." In *A History of Private Life: V. Riddles of Identity in Modern Times.* Edited by Antoine Prost and Gérard Vincent, 450–501. Cambridge, MA: The Belknap Press of Harvard University Press, 1991.

Savorra, Massimiliano. *Enrico Agostino Griffini – la casa, il monumento, la città.* Naples: Electa, 2000.

– "La legge e la natura – Strategie istituzionali per la salvaguardia del panorama (1922–1939)." *Bollettino d'Arte* 113 (2002) 101–12.

Scalvini, Maria Luisa. *L'immagine storiografica dell'architettura contemporanea da Platz a Giedion.* Rome: Officina, 1984.

Scarano, Rolando, and Antonietta Piemontese. "La ricerca dell'identità mediterranea nell'architettura italiana degli anni Trenta." In *L'architettura del Mediterraneo – Conservazione – Trasformazione – Innovazione,* edited by Paolo Portoghesi and Rolando Scarano. Rome: Gangemi Editore, 2003.

Schnapp, Jeffrey T. "Between Fascism and Democracy: Gaetano Ciocca –

Builder, Inventcr, Farmer, Engineer." In *Modernism/Modernity* 2:3 (1995): 117–57.

– *Gaetano Ciocca: Costruttore, inventore, agricoltore, scrittore.* Milan: Skira, 2000.

– "The Mass Panorama." In *Modernism/Modernity* 9:2 (2002): 243–81.

– *Gaetano Ciocca: Architect, Inventor, Farmer, Writer, Engineer.* Stanford, CA: Stanford University Press, 2003.

– *A Primer of Italian Fascism.* Lincoln: University of Nebraska Press, 2003.

– ed., with Matthew Tiews. *Crowds.* Stanford, CA: Stanford University Press, 2006.

Scott, Felicity. "Architecture without Architects: Short Introduction to Non-Pedigreed Architecture." *Harvard Design Magazine* (Fall 1998): 69–72.

– "Bernard Rudofsky: Allegories of Nomadism and Dwelling." In *Anxious Modernisms: Experimentation in Postwar Architectural Culture,* edited by Sarah Williams Goldhagen and Réjean Legault, 215–37. Montreal: Canadian Centre for Architecture, and Cambridge, MA: MIT Press, 2000.

– "Functionalism's Discontent: Bernard Rudofsky's Other Architecture, Austria." PhD dissertation, Princeton University, 2001.

Scudiero, Maurizio. *Giorgio Wenter Marini, Pittura, Architettura, Grafica.* Trent: L'Editore, 1991.

– *Fortunato Depero – Stoffe futuriste, Arazzi e cuscini, Moda, Costumi Teatrali, Tessuti.* Trent: Manfrini Editori, 1995.

Scully, Vincent. "Architecture and Ancestor Worship." *Art News* 10 (1956): 26, 56–7.

– Introduction to *The Paintings and Sketches of Louis I. Kahn,* by Jan Hochstim. New York: Rizzoli, 1991.

– "Marvelous Fountainheads: Louis I. Kahn: Travel Drawings." *Lotus international* 68 (1991) 48–63.

Sereni, Emilio. *Storia del paesaggio agrario italiano.* Rome: Laterza, 1961. English translation, *History of the Italian Agricultural Landscape.* Princeton, NJ: Princeton University Press, 1997.

– "Agricoltura e mondo rurale." In *Storia d'Italia.* Vol. 1, 132–304. Turin: Einaudi, 1972.

Silva, Umberto. *Ideologia e arte del fascism.* Milan: Mazzotta, 1973.

Simeone, William E. "Fascists and Folklorists in Italy." *The Journal of American Folklore* 91 (1978): 543–57.

– "Italian Folklore Scholars." *The Journal of American Folklore* 74 (1961) 344–53.

Sparke, Penny. *Italian Design: 1870 to the Present.* London: Thames and Hudson, 1988.

– "'A Home for Everybody?' Design, Ideology and the Culture of the Home in Italy, 1945–1972." In *Modernism in Design*, edited by Paul Greenhalgh. London: Reaktion Books, 1990.

– "The Straw Donkey: Tourist Kitsch or Proto-Design? Craft and Design in Italy, 1945–1960." *Journal of Design History* 11:1 (1998): 58–69.

Stabile, Romano."La borgata giardino 'Garbatella' 1920–1929." In *Architettura moderna a Roma e nel Lazio, 1920–1945*, edited by Luigi Prisco, 151–2. Rome: Edil Stampa, 1996.

Stone, Marla. *The Patron State: Culture and Politics in Fascist Italy*. Princeton, NJ: Princeton University Press, 1998.

Tabor, Jan, ed. *Kunst und Diktatur – Architektur, Bildhauerei und Malerei in Österreich, Deutschland, Italien und der Sowjetunion 1922–1956*. Baden: Verlag Grasl, 1994.

Tafuri, Manfredo. "Design and Technological Utopia." In *Italy: The New Domestic Landscape. Archievements and Problems of Italian Design*, edited by Emilio Ambasz, 388–404. New York: Museum of Modern Art; Florence: Centro Di, 1972.

– *Teorie e storia dell'architettura*. Bari: Laterza, 1968. English translation *Theories and History of Architecture*. New York: Harper, 1980.

– *Architecture and Utopia*. Cambridge: MIT Press, 1976.

– *History of Italian Architecture: 1944–1985*. Cambridge: MIT Press, 1989. Italian edition Turin: Einaudi, 1986.

– "Architettura e Realismo." In *Architettura moderna. L'avventura delle idée 1750–1980*, edited by Vittorio Magnago Lampugnani, 123–36. Milan: Electa, 1985.

Tafuri, Manfredo, and Francesco Dal Co. *Modern Architecture*. Translated by Robert Erich Wolf. New York: Harry N. Abrams, 1979.

Talamona, Marida. *Casa Malaparte*. New York: Princeton Architectural Press, 1992.

– "Primi passi verso l'Europa (1927–1933)." In *Luigi Figini. Gino Pollini. Opera Completa*, edited by Vittorio Gregotti and Giovanni Marzari, 55–81. Milan: Electa, 1996.

– "Modernité et Fascisme: illusions croisées." In *Les années 30 – L'architecture et les arts de l'espace entre industrie et nostalgie*, edited by Jean-Louis Cohen, 127–39. Paris: Éditions du patrimoine, 1997.

Tonelli, Maria Cristina. "Il folclorismo." In *Artisti e cultura visiva del Novecento*, edited by Barbara Cinelli, Maria Cristina Tonelli, and Carlo Sisi, 49–51. Pistoia: Comune di Pistoia, 1980.

Tozzi Fontana, Massimo. "Il ruolo delle mostre etnografiche in Italia nella organizzazione del consenso. 1936–1940." *Italia contemporanea* 137 (October–December 1979): 97–103.

Varnedoe, Kirk, ed. *High & Low: Modern Art and Popular Culture.* New York: Museum of Modern Art, 1990.

Vergine, Lea, ed. *Capri 1905–1940.* Milan: Skira, 2003.

Veronesi, Giulia. *Difficoltà politiche dell'architettura in Italia 1920–1940.* Milan: Libreria Editrice Politecnica Tamburini, 1953.

Vivarelli, Pia. "Classicism and Tradition in Italian Art of the 1920s," In *On Classic Ground: Picasso, Léger, de Chirico and the New Classicism 1910–1930,* edited by Elizabeth Cowling, and Jennifer Mundy, 371–82. London: Tate Gallery, 1990.

Wall, Alex, and Stefano De Martino, eds. *Cities of Childhood – Italian Colonies of the 1930s.* London: Architectural Association, 1988.

Zucconi, Guido. "Gli anni dieci tra riscoperte regionali e aperture internazionali." In *Storia dell'architettura italiana – Il primo novecento,* edited by Giorgio Ciucci and Giorgio Muratore, 38–55. Milan: Electa, 2004.

Index